T0383194

The International Manager

The International Manager

Manager

A Guide for Communicating, Cooperating,
and Negotiating with Worldwide Colleagues

Frank Garten

CRC Press
Taylor & Francis Group
Boca Raton   London   New York

CRC Press is an imprint of the
Taylor & Francis Group, an **informa** business

CRC Press
Taylor & Francis Group
6000 Broken Sound Parkway NW, Suite 300
Boca Raton, FL 33487-2742

© 2015 by Frank Garten
CRC Press is an imprint of Taylor & Francis Group, an Informa business

No claim to original U.S. Government works

Printed on acid-free paper
Version Date: 20150109

International Standard Book Number-13: 978-1-4987-0458-8 (Hardback)

Library of Congress Cataloging-in-Publication Data

Garten, Frank, 1970-
    The international manager : a guide for communicating, cooperating, and negotiating
with worldwide colleagues / Frank Garten.
        pages cm
    Includes bibliographical references and index.
    ISBN 978-1-4987-0458-8
    1. Management--Cross-cultural studies. 2. Intercultural communication. 3.
International business enterprises--Management--Cross-cultural studies. I. Title.

    HD62.4.G373 2015
    658'.049--dc23   2014048671

Visit the Taylor & Francis Web site at
http://www.taylorandfrancis.com

and the CRC Press Web site at
http://www.crcpress.com

Contents

Foreword

Why a book on how to manage, communicate, and cooperate across cultures?

These days we all face international connections in our everyday lives. Whether we buy raw materials from a supplier in Australia, sell end products to a client in Brazil, or form a joint venture with a company in the United Arab Emirates, we have to connect with people from other cultures. Privately and professionally we deal frequently with people who think and act differently from the way we do. And most of the time we rely on our intuition and experience to handle our interactions with others. Often this is successful, but just as often, we feel a degree of tension: unclear communication, misunderstandings, and lack of trust. All too frequently I see that cultural barriers and poor communication stand in the way of achieving great results.

This can be avoided, and I believe that this book will help clarify and resolve many of these problems.

In Borealis, I see the importance of strong cross-cultural cooperation. We are an international company where people maintain daily contact between European innovation centers and manufacturing facilities in Austria, Finland, Sweden, and Belgium. Our Borouge facility is a joint venture with the Abu Dhabi National Oil Company (ADNOC) in the Emirates, and we run compounding units in Brazil, the United States, and Italy. We recently acquired a French company, and our 6,000+ employees represent many different nationalities. Our global operations are strong: we operate in more than 120 countries.

We take pride in the things we realize with so many different people. This reflects one of our core values: respect. We are one company, building on diversity.

I remember one of the first times I went to the Emirates. I had to learn that whereas we believe that "time is running" and "time is money," they believe "time is coming"—so the sense of urgency is completely different. You need to understand this if you want to be effective.

Frank Garten knows our company, and has been a facilitator in one of the leadership programs for our multinational talents. Some of the topics we deal with in the context of that program resound in this book: open and honest communication, conflict resolution, motivation and evaluation of people, and change management are all daily activities for many Borealis managers. And doing all of that against a backdrop of a variety of cultures is a challenge. It is a challenge we are delighted to accept.

I like this book, for the reason that it reveals the critical communication steps that are essential in building up successful international cooperation:

- The willingness to invest in a long-term relationship of mutual trust (we-dimension)
- The openness to really listen to what is going on in the life of the other person (you-dimension)
- The clarity to express your own contributions and intentions (I-dimension)

The book convinces the reader that in order to work successfully across cultures, you need to understand the other culture and invest time in decoding a different way of working. But knowledge is not enough. A solid basis of communication skills helps to navigate cultural barriers smoothly. The first part of the book deals with this topic. The book ends with four chapters dedicated to what managers in my company face on a daily basis: managing teams, managing performance, managing change, and negotiating across cultures.

The title of the book is well chosen; it's very human to blame external factors for the things that are not going well in our lives. And when cultural difficulties come up, our own superiority drives us into the mode of "I'm right, so the other person must be wrong." Managing others effectively across cultures requires a manager to look in the mirror, and find the tools in himself to deal with the problems that emerge.

Although well researched, the book is mainly practical; 100 concrete tips help the reader to apply effective measures in his or her daily work. These tips actualize the options: they are reflective, yet practical.

I recognize that this book has been written by someone who understands the international business context, and who has worked in the field himself. It is my pleasure to recommend *The International Manager*, and I wish the reader every success in applying the useful tips in his or her own international ventures.

Mark Garrett
CEO Borealis

Introduction

It was during one of my travels for Philips in South Korea that I missed my flight back to the Netherlands. Rather than spend an extra day in the hotel in Seoul, I booked a day trip to the border with North Korea. The next day, I was standing at the frontier with this mysterious and inaccessible country, in the village of Panmunjom in the middle of the demilitarized zone. The border is drawn on the ground. Stepping forward and crossing the line was unthinkable. At that moment, my challenge became to return to that same spot, at some point in my life, but to approach it from the north on that occasion. Because that seemed impossible. And because I was fascinated by North Korea that, in spite of all the negative things we hear about it in the news, is also a beautiful country.

A few years later this became reality. It had been a fascinating trip through the mysterious, closed, but also intensely beautiful *Chosŏn* (as the North Koreans refer to the whole of Korea). Standing at the same border as a few years earlier—but now on the other side of the line—was unreal. It was in that period of time that I knew that cross-cultural work would become the focus of my professional life. The experience of traveling through North Korea reinforced what I knew already: my truth is only my truth, and another person growing up in a different culture has a different truth. My truth is based on what others have told me. In the same way, North Koreans have also been told certain things, and these things form their truth. They have been told that South Korea has been occupied by the Americans (the "U.S. imperialist aggressor") since 1953. We know better. But only because we have been told differently. And we think that is better.

Reading stories like this often leads unwittingly to moral judgment: better rather than different. Our way of doing things is what has become natural to us, and other ways of doing things are quickly qualified as inefficient, irrational, or simply stupid and wrong. As Lewis says in his splendid book *When Cultures Collide* (Lewis 2006): "These various manners and mannerisms cause us great amusement. We smile at foreign eccentricity, congratulating ourselves on our normality."

For any global company, internationally dispersed teams are commonplace these days. Employees in different countries and different time zones work in project teams, their success relying on smooth cooperation between the members of the team. Even when the language barrier can be overcome, the different time zones and dissimilar cultures can easily cause the team to function in a nonoptimal manner. And even if your company itself does not have globally dispersed teams, almost all companies these days work with suppliers, customers, and partners from other cultures. This trend will further intensify in the years to come: the professional of the future does not work in an office, but works office-free in a network of other professionals, connected online, independent of the time zone and culture in which they all reside. The success of a company increasingly depends on the ability to coordinate its activities across a connected network of professionals.

Problems do arise in this context. My experience is that difficulties with cross-cultural work can often be prevented. It all starts with the willingness to understand the other person who is so very different. The Korean manager is part of one or multiple interconnected groups. The Russian engineer works in a strictly hierarchical context. The West African salesman relies on strong interpersonal relationships. And the Hungarian project manager has grown up with typical masculine habits like competitiveness and assertiveness. We can hope that the Korean, Russian, West African, and Hungarian professionals will change their behavior and become more like us, but this is unlikely to happen. Fortunately. But what can change is our willingness to understand them, and the behavior we choose to adopt in our response to them.

This rationale became the basis of a model I use in every intercultural awareness program I run. It relies on a three-step approach:

1. Look in the mirror. Understand the impact of your own behavior—whether determined by your culture, your organization, or your personality—on others.
2. Understand the other person. Develop understanding of the other culture you deal with.
3. Make a conscious choice. Take personal responsibility for the behavioral choices you make. Decide to adjust to the other culture. Or decide not to. As long as this is a conscious choice, you have acted responsibly and constructively.

Many companies—when dealing with intercultural difficulties—organize an "intercultural awareness" training for their employees. These trainings often deal only with step 2: theoretical knowledge about other cultures. I believe that a more advanced approach yields better and lasting results, as becomes clear from the three steps described above. This has also become the focus of this book: understand your impact on others, learn about the others, and make a conscious choice.

Many people hope they can rely on the experiences they have previously gained when working with other cultures. As S.P. Verluyten states in the book *Intercultural Skills for International Business and International Relations* (Verluyten 2010): "But there is still the naïve idea that intercultural skills are easily acquired 'on the spot' through travelling and experience. But there is ample empirical evidence that simply exposing people to different cultures does not automatically lead to mutual sympathy and improved understanding."

When adjusting to the other—different—person you have to step out of your own frame of reference, and accept that the frame of reference of the other person is different. Not better, not worse: just different. Not strange, not irrational: just different. To step into this unknown frame of reference enriches your world, and prevents hasty judgment and an unjustified—and occasionally cruel—exclusion of others who are not like us.

SETUP OF THE BOOK: READING TIPS

The International Manager starts with a reflection on your own communication style: Chapters 1 and 2 describe models of influencing and methods to breach ineffective communication patterns. Having examined the nonverbal part of interpersonal communication in Chapter 3, we subsequently address personal preferences in Chapter 4. These four chapters form the basis of *The International Manager*: looking in the mirror and becoming aware of the effect of your own communication, and building up a toolbox to communicate effectively in difficult situations (step 1 in the above three-step approach).

Only in Chapter 5 do we activate the dimension of culture. After describing what culture is and the general characteristics of culture (Chapter 5), we become acquainted with the dimensions of culture as defined by Hofstede et al. (2010) in Chapter 6. We see how people in different countries have been programmed differently, and we examine these mental programs through the lenses of the five independent dimensions of culture. Chapter 7 takes this one step further, and describes the most relevant cultural characteristics of several countries with which a lot of business interactions take place.

The last part of the book applies this knowledge to specific job aspects that every manager has to deal with. The models for performance management, team management, change management, and negotiation are discussed against a backdrop of different cultural programming. Here we see that most management models find their origin in Western (predominantly American) culture. These models only become meaningful in a global context once the manager looks in the mirror, recognizes where his own models no longer apply, and then adopts a flexible attitude to adjust his approach where needed.

This book targets managers in companies whose business takes place in a global context. The insights and tips are of benefit to any manager, regardless of cultural programming. The last four chapters of the book, in particular, come to life most of all when you continuously translate the insights to your own cross-cultural experiences. This should benefit globally operating product and marketing managers, engineers, project leaders, program managers, change managers, and specialists. The book benefits professionals at all levels, from the boardroom to the workfloor. Two subgroups can be identified within the overall target group: managers who steer intercultural teams consisting of members from multiple nationalities, and managers who manage their company's interaction with suppliers, customers, and partners from other cultures.

I have assumed that the reader will start at page 1 and systematically proceed to the last page. But that assumption is based on my own preferences of handling tasks orderly and systematically (my cultural programming). The chapters can also be read independently, and accordingly, the amount of cross-references between the chapters has been limited. Appendix A helps the reader to move through the chapters without consistently having to refer back to the definitions of culture given in Chapter 6 (which presents the Hofstede classification of cultures), and is a good reference when reading Chapters 8–11.

Each chapter contains a number of practical tips that can be applied immediately in your own work environment. The tips also challenge you to question the effectiveness of your own interpersonal and intercultural communication. The tips add up to the nice round number 100. Most of the tips invite you to look into the mirror, and to study the effect of your own cultural programming on others. I trust these tips will make your business communication more successful when cultures meet.

The examples I have used throughout the book have originated from my own international experiences. But I realize that my experiences are just that—mine. Therefore, I have asked some people from completely different professions and industries to share their experiences with cross-cultural cooperation. These "Sharing Experiences" sections can be found throughout the book, and also contain practical advice for the international manager.

A book about culture inevitably contains generalizations, which can be countered by specific personal experiences that differ from such generalizations. I invite you to think about these personal experiences, to critically examine them, and compare them to what I state in the book. My intention is not to write "the ultimate truth about culture"; rather, I intend to help you to look at other cultures in a constructive way, and provide you with effective communication tools that help you navigate cultural differences more effectively. When your own cultural observations contradict those described in the book, I would very much welcome your feedback. I will respond.

Frank Garten
Utrecht, the Netherlands

REFERENCES

Hofstede, G., Hofstede, G.J., and Minkov, M. (2010). *Cultures and Organizations: Software of the Mind: International Cooperation and Its Importance for Survival*. New York: McGraw-Hill.

Lewis, R.D. (2006). *When Cultures Collide: Leading across Cultures*. London: Nicolas Brealey International.

Verluyten, P.S. (2010). *Intercultural Skills for International Business and International Relations: A Practical Introduction with Exercises*. Louvain, Belgium/The Hague, the Netherlands: Acco.

1

Interpersonal Communication: Taking, Giving, and Sharing Space

> There are people who, instead of listening to what is being said to them, are already listening to what they are going to say themselves.

> **—Albert Guinon**[*]

On a Saturday morning in November 2004, we entered a gray and sober conference room in Seoul, South Korea. We were tired, which was a direct result of jetlag combined with too much alcohol. Only a few hours ago, our client had dropped us off at the hotel after an exalting night of karaoke. A pastime that—for some of us—had felt like a severe punishment, but had been great fun for others. We were still joking about last night, assuming we would rapidly reach a favorable deal with our Korean client. Our Korean counterparts seemed, however, to have completely forgotten our night on the town together: they looked at us indifferently, and adamantly proposed conditions with which we could not possibly comply. We could hardly recognize our "friends" of last night. It turned out to be a difficult meeting. The price of our semiconductors seemed to be the only discussion point for this television set manufacturer. None of our concessions—which grew in number as the day proceeded—seemed to raise even the slightest hint of enthusiasm. We began to believe that the word *concession* itself was nonexistent in the Korean language.

It only came to a breakthrough when we casually mentioned that this product was to be phased out next year, as most of our clients had already switched to newer models. From that moment on—by then we were already well into the afternoon—the discussion stirred up. The negotiation was no longer done by Mr. Kim, who had been the sole speaker so far, but was

---

[*] www.quotationspage.com

1

taken over by Mr. Ho. Several Koreans suddenly seemed to be engaged in intense discussions and were eagerly making notes of every word we said. The majority of the Koreans seemed to be working in research and development and were very interested in discussing new models and future projects. The price discussion vanished. In fact, after we agreed on the steps to be taken in the future, price was not even mentioned.

When we took off from Incheon, Seoul airport, at 6:30 p.m., we felt satisfied. We would spend the next 10 hours evaluating and catching some much needed sleep.

It was only afterwards that we understood what had happened. From the start, we had assumed that the client only wanted to discuss the price, that the people on the other side of the table were mainly commercial professionals or purchase managers, and that the purchase price would be a result of concessions on either side. All of these assumptions proved to be false: our negotiation partners wanted to discuss a long-term relationship in which business was generated jointly, the delegation consisted of technicians and R&D managers, and price was not even an issue. This mistake could have been avoided, though. It had nothing to do with intercultural differences or a lack of negotiation skills. It had everything to do with the way we communicated. An important part of communication is checking the assumptions you make about "the other side." In our case, refraining from doing so could have proved to be very costly: it could have cost us 5–10% of our total business with this client.

Many problems we encounter while doing business internationally seem cultural, but in fact are a result of poor interpersonal communication.

TIP 1: VERIFY ASSUMPTIONS

In any cross-cultural situation you find yourself in, write down the three main assumptions you have made about the other person. Now put these assumptions to the test: How valid are your assumptions? There is a good chance that one or more of your assumptions will be flawed. What would have been a better assumption to make in this particular situation? Now, ask yourself: "What would I do now if my assumptions proved to be wrong?" Act on the basis of these insights rather than on your previous assumptions.

1.1 COMMUNICATING EFFECTIVELY

This chapter deals with effective interpersonal communication. It forms the introduction to intercultural management, as the problems we encounter in working with other cultures are often simply communication problems. You cannot overcome these with more knowledge of the other culture: clarity, careful formulation, intense listening, and investment in a solid interpersonal relationship are what are needed.

We communicate in order to influence others. We want to understand others, and we want them to understand us. This occurs unconsciously. When communication flows naturally, we don't think about it, but we talk, listen, and "twitter" away. However, when misunderstandings arise and emotions get the upper hand, we suddenly become conscious of our communication. By the time we realize there is a misunderstanding, we are in the middle of it. Mutual accusations dominate the interaction, conflicting interests lead to stagnation, and emotions prevent us from thinking clearly about what is being said. It becomes necessary to restore an effective way of communicating with each other, which can only be achieved by changing our style of communication.

Even when we look someone in the eyes and communicate face-to-face, it may already be difficult to influence that person effectively. Such difficulties increase with the use of modern communication tools: in using email and chat functions we tend to miss the valuable information that is hidden in the tone of voice and the body language. Much international communication happens by phone, video conferencing, or email, making it even harder to communicate effectively and satisfactorily.

All aspects of the manager's daily work—managing performance, teams, change, or negotiation—rely on effective communication. Repeating your wishes loudly and relentlessly is usually not the most effective communication strategy: intense listening and building up mutual understanding should be essential parts of the communication mix.

My experience is that communication is effective only when a number of conditions are fulfilled:

- There should be an open relationship based on mutual trust.
- People should speak clearly and confidently about their visions and expectations.
- People should act respectfully to each other.
- People should be prepared to really listen to the other person.

TIP 2: BE RESPECTFUL AND CLEAR

When confronted with other cultures, be respectful to the other person or party. This comes by fully accepting and respecting their communication habits. At the same time, be very clear about your own communication preferences as well. Be understanding and respectful about their way, while being assertive and clear about your way.

1.2 THE THREE DIMENSIONS OF COMMUNICATION

The three dimensions of communication model (Swaan and Boers 2012) comprises all of the above-mentioned conditions. The model presents three dimensions, referring to three specific aspects of influencing: the I-dimension, the you-dimension, and the we-dimension (Figure 1.1):

- I-dimension: About my position in a conversation. What are my interests? What message do I want to get across? I want to be understood.
- You-dimension: Concerns the other person in the conversation. What is his or her concern? I want to understand.
- We-dimension: Covers our relationship. We would like to connect and establish mutual respect and trust. We want to connect.

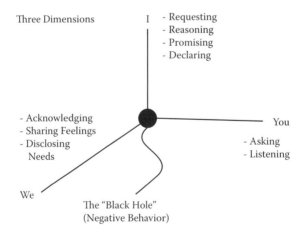

FIGURE 1.1
The three dimensions of communication. (From Swaan and Boers, *Making Connections: Getting Things Done with Other People*, Great Yarmouth, UK: Bookshaker, 2012. With permission.)

An effective way to describe the relationship between the three dimensions is the following. In the I-dimension, you try to get the other person to see the world through your eyes, whereas in the you-dimension, you try to see the world through the eyes of the other person. In the we-dimension, you look into each other's eyes (Swaan and Boers 2012).

Addressing only one of the three dimensions does not ensure effective communication: the conversation will lack depth. We may still call it communication, but some essential parts are missing. A person who presents his or her own (brilliant) point of view (I-dimension only) will quickly lose audience. On the other hand, placing yourself completely in the other person's shoes (you-dimension) might be interesting, but will not get your point across. And only working on the mutual relationship (we-dimension only) is nice, but you will not get much done. In order to influence effectively, you must be able to switch flexibly between the three dimensions. This way you will assertively present your own agenda, truly understand the other person's agenda, and build the kind of relationship in which you want to have a shared agenda.

When you master all three dimensions of this model, communication can be a more conscious process in which you choose to either take, give, or share space. The more familiar you become with the model, the more this becomes an unconscious process in which you will switch between the dimensions frequently and naturally. Training yourself in the use of those dimensions that do not come naturally is a particularly enriching process, in which a whole new world might literally open up to you: the other person's world.

Many people in office environments are familiar with communicating in the I-dimension. Clearly stating your message, making sure you are heard, and actively working on your visibility are of great importance in

TIP 3: RECOGNIZE THE THREE DIMENSIONS OF COMMUNICATION

For one full day, reflect on every conversation you have with other people. Which dimension do you use most? Do you switch? Do you mainly send, receive, or are you actively building a relationship? Which of the styles do you prefer? And which style do you avoid or use too little? A successful influencer can instantly switch between the three dimensions.

many (Western) business circles. In order to reach the higher echelons of the organization, you need to be visible. When it comes to interpersonal communication and enhancing your career opportunities, it is often assumed this concerns eloquence, confident presentation, and an assertive formulation of your point of view. This assumption is wrong. Much of the improvement in communication is reached by listening to the other person and building a relationship of trust and respect.

It is important to notice that the I-dimension is used a lot. For example:

- Making clear to the department in India that it should comply with the procedures that we at headquarters have designed
- Convincing the customer in Taiwan that our software architecture is the best solution to their problem
- Convincing the Russian purchasing manager that the price-quality ratio of our product is better than that of our rivals

These are all displays of our assumption that in order to be more effective, we have to improve our communication in the I-dimension. Assertiveness, clarity, firm action—we assume—will lead to more understanding of our viewpoints and ultimately to compliance with our ideas and processes.

The you-dimension seems detrimental to our skilled efforts to influence the other person: letting go of our own agenda and replacing it with someone else's may not feel like a very effective way to convince. Nevertheless, this is a very important dimension, as the effectiveness of our communication relies on both understanding and being understood.

In interpersonal communication within the same culture, it can be difficult enough to understand the other person, but understanding someone with a completely different way of thinking is far more complicated. It

TIP 4: PREFERRED DIMENSIONS OF COMMUNICATION

Make a list of your 10 most important colleagues and business contacts in other countries/cultures. Ask yourself what characterizes their communication style: Active or passive? Assertive or modest? Short and purposeful, or loquacious with many sidesteps and examples? Note which of the communication dimensions certain people tend to use most. Compare this to your own style. What style should you use more to improve your communication with these people?

takes curiosity and genuine interest in order to comprehend how people from so-called collectivistic cultures (see Section 6.3) come to a decision: to understand what drives someone with long-term orientation, to understand why the other person is continuously talking about aspects that do not seem relevant at all to the business we are trying to discuss.

The key to improved interpersonal communication is the willingness to set aside your own agenda and move your focus to the department in India, in order to understand why flexibility is so important to the people there. Really identifying with the needs of the Taiwanese customer, which concern a low-cost solution to win the very project that will save his factory, rather than create the superior software architecture that everyone may buy later. Really placing yourself in the shoes of the Russian purchase manager, who has committed himself to a certain price level in his dealings with his superiors and is now confronted with hard targets in terms of lead times and payment periods. These examples show us aspects we will never discover if we are not willing to "read into" the person who seems so completely different from us. More knowledge of etiquette and manners (the dos and don'ts) in India, Taiwan, or Russia will not get us there. We need to build a solid relationship with the other person and learn to think like him or her.

Building a relationship based on mutual respect, in which there is room for feelings and emotions, does not dovetail easily with Western business cultures. So for Western business people, it is particularly important to understand and accept that in Latin America, the Middle East, and Asia a personal relationship is essential to doing business. Emotions play a major role in the business process, and a deal will only be closed when the relationship is healthy and when both parties have visibly invested

---

TIP 5: REFLECTION TIME

When you feel annoyed by the behavior of one of your cross-cultural contacts, step back from the situation and think about it (reflection time). Put your own agenda and worries aside for a moment. Now suppose that he also has perfectly good intentions and that he is working to the best of his abilities. Can you understand why he is doing what he is doing? What could be his reason for displaying this behavior? Do you have the kind of relationship with this person in which you can openly discuss this behavior?

in the necessary levels of trust. Vice versa, people in non-Western cultures should not read the wrong signals in the apparently cold and distant behavior of Western counterparts.

The crux of effective cross-cultural communication (or in a broader sense what we refer to as diversity) lies in acknowledging the power and added value of those who are different from us—a point we will elaborate on further in this book. In other words: letting go of one's perceived superiority and accepting that great value lies in appreciating the other person. This does not mean that whatever we conceive in many head offices is not valuable, but it means that we lose the unjustified, often automatically attributed superiority. It means we have opened the door to true learning about Japanese quality management, Indian pragmatism, or Chinese entrepreneurship.

The rest of this chapter is devoted to an elaboration of the three dimensions of communication. Knowing them well provides a solid framework for interaction in an intercultural context.

1.3 THE I-DIMENSION

Presenting your ideas, giving your opinions, and contributing to discussions are central features of the I-dimension. You expect others to take you seriously and to pay attention to you. The way to create such a situation is to present your case convincingly: articulate clearly, choose the intensity of your voice carefully, and emphasize your points nonverbally. Mumbling something with your hands in your pockets will not help you to broadcast your vision. Communication in the I-dimension is often applicable when addressing a crowd or delivering a speech for a room full of people. In these settings, people are automatically drawn into the I-dimension, and this will mostly consist of one-way communication. However, communicating in the I-dimension should not be the default setting. It should rather be a conscious choice, and it requires the other person to allow you the scope to do so. Your nonverbal communication is congruent with your words. You radiate the message: "I wish to contribute to this conversation and I am taking the space to do so."

I often use the analogy of a theater: In the I-dimension you step up onto the stage and, as of that moment, everything revolves around you. You enter the spotlight, the curtain rises, and you present your ideas. You expect the audience to be quiet and to "turn on its receiver" while you are "broadcasting."

Communication in the I-dimension can consist of:

- A request: "I suggest we take a break now, before we continue this discussion."
- A claim/assertion: "Your price is 10% higher than the price of your competitors. You are asking much more than the average market price."
- A promise: "After the break I will present a new proposal that will address your wishes."
- An evaluation: "It was the right decision to take this break, we would not have wanted to rush things."

Some guidelines for effective communication in the I-dimension (Swaan and Boers 2012):

Short and simple. Short and clear statements make more of an impression and are better remembered. Political campaigns are good examples of this: remember the one-liners that fly around from all candidates and parties like "Yes, we can!" Politicians are trained to explain their entire program to an audience in just 30 seconds. If you are not able to formulate your message in short and simple terms, you lose votes.

Choose position. In the I-dimension you choose position. The other person should know what your position is. Simple and accessible language helps achieve that. You should be frank about your position or opinion, and not make things more difficult than they need be. A statement such as "Our country is full" is quite clear, whether you agree with it or not.

Be precise and specific. Short and sharp facts are better received than long-winded, general, and abstract statements. You could state: "The competitive landscape is changing, and when you carefully consider the increase in the number of active parties in this segment of the market, you will see that the average price is decreasing." Or you could say: "There is more competition, so the price has dropped from $1.20 to $1.05." Much clearer. Abstractions and indistinct formulations distract from the essence and suggest that you don't have a clear vision or have something to hide. Long, abstract formulations often mean the speaker is afraid to take a position. In order to get your message across in the I-dimension, it is better to be specific. If for good reason you might not want to become specific, then say something like "This is not the right moment for me to go into the details of this. I would like to get back to you on Friday."

Label your contribution. By labeling your contribution, you announce what you are going to say. "I would like to propose how to proceed with this meeting." This works wonders: it clarifies, draws attention, and structures the conversation. Curiosity is aroused and the other person "switches to the receiving mode." It is also effective when you want to stress your contribution: "I will explain this to you" labels your contribution, and gives it more weight. If you would like to train yourself in this, listen to debates and speeches by campaigning politicians: they often use the technique of labeling to get their points across effectively.

Consistency in verbal and nonverbal communication. Your nonverbal communication should support your words. The verbal and nonverbal should be congruent. A manager stating that we should all show more initiative, while he himself is leaning against the doorpost with his hands in his pockets, does not succeed in making his point. By doing so, he actually weakens the credibility of his statement. The nonverbal aspect of communication is always present and generally tells the world exactly what is going on in the inner world of the speaker.

Apply appropriate pressure. A typical element of the I-dimension is putting pressure on the receiver: surely you want to make your point clear and you expect your audience to give you the room to do so. That is why you—both verbal and nonverbally—apply pressure. Striking a balance is crucial: if you apply too much pressure, you will make yourself look ridiculous ("I expect you to vote for me!"). It will turn you into a caricature of a speaker. If you apply too little pressure ("It would be very nice of you if you consider giving me your vote"), your message will evaporate and go unnoticed.

Be aware of wrong assumptions or misconceptions. No matter how convincing you are in your I-dimension communication, there is always the chance that you may not be right when it comes to the content. Yes, even you! Make sure you always allow for the possibility that you do not have all the facts, or that the arguments on which you base your conclusion are not correct. When selling something, you benefit from a strong formulation of your proposition: "The market price of this product ranges from €1.30 to €1.50, and the quality has been demonstrated to be much higher than that of our competitors. I will not accept anything under €1.45." This is a very clear statement indeed. In practice one should take into account the possibility that the other person is better informed of the market price, or might not be interested in the highest possible quality, or knows (from a competitor) that ordering volumes over 500,000 items will reduce the price to somewhere between €1.27 and €1.34. Make sure you present you case confidently, but don't be overconfident about being right.

Managers often assume that the I-dimension is the only dimension they need to convince others. This assumption is wrong. When working with colleagues in Qatar, for instance, many Westerners are inclined to impose their own processes and procedures upon them. And no matter how difficult the cooperation may be, they keep telling these colleagues how they are expected to behave in their jobs. The Westerners are very surprised that people do not simply abide by their standards in the Middle East. And in their attempts to get them to comply, they keep on repeating their ineffective message. This was exactly what Einstein called insanity: doing the same thing over and over again and expecting different results. We often see this in conflicts. One of the parties continuously repeats the same point of view, which does not seem to have any effect on the other party. You will need to break this pattern and do more than just send: check whether your message is understood, find out what the other person's viewpoints are, ask whether you were clear in explaining your point, and try to clarify the

TIP 6: BE CLEAR AND CONCISE

Ensure that in daily communication with your (virtual) team members you practice the above-mentioned aspects of the I-dimension. When making a request, ordering work done, making a promise, or arguing your case, ensure that you make short and unambiguous statements. Label your contribution to the conversation, and be precise and to the point. Members of your team will prefer clarity above vagueness and ambiguity. Ask one of your team members to give you regular feedback about how clear your directions are.

stance of the other person by finding out what his underlying intentions are. It is time to "park" the I-dimension and move to the you-dimension.

――――――――――

1.4 THE YOU-DIMENSION

In the you-dimension, the focus is on your understanding of the other person. This requires more than merely asking questions. The you-dimension requires an active attitude: it can be hard work to fully understand someone else and to find out where his arguments originate. Try placing yourself in the other person's shoes. Using the parallel with the theater again, you now take a seat in the audience, invite the other person to take the stage, and intently follow the "performer" in order to understand what he is doing and why. The spotlight and your full attention are devoted to the other person until he indicates that it is time for a break. Sit down, set aside your own agenda, and enjoy the show.

The you-dimension is the most important dimension in conflict or disagreement. You will need to understand the other person's position to be able to interpret his behavior correctly and make the most effective interventions. You will have to listen actively. However, it is not uncommon to forget this theoretical knowledge quickly once the reality of everyday work or the intensity of discussion takes over. In the heat of the moment, our good intentions evaporate and the fighting spirit that most of us erroneously associate with debate prevails. On the other hand, an effective communicator frequently parks his own agenda. An effective international manager does that even more often.

Placing yourself in the other person's internal world is not easy, as it requires you to put aside all the assumptions or ideas that you may unconsciously nurture about the other person. You will need to engage openmindedly and ensure that you understand the other person without bias. Such moments can provide you with important information about the other person's frame of mind and motives and often lead to clear insights. This is exactly what happened in the negotiations with our Korean clients, described in the beginning of this chapter.

The you-dimension can only be applied effectively if it is based on genuine curiosity and willingness to understand the other person's way of thinking: merely suggesting or acting as if you are interested will not fool the other person. Nevertheless, we often encounter: "I understand what you are saying, but….” This phrase usually implies that you are not really listening, but instead feel the urge to claim more I-time. In order to really absorb what the other person is saying and understand what drives him, you should no longer try to find quick confirmation of things that you already know, but you should strive to find out how this works for him. Is your curiosity strong enough to embark upon frequent exploration? Unfortunately, many communicators are not such good explorers.

Listening actively, directing all your attention toward the other person, indicating that you understand what the other person is saying, asking questions, and continuously asking “Why?”—the you-dimension goes beyond asking questions. When saying, for example, “Thanks, but do you really think that your approach makes any sense?” you are technically asking a question, but you are clearly thinking in terms of your own agenda. You imply that the proposed solution does not make sense. The question was not posed in order to gain more insight into the other person's position. “Would you elaborate on your proposal? I am interested in your reasoning and your vision behind it” will certainly be more of an invitation to the other person to share his thoughts.

In practice, we often believe that we are better listeners than we actually are. The gap between “picking up words” and really listening “with your heart” is enormous. To participants in our training sessions, learning to listen with your heart most of the time is a wonderful experience. And although, as an experienced trainer, I possess this knowledge at the theoretical level, I still often find myself thinking that I can keep reading the paper while my wife is trying to tell me something. Effective communication benefits from giving full attention to the other person and his or her message. Bringing this into practice requires inner calm and genuine attention.

TIP 7: UNBIASED AND OPEN-MINDED

Have a conversation today with one of your team members who, at first glance, you don't perceive as very interesting. Start a genuine conversation, ask this person about his motivation to do what he is doing, identify with him, and actively put yourself in his shoes. Start to appreciate the other person by placing yourself in his or her (inner) theater. You will discover that the person in front of you is actually a very interesting human being.

Communication in the you-dimension can consist of:

- Listening: "I get the impression you are not happy with the way we are progressing. Am I right, Nick?" invites the other person to share what is on his mind.
- Exploring: "Would you elaborate on your reasons for requesting a delivery period of two weeks?" invites the other person to tell you more about his point of view. You explore by inquiring further: "What would be the consequence of allowing a delivery time of four weeks?" and "What if we could realize a period of three weeks? What would that bring you?" You will, without doubt, understand much more of the other person's reasons to emphasize a short delivery time.

Some guidelines for effective communication in the you-dimension (Swaan and Boers 2012):

Genuine interest. Your attention is completely with the other person and you have parked your own agenda for the time being. You can only do this when your interest in the other person—and his position—is real. Pretending that you are interested will give the other person that impression to some extent, but the nonverbal signs that you send will display that your mind is actually focused on something else, i.e., on your own arguments and interests. Not a good impression.

Curiosity. Curiosity is absolutely vital to understanding the other person. In order to find solutions to everyday problems, it is important to really understand where others come from. You can only do this when you are curious and take a real interest in the other person. I know from experience that people with a curious mind are among the most successful in working with other cultures.

Take the time to understand. Many Western cultures strive to get to the point and do business quickly. Western culture revolves around this principle, which is reflected in phrases such as "time is money." The end result is often the main focus of discussion, and people strive to reach that goal as quickly as possible. The other person is assumed to share the Western interest in reaching a deal quickly. This assumption often proves incorrect: in most Asian, Latin American, and Middle Eastern countries, the relationship between partners is of great value, and that relationship is constructed carefully. It is of less concern that this may take time. In that framework, getting to know each other is an investment. Understanding each other is actually a prerequisite for being invited into a business discussion at all.

Think like the other person. It is quite common—particularly in conflicts—to disagree on the content. Different points of view need to come together; consensus needs to be found among viewpoints that initially differ. But even when you differ greatly on the content, it is still possible to find out how the other party comes to his or her stance. Ask loads of questions; then stop sending and go into receiver mode. Following the other person's train of thought provides you with crucial information for any business encounter.

Park your own ideas and objectives. In the you-dimension you literally park your own agenda. By doing so, you choose to focus on the other person's agenda. Train yourself to literally park your views and assumptions, hereby creating room for another reality in which other things are important. Close your eyes and visualize a parking space with a great big P-sign. Imagine shoving all your concerns and interests onto that space. Having done so, you can really focus on the other person.

The other person's frame of reference differs from yours. In the context of real understanding, another Neuro-Linguistic Programming (NLP) concept is relevant. A principle of NLP is that the map is not the territory. Based on our experiences, we build our own idea or map of the world; we attach a personal and unique meaning to everything we encounter. When two people are in the exact same situation, they "save" a completely different version of the event. They create different pictures in their minds and remember different things. When two people participate in a discussion, they remember different moments and events. "My map looks different than yours, even though we base it on the same facts." In this context, the you-dimension can be a treasure hunt. Your quest is to unravel and decode the other person's map in order to find the treasure.

Investigate what the other person is saying. Investigation by asking questions provides you with important information, particularly in important business meetings. "When will this model go into production?" "Have you received orders for this product yet?" "What price have our competitors asked for?" You would be surprised how often you actually get a straight answer to such questions. "On which criteria is the final decision based? What do you need from me to make your decision?" Keep investigating the answers to these questions, repeat what the other party is saying, and test your understanding by summarizing what you just heard. "If I understand you correctly, what you really need to take back to your managers is...."

These techniques ensure that communication in the you-dimension, of which the other person is the focal point, is effective. Yet, putting your own agenda in second place (even temporarily) is often perceived as soft. Many people believe it conveys a subordinate attitude. People in the United States, for example—just like in Western Europe—have an image of a successful manager as someone who clearly possesses many features of the I-dimension and who assertively (single-mindedly) focuses on his goal. However, there is a lot to gain by letting go of this image. Spending your power of thought on trying to really understand the other person's interests has nothing to do with soft. On the contrary, it is a prerequisite for (getting) hard results.

Once our company could not deliver enough products to a client, thereby putting at risk the continuity of his business. In the discussions that followed on the compensation for his financial losses, my manager—who led the discussions—spent his time solely asking questions and inquiring about the market and the dynamics in the client's business. At the time this made no sense to me; the only thing we had to do was come to an agreement on the actions that would adequately compensate our client for his loss. However, the investment my manager had made that first hour proved very valuable: based on what he had learned, he concluded that if we could temporarily supply the client with the semifinished products and take over the quality

---

TIP 8: LISTEN WHEN YOU DON'T WANT TO LISTEN

When you disagree with one of your team members on something (this might even be something completely technical), apply the you-dimension and stop arguing about your position, at least temporarily. First aim to understand. Put your own thoughts and solutions aside, listen actively, ask questions, and summarize what you have heard. Then ask more questions. And more. Do you now fully understand the position of the other person? Only when you are sure that your own position is still valid should you decide to return to it.

control, the factories would be able to keep running. Accordingly, we would not have to compensate him financially and the factories would not have to pause the production. This outcome would not have been possible without my manager's in-depth inquiry and genuine interest.

It should be clear, though, that identifying with the other person and listening intently does not mean you have to accommodate the other person's wishes. You will repeatedly need to decide what you wish to do with the information you receive. However, this decision only should be made after you have completely understood the other person.

The you-dimension enriches processes of interpersonal communication, communication with other cultures, and intercultural cooperation. When you put your own agenda aside, you may discover that a most interesting person is there in front of you. A person who deserves to be heard. A person with whom you actually want to build up a valuable relationship so that you can communicate effectively. Someone with whom you would like to enter into the we-dimension.

Sharing Experiences

Kenneth Hansen, International Marketing Manager, Royal Unibrew A/S, Denmark
LinkedIn: https://www.linkedin.com/in/kennethhansen

Kenneth Hansen *is international marketing manager at Royal Unibrew A/S, second largest brewer in Denmark and category leader in multiple*

overseas markets. The company serves customers and consumers across the world in both emerging and developed markets with a wide range of alcoholic and nonalcoholic beverages. Since the beginning of his career in marketing he's been determined to build premium to super premium brands and beverages in the eyes of consumers, shoppers, and customers. Kenneth has managed brands such as Pilsner Urquell, Peroni Nastro Azzuro, Ruinart Champagne, Robert Mondavi, Rothschild (Lafite), and Camus Cognac to name a few and has lived and worked abroad for several years. In short, the role of the international marketing manager is to shape and own the marketing agenda across export markets. One crucial component in the role includes the responsibility to drive the portfolio in markets with the individual market teams or key partners ensuring strong brand development.

One of my key tasks and challenges is to expand the business worldwide, enter new markets, and build profitable premium brands in these. One of the many things I've learned and realized throughout my years in international trade, working with all these different brands, markets, and cultures, is that we sometimes tend to stop with knowing and not go into understanding—or we fall into the trap and simply think we understand. For me it's absolutely fundamental to understand and to just get to know about the different culture we work with. At headquarters level we tend to talk in general terms about the consumer, but that abstract description of the consumer is meaningless. The challenge is to accept that every consumer is a real human being, with his or her own individual experience and own individual culture. Getting to understand that is hard work, and it comes down to one key skill that Frank refers to in this book as the you-dimension.

Me personally, I always ask (a lot of) questions, listen, ask more questions, listen, then ask questions again—because that way I really get to understand my specific target market, sometimes target city or neighborhood, about the human beings and how they live. What do they think of first thing in the morning? What hobbies do they have? What magazines do they read? What inspires them? Why do they buy what they buy? What do they expect of a brand? Are they even into brands? You need to put yourself in the shoes of the human being. There is only one way to learn: ask plenty of questions and listen. This way I get into the heart and mind of these people. And that's what a brand must appeal to in the end.

For this reason I travel more than 80 days in the year, visiting key export markets in Europe, Africa, Asia, South America, etc. On top of my specific commercial agenda, I visit these markets, talk to local partners, engage with consumers and key customers, observe, ask questions, listen, and evaluate. You can only learn about their real needs by asking. This questioning and answering also helps them to stay on track, as often local markets have a hard time to specifically formulate their real needs. It's all about spending a week there, and come back regularly.

I recall some years back, in a previous role on another blue-chip company, we launched a brand into Italy with clear positioning, imagery, and all the possible above- and below-the-line assets you can think of. It became a very emotional campaign, with vivid images of consumers, lots of storytelling and romance around it. We witnessed a successful launch, but then we made the mistake of extrapolating the success: launching the same campaign into Germany. Only to find out that nobody bought into it. Touching the heart—that was key in Italy—did not appeal to the Germans, who in the end were just looking for good quality beer, one that was only that and one that hadn't changed. We learned that an approach that works in one country will not automatically work somewhere else.

The African markets I today work with pose another challenge. Data are very limited, so when I do above-the-line advertising there (TV commercials), I invest money without knowing the real impact of my campaign, as these statistics are hard to get. My Western mindset would tell me not to do that: investment decisions are made with business cases, and if you don't know the impact, you don't have a case. But to succeed in those markets you really have to put your (Western) headquarters mentality aside sometimes. A long-term mindset is needed: investing without knowing the return is a necessity if you want people in Ghana to drink your beer one day.

My practical tips for the international manager:

- Managers have the challenge to learn to listen. You can have worked many years in headquarters, you may have experience with all the cultures in the world, you may have understood

> markets and distributors for years, but it's still your job to listen, not tell. Brands are built when you have understood the human beings that form your market, and understanding follows listening. Always listen first.
>
> - Do not assume an approach that will work in one market will work in another market. Success stories in one country can become a failure in the other. The lesson for international managers is that headquarters can decide for one approach—for example, a way of working, a procedure, or a brand campaign—but this will always work differently in different markets. Accept that local flavors need to be added to every work process to make it work.
>
> - When processes that are designed at headquarters do not get accepted in local markets, our human response is that we think we need to convince the local markets: we explain again, we rationalize, and we give more arguments. The assumption often is: if we explain better, in the end they will understand and start to work like us. I have learned that this is the wrong approach. When local markets do not accept your work processes, it simply means you did not listen well to their wants and needs. It's not them who don't understand—it's you.

1.5 THE WE-DIMENSION

The third dimension of communication is all about creating a climate that stimulates understanding. It is about building bridges across worlds of thought and feelings, and engaging in true and valuable contact. In this dimension, you communicate that you respect the other person by investing in the relationship with him or her.

This relationship requires trust, which is more than merely being trustworthy or even being trusted. Trust goes beyond skills and capabilities, and is about putting trust in the other person's character (see also Section 9.2). By doing so, you can build a valuable relationship based on mutual dependence. The atmosphere of trust that is established is the result of noticing, acknowledging, and respecting the feelings of the other person, and being open about your own feelings and needs.

TIP 9: QUALITY OF RELATIONSHIP

Go back to the list of 10 names you made when working on Tip 4. Give a score of 0–10 for the quality of the interpersonal relationship you have with that person. For the people with the three lowest scores, ask yourself what has caused the quality of the relationship to be this low. When done, ask yourself what *you* do that has caused this relationship to be nonoptimal (this time you cannot say anything about the other person, it is about you now). Resolve to do one thing today that contributes positively to the quality of the relationship with each of these people.

Aspects that contribute to the we-dimension are:

- Acknowledging: "I do understand that it might be rather difficult for you to just accept my proposal. I know I would be the same if I were in your shoes. Is there anything I can do to make it easier for you?"
- Sharing feelings: "I am frustrated about the lack of progress so far and it makes me feel anxious."
- Sharing needs/interests: "When we discuss this proposal, it really helps me to build up full understanding of your intentions first."

You may have noticed that in these descriptions the terms *I* and *me* are used a lot. Nevertheless, while sharing feelings and needs, you are in the we-dimension; you are actively building a bridge between the worlds of you and I or me.

It should be clear that this dimension comprises more than listening to the other person intently and letting him know that you have heard him. It is about the willingness to put yourself in a vulnerable position in the presence of another person, and basing your future cooperation on the relationship that has been established. Sharing your own feelings is often a powerful invitation for the other person to share his thoughts and feelings as well.

Some guidelines for effective communication in the we-dimension (Swaan and Boers 2012):

Openness and trust. Putting your trust in someone and generating a climate in which the other person is willing to put his trust in you. Honesty and openness predominate in such a climate, and they are essential when you want to establish a mutual basis of interdependence with which to work.

Willingness to be vulnerable. In business environments, it is quite common to hide our insecurities—which we all have—and put on a mask of confidence. We do this because we assume that vulnerability is not appreciated. This assumption proves to be false, however, in a healthy business culture; showing one's vulnerability can contribute to a climate of mutual trust. Paradoxically, willingness to be open is based on (self-)confidence; when you trust yourself and your own values, not knowing something or making a mistake is no longer a threat. This has everything to do with attitude: being able to bring yourself into a state of tranquility and self-confidence, allowing yourself the vulnerability and sympathy that you need to engage in profound relationships with others.

When involved in discussions, we often assume that we have a monopoly on the truth, the ultimate and only truth. We assume that we are fighting for our own opinions, and you are fighting for yours. The manager who knows how to build bridges between different worlds and who puts effort into establishing mutual respect is often the one who succeeds in bringing parties together. The more vulnerable attitude that comes with that radiates: "I don't have all the answers, but I trust that we will find a solution that will help us both." You will be surprised by the willingness that the other person/party demonstrates in an attempt to achieve a joint result. As of that moment, you are a team with the other party instead of an opponent: a very healthy basis for successful cooperation.

Consider relationships to be equal. In order to do this, it is essential that you do not feel or act superior. We often do this, especially in intercultural contacts: based on perceived technological advantage, proven processes, proper education and training, and excellent proficiency in the English language, we can feel superior to the factory worker from Bombay, the quality engineer from Qingdao, or the supply chain manager from Bratislava. This superior attitude obstructs the establishment of a deep and worthwhile relationship. The we-dimension is effective when both parties see each other as equal.

Take the time to build a relationship. It takes time to establish a rich relationship with someone else. Westerners tell themselves they do not have the time: chitchat and small talk do not pay off. Compare this to the concept of time in other cultures: the Japanese seem to have all the time in the world to establish a profound and valuable relationship. In fact, "having time" is not a known concept for the Japanese. Time is not scarce; there is more than enough of it (for the full story read Chapter 7). Many Arabic-speaking countries and Islamic cultures will invest time to build a good relationship, based on mutual trust. In order to establish a valuable relationship with people from other cultures, most Westerners therefore will have to leave their comfort zone and invest the time that they think they do not have. The Western rushed concept of time—and the little value people attribute to deep relationships with others—is actually more of an exception than a rule: in most cultures, building a strong relationship is a condition that needs to be fulfilled before one can even start any cooperation.

Show your emotions, but prevent an outburst. In discussions with other cultures, expressing emotion is often appreciated. But, on the other hand, an outburst of emotions is not. Keep your emotions under control, but do not hide them. In Chapters 3 and 7, we see that different cultures deal with emotions in different ways. "The way you speak makes me feel a bit insecure; it comes across as rather rigid" is an effective intervention, which will help you especially in cultures in which emotions are not openly shown normally.

Unfortunately, the corporate world appears to believe that sharing your emotions is not done in an office environment. If sharing your feelings and showing your vulnerability gives rise to irony and mockery, it means you are working in a (office) culture in which there is no trace of inner motivation or commitment. Meaningful and effective interpersonal communication will never be established. This will have direct consequences upon the organization's performance: creative new product ideas will never see the light of day, relationships with clients will remain superficial, and decision making will be sluggish. This is not a good basis for effective cross-cultural interactions.

Communication based on genuine respect that leaves room for emotions is not hard. We only refrain from it most of the time because we believe it is not done. And by sticking to that thought, we remain safely in our collective comfort zone. Anyone who frequently deals with other cultures will have to let go of this idea. When we give room to feelings and commit to relationships in our work environment, diversity and honesty

TIP 10: SHARING FEELINGS

The next time you are in a conversation and you notice that emotions like disappointment, insecurity, happiness, doubt, or enthusiasm come up, share these emotions. I know your first response is: "You don't know where I work. This is not done in our work environment." Nevertheless, you should move out of your comfort zone and practice sharing these emotions. See a few examples below. Reflect on the response of the other persons who were involved. Did your sharing lead to more openness and trust?

Examples:

- "I feel disappointed we did not finish in time. Am I the only one feeling like that?"
- "I'm really not sure what to do, and it makes me uncomfortable to have so much doubt."
- "I am so happy we passed the milestone within the deadline. This is great!"
- "I doubt about the next step, and I feel bad about doubt and uncertainty. Can you help me?"
- "Enthusiastic about joining this team, it feels wonderful to be on board!"

will flourish. Strong business performance thrives on a basis of diversity and mutual respect.

It is fascinating to see how, in many countries in the Middle and Far East/Asia, an expression of feelings and emotions actually contributes to relationships based on respect and trust: it is the only way to establish long-term relationships. To Westerners, it is important to realize what a long-term relationship often means in the Western view: it means people tolerate each other despite their differences. In this interpretation, the West is the exception to the rule. The fact that you don't show your sincere satisfaction with the result feels less comfortable to many Westerners than to most other cultures.

The importance of a valuable and deep interpersonal relationship in a business environment is evidenced by research by Leigh Thompson and Janice Nadler (2002) of Northwestern University, for example. They simulated one-to-one negotiations that were conducted by email. The group that had had time to get to know one another beforehand was more cooperative and achieved more and far better outcomes.

The three dimensions of communication offer a powerful tool to strike the right balance between sending, receiving, and establishing the strong relationship that is needed to really understand each other. A manager must learn how to alternately give room, take it, and share it. The three dimensions model has proven itself in many communication courses and real-life settings, and in a variety of organizations.

This experience forms a valuable lesson for HR managers and learning and development professionals: do not send your employees to just any training in intercultural awareness when problems arise, but first find out whether they speak clearly, listen carefully, and build respectful relationships. If not, you can maximize the return on learning by addressing those problems first, instead of randomly training intercultural competencies.

In Chapter 2, we look into the techniques we can use when communication is not effective and we need to break through the pattern in order to obtain good results.

REFERENCES

Swaan, N., and Boers, E. (2012). *Making Connections: Getting Things Done with Other People*. Great Yarmouth, UK: Bookshaker.

Thompson, L., and Nadler, J. (2002). Negotiating via Information Technology: Theory and Application. *Journal of Social Issues*, 58(1), 109–24.

2

When Communication Fails, Break the Pattern

> Creativity involves breaking out of established patterns in order to look at things in a different way.
>
> **—Edward de Bono**[*]

The Korean delegation in Chapter 1 was still sitting at the other side of the table. Our frustration about the lack of progress was growing, not in the least due to increasing tension within our own team. During the last few breaks, we had racked our brains deliberating on what the other party really wanted to achieve. The views within our team ranged from an outright "These guys are always asking too much, they really play unfairly" to a more nuanced "Apparently they have not achieved the result they need to report back to their management without loss of face."

At a certain moment Mr. Kim repeated his position that a reduction of 25% on last year's prices was necessary for their organization to remain competitive. He consistently emphasized that if they did not meet their target, it would have major consequences for their personal positions within the company. We took such remarks as tactics. On the other hand, we knew very well that in Korean *chaebols* (conglomerates of businesses usually controlled by families), individuals sometimes need to leave if they have failed to negotiate and bring home the best possible outcome for the collective.

We also knew that the average outcome of our negotiations over the past few years had been a yearly price erosion of 3.5% and occasionally even 5.5% to 6%. The 25% to which the other party kept referring was absurd.

---

[*] www.brainyquote.com

It was a random number, which might be realistic on other planets (such as planet Korea), but definitely not in the universe in which we conducted business. We had already made various concessions with regard to our initial offer (an overall price reduction of 3%) and were readily approaching the limits of what we could and wanted to agree to.

Our client clearly disagreed. No matter how often we repeated that we had no more flexibility in terms of price, they kept insisting, "But you have to give us more." In principle, we had no problem with this tactic: to Asians in particular, the statement "You have to give us more" followed by a long and heavy silence is an effective way of negotiating. Westerners readily break those silences, by making another concession, for example.

Our spokesperson Carlos remained outwardly calm, but it was obvious that he too was completely fed up with this exhausting process. We had not seen any effective communication for at least 45 minutes: the CD was on a loop. When we explained our position again and threw in a final concession, the reaction was hardly surprising. Consistent with the pattern of the last hour, the stoic response was: "We expect more from you."

Carlos's reaction came as a big surprise to all of us. Instead of calmly proposing to take a break in order to confer, Carlos did something rather unexpected. He picked up his pen that he had used to industriously take notes, which had our company's logo on it. He elegantly presented this pen across the table to Mr. Kim and said: "Mr. Kim, this is all I can give you today."

In doing so, he broke various communication patterns. To us, it was so unexpected that we were having trouble not laughing, and our Korean friends were visibly surprised by this move. As of that moment, the atmosphere changed. Both parties seemed to understand that by continuing the way we were negotiating we would not get anywhere. This realization created a connection.

"This is all I can give you" had nothing to do with the content of the negotiation itself: a plastic pen with a market price of 35 eurocents as a concession obviously was not all we could give. This negotiator broke the pattern, the pattern in which the communication had been stuck for some time. Humor can be a very effective means to do so. There are various other methods or techniques to break through ineffective communication patterns, and a good international manager is prepared to use these. In this chapter we discuss the most important ones.

2.1 TECHNIQUES TO BREAK THROUGH INEFFECTIVE COMMUNICATION PATTERNS

No matter how effectively you may use the three dimensions of communication that we discussed in the previous chapter, meetings can grind to a halt and communication can stall. Parties may not understand each other, may not want to understand each other, or human emotions such as anger or frustration hamper progress. In intercultural environments, negotiations often end in deadlock as a consequence of a lack of understanding. This may be a matter of tactics: allowing negotiations to get stuck can be an effective way to emphasize your demands, and force the other party to make a concession. Negotiation—just like other business processes in the office—is ultimately about bridging gaps between conflicting views and positions. These kinds of bridges will never be built easily.

The models we present in this chapter share the feature that they help prevent escalation of communication conflicts and build bridges between two parties. The solution always lies in creating a breakthrough in common patterns of communication. A person who wants to persuade people from other cultures and discuss complex deals with international parties will have to recognize communication patterns and conduct effective interventions in order to breach those patterns that are ineffective.

You will only succeed in breaking through ineffective patterns when you recognize them. And to recognize them, it is essential that you are open to the fact that you yourself may actually be part of the problem. In practice, this is rather difficult, because we all assume that problems are primarily caused by the fact that the other person does not think like us. "If only he thought like I do, there would not be any problem," we keep saying to ourselves.

In his book *Discussing the Undiscussable,* Bill Noonan (2007) explains that it is entirely human to react defensively when we feel threatened or ashamed. We adopt this attitude because we believe that the problem lies with the other person and not with us. In our minds we are sure of ourselves and our position. We do not communicate with the other person or party about what we think his or her intentions are, nor do we discuss the problem. Instead, we cover the issue with a thick layer of small talk and politically correct phrases. "That's just how things work over here." This is how we externalize the problem: we can't help it—this is just how we normally behave toward each other.

In his book, Noonan (2007) argues that breakthroughs start with curiosity. To find out why we look at things differently, we need to be sufficiently curious to discover which information we may have missed when the other person was stating his case and what we can learn from his perspective. This attitude can lead to tremendous breakthroughs when discussions get stuck: get both parties to sit on the same side of the table and try to understand each other's needs.

We will discuss three ways to break out of conversations that have stagnated or ineffective communication patterns. Mastering these techniques is essential for anyone who endeavors to influence people from other cultures.

2.2 FRAMING AND REFRAMING

A frame is the unique way an individual perceives a certain situation. In the example at the beginning of this chapter, my frame encompassed the fact that a price reduction of 3.5% is reasonable in this market. I believe this is legitimate: other clients accept 3.5% as well. The frame of the Korean client is totally different: he foresees increasing price erosion in the market for traditional TVs when new technologies enter the market. In addition, he wants to gain a substantial market share and ultimately dominate the TV market. This firm is prepared to give it all to get there. In Korean culture, it is quite common to jointly engage in this kind of ambition with your most important suppliers, and to support one another in reaching that goal. From that perspective, our client's request for a price reduction of 25% is understandable. Our frames differ completely, and if we do not make an effort to understand each other's frames, we will definitely not reach a satisfactory result.

Every person deals with discussions based on his or her own frame of reference: whether that frame is a personal point of view or a cultural one, it is and will remain your frame of reference. The frame will never be exactly the same for two people. Sometimes the frames will differ only slightly, and sometimes they will differ completely: "I would like to come to an agreement on price, while you are only interested in finding out how much I am willing to lower my price, because you already have a deal with another supplier." An effective manager is able to place himself in the frame of the other party and to adapt when he needs to.

There are several frames through which you can look at things. In their *Handbook of Global and Multicultural Negotiation*, C.W. Moore and P.J. Woodrow (2010) make the following distinction, which can easily be applied to frames in other situations as well:

- Neutral framing: "Today, we will discuss the total price of the package consisting of 10,000 products for 2012."
- Framing based on position: "Today I would like to discuss a price reduction of 10% on your products in 2012."
- Framing based on interest: "I would like to discuss your price in 2012; as we have not negotiated a price reduction for the last few years, we are seriously out of sync with market prices." In this case, you haven't adopted a position yet, but you do tell the other party what you're after.
- Framing based on mutual interest: "We'll discuss your prices in 2012, looking for ways to keep both our production costs as low as possible and your compensation competitive."

When both parties are glued to their own frame, tunnel vision occurs; each party explains everything that happens in terms of his own frame of reference and sees everything that happens as proof of the fact that his frame is the right one. When one of the parties is willing to step out of his own frame—even if only temporarily—a breakthrough can be created. However, this requires you to first recognize your own frame of reference. This can only be accomplished by stepping back and analyzing the situation from the position of an independent observer (the so-called meta-position). Only when you are able to accept such an independent point of view will you be able to reframe and work toward a win-win situation, toward a frame where the interests of both parties are united.

TIP 11: GET INTO A META-POSITION

When you and your team are in a difficult discussion, learn to step out of your own position and move into meta-position. Here, you are an independent observer of the conversation. You detect—just as a camera and a microphone would—what is going on in the conversation. This position of the independent observer helps to take a new perspective and propose a creative way forward.

When a Dutch company sets up a joint venture with a Taiwanese company and the location for a new production site must be chosen, much time can be spent discussing the pros and cons of a location in the Netherlands in relation to one in Taiwan. Costs, quality of infrastructure, training of employees, and local labor laws in both Taiwan and the Netherlands can determine the narrow frame of the discussion. When framing is based on mutual interest, the business goals of the joint venture will become leading: based on the growth ambition of the joint venture in India, setting up the production site there suddenly seems more realistic than in either the Netherlands or Taiwan. The costs are certainly lower, the production is closer to the customer, and highly trained personnel are available.

TIP 12: MY FRAME OF REFERENCE

When you find yourself in a disagreement or conflict, ask yourself what your frame of reference is and which alternative frames you could consider. So ask yourself: "What assumptions am I making about the other person?" or "If I wished to describe this conflict in 100 words, what would I write?" Is your frame neutral, or is your frame based on positions or interests? Initially it is sufficient just to know the alternative frames, even though you find them completely unacceptable. When you have mastered this technique, you should regularly ask yourself: "What would be the consequence of accepting an alternative frame of mind?" Ask yourself: "If his frame were my frame of reference, what would be a possible next step to reach consensus?"

TIP 13: THEIR FRAME OF REFERENCE

Your team members in different cultures all have different frames of reference. They are all in a different time zone, in different offices, with different cultural bias, and hence in a different state of mind. Get into their frame of reference directly at the start of your phone conversation. Where are they? What does the world look like from their position? What is occupying their mind? What is their goal in the upcoming discussion?

2.3 THE FOUR LEVELS OF COMMUNICATION

Communication usually is not as straightforward as we would like it to be. A remark can be interpreted in different ways, and the exact same wording can mean completely different things. The remark "Time is nearly up" can be intended purely as a factual observation: "Only five minutes remain to finish what we are doing." However, it can also be meant as a warning that we had better change our priorities: "If we continue like this, we will not achieve what we want within the given time frame; we should use our time differently." Alternatively, the remark can be made in order to express irritation at the slow progress of the discussion. In that case, we accompany our remark with a deep sigh while rolling our eyes and wearily positioning our right arm against the doorpost.

A very useful model to classify between these various levels of communication distinguishes between:

- Content: The subject of the discussion.
- Process: The way we talk about the subject of the discussion.
- Interaction: The way people deal with each other during the conversation.
- Climate/feelings: The atmosphere in which the conversation takes place and the feelings people have during the conversation.

Literature on communication and conflict management often distinguishes between task-oriented and people-oriented communication styles. Task-oriented communication focuses on the objective of the communication, while people-oriented communication focuses on the atmosphere during the conversation and the relationship between the parties. We can recognize this distinction in the four levels of communication: the upper two levels focus on tasks and how you go about them, and the lower two focus on people and the relationship between them.

In Figure 2.1, the two upper levels are above the surface, just like the figurative iceberg suggests. The content of the conversation and the rules of play of the conversation are public. The two lower levels are below the surface: the way in which the interaction is perceived, and the feelings and emotions that play a role are often not mentioned. An observer can only guess what is happening at these levels.

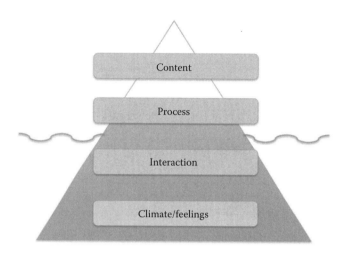

FIGURE 2.1
The four levels of communication.

In the Korean-Dutch negotiation at the start of this chapter, the following wording could be appropriate: "I keep on doing concession after concession and you keep looking at me without any reaction. I hate that! You stick to your position, while I am doing all the hard work trying to be reasonable. This is no way to do business!"

Various reactions are possible, none of which are very productive:

- "Yes, you may be doing concessions, but they are worthless and do not help us."
- "Call it a 'fair deal'? You totally ignore our interests."
- "That is absolutely not true. I really want us to reach consensus."
- "Reasonable? You are only thinking about your own interests."
- "Indeed, if you keep talking like that we will not do business together. We will be talking to your competitor next week."

As stated, these are ineffective reactions. None of them will lead to a constructive solution. At this point we should apply more structure to our reaction. We can choose to base our reaction on either:

Content: "Indeed, if we want to come to an agreement, concessions must be made. Let me tell you that my situation is such that I have come to the limit of what I can offer. My CEO would not accept it if I were to agree to a lower offer. And furthermore, my price is entirely in line with market prices I am aware of."

Process: "I propose that we take a step back and park the problem, then calmly repeat our positions and explain why we are taking that position. After that, we can see whether we are able to meet each other half way."

Interaction: "It seems to me that our conversation is repeating itself. You keep on proposing solutions that I cannot accept, while I turn down your offer time and again. Furthermore, we are continuously interrupting each other. Do you agree?"

Feelings: "When I try to put myself in your position, I can fully understand your irritation and frustration. To be honest I find it quite difficult to take my position, but I feel like I am stuck between, on the one hand, what my superiors want and, on the other, you and your company's interests. That feels rather uncomfortable."

These reactions—although constructive—are not common, as we tend to feel more comfortable continuing the discussion on the content rather than daring to mention process, interaction, or feelings. It takes practice and patience to recognize your own emotions at these critical moments, to take a step back and decide at which of the four levels of communication your reaction should be.

An effective manager will have to develop the skill to take a step back mentally in order to recognize the patterns of communication and make a breakthrough in process, interaction, or atmosphere.

Focusing on the content is very legitimate: ultimately our work in the office is about reaching agreements on certain topics. However, discussions often come to a standstill due to the clash of different points of view. Both parties start digging their trenches from which they can open fire on the other party. What remains is communication at the level of "I do! No,

TIP 14: RECOGNIZE THE FOUR LEVELS

Take one whole day to train yourself to recognize the four levels of communication. In every conversation, ask yourself about the level at which you and the other person are communicating. You will see that you often work and communicate at the level of content. Next, ask yourself: "What would I say if I were to operate at the level of process, interaction, or feelings? What would be the result of each intervention?"

you don't! I do! No, you don't! ..." The pattern is that you stubbornly stick to the level of content, and the discussion turns into a pointless exchange in which you fire back and forth. It would be more effective to break this pattern. Step out of your comfort zone and leave the content. Continue the conversation by talking about the communication at the level of process, interaction, or feelings.

Compare the discussion in a conflict situation with two people physically putting pressure on each other. The normal mechanism is: "If you push me, I will push back." Pushing back is a natural, automatic response. A good manager has learned to refrain from pushing when he feels pressure: he concedes and takes the position of an independent referee. Only after analyzing the arena can he decide what the most effective next step should be. Often it is all about not pushing, but knowing how to refrain from pushing or how to prevent it.

The rule of thumb is that problems at a certain level can be solved at a lower level, usually one level below. Disagreement on the content can be solved by discussing the process: "First you explain what you want, then I will explain what I mean, and then we will take a short break to formulate possible solutions in our mutual interest. Is that OK for you?" If you get stuck at the process level, it often helps to formulate your observations at the level of interaction between the speakers: "It strikes me that we are continuously interrupting each other and that we are not really listening to each other. Do you experience that too?" In this way, you propose changing the way you interact and agree to new rules to which both parties adhere in further interaction. And when an intervention at the level of interaction does not do the trick either, a last level remains: sharing your frustrations, anger, disappointment, and other feelings, and acknowledging similar

TIP 15: GET OUT OF CONTENT

As the manager of an intercultural team, you steer the contributions of others. This involves frequently switching levels of communication: you often have to leave content and propose process, observe interactions, and share feelings. For many managers this involves getting out of the comfort zone of content. As the manager of a team, your biggest contribution to the success of your company is to no longer stay with content; instead, it is better to steer the (content-level) efforts of others by using the other levels of communication.

feelings and emotions on the other side of the table. This can be a powerful way to mend the relationship between parties.

I remember one of the first meetings in which I used this principle without actually being familiar with the model. Two groups with conflicting interests had been working together rather unsuccessfully for quite some time, and they did their utmost to annoy each other. When finally a meeting was scheduled to discuss the cooperation, we were very civil and amicable to each other: we listened to each other understandingly and exchanged nice words. In the meantime our body language said it all. Our mouths said, "We agree, as of today we will improve the way we collaborate," while our hearts said something that we would prefer not to repeat here. Readers working for large companies might recognize such situations.

At the end of this meeting we kept exchanging pleasantries: "It had been such a productive meeting" and "We should definitely do this more often," and countless similar expressions. A quick glance from the perspective of an external observer (meta-position) told me how absurd this situation was. Nobody really believed all those declared intentions to change. I decided to intervene, and this turned out to be a very effective intervention. I proposed doing a quick round to inventory how everyone had personally experienced the meeting, and invited everyone to be honest about how he or she felt. I kicked off by stating that I believed that on our way home we would all say to each other, "See, they cannot be trusted, they say one thing, but they mean something else." I shared that I felt rather frustrated about this, especially since I was doing exactly that myself, but I wasn't able to turn the situation around. And I asked whether anyone had any ideas on how to address this unproductivity.

The meeting continued for another hour—the most productive hour we ever spent together. Even though I wasn't aware of it at the time, the issues in our cooperation had been brought back to feelings and climate, and there and then they could be discussed and ultimately solved.

Issues can be solved with interventions at a different level from that where they originated. The way to do this and the results that can be expected are listed in Table 2.1.

In summary, the conclusion of the four levels of communication is that as soon as we notice that our communication is no longer effective, we need to break away from content and intervene at a different, lower level. Leaving the level of content and moving to a deeper-lying level often creates breakthroughs and leads to valuable results.

TABLE 2.1

Interventions at Another Level, and the Expected Results of These Interventions

Intervention at Level of…	How	Result
Process	Make a proposal on how to continue the meeting.	Clarity and structure in the discussion and active participation by all members.
Interaction	Observe from the perspective of an independent observer (meta-position) and describe what you see and hear. Do not mention feelings and emotions.	Awareness of the ineffectiveness of the current interaction, awareness of own blind spots, intention to come to consensus at a higher level (process) in order to come to an agreement (content).
Feelings	Not mincing words about how you feel. But also not describing how you feel about someone. Talk purely personally: "This is how I feel. This is what is happening to me right now." Acknowledge the feelings and emotions you recognize in the other person/party.	Openness, stronger mutual relationship, warmth and commitment, honesty, sincere intentions to come to consensus on how to talk to each other (interaction), according to which rules (process), and come to an agreement (content).

TIP 16: INTERVENE WITH PROCESS

In your team meetings ensure that you always start the meeting with a procedural remark rather than dive into content straight away. Start any meeting by explaining the purpose of the meeting, your aim (sharing information, seeking inputs, informing, taking a decision), the time you have reserved for the meeting, and what you expect from the participants. Especially in virtual team meetings with other cultures, be clear about your expectations of others in the meeting. In the same way, you should always end the meeting with a summary of what was discussed: be clear on the actions to be performed and who is to take the actions.

2.4 THE COMMON REALITY

Whenever we are communicating ineffectively and we do not succeed in reaching agreement on the content, it is advisable to descend step-by-step to the level at which the problem arose. This principle offers a third technique (the common reality) to breach ineffective patterns of communication. This technique is based on the so-called ladder of inference (Argyris 1990, 1993). Figure 2.2 presents the model, in which we refer to the information and facts that underlie our reasoning and conclusions.

From bottom to top, the ladder of inference describes our process of obtaining objective data (facts, events), which turn into subjective experiences. Our senses only take in part of all the observable data (facts, events) available around us. Not everything around us is registered by our senses. Even less is processed: sometimes consciously—but mostly unconsciously—we determine which observable facts are going to constitute reality. We give meaning to the filtered information: we interpret the selected data based on earlier experiences. In doing so, we make assumptions about the world around us. These assumptions lead to conclusions

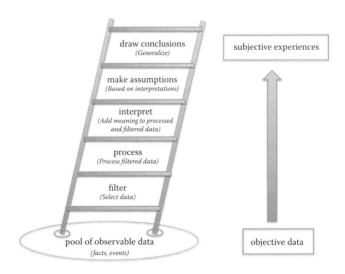

FIGURE 2.2
The ladder of inference.

and generalizations, which are usually no longer checked against the observable facts: our generalizations become our reality.

These generalizations and conclusions are usually rather blunt: "Eric is unreliable." It is based on something we have seen Eric do once upon a time: Eric of course does a lot more, but we filter that out. We have made assumptions about Eric, which lead to the conclusion that Eric is unreliable. During this process we have already forgotten the observable facts on which we based our conclusion that Eric cannot be relied upon.

The analogy with how we generally discuss things in the office is evident. Often discussions turn into an ostensibly polite exchange of opinions and positions, characterized by the famous "Yes, but…." The two discussion parties exchange data. These data are filtered (unconsciously or consciously), so that only part of the available data are processed, such as the information that supports our position, for example. The significance that each party gives to these data and the assumptions they make mutually differ. This happens inevitably in daily life, but even more in situations in which meanings and assumptions are biased, such as negotiations. When I want the lowest possible price, I will have surely made the assumption, in the heat of negotiation, that the other party wants the highest possible price. In line with that assumption, I will assign a particular meaning to every price the other party mentions (outrageously high) and attach conclusions (they are in it purely for their own benefit). My conclusions, which are the basis of my actions and behavior during the negotiation, will be totally different from the conclusions the other party draws from the same data (they do not understand that our prices are such a good deal for such quality products).

TIP 17: DOWN THE LADDER!

When working with people from other cultures, always make sure that you see the difference between facts, interpretations of facts, assumptions about reality, and conclusions. Are your statements and those of others based on facts, on an interpretation of facts, or are they general conclusions based on filtered data and personal interpretations? Bring difficult discussions back to the shared facts you are discussing. Agree which facts are relevant (filter), jointly assign meaning to the facts (interpret), and draw common conclusions.

I remember years ago we found ourselves negotiating for some time with a French client, who had been buying our products for years. One day, the negotiations had to be concluded. While I was presenting a concession to our client, I noticed François, the spokesperson from our client's side, looking at his colleague Dominique with raised eyebrows while glancing at his watch. At a certain moment he interrupted me, saying: "I think this is the moment to call Mr. Lacroix, the purchasing manager." Shortly afterwards Lacroix entered the meeting room, started talking, and explained to us that if we did not reduce our prices by 15%, our partnership would be abandoned. François and Dominique looked at each other and seemed uncomfortable.

To me, the situation was clear: François thought my proposal worthless. He interrupted me in mid-sentence, so he obviously did not hear what I was saying. Therefore, he cannot have understood what I was proposing. He brought in his superior to put more pressure on us. This is exactly what he did last year. These are unprofessional and transparent tactics, and it was clear that I was wasting my time with François and Dominique. They were not even authorized to make these kinds of decisions. Dominique was sly, he did not listen, and was obviously incompetent. His boss needed to come and help him when it came to a decision on the price. My conclusion—at the top of my ladder—had been drawn. I closed my laptop and sat down again: I was not making any more concessions that day, and these guys would certainly not receive any more information from me than was absolutely necessary. "If Lacroix wants to play the boss, he should attend the negotiation himself the next day, in order to come to a fair deal. A bunch of rats with transparent, dirty tactics from shallow negotiation books—that is what they are!" When I draw such blunt conclusions, I am on top of my ladder, and certainly no longer constructive.

A lot happened between the moment Dominique proposed to bring in Mr. Lacroix and the moment I was silently referring to my opponents as rats. I filtered my data: François raising his eyebrows to Dominique, François looking at his watch and leaving the room to get Mr. Lacroix, me shutting my laptop. The information I filtered out the fact that Eric, the research and development manager, looked up from his laptop and looked at me eagerly, and the fact that Caroline, the quality manager, was listening carefully and nodding approvingly. Next, I gave my own interpretation to what had happened (this is tactics—Lacroix is playing a game with us) and made assumptions about François (he does not have

> **TIP 18: CHECK YOUR FILTERS**
>
> Realize that behavior is based on conclusions (generalizations) that you draw yourself. Be aware that these conclusions do not represent universal truths but are merely your own interpretation of reality. Learn to descend your ladder: personally check your filters, representations, and assumptions, and analyze the objective data in conjunction with your counterpart.

the authority to make a decision; he needs Lacroix for that). My conclusion was that François is incompetent, has no authority, and relies on dirty tactics.

Had a camera been installed in the negotiations room, various things would have been recorded: François looks at Dominique, glances at his watch, walks out of the room. After Lacroix's statement, I close my laptop and I keep my mouth shut. These are observable facts. All else is based on my unconscious filtering of data, my interpretations based on past experiences, and the conclusions I decide to draw. Without being aware of it, I have become so selective that I don't even notice Caroline's approving nods or Eric's genuine attention.

Similar processes take place inside François's head. Based on the same observable facts; he might conclude that I am no longer interested in a partnership with their company (after all, I closed my laptop) and that I lack respect for his superior. The latter is, of course, quite true, as was plain from my nonverbal behavior. However, from these facts, we cannot know which conclusion the other person has drawn: they are not exactly conclusions for sharing openly. A breakthrough can be realized by constructively engaging in a conversation, restoring our relationship, sharing our assumptions and generalizations, and checking them with the other party.

Train yourself—when discussions stall and escalate—to pursue the following three steps before you continue:

Reflect: Recognize the rungs you climb on the ladder from observable data to generalizations and conclusions.

Share: Make your thoughts and reasoning transparent to others, so that you can have a constructive dialogue about the way you come to certain conclusions.

Understand: Try to genuinely understand the other person's thoughts and reasoning. Check if you've understood them correctly, ask more questions, and shut out your own interpretations and opinions for a while (you-dimension; see Section 1.4).

With these three steps, we have a tool that can help us break through nonconstructive dialogues and get us both out of our trenches. The process has come to open discussion and we can seek to establish mutual understanding:

> "François, I see you are exchanging looks with Dominique. Would you share with me what you think about my proposal? I would not want to misinterpret your intentions."
>
> "François, I am under the impression that Mr. Lacroix is the one who ultimately makes the decision on my proposal and that you advise him. Is that correct?"

If François has also read this book, he will ask you what the basis is for your impression and why you think he is not authorized to make decisions. The dialogue has been resumed and François, Dominique, and Mr. Lacroix will certainly not declare you an idiot and completely misguided.

Sharing your reasoning and inner processes—the mutual search for how observable facts became individual conclusions—is a very powerful intervention in discussions that break down. First of all, everyone is made aware of his own processes of thought, assumptions, and beliefs. Even more important is the fact that trust (see we-dimension in Section 1.5) has been restored, which allows the constructive taking and giving of space: the I-dimension and the you-dimension, respectively.

When searching for mutual reality, it is necessary to apply the you-dimension: you focus on the position of the other person and try to understand his or her point of view. In terms of Argyris's model, you are descending the ladder: you wish to understand the other person's reasoning that leads to his position, as well as the data and facts that form the basis of his point of view. This reasoning holds the key to understanding his real interests, rather than his position at that very moment.

How did it end up with our French client? After Mr. Lacroix's visit we looked at our mutual reality and we exchanged data about the market and market prices. We also openly shared our frustrations about the process. Not only did this do miracles for the relationship we had—which had always been quite good with this client—but it also eliminated a couple of misconceptions. When I proposed my last concession, François did raise his eyebrows and looked anxiously at Dominique. However, he did not do so because of any discontent with my proposal. On the contrary, he was very pleased with my proposal. This was exactly the reason for him to invite Lacroix: after all, his superior had to approve the deal with me. Subsequently, Lacroix refrained from checking the status of the negotiation when he entered the room, and he defended a rather extreme position in order to put pressure on us. This put François and Dominique in an awkward situation, as they were very satisfied with our results so far, and they realized they should have briefed Mr. Lacroix before he joined the meeting.

Our frankness resulted in more understanding. That night, in the bar, we could make jokes with François and Dominique about this episode, and we had learned a lot. The deal had been closed with a price erosion of 4%: a very acceptable rate to both parties.

In this chapter, we have discussed three ways to breach fixed patterns of communication: framing and reframing, the four levels of communication, and the common reality. We could add a fourth one: humor. No matter how serious the discussion we are in or how big the interests may be, a difficult moment can be turned around by a humorous remark. However, the appreciation of humor can differ per country or region, so make sure you do your homework.

What all methods in this chapter have in common is that when the conversation stalls, you should change your behavior: abandon your own frame of reference, your own level of communication and ladder, and suddenly you will be open to another perspective, sincerely and curiously. No matter how experienced you are in applying these techniques, the international manager will have to be open to the fact that all cultures are unique and that this determines how people communicate.

So far, we have discussed techniques that help us structure verbal communication (Chapter 1) and breaching patterns of verbal communication (Chapter 2). In Chapter 3, we shift our focus to nonverbal communication.

REFERENCES

Argyris, C. (1990). *Overcoming Organizational Defenses: Facilitating Organizational Learning.* New York: Prentice Hall.

Argyris, C. (1993). *Knowledge for Action: A Guide to Overcoming Barriers to Organizational Change.* San Francisco: Jossey-Bass Wiley.

Moore, C.W., and Woodrow, P.J. (2010). *Handbook of Global and Multicultural Negotiation.* San Francisco: Jossey-Bass.

Noonan, W.R. (2007). *Discussing the Undiscussable: A Guide to Overcoming Defensive Routines in the Workplace.* San Francisco: Jossey-Bass.

3

What We Do Not Say: Nonverbal Communication and Emotions

He liked to observe emotions; they were like red lanterns strung along the dark unknown of another's personality, marking vulnerable points.

—Ayn Rand[*]

3.1 SOMETHING IS NOT QUITE RIGHT— BUT I AM NOT SURE WHAT

In the previous chapter we described a meeting between two teams from the same company, both of which had the aim to achieve the commercial objectives of their companies (turnover, margin, profit growth of a product line). At the end of the meeting, the teams politely exchanged remarks about how wonderful it was to have such good cooperation and how valuable the meeting had been for the continuation of their partnership. The rhetoric was impressive, and if you had only listened to the words, you would have genuinely thought that these two teams were selling each other the world. The reality was different, however, and a rather confrontational intervention was required to ensure that the participants could be frank with each other. Had they been honest, they would have told one another that they found this "ritual" completely useless and a waste of time. There was no trust and everyone doubted the other team's intentions.

In this case I state that—as if it were a tangible fact—there was no trust among the participants. But how do I know?

---

[*] www.searchquotes.com

Literally examining every sentence spoken is a tricky business, and had we recorded what was said, it would not have indicated any inappropriate use of language. So, what made me come to the conclusion that there was no trust? I have no idea; it seemed intuitive. After all, I did not descend the ladder of inference (see Section 2.4) step-by-step, rung-by-rung, to find out what formed the basis of my conclusion. I suppose my senses must have registered things that undermine trust. The nonverbal communication had already told me that the other party did not trust us. My conclusion was based on observation of subtle contractions of the muscles around the eyes, glances of understanding, the closed and guarded body language of the people around the table, and the intonation in their voices. All of this disclosed deep distrust.

In cases of incongruence between the verbal (the exact words spoken) and the nonverbal (the tone of voice and the body language), we choose to regard the nonverbal signals as correct. A voice in our head tells us: "Nice story, but I don't buy any of it." The nonverbal communication—which is expressed in the behavior of the person—reveals the true intentions.

The devastating power of incongruence plays a major role in organizations, when initiatives for change fail miserably and management does not understand why people are so critical of the plans for change. The employees express the fact that communication has not been clear, while the management is convinced they have taken the right steps: info sessions have been held in the canteen, the CEO has addressed the employees, and the internal communication department has sent emails and distributed shiny brochures. The words spoken and written are all correct and the corresponding sentences not only are grammatically sound, but also convey the right message. That message, however, has not been accepted, because the behavior that the employees observe on a daily basis does not support it. Then what do you do as an employee? Do you trust the eloquently spoken words, or go with your own feeling of discomfort based on the nonverbal?

When the verbal and nonverbal are congruent, you don't realize that nonverbal communication is of any importance. It is just there—it goes unnoticed. Only when incongruence plays up and you are thrown off track, does confusion set in. This is exactly what happened to us a couple of years ago, when we were discussing a partnership with a large Indian family-owned business. Our discussions went on for hours, but we could not come to agreement on a few smaller details. After I had elaborately explained our intentions and made a new proposal, I saw the men opposite

> ## TIP 19: WHAT DO YOU NOTICE?
>
> Each time that you notice that something is not right, avoid immediate interpretation of the nonverbals. First try to enter into the frame of reference of the other person. Become aware of the facts and hard data that are causing your discomfort: What do you see and hear that is making you feel uncomfortable? Train yourself to detect these signals! Now very carefully observe the facts and data (lowest rank on the ladder of inference; Figure 2.2). Understand what causes your discomfort. Is your conclusion about the other person still the same?

me wobble their heads from side to side. My heart sank: they seemed tired and I wondered whether they had actually understood what I had said. Later, my colleague explained to me that in India and Pakistan, wobbling the head is a confirmation that they have heard what you are saying and that they may even agree. To me, things didn't seem right. I was seeing things that were not in line with my expectations. To them all was fine.

The way you let the other person know that you have heard him differs per culture, especially because of the different meaning we give to nonverbal signals. One culture nods and another culture makes small circular movements with the head. Confusion and irritation resulting from different nonverbals should be taken as a warning sign that you might be building up incorrect interpretations. Equivalent to the common reality described in Chapter 2 (see Figure 2.2), my interpretation could have easily led to the conclusion that Indians are not to be trusted—which would have been a pretty unfair conclusion.

3.2 WHAT IS NONVERBAL COMMUNICATION?

Nonverbal communication—that is, the *way* something is said—can be made up of many signals. In their book *Global Business Negotiations*, Cellich and Jain (2004) identify the following forms of nonverbal communication:

- Body language: Gesture, body movement, facial movement, eye contact

- Vocalics (paralanguage): Tone, volume, sounds that are not words
- Touching
- Use of space
- Use of time
- Physical appearance: Body shape and size, clothing, jewelry
- Artifacts: Objects associated with a person, such as office size, office furniture, a personal library, and books

These aspects of nonverbal communication vary in significance according to the extent to which they are used consciously or unconsciously. Do you consciously emphasize those phrases that contain hard numbers, or is that just your way of talking? Do you consciously leave the negotiators from the other party waiting in the cold and gloomy lobby, or do you not pay attention to such things in general and are all visitors welcomed like that? Did you consciously wear a black suit with a plain tie because that harmonizes with the formality of signing a contract, or was that coincidentally the first thing you found in your closet when you got dressed this morning?

On the importance of nonverbal vs. verbal communication, you hear the wildest numbers. It is often stated that communication is mainly determined by body language, only partly by someone's voice, and hardly at all by what someone actually says. An array of academic research is quoted to underline that the nonverbal determines 70, 80, 90, or even 95% of the total message. Most references lead to Borg (2008), who concludes that 93% of our communication is nonverbal, or Mehrabian (1971), who—in the context of addressing feelings—gets to 7% for the impact of words, 38% for the tone of voice, and 55% for body language. In the book *Praten en iets zeggen* (Talking and Saying Something), Sander Wieringa (2010) states that only in cases of incongruence between the verbal and the nonverbal is the impact of the latter substantial. In cases where incongruence is limited—that is, where there is little to no discrepancy between the words you say and the signals you transmit nonverbally—the solid content of your argument and the exact words are still of great importance.

For the moment, it suffices to state that the nonverbal tells us everything about the effectiveness of a dialogue and that these signs usually remain beneath the surface in Figure 2.1. Issues at the level of interaction and feelings are revealed through nonverbal communication. The importance of nonverbal communication is also determined by our culture. In

TIP 20: PRACTICE DETECTING THE NONVERBAL

Study, for one whole day, the way in which the people around you express their emotions nonverbally. Take a piece of paper and divide it into two halves: on the left side you write down what you have noticed about the other person (such as anger or nervousness), and on the right side, write down which nonverbal signals you have observed that are congruent with this emotion. You will see that—by training yourself—you learn to detect and interpret these kinds of signals better. It becomes a habit: a very useful habit in intercultural encounters!

a culture where people communicate rather directly (they "tell it like it is," which is quite common in Dutch, German, and U.S. cultures, for instance), you can easily deduce what is meant on the basis of the exact words used: the influence of the nonverbal is relatively limited. In many other countries—where the communication is less direct—you have to pay more attention to nonverbal communication. In such countries, the context of the sentences determines what is meant. Saudi Arabia is a good example here. Direct expression of emotion and feelings should be avoided: you need nonverbal communication in order to understand what the other party really means.

The fact that feelings govern nonverbal communication is well illustrated by movies. When we turn off the volume and don't hear the words, we are left with most of the nonverbal behavior (apart from the intonation). We still understand exactly what kind of conversation is being held, whether the speakers agree with each other or not. We recognize the kind of feelings involved and whether the parties like each other or not. The same can be observed in comic books: when you pay attention to the way in which the emotions of the characters are translated into pictures, you realize that the whole nonverbal game is actually quite subtle and tells a big part of the story.

Two aspects of nonverbal communication in the context of intercultural interactions deserve special attention: facial expressions and body language.

3.2.1 Facial Expressions

Several basic human emotions are biologically determined; we call them universal emotions. They are the same in Congo, Singapore, and any other place. These emotions are happiness, surprise, disgust, sadness, anger, and fear, and they are mainly expressed by the face. In business settings, the face is the most visible part of the human body, so that is convenient. Countless small details in our face reveal which universal emotion is currently exerting influence on the owner of the face: eyes open or nearly shut, the size of the pupils, raised or placid eyebrows, blinking, staring, mouth open or closed, curling lips, subtle blushing, or contraction of the skin. Some consequences of these basic emotions are just as universal: laughing and crying are expressions of feelings, and everyone from Iceland to Papua New Guinea knows them. The facial expressions that are related to emotions have been studied extensively by Paul Ekman (2003): he concluded that facial expressions or basic emotions are not culturally but physiologically determined.

This is an important truth for those who work with people from other cultures: the basic emotions are a fact, and they can be neither avoided nor prevented. However, it is worthwhile studying situations that lead to certain emotions, and the rules that determine whether or not emotions can be shown in different countries. For example, the Japanese have learned from childhood onward that negative facial expressions should be avoided. They are taught to mask these expressions with smiles and laughter, or they make their facial expression completely neutral. This leads to Westerners often describing the Japanese as cold and unemotional, which is a very wrong description of the Japanese. In reality they are emotional and often warm people.

When giving feedback to others, we often mistakenly assume that the facial expressions we see are conscious and voluntary choices. However, many expressions of emotion are generated unconsciously and can hardly be prevented. Feelings of disgust, for example, are almost instantaneous and can only be neutralized afterwards (after we have become aware of them). In that sense, we can state that nonverbal communication through facial expressions is much more honest than verbal communication: the face reveals what is really going on inside. Facial expressions cannot be faked.

The extent to which we can read emotions from a person's face differs. Anger and content are generally quite easily read, even though we hardly know the person in question. However, expressions of disgust and fear are

---

TIP 21: ACT ON NONVERBALS

In team meetings where you notice strong nonverbals, address these immediately. Although it may initially be uncomfortable to do so, it becomes progressively easier when you train yourself to do so and when you act with respect. Addressing nonverbal expressions is a powerful catalyst, as it invites people to speak up and share their worries. "Eric, I notice you are sitting backwards in your chair, with a critical frown on our face. What's bothering you?" When done in a respectful way, all cultures can handle this type of feedback.

---

more difficult to recognize, even when we know the person quite well. You cannot expect an international manager to detect all the nonverbal signals of his employees and interpret them correctly in all situations. But he should be sensitive and ideally, even in difficult circumstances, he should be able to imagine what is going on in people's minds.

3.2.2 Body Language

Another important aspect of nonverbal communication is the posture or positioning of the body and how this comes across. When I started out on my international negotiation career—in possession of an Amsterdam–Manila–Seoul–Tokyo–Amsterdam ticket, but without any knowledge of intercultural business or negotiation skills—nonverbal communication was my biggest problem. I was very nervous and I thought I had to be a tough negotiator. In my mind I had an image of how a tough negotiator behaves, and I had to resemble that figure as much as possible. The greatly exaggerated effort I put into appearing tough (loud voice, leaning forward at the table whenever I spoke, underlining my words with gestures) was not very convincing; it looked rather unnatural. Luckily I was part of a team that was amicably candid and a colleague gave me plain feedback: he warned me that I was giving out the wrong signals.

Improving your nonverbal communication cannot be realized by merely paying attention to it and adopting stereotype behavior: acting is not the solution. Your behavior and expressions should be authentic. Check frequently what you see in the mirror: make sure you learn from others how you come across, and make adaptations where needed.

3.3 THE ROLE OF THE NONVERBAL IN WORKING WITH OTHER CULTURES

When we work with people from other cultures, three aspects of nonverbal communication are relatively important:

1. Most nonverbal behavior is unconscious.
2. You should be aware of the impact of your nonverbal communication on others.
3. The meaning assigned to nonverbal expression differs per culture.

3.3.1 Most Nonverbal Behavior Is Unconscious

Earlier in this chapter I explained that much of your body language is automatic; your posture is a reflex, not a conscious choice. Thinking too much about the signal you are nonverbally transmitting often leads to disappointing results and to the conscious adoption of a certain posture or to placing your hands somewhere that looks rather artificial to both yourself and the receiver of the signal. As most nonverbals are automatically generated, people are usually not aware of the pointers they are sending. Feedback is an effective means to make people realize how they are perceived. People who are confronted with video recordings of their nonverbal communication in leadership courses often remember that moment for a long time, which is an indicator of the fact that we are usually not aware of the effect of our behavior.

People often find it difficult to give proper feedback. Telling someone "You come across as rather uncertain" is not constructive feedback and will not help the other person, even though it is the first thing that comes to mind. In training courses you learn that feedback is about observable data: describing what you observe and how that affects you. But what are you actually seeing? Even though you have registered the twitching eyelids, the heavy breathing, and the straying eyes, you are not immediately aware of this observation and how it affects you. But you have inadvertently drawn a conclusion based on these observations, and you feel something is not right. It is only when you become consciously aware of the situation that you can provide the other person with constructive feedback. And this can be learned.

TIP 22: ASK FOR FEEDBACK

In the next team meeting you host with your team, ask one of your team members to observe you and give you feedback afterwards. Ask the person to watch especially for nonverbal signals. Although this may feel difficult to ask at first, the feedback generally provides you with important insight. The only situation in which I would not advise asking team members is when they are from a country with so-called high power distance (see Section 6.2); it will be uncomfortable for them to give open feedback to somebody in a higher position.

3.3.2 You Should Be Aware of the Impact of Your Nonverbal Communication on Others

In your daily work, your manager, clients, and colleagues are continuously paying attention to the signals you send. However, you yourself are usually not aware of the impression you are making. How often do we fiddle with a pen during a meeting, do we scratch our heads, and do we look around to see what other people are doing? In a camera registration of the meeting you would come across as a very nervous person if you display such a combination of signals. But, as you are doing all these things unconsciously, you have no idea how you come across. Still, based on your nonverbal signals, another person has already drawn his conclusions.

The good news is that you can learn how to become aware of your body language and its effect on others. This is important in a business setting.

TIP 23: OBSERVE YOURSELF

The next time you are in a meeting, pay attention to your own nonverbal behavior. Ask yourself what you are doing in terms of posture, the position of your hands, intonation of voice, and gestures. You will realize you are suddenly more conscious of the nonverbal signals you are sending. Next, ask yourself: How will the other person interpret my signals? What alternative nonverbal behavior can I choose? And what would the impact then be? Experiment and you will notice that—although this feels a bit awkward at first—it will also give you some grip on, or clues about, the impact you have on others.

When discussing complex deals or large contracts, the other person's nonverbal signals tell you whether you are making progress or not.

3.3.3 The Meaning You Give to Nonverbal Expression Differs per Culture

The meaning of nonverbal communication differs immensely per culture. A nice example of this is the significance we assign to eye contact. In many Western cultures, direct eye contact is appreciated; it is a sign of trust and honesty. However, the same direct eye contact should be avoided in many Asian cultures, as this is perceived as confrontational and therefore undesired. In some cultures, avoiding eye contact is even a sign of respect for the other person, as is the case in Nigeria, for example. Always be wary of well-meant advice from people who are not familiar with such subtle cultural differences: for instance, there are books that state that you can detect whether or not the other party is lying by checking the amount and intensity of eye contact. This may be so in cultures where direct eye contact is considered to be a sign of trust, but I would not advise using eye contact as a "lie detector" when working in Japan or Thailand.

The significance of muscle contractions, gestures, raising your voice, and hand movements differs per culture. Everyone understands intuitively what is meant by certain nonverbal signals within one culture, but between two or more cultures misunderstandings easily arise. For example, to Dutch people, tapping your temple with the index finger means that something is smart, well thought through, or intelligent. To French people, the same gesture means that someone is mentally out of order. Fervent hand gestures in South America are used to emphasize our words, whereas in Thailand they are classified as aggressive and rude. You can think of many examples in this category.

Western managers should pay particular attention to their tone of voice. It is only natural to speak a bit louder when we feel we are not being understood. Signals of confusion and misunderstanding on the part of the other person often trigger us to repeat our words with more emphasis and at a higher volume. However, in countries where people speak softly, raising your voice is soon interpreted as aggressive. In many Asian countries, keeping your voice down is a sign of modesty and respect for others. You will gain more appreciation and be trusted more if you assume a modest approach. To many American managers, this is a challenge: in their culture they have learned to be assertive, up front, and clear.

TIP 24: DON'T RAISE YOUR VOICE

If you notice that someone from another culture does not understand you, quietly repeat what you said, but a little bit slower and with the appropriate emphasis on the important words. Learn to resist the temptation to speak louder in order to clarify your point, as this comes across as overly assertive or even aggressive. Modesty will be more effective, and in most cultures of the world a cool, calm, and collected tone of voice will be more appreciated.

Greetings in different cultures are particularly fascinating. The verbal part is not so exciting ("It's good to see you again, Mr. Kim"), but what happens on the nonverbal front is intriguing. In Japan, for instance, respect for the other person's status is expressed by the depth of the bow people make to each other. In France, people kiss when they meet (the unwritten rule that determines the number of kisses is incomprehensible to the non-French), and in a French or Belgian business environment people shake hands every morning at work (where a Dutch person would not even think of it). As a greeting people in India, Nepal, and Thailand express their respect for each other by pressing the palms of their hands together, while Russian people hug one another.

Graham (1983, 1985; Ghauri and Usinier 2008) conducted a systematic study of negotiation styles in businesses in 16 different countries, in which he used observations gathered in simulated negotiations, behavioral scientific laboratory simulations, and interviews. Graham's findings may be based on simulation of negotiations, but they reveal patterns that are characteristic of many intercultural business interactions. Table 3.1 lists how

TIP 25: UNKNOWN NONVERBAL BEHAVIORS

Address unknown nonverbal behaviors openly. "I notice you never look somebody in the eye, while in my culture we do this all the time. I'm curious: What do people think about direct eye contact in your country?" When neutrally formulated, everybody will take your observation as an invitation to share experiences, and hence to connect. You set the example of addressing cultural habits for your team members: in this way, you indirectly stimulate them to do the same.

TABLE 3.1

Verbal, Linguistic, and Nonverbal Negotiation Behavior in a Number of Different Cultures

	Japan	Korea	Taiwan	China	Russia	UK	France	Spain	Brazil	United States
Promise	7	4	9	6	5	11	5	11	3	8
Threat	4	2	2	1	3	3	5	2	2	4
Recommendation	7	1	5	2	4	6	3	4	5	4
Warning	2	0	3	1	0	1	3	1	1	1
Reward	1	3	2	1	3	5	3	3	2	2
Punishment	1	5	1	0	1	0	3	3	3	3
Positive appeal	1	1	0	1	0	0	0	0	0	1
Negative appeal	3	2	1	0	0	1	0	1	1	1
Commitment	15	13	9	10	11	13	10	9	8	13
Self-disclosure	34	36	42	36	40	39	42	34	39	36
Question	20	21	14	34	27	15	18	17	22	20
Command	8	13	11	7	7	9	9	17	14	6
No	1.9	7.4	5.9	1.5	2.3	5.4	11.3	23.2	41.9	4.5
You	31.5	34.2	36.6	26.8	23.6	54.8	70.2	73.3	90.4	54.1
Silence	2.5	0.0	0.0	2.3	3.7	2.5	1.0	0.0	0.0	1.7
Overlaps	6.2	22.0	12.3	17.1	13.3	5.3	20.7	28.0	14.3	5.1
Gazing	3.9	9.9	19.7	11.1	8.7	9.0	16.0	13.7	15.6	10.0
Touching	0.0	0.0	0.0	0.0	0.0	0.0	0.1	0.0	4.7	0.0

Source: Reprinted from Graham, J.L. (1985). The Influence of Culture on the Process of Business Negotiations. *Journal of International Business Studies, 16(1),* 84–88.

often people from different countries used typical verbal and nonverbal expressions.

The upper 12 rows in Table 3.1 are percentages (7% for "promise" means that 7% of all expressions were promises). The lower 6 rows show the frequencies (how often this behavior was observed over a period of 30 minutes).

First of all, what these studies show is that expressions of verbal behavior are comparable in nearly all cultures included in the study. In negotiations, the relative number of times that questions are asked, that promises or recommendations are made, or that people share information about themselves, shows the same pattern, even though there are differences. The subtle differences confirm the image we generally have of certain countries: the Japanese hardly share information about themselves, people from the UK will use many expressions that are intended to be received positively by the other party, Koreans relatively often employ a so-called punishment (the use of expressions that are experienced negatively), and Chinese ask many questions for clarification in trying to understand the other party.

The differences between cultures become apparent when the use of words is analyzed carefully: the word *no* is used often by Brazilians and Spaniards, but not by Japanese and Chinese. The latter consider the direct rejection conveyed by the word *no* as confrontational, while public opposition must be avoided. The Japanese language does not even have an exact word for *no*.

Even clearer are the differences in nonverbal behavior. Japan, the UK, and Russia are examples of cultures that often use silences in their encounters, whereas to Brazilians and Spaniards, that would be almost impossible. The number of times that conversations overlap and where one person starts talking before the other person has actually stopped talking are numerous in Spain, France, and Germany, but significantly less so in the United States, the UK, and Japan. At the same time, the Japanese look at the face of their opponent relatively infrequently: they avoid eye contact, which can be perceived as confrontational. On the other hand, the Taiwanese, French, and Brazilians often do that. The expressive character of Brazilians becomes very clear from the number of times they touch the other person when speaking: this happens more than in any other culture.

When working with other cultures, it is important for international managers to:

- Prepare and be aware of the other culture and its characteristic habits
- Be able to recognize the common nonverbal communication of that culture
- Continuously be conscious of the nonverbal signals he or she picks up
- Continually consider: What is my impression of the other person, which nonverbal signals lead to this impression, and am I interpreting the nonverbal behavior correctly?

In cases the manager does not prepare in advance—which is often the case in hectic international business—he will most likely be annoyed by the apparent utter lack of sense of urgency on the part of the other party (different time orientation), he will be confused by the warm hug his Brazilian counterpart treats him to (personal space), and he will not discern that the Taiwanese partner at the table is actually very angry (after all, you do not deduce this from the tone of voice). These signals can—if they are noticed—be a valuable contribution to preventing or solving conflicts.

3.4 THE ROLE OF EMOTIONS IN DIFFERENT CULTURES

We previously stated that so-called basic emotions are biologically determined and therefore present in every cultural context. However, the appropriateness of these emotions differs per culture.

In so-called individualistic cultures (see Section 6.3) emotions that emphasize a person's uniqueness and authenticity play a large role. Collectivistic cultures, where the interests of the group are more important than the interests of the individual, are more about the relationship with others and how the individual relates to his social context. In other words, emotions in individualistic cultures are subjective (in a similar situation, different people will have different emotions), whereas in collectivistic cultures they are more objective (everyone experiences the same emotions).

The appraisal of certain emotions differs per culture too. In general, emotions are classified similarly across the world: happiness is a positive emotion that people seek, while sadness is undesirable and is better avoided. However, some emotions such as pride have a very different meaning in different cultures: pride in Western cultures is a positive emotion, but in India it has a negative ring to it and an expression of pride is not appreciated.

Furthermore, there are social conventions that dictate whether or not you can express emotions. In the above-mentioned individualistic cultures, the norm is that people pursue positive feelings and happiness: the culture dictates this. There are hardly any rules that tell you when you can or cannot express such feelings. Our personal preferences determine how we do this in countries such as the United States, the UK, or the Netherlands. In contrast, in collectivistic cultures there are no strict expectations as to how someone feels or what he should strive for in life. Emotions that occur are what they are and they don't have different values. Nevertheless, there may be strict rules for showing emotion in certain contexts. In many Asian countries, the norm is that emotions should not be displayed publicly. Expression of emotions can be confrontational and may threaten social harmony: the individual will not show them openly.

Confusion often kicks in when it is not clear how the other culture deals with emotions, and how that culture will react to your emotions. In some cultures (Japan, Thailand, Philippines), people will do everything to avoid emotional confrontation. In other cultures, though, people will express their points of view emotionally and theatrically in cases of conflicting interests. Such discussions just have to be accompanied by strong emotions; otherwise, you have not given your utmost. This is the case in many Latin American countries. In other cultures—such as those in many Arabic countries—people use their emotions to strengthen their

TIP 26: DEALING WITH EMOTIONAL OUTBURSTS

In order to cope with strong emotions from other people, you should find out about the display and significance of emotional conduct in that country. It is good to know whether the emotions with which you are confronted are characteristic of the culture (this frequently happens in business meetings in Russia or the Middle East, for example) or of the person. If they are the result of general cultural programming, you may decide to let them be. If the emotions are personal, you should confer with the person about the cause of his behavior and perhaps ask if there is anything you can do to help.

demands. A complete description of all these emotions in the various cultures is beyond the scope of this book. Nonetheless, in Chapter 7, in which we describe many business cultures, we frequently refer to the role of emotions.

It is important to distinguish between the extent to which emotional sensitivity is appreciated and the extent to which emotions are shown. In Japan, emotional sensitivity is highly rated, but in business settings emotions are hidden behind a calm and opaque exterior. The negotiators exhibit socially desirable behavior; there is even a Japanese word for this: *Tatemae*. The fact that the emotions do exist and need to be vented becomes clear when your Japanese counterparts take you out for a night of karaoke in the bars of Roppongi in Tokyo, for instance. Here they allow their emotions (and a fair amount of emotion-inducing alcohol) to flow freely. In these situations, they are permitted to show their true feelings and emotions: the word for this is *Honne*, which is inconceivable when in the *Tatemae* state. The next day, when everyone is once again *Tatemae*, everyone has also forgotten what was said (or sung) the previous night: it seems as though it was a completely different person who said those things.

Finally, we need to be aware of the fact that the recognition of emotions—although some basic emotions are universal—is indeed culturally determined. Research (Elfenbein and Ambady 2003) has shown that people are better at recognizing the emotional expressions of others within their own "in-crowd" than of those of people outside that group. For example, Americans are better at reading the facial expressions of other Americans than the Japanese are. It is known that people who work abroad experience that their communication is more often misinterpreted than occurs within their own culture. When working with people from other cultural backgrounds, you should take it as a given fact that emotional expression is harder to recognize in the other culture than in your own culture.

We have argued that the expression of basic emotions and nonverbal signals happens practically automatically and is determined mainly physiologically, at least in the case of many emotions. Another instinctive aspect—one that has a great influence on the way we communicate and cooperate—is our personality. The way our personality deals with its surroundings determines the success of intercultural business. This is the subject of Chapter 4.

REFERENCES

Borg, J. (2008). *Body Language: 7 Easy Lessons to Master the Silent Language.* Harlow, UK: Pearson Education.

Cellich, C., and Jain, S.C. (2004). *Global Business Negotiations: A Practical Guide.* Mason, OH: Thomson South-Western.

Ekman, P. (2003). *Gegrepen door Emoties. Wat gezichten zeggen.* Amsterdam, The Netherlands: Nieuwezijds.

Elfenbein, H., and Ambady, N. (2003). Universals and Cultural Differences in Recognizing Emotion. *Current Directions in Psychological Science,* 12(5), 159–64.

Ghauri, P.N., and Usinier, J.C. (2008). *International Business Negotiations.* 2nd ed. Bingley, UK: Emerald Group.

Graham, J.L. (1983). Brazilian, Japanese and American Business Negotiations. *Journal of International Business Studies,* 14(1), 47–61.

Graham, J.L. (1985). The Influence of Culture on the Process of Business Negotiations. *Journal of International Business Studies,* 16(1), 84–88.

Mehrabian, A. (1971). *Silent Messages: Implicit Communication of Emotions and Attitudes.* Belmont, CA: Wadsworth.

Wieringa, S. (2010). *Praten en iets zeggen.* Schiedam, The Netherlands: Scriptum.

4

Personal Preferences in Communication

> In all the woods and forests, God did not create a single leaf the same as any other.... People go against nature because they lack the courage to be different.
>
> **—Paulo Coelho**[*]

A couple of years ago, my job required me to purchase training courses in communication and leadership for a multinational firm. These courses were purchased by the head office and then offered to employees in many different countries so that they could improve their interpersonal skills and their personal effectiveness. In discussions with suppliers who were eager to sell their training courses to us, I often found them annoying. To me, they seemed quite unprofessional and had hardly anything concrete to offer. I was irritated by their lengthy stories, their abstract views on learning, their strategic arguments about the courses being for our own good, etc. To me, the limit was the fact that they were lost whenever I asked about the exact price of one of their training courses, the number of people per group, or the agenda for the second afternoon of the course.

Only later—when I became better acquainted with one of the suppliers—I learned that they were very annoyed with me too. They had gone to great lengths to acquire my company as a client, and they had carefully formulated arguments to convince us to work with them. They had developed a vision and strategy that dovetailed with our current challenges. But, in their view, every time they tried to convince me with their vision and plans, I assailed them with questions about insignificant details. They

---

[*] Coelho, P. (1998). *Veronika Decides to Die*. New York: HarperCollins Publishers.

did not understand why I had wanted to discuss such practical issues with a potential supplier at such an early stage.

We obviously had completely different needs for information during those conversations: the supplier was after general direction, a vision for the future, and a coherent strategy in order to improve the learning capacity in our company. My need amounted to concrete steps we could take, the sooner the better, and I wanted to know the details of those steps so that I could get a picture of the training course itself.

We were all annoyed and confused, as we just did not understand what the other party was after.

4.1 CONFUSION ABOUT PERSONAL PREFERENCES

Confusion is part of international cooperation. After all, we all have a set of rules in our head that tell us how conversations are to be conducted. We learned these rules as a baby, as a child, as a student, as an employee of a company, etc. Slowly but surely this set of instructions became embedded in our system, after which we felt comfortable with it and started to expect others to abide by these rules as well.

Confusion sets in when someone behaves differently from what we expect. If the other person does not do what we want, we think he is weird or does not know how to behave properly. We label this as conscious manipulation, we find it reprehensible, and we may even become angry at such "uncivilized" behavior. When we continue to reason like that, we end up—referring back to Section 2.4—on top of our ladder. Meanwhile, we have drawn various rather unfounded conclusions about the other person. We have become convinced that if this person only behaved a bit more like us, we would not have any problems. It is his behavior that is the cause of the problems, certainly not mine.

The perspective of our counterpart is generated in a similar way. He too has been brought up with a certain set of rules. These rules have formed his frame of reference, and based on his rules, we are the one acting in a strange and uncivilized manner.

This is exactly what happens when two cultures—each with its own unwritten rules—come into contact. When the participants judge each other on the basis of their own frames of reference, little successful work can be done. Besides our national culture, we also bring along our personal preferences. And whereas culture is something that is taught and develops throughout our lives, our personality is something that is determined at birth. Our personality, too, is built up of various predilections, rules, and norms, and we prefer others to behave in accordance with these. When they do not do so, we become confused and irritated. It is quite clear where the problem lies: somewhere else, but not with me.

Whether it is the culture of your country, the culture of your organization, your own culture (which you have built up during your life), or your personality (which has been hardwired since you were born), all these forms of culture will influence your communication with others. And when confusion sets in because someone else does not abide by your rules, you will have to take a step back and look at yourself from a meta-position and ask yourself: "What is going wrong here? What behavior and beliefs are responsible for the fact that, at this moment, I am not getting the result I want?"

We all have personal preferences and the limitations that come with them. This also applies to the international manager: he will feel at ease in certain situations and rather uncomfortable in others. A successful manager knows his own preferences and knows how these impact his behavior. As Raymond Saner (2008) states in his book *The Expert Negotiator*: "Obviously, each individual has his own style…. But a really practiced negotiator can ring the changes on his own inclinations to the point that—like a good actor—he can play every part competently. The choice of communication style will then depend solely on the situation at hand, and not on his personal limitations."

The manager who does not consciously choose his behavior in relation to the situation, but whose behavior purely reflects his personal preference, will probably show the same familiar behavior in any given situation. This

---

TIP 27: BE PART OF THE SOLUTION

Always analyze confusion, irritation, and misunderstandings. Understanding the different expectations people have is the key to better cooperation. When things do not go the way you want, there is a solution that improves the cooperation. When things do not yield the result you expect, realize that you are not an external observer: you yourself are part of the problem. This gives you the ability to take action and break the pattern. Only your own actions will determine whether or not you will get what you want.

is far from effective, as different situations require different reactions and behavior.

Intercultural settings, in particular, require managers to be flexible in their choice of behavior, since the intercultural setting is more complex. There are many different interests to be taken into account, and the intercultural context limits the array of behavior to choose from. This means international managers, apart from knowing their own specific personality and the impact it has on their behavior, must possess certain skills. They must be flexible: their behavior is a conscious choice, based on the circumstances. Their personal preference is then of minor importance.

In this chapter, we describe the personal preferences that are relevant when working with other cultures. We cover conflict styles (Thomas Kilmann) and personality types (Big Five and some other relevant personal characteristics) and we relate these styles and characteristics to various aspects of international business.

4.2 DEALING WITH CONFLICT

On a daily basis, the international manager will encounter situations in which seemingly conflicting interests need to be reconciled. Consensus should be reached: a solution must be found that is acceptable to the people involved. Two main constituents can be identified in the way a person prefers to deal with conflicts: the degree to which he takes care of his own interests (assertiveness) and the degree to which he takes care of the interests of the other person (cooperativeness). Thomas and Kilmann (1974)—following up work by Blake and Mouton (1966)—used these constituents to create a grid in which five conflict styles (Deutsch et al. 2006) can be plotted (Figure 4.1).

As mentioned, there are five styles or ways in which people deal with conflicts, as identified in the Thomas-Kilmann model:

1. Avoidance. This situation is sometimes called lose-lose, in contrast to the well-known win-win situation. When both parties avoid confrontation, there is not much to win. This choice upholds the status quo, and there is consensus about the fact that there is no agreement. A frequently used phrase to conceal this negative situation is: "Let's

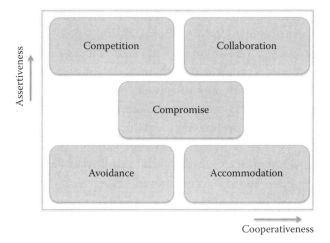

FIGURE 4.1
The Thomas-Kilmann model of conflict resolution.

get back to that later." The person saying this is clearly not taking any initiative to specify "later," and he knows that there will be other things later that need to be dealt with.

Though avoiding may sound foolish and weak to many readers, it can be the most effective strategy in some cases, as when you suspect that the effort you put into a conflict will not pay off (the return on conflict is low), for instance. Other reasons for avoidance are: it is in your interest to maintain objectivity and thus not take sides, or your interests are limited, or it is wise to buy time, or you can prevent emotions that are likely to arise in a confrontation.

2. Competition. This quadrant, in which you focus on your own interests and less on the other party's, is called dominance, or win-lose: one of the parties wins at the expense of the other. We all know a person who always concentrates only on his own interests and does not seem to bother about the interests of the other party. This is an attitude that you might even be envious of: such people have a clear focus and can achieve a lot in a short span of time. In the long run, however, this strategy rarely pays off. The same goes for managers who solely pursue their own interests.

Dominance can be the strategy of choice if you have a great interest in getting what you want and, at the same time, there is little room for mutual benefit. This may also be the case if a good relationship or long-term partnership is of no importance. If you are quite sure that you are right, you can choose to dominate, regardless of the needs and agenda of the other party. This is certainly a risky strategy, as you can never be absolutely sure that you are right. Another reason to choose win-lose can be that you do not have leeway for a more time-consuming strategy, or at least you think that you don't.

3. Compromise. Compromise is a solution that is quite well known in some cultures (Scandinavian, Dutch), whereas it is seen as suboptimal or even weak in others (Russia). Compromise means that the parties settle (quickly) in the middle: both win some, but they also pass up opportunities to forge even better deals. Dutch people see this type of solution as the most reasonable way to meet everybody's wishes. In many other cultures, though, people will describe this solution as something negative, something that should be prevented: after all, neither party has achieved what it was after. Making a compromise often seems reasonable: the seller asks for 10,000 euros, the buyer only wants to spend 4,000 euros, so let's meet each other halfway, at a price of 7,000 euros. However, if the current market price is 6,000 euros, the seller started with a very high bid and the buyer has paid 1,000 euros too much.

   Nevertheless, a compromise can be a favorable solution when you find yourselves in a deadlock and you want both parties to go home with something with which they can be satisfied, when the stakes are not too high and you have the good sense to support the other person's interest, or when one of the parties has nothing to win. Furthermore, a compromise can be an adequate temporary solution, waiting for a better moment to conjure up a solution that fulfills the wishes of both parties better.

4. Accommodating. Accommodating means adjusting: you comply with another person's wishes while relinquishing your own interests. You mumble, "My pleasure," and in doing so, you are choosing a solution that does not cost much effort, as the other party sees all its wishes fulfilled. This "easy" solution will not be very popular in so-called masculine cultures (a more extensive description of masculinity can be found in Section 6.4). These cultures are oriented to competition, to pursuing and winning the best possible result. In these cultures, the accommodating solution (less positively dubbed lacking backbone) is the least acceptable.

   However, adjusting to the other person's wishes can be a wise choice. For instance, when a good relationship with the other person is more important than getting your way. But take care: when the relationship is solid, it can take a hit, and by conceding without a fight, you can easily lose respect. In situations where the stakes are limited, whenever you want to acquire credit for later, or you want to keep the peace no matter what, adjusting can be a wise choice. Finally, this is a temporary solution in many cases: your gain in the long run can far outweigh the lack of short-term gain. Asians understand this much better than Western cultures: see Section 6.6 about long-term orientation.

5. Collaboration. This is the integrative win-win solution, in which both parties gain and achieve mutual benefit. A compromise is avoided, by first jointly increasing the size of the pie before dividing it. It entails a genuine belief that the parties are stronger when united, but it requires leadership and courage to realize such a solution.

   Collaboration or cooperation—when feasible—is usually the most attractive option. The integrative potential (that extra piece of the pie that is valuable to both parties) is tremendous. Both parties gain in a way that is genuinely attractive to both. Moreover, the joint solution can be valuable when parties need each other in the future, or when the interests of both parties are of equal weight.

   A situation of collaboration can be illustrated in the sale of a car. It is in the interest of the salesman to increase his annual turnover and generate steady revenue in the long run. When my interest is to have independent and reliable transportation at my disposal, we do not help each other by finding the lowest price (his loss) or going for a car that will fall apart after a month (my loss). What will help us both is collaboration: we strike a deal for a good price and we combine it with a maintenance contract and a free replacement car in case of a breakdown. The salesman wins because a good price supports his turnover and the maintenance contract is a steady flow of income in the long run. I win as well, as I am paying a fair price and I have my independence in terms of transport guaranteed, even when my car breaks down.

The choice of conflict management style in a given situation depends both on a person's strategic choice (a rational choice for a certain approach) and on his preference for certain styles (that are important to him personally).

TIP 28: CHOOSE YOUR APPROACH

At moments of conflict or disagreement in your team, you will notice that most people continue to discuss content: they adopt a stance and stay with it. Your added value should be in helping them find a solution. A helpful way to do this is to describe the conflict (take meta-position and describe this as if you were an external observer). After this, write down a few possible actions you could take within each of the five conflict styles. Suddenly the conflict becomes an interesting puzzle: Which of the options you write down is the most desirable one in the long run?

Researchers have demonstrated that people who take conflict personally often avoid conflicts and go for a compromise at best. It is quite clear that using this approach, a manager will not be successful in the long run. After all, you are letting advantageous opportunities pass by. You will have to learn to be tough on the content and not shun conflict about the task at hand, while still maintaining or building up the relationship with the people involved. You are not damaging the relationship with others when you are tough on the content, but going easy on the people.

TIP 29: DO NOT AVOID CONFLICT

Many people fear conflict, as they are afraid the other person will no longer like them and the relationship between the parties will deteriorate. This is the wrong reason for avoidance or accommodating strategies. Judge every situation of conflict on its content: What kind of solution does the situation at hand require? When this is done you should be able to decide on the right strategy (which could also be dominating, compromising, or often better, cooperating). Only when this choice has been made and you are clear on your strategy to deal with the conflict should you start thinking about the relationship with the other person and the way you will communicate about the conflict. See Section 9.5 about dealing with intercultural conflicts within your team.

4.3 PERSONALITY

One of the most popular models with regard to personality traits is the Big Five (Goldberg 1993): this model identifies five dimensions or factors. These five independent dimensions jointly give a clear idea of a personality: every person has a certain score on each of the five dimensions.

Before we go into the role of these dimensions in international business settings, we introduce the five dimensions themselves:

Extroversion vs. introversion: The degree to which a person has a need to be in contact with others is indicated by extroversion: a person is an extrovert when his attention is focused outward, to his environment. Extroverts are often described as active, social, spontaneous, and talkative. They like to be in the company of others and they actively seek it. The other end of the spectrum is introversion: we call a person introvert when he draws his energy from himself. This person often mentally retreats into himself and is therefore often called reserved, distant, and quiet. He has no difficulty with being alone, and avoids the hustle and bustle that the extrovert needs to feel at ease.

Agreeableness: An agreeable person is friendly, pleasant, and kind, and easily adjusts to others. He likes to work with others and is usually modest and attentive. His character is typified by dependence on his environment: it is very important to him to live and work in harmony with his environment. He is tolerant. His antipole is someone with a dominant personality, who likes to compete with others and claim his own space. This person acts independently and likes to take the lead. He can also be characterized as confident, commanding, and sometimes as domineering.

Conscientiousness: The degree to which a person wants to control his environment is termed conscientiousness. Someone who scores high on this dimension likes rules and structure, and works orderly and systematically. He will always honor commitments. These people are often described as reliable, organized, careful, and hard working. On the opposite side of the spectrum we find people who are flexible, who accept disorder, and who like to improvise. They have less need for rules and structure, as they believe that this limits their possibilities.

Emotional stability: This dimension is termed emotional stability and expresses the way in which people deal with stressful and emotional situations. On the one hand, there are people who score highly on "stable": they are calm and relaxed and come across as being carefree and balanced. On the other hand, there are people who are restless, who worry and suffer from insecurities and nerves. These people have emotional highs and lows, can be irritable, but are often also very driven and passionate. This other extreme is also dubbed neuroticism.

Openness: The open, innovative person is curious and adventurous, is open to new experiences, and is blessed with a sense of imagination. He is a creative and out-of-the-box thinker. At the other end of the spectrum, there are the people who are much more conservative, traditional, and also more realistic: they look at things from a more practical angle and are down to earth and conventional in their own manner. In ultimo, this is called rigidity.

By identifying the extremes of the dimensions, we run the risk of trying to put people in boxes and to think in black-and-white terms and label them either extravert or introvert. In practice, however, nearly everyone will score somewhere between the extremes, and the subtleties of the personality will hardly ever be as clear as described above.

The five dimensions are obviously not adequate to describe all the subtleties of a personality. The model is merely an instrument that can be

TIP 30: PERSONAL OR CULTURAL?

When confronted with undesired behavior displayed by members of your team, ask yourself—using this chapter on personal preferences and Chapter 7 on cultural characteristics—whether the behavior of the person is driven by aspects of personality, or whether the person has learned that this behavior is appropriate within his culture. Undesired personal behavior can first be dealt with by accepting and appreciating individual differences between people. When this is done, you can decide on desirable behavior for the future. If the behavior is culturally determined, you will first have to understand the cultural bias before deciding whether or not a behavior change is desirable and realistic.

used to interpret certain personality traits, but it is always incomplete (just like any other instrument). It is even more complex when we investigate how personality traits affect intercultural management: we cannot be sure whether a person's behavior can be attributed to his personality, to the culture of his organizational environment, to the national culture in which he grew up, or to the culture of other groups to which he belongs. More than in any other chapter, the reader should take care not to generalize here, since that will not do justice to the complexity of a person and his culture.

Even though all aspects of personality play a role in an international manager's daily job, particularly the first three traits described above apply to intercultural business. Accordingly, we first describe how extroversion, agreeableness, and conscientiousness play a role in intercultural management.

4.3.1 Extroversion vs. Introversion

In his daily work, the extrovert will readily and frequently be in contact with others: he loves interaction and consequentially contributes to the establishment of good relationships with others. It is often stated that for managers, extroversion is a more desired trait than introversion. This is not the case. Even though we can state that interaction comes more easily and naturally to the extrovert manager than to the introvert manager, this does not say anything about the quality of the interaction. A lot can be said for the careful, quiet, and profound analysis of the introvert before engaging in interaction with others.

In general, it can be claimed that extroversion is seen as a stronger and more desired personality trait than introversion, and many subjective performance appraisals by extrovert managers reinforce this idea. *Quiet: The Power of Introverts in a World That Can't Stop Talking* by Susan Cain (2012) is a book that I would gladly make mandatory reading for any business leader.

Extroversion can help a manager in establishing contacts with superiors, employees, colleagues, and external parties in a smooth and easy way: he is skilled in connecting, which stimulates discussion and exchange of information. Extroversion can also be a handicap: the extrovert is more prone to being influenced by the opinions and extreme positions of other people. Adjusting your own aspirations and position in response to the other person's stance is called anchoring: the response of the second

TIP 31: ALLOW THE INTROVERTS TO BE HEARD

An important aspect of managing an intercultural team is to ensure that all team members contribute as much as they can. Introverts often have difficulty contributing publicly, especially when overwhelmed by the energy of extroverts in meetings and discussions. Actively invite the introverts in your team to speak up: they need this impulse. The question "What do you think about it, John?" can do miracles.

person is anchored to the first person's position. As a rule, extroverts are more affected by this anchor and will more easily adjust their aspirations. In terms of the Thomas-Kilmann model that we discussed earlier, extroversion leads to a more cooperative and less assertive style.

In intercultural management, extroversion is primarily a trait that helps the establishment of connections with others: the extrovert manager is more visible to his team, is more pronounced, shares more information, and is continuously in contact with his environment (e.g., other disciplines, departments, and external partners). However, it should be noted that the introvert, too, may equally be a highly successful manager: his thoughtful approach can protect him from judging others too quickly and can lead to a careful analysis of the situation at hand.

4.3.2 Agreeableness

The dimension agreeableness or friendliness immediately reminds us of the cooperative axis in the Thomas-Kilmann model (Figure 4.1). This Big Five dimension indicates the way in which a person perceives conflicts, the degree to which they are desirable, and the manner in which a conflict is settled: the more agreeable a person is, the more he will have a personal preference for the quadrants on the right-hand side of the model (cooperation or accommodation). The agreeable person is less focused on competition and individual gain, and will be inclined to make more concessions than people with a more individualistic and competitive orientation. Agreeableness is often linked with taking others into account, being tolerant toward their position, and trusting them. Agreeableness and friendliness are traits that are therefore beneficial to mutual gain.

In cultures that are more focused on harmony (the so-called collectivistic cultures, in which the group is most important; see Section 6.3), agreeableness is a greatly appreciated personality trait. After all, harmony is maintained when you refrain from adopting a strong or extreme stance and when there is room for consensus and adjustment of positions. In many Asian countries (almost all of them are collectivistic) an agreeable, modest attitude is much valued. Agreeableness enhances trust, which is of great importance in cultures that are primarily concerned with building long-term relationships.

In contrast, dominance is the norm in many individualistic, masculine cultures (such as the United States): do not adjust too easily or comply too much with someone else's ideas, but try to debate and influence the other person to embrace your idea.

Agreeableness often means that people find it difficult to state their own wishes clearly and convincingly (they have difficulty with the I-dimension described in Section 1.3). An agreeable manager will be more inclined to make concessions, and generally uses the you-dimension and the we-dimension more naturally (listening to others, building relationship). He is less comfortable with the I-dimension (in which he takes responsibility for his own position).

4.3.3 Conscientiousness

The first two personality traits of the Big Five, extroversion and agreeableness, are related to the social aspects of a personality that can impact the negotiation process and its outcome. Now we shift our focus to a more organizational aspect of personality: the degree of conscientiousness.

This dimension indicates the degree to which a person is organized and task-oriented. In practice, this is usually related to behavior described as careful and loyal. A thorough, well-considered approach to work and careful consideration of interests and positions benefits cooperation. This is a useful trait that enables international managers to bring structure to international ventures. Chapters 8 to 11 indicate that fruitful interaction across borders requires much preparation, in which the manager needs to consider the different cultural aspects carefully, as well as the most effective approach per culture.

The international manager with a high score on conscientiousness is generally more task-oriented than people-oriented. He focuses more on process and progress than on connection, cooperation, and relationship.

TIP 32: WHO ARE YOU AND HOW DO OTHERS SEE YOU?

Be aware of your personal preferences on the dimensions of extroversion, agreeableness, and conscientiousness, as described above. Decide where your own preference lies on each of these personality traits, and consider how this comes across to the outside world. What image do others have of your management style? Check your insights with people from your team: How do they perceive you? Knowing your own style and impact on others increases the cooperation within the team. Help your team to work effectively with you.

4.3.4 Other Relevant Personality Traits for International Managers

Besides the personality characteristics of the Big Five, there are other ways to classify personalities. We discuss some that are relevant to doing business across borders.

4.3.4.1 Taking in Information: Detail or Big Picture?

Managers need to make proposals all the time, in order to get others to engage in working with them. They know—hopefully—that people differ in the way they absorb information: Does someone prefer details and concrete information about what is here and now, or does he opt for the big picture, concepts, and visions of the future?

When presenting information and arguments at work, it is advisable to take this aspect into account: Whom do I want to convince and what do I know about their needs in this area? If you are dealing with only one or two people, you can choose to adapt to his or their preferences. When addressing groups, it is wise to make sure that people with both preferences can associate themselves with your proposal: you will have to present a mixture of the big picture and the details.

When dealing with hierarchical cultures, it is important to find out the preference of the person who makes the decisions. In these cultures it is usually quite clear who that is. Adjusting your communication to his preferred style of dealing with information can be an effective strategy.

Knowing other people's preferences is also valuable to managers who lead heterogeneous intercultural teams: Do you motivate your team members by presenting facts, dates, and details as systematically as possible, or by sketching the big picture and the vision behind it?

4.3.4.2 Making Decisions: Logic or People?

The way someone makes decisions can be a purely rational, logical process, in which facts are analyzed. Or it can be a process in which the interests of the people involved are more important. If you wish to convince someone in the first category, it is wise to make sure you have your facts straight and that your reasoning is logical. Make sure the logic you present is impeccable, and present your proposals in a structured way.

Alternatively, if you need to convince a person who finds other people's interests important, you ought to ask yourself how the decision maker's environment will react to your proposal and how he will respond to this. In this case, you will have to focus on the other person's interests. Establishing a relationship before getting down to business is advisable.

Even though it is difficult to cluster countries, feelings about cooperation and trust are much more important than logic in places such as South America, for instance. Whether or not you will do business with someone depends on whether or not you trust him and your relationship. In most Scandinavian countries, it is the other way around: even though people may appreciate a good relationship, decisions are made on a basis of facts and logic.

4.3.4.3 Self-Interested or Mutual Orientation?

The extent to which you are focused on your own interests or on the interests of the other party differs per person. The self-oriented person is focused on his own well-being. This person primarily refers to his own interests and lets them prevail. He wants to be in the driver's seat and to force others to accept his proposals.

At the other end of the scale is the cooperative orientation, which focuses on jointly attaining the best result for all stakeholders. This person is, by definition, more interested in cooperation, where all parties' underlying interests are carefully addressed before a decision is made.

In Section 8.2, we see that this personality trait is also very important to the international manager and to the way he motivates his team. Some people on your team may be motivated by an understanding of the importance of mutual interest. You can stimulate them to contribute to the whole, whereas others are motivated by the rather personal question: "What's in it for me?"

4.3.4.4 High or Low Trust?

People differ in the degree to which they are inclined to trust others. Whereas one person may have a lot of confidence in the good intentions of others (until the trust is broken), another person may primarily assume that people cannot be trusted; it will take some time and effort to win his trust. In effectively cooperating with partners from other cultures, and in managing international teams, trust is an important aspect of building a solid interpersonal relationship (see Section 9.2).

Your personal history is an important aspect in this choice: Has your trust in others often been broken or affirmed? People who score low on trust are more careful in committing to long-term relationships and find it more difficult to establish a relationship in which the interests of both parties are nurtured.

In international business, every manager has to make sure he knows how trust is established in the particular culture he is addressing. What does trust really mean in that culture, and what can you do in your interaction to build up that trust (or at least not to break it)?

4.3.4.5 Effective Action and Locus of Control

Some people have the skills and conviction to act effectively given a certain situation. They generally formulate higher goals and they have faith in their capability to influence and to turn every situation into a favorable one. In terms of the Thomas-Kilmann model, this can be seen as a style that is characterized by cooperation. On the other hand, we find people who believe that their power to influence or control a situation is very limited and that things simply are what they are. They will approach situations of cooperation with less drive and will generally achieve less, in terms of their own benefit and that of others.

The so-called locus of control is related to this phenomenon. Some people place that locus externally, and believe that the causes of events lie beyond the individual's own power (most people in the Middle East and Asia), whereas others think they can control their life and conceptualize the locus of control as internal: whether or not events occur depends on the choices an individual makes (most people in North America and

TIP 33: THE LOCUS OF CONTROL OF YOUR PEOPLE

Be aware of the personality characteristics of all your team members. Driven by their culture or by their own preferences, some people may not easily show initiative or take responsibility. Do not wait a year before addressing this in a performance appraisal meeting: not only is this too late, but also it is an aspect of culture or personality that cannot easily be changed. People with a low locus of control rely on your guidance and drive: stimulate their creativity, assign them tasks, and explain clearly what you expect of them. Discuss the locus of control concept, and offer your help in dealing with the assigned tasks.

Europe). However, this differs for every person in your intercultural team. The manager will have to be aware of this aspect of personality as well: Will my employee proactively seize the initiative as soon as he sees an opportunity because he believes in the malleability of life? Or am I dealing with someone with a lower level of ambition, who takes life as it comes and is less convinced of an individual's ability to influence reality? These two kinds of people require two different approaches.

4.3.4.6 *Argumentativeness or the Pleasure of Arguing*

Not everyone feels comfortable with taking a pronounced position and defending it. Some people get satisfaction from a heated debate: they enjoy assuming controversial positions and look forward to the lively discussion that will follow. These are usually people who present their own point of view passionately, and who enjoy countering the other person's standpoints. They appreciate a verbal fight. Others would rather avoid a fierce debate: they see firm statements as conflicts, find them uncomfortable, and are happy when harmony is regained. No matter how trained they are in communication and conflict resolution, they will not derive much pleasure from it. The appropriate word for this is *argumentativeness.*

This personality preference is particularly strongly influenced by cultural context. The so-called low-context cultures (Hall 1976)—where participants in discussions are forthright—tend to appreciate a debate. The Netherlands, the United States, and the Scandinavian cultures are good examples here. On the other hand, there are the high-context cultures

(Hall 1976)—where statements are made indirectly in order to avoid confrontation and loss of face—that enter discussions more reservedly, and only when a relation of trust has been established. This category includes the Arabic cultures, Japan, Russia, and several Mediterranean countries.

Managers who enjoy argument and debate have to take into account that their preferred style is not appreciated in high-context cultures, where it will be perceived as aggressive and hostile. Attacking someone's position should be particularly avoided and positions need to be chosen carefully. This can be quite difficult for Dutch or Americans who like debating: they are famous worldwide for their direct manner of communication. The classic example of the American bull in a (Japanese) china shop is quite apt here. If you do not carefully prepare your business with a Japanese company, your directness will generally cause a trail of destruction, leaving you wondering why there is so little progress in your cooperation with this partner.

Someone who does not enjoy debate should take into account that his voice may not be heard in the midst of all the noise others produce. He will have to exit his comfort zone in order to convince others in a low-context culture. His modest way of communicating will be highly appreciated in high-context cultures, though, where saving face is important and open debate and controversy tend to be avoided.

4.3.4.7 Aggressive or Not?

People differ in assertiveness and its use in communication. A very assertive style can be perceived as intimidating or even aggressive. Verbal aggression is an extreme and destructive form of communication aimed at attacking another person's self-esteem. Fortunately, this is not the most frequently used style, although some people will choose to manipulate another person by means of personal attack when the stakes in the office are high. This aggressive style is expressed both verbally and nonverbally: a dominant and aggressive tone of voice (loud!) and body language complement the sharp words. In every international venture where stakes are high, times of pressure and escalation are common, and the extent to which you resort to verbally aggressive behavior depends on your individual assessment of whether that is apt or not.

People who receive feedback that their style is perceived as aggressive should take into account that conflicts can easily escalate when the other person adopts the same style. Cultures that seek a long-term cooperation

TIP 34: HAVE A SHARP EYE FOR THE PERSONAL PREFERENCES OF YOUR PEOPLE

Draw up an overview of all above-mentioned personality character-istics of your people. By comparing these observations to your own personality profile, you will notice many differences that explain some of the difficulties at work. These difficulties probably have little to do with culture, but much more with personal preferences. These can be discussed and mutually understood. Make a habit of discuss-ing personal work preferences in your team: it may feel unnatural at first, but when people get used to it, they will see the benefits. Making personal preferences discussable is an essential step to resolving cross-cultural problems.

will quickly lose trust and pull out. They will not explicitly say so, but you will find out in the next few months when you try to arrange a follow-up meeting and the other party has no time or circumnavigates the issue. There is no relation of trust and they are letting you know indirectly that a next appointment is of no use for now.

People with low willingness to resort to aggressive behavior will always avoid confrontation and personal attacks. Interestingly enough, they are usually the only ones who can come to proper agreement with a verbally aggressive person: they can see behind the aggressive mask and breach the pattern of escalation by openly working toward a good relationship.

4.3.4.8 Self-Awareness

The capacity to analyze your own behavior and adapt it when the social situation requires it can benefit any interpersonal communication. But some people are more self-aware than others. And people differ in the extent to which they look for feedback to increase their self-awareness.

People differ in their capacity to adjust their behavior to the situation. People who have the ability to do so have an antenna that detects social signals telling them what kind of behavior is appropriate and what kind is not. Generally these people are quite strong communicators. People with-out such alertness pay little attention to their own presentation and usu-ally do not pick up those signals. They are less concerned with the impact of their communication on others.

TIP 35: MAKING YOUR TEAM WORK

When managing a team of professionals, it is helpful to spend some time on the personality traits of all your people. There are very helpful personality tests, such as Myers-Briggs Type Indicator (MBTI), Big Five, MOTIV (Marketing, Offbeat, Thinking, Interpersonal, Vital), and the R-Drive test, that give lots of insight into personal differences. Discussing these differences opens the discussion on behavior, and facilitates people speaking openly about their personal preferences. This benefits intercultural cooperation.

Highly individualistic cultures are usually very skilled in adjusting their communication: giving feedback—although not much appreciated in most business cultures—is common. In collectivistic cultures such as Japan and Korea, people are less open to personal feedback. However, they are generally more effective when it comes to communication with other collectivistic cultures—a good example of "birds of a feather." But it is also an important reason to team up with local representatives if you wish to start a venture in far-away countries.

To the international manager, it is very important to be aware of his own preferences and to consistently deliberate on the aspects of his style that are appreciated by people from the cultures with which he is doing business. The question as to whether or not your personal style harmonizes with the culture you are working with should be answered beforehand—only then can cooperation be effectively organized. An effective international manager will adjust the formation of his team as soon as he realizes that personalities are impeding a good result.

In this chapter we have focused primarily on personality traits and their impact in international interaction. Apart from possessing a certain trait, cultures can determine if it is appropriate to actually show that trait. Socially accepted behavior can be of great importance.

The culture dimension will be the main topic of the next few chapters, in which we turn our attention to what culture really amounts to and to the way in which culture manifests itself in the daily business of an international manager.

Sharing Experiences

Carmit Yadin, Director of Marketing and Sales North America at Silicom, Israel
LinkedIn: https://www.linkedin.com/in/carmit yadin

Carmit Yadin *director of marketing and sales at Silicom, is responsible for business development of high-performance networking and data infrastructure solutions in the North American market. The company sells to major Original Equipment Manufacturers (OEM) across the globe, and Silicom's solutions help customers to improve the throughput and availability of their networking appliances and other server-based systems. In her work as a sales leader and business development specialist, Carmit helps organizations to stand out in competitive markets. Her focus on this specialty resulted in her being frequently asked to be an international speaker, author, and blogger.*

I have learned over the years that performing cross-Atlantic sales is not an easy task. It requires business skills, as well as strong understanding both of your origin country (Israel for me) and of the country where your business operates and grows. Learning this takes time and lots of experience, and for this reason companies choose to hire salespeople that live in the target market. My story nevertheless is about building up a business in the United States while being located myself in Israel. I managed to double my revenue working for an Israeli high-tech company while executing sales in the U.S. market.

In order to do that I used the power of social media, and focused on establishing strong interpersonal communication. In spite of the different culture and the huge time differences (about 10 hours), I managed to gain credibility, never-ending sales cycles, and some new and wonderful friends, and I'm proud to say that my competitors based in the United States had a hard time keeping up!

To be honest, the first six months on the job were difficult. I didn't gain a single dollar in sales! It took me time to realize that I needed to learn many sales skills (so I read tons of books), and that I needed higher understanding of transatlantic (cultural) differences. In the long run, however, I definitely did benefit from the cultural similarities between Israeli and the U.S. cultures. For example, we are known abroad for being very direct and to the point; we get to business quickly and minimize small talk. This is something the Americans are known for as well, and I think this worked in my advantage when building up a personal connection. Another character trait many people attribute to the Israeli people is to be very persistent: we have an inner drive to succeed; we work very hard and don't give up. This is the second thing the masculine Americans liked about me and my culture, and the fact that I did not give up in spite of all the roadblocks and difficulties gained me a lot of respect. In the end this paid off.

I also found that American people like and appreciate authorities, and people who speak their language. And although very task-focused, Americans are informal and personal in social interactions. I found that they spend much more time on social media than people do in my country, and that was my way in. Using social media, I built my own brand and became an authority in my arena. The best possible thing happened. Not only did I not have to pursue my customers with cold calls in the middle of my nighttime; I actually turned the whole thing upside down and made potential customers come after me!

Practical advice for the international manager:

- Do not focus on cultural differences only. Make sure you understand the differences, but even more, make sure you understand the similarities. Take advantage of these similarities between two cultures to reach your goals.
- Use social media in order to build your brand as an authority. Use your authority to bring potential customers to your door, instead of you chasing after them. That will make sales easier and solve the problem of working in a different time zone and a different culture.

- "Don't let anybody kid you. It's all personal, every bit of business. Every piece of shit every man has to eat every day of his life is personal. They call it business. OK. But it's personal as hell" (Mario Puzo, *The Godfather*). Everything you do and don't do with your customers, how you handle situations, everything is personal. You have to know and remember that business is between people, not between companies or cultures.

REFERENCES

Blake, R.R., and Mouton, J.S. (1966). Managerial Façades. *Advanced Management Journal*, 31(3), 30–37.

Cain, S. (2012). *Quiet: The Power of Introverts in a World That Can't Stop Talking*. New York: Crown Publishers.

Deutsch, M., Coleman, P.T., and Marcus, E.C. (2006). *The Handbook of Conflict Resolution: Theory and Practice*. San Francisco: Jossey-Bass.

Goldberg, L. (1983). The Structure of Phenotypic Personality Traits. *American Psychologist*, 48, 26–34.

Hall, E.T. (1976). *Beyond Culture*. New York: Doubleday Anchor Books.

Saner, R. (2008). *The Expert Negotiator: Strategy, Tactics, Motivation, Behaviour and Leadership*. Boston: Martinus Nijhoff.

Thomas, K.W., and Kilmann, R.H. (1974). *Thomas Kilmann Conflict Mode Instrument*. Mountain View, CA: Xicom, a subsidiary of CPP Inc.

5

Culture and Its Impact on Communication

> Culture is the accumulated wisdom of a group of people. But then also, it is the accumulated stupidity of a group of people.
>
> **—Steve Andreas**[*]

"That's just the culture of this organization" is a familiar phrase, and is especially useful when we are painfully confronted with too much inefficiency in the management of our business. Or when someone is looking for an excuse not to meet expectations: "In my culture, it is considered very impolite to act assertively and proactively." We often refer to culture, and many quotes suggest that culture is something unchangeable and fixed: an excuse that can be used as an explanation for anything that does not go according to plan. In this chapter we delve into the concept of culture and the way in which culture affects business processes and communications.

We often think of culture in terms of geographical location: we talk about Saudi Arabia as a desert culture, and we view people in Siberia as cold and remote. A real definition of culture goes far beyond geography alone. In 1871 culture was defined by E.B. Taylor (Taylor, 1871) as "that complex whole which includes knowledge, belief, art, morals, law, customs, and many other capabilities and habits acquired by members of society." This sounds rather theoretical. A more recent and much shorter definition of culture has been used by Dutchman Geert Hofstede (1980) (see Chapter 6): "Culture is the collective programming of the mind." Culture as a collective programming of our minds allows the identification of groups and differentiation between these groups and their members. Hence, one

---

[*] Andreas, S. (2002). *Transforming Your Self: Becoming Who You Want to Be.* Moab, UT: Real People Press.

of Hofstede's books is called *Cultures and Organizations: Software of the Mind* (Hofstede et al. 2010). The question is: "Who is the programmer?" The answer is: "We are."

Instead of digging into the various definitions of culture, it is more appropriate, for application in intercultural business, to see what these definitions have in common. We identify four aspects:

1. Culture is acquired or learned. Culture is not "built in" when we are born, but is something that we learn gradually through our environment. Our environment consists of parents, family, the tribe to which we belong, or other people within the same culture. Only part of this learning happens consciously: through education at school, in local and national laws that you are expected to know and abide by, and through role models that show us exemplary behavior. Culture is mainly taught unconsciously: you copy other people's behavior and you pick up what people around you think is appropriate behavior and what is not. This "programming" begins immediately after we are born and is mainly formed in our early years, but is refined throughout our lives.

2. Aspects of culture are not independent: they form a whole. For example, a person's status in some cultures is based on the position of the family into which he was born, which also determines his status jobwise (such as the caste system in India). Similarly, religion influences culture in determining the role of marriage in society, for instance, morally acceptable behavior, or the significance of material things. Thus, culture consists of a rich mixture of aspects that collectively comprise the overall social environment.

3. Culture is shared within the group. A certain group of people primarily behave according to the same unwritten rules that give the group the characteristics that distinguish it from other groups. Culture is thus a quality of the whole, not only of one individual. This aspect conveys the risk of prejudice: we immediately project onto individuals any characteristics that we recognize as belonging to a certain group. Germans are punctual, the Japanese have no emotions, and the Dutch are blunt. And even though I recognize these features when I compare German, Dutch, and Japanese cultures to other cultures, I do know Germans who take their time (yes, they exist), I have met Japanese who showed emotions (I admit, it took a while), and not every Dutchman is blunt or rude (the author is not).

4. Culture is internalized: you have acquired and mastered it. You behave according to the rules and standards of your culture. You perceive the various aspects of your culture as the ultimate truth: you are convinced that you must be on time, that it is absolutely inappropriate to show feelings and emotions in public, and that it is right to be open and direct about something. The behavior relating to the culture is so familiar and normal that you are convinced that everyone should behave in that way. For instance, the Dutch are generally convinced that problems can be prevented if everyone would just speak his mind openly and honestly. Similarly, Germans think that things would be better if everybody respected and complied with the rules. This is exactly the element of culture that causes many problems: the normal behavior for a group is projected onto other groups. If only they behaved more like you, everything would be better.

Based on the above we can conclude that culture is something that evolves or develops over time and can change. It is developed collectively and maintained by a group that itself is a part of that culture. Since the fall of communism in Eastern Europe, the culture in those countries has been changing slowly but surely. Likewise, China, Russia, and several North African and Middle Eastern countries have recently experienced irreversible change. Factors such as frequent intercontinental air traffic, international telephone and Internet services, and the global mindset of new generations are pushing typical national characteristics into the background, as a more universal business culture seems to be emerging. However, the typical culture of a country does not disappear: it continues to define how people think and behave.

I once read the description of culture as: "Culture teaches one how to think, conditions one how to feel, and instructs one how to act, especially how to interact—in other words: how to communicate." I do not have the proper reference of this quote anymore, but the author should take pride in this sharp view on culture.

Referring to the quote at the beginning of this chapter (Andreas 2002): "Culture is the accumulated wisdom of a group of people. But then also, it is the accumulated stupidity of a group of people." The power of this quote—apart from the humor—lies in the judgment inherent in the term *stupidity*: besides the wisdom that the group has established down through the years, it has also shown behavior that can be qualified as downright stupid. And that is a good thing, because if they are aware that they are learning certain

TIP 36: DO NOT BLAME CULTURE

When dealing with problems between two people or two organizations with different cultural backgrounds, never accept the explanation "It's the two cultures that do not match." Culture cannot be blamed. Any problem dressed up as an intercultural problem can be solved at the communication level: make the two parties communicate about their differences, work on a mindset of respect for, and acceptance of, what is different, and proceed with taking the right set of actions.

behavior, they can also break certain habits. Therefore, culture is something that we should never use as an excuse, since we do have a choice. Where a business merger of two companies fails and cultural problems are blamed, the real problem has been covered up. The cultural integration has not been well managed. There has been no communication about the differences between the cultures and their impact on various work processes. And due to a lack of open dialogue, a minimum amount of trust has been built up between the cultural entities that had to be integrated. Of course, it is difficult to implement effective communication patterns and overcome trust and communication problems, but it can be done.

5.1 HOW CULTURE IS EXPRESSED

Culture is expressed in many forms. The iceberg in Figure 2.1 represents the part of our culture that is openly visible above the water surface: what we say to each other and how we treat each other. However, much is going on under the surface: values, norms, beliefs, and feelings dominate at that level, and they determine the way we actually treat one another. The visible characteristics of culture are symbols, rituals, and the people's heroes. The symbols are recognized by everyone within a certain culture: a lion is the symbol for courage in ancient China, the Star of David is the symbol for Judaism, and the yin-yang symbol is famous all over the world as a representation of Taoism. Rituals are expressions of culture (think of Indian rituals such as setting fire to the houses of those who have passed away), as are values (respect and harmony are important values in many Asian

TIP 37: KNOW YOUR TEAM CULTURE

Spend time with your team discussing the typical culture of your team. Apart from country culture, organizational culture, or personal preferences, what would you say is the typical culture of your team or department? What would an outsider observe when arriving in this work environment? Which typical behavior patterns would he notice? What is really typical of "the way we do things around here"? The observations of newcomers in your team are particularly relevant in this respect. Stimulate the discussion about the expectations people have, and whether or not some behaviors are desirable.

countries). Frequently, culture is expressed by the collective worship of heroes, use of language, joint activities, social structures, and norms for social intercourse and communication.

No matter how conscious you are of your own culture, you cannot simply switch it off. It is inevitable that cultural aspects will be visible to others when you interact, when you communicate in the office, or when you make a decision. A trained person can quite easily detect verbal and nonverbal signs, albeit usually not at first sight, and link them to a certain culture.

Just as culture is expressed in every aspect of social discourse, many aspects of culture are present in the workplace. Where two people from different cultural backgrounds work together, confusion, misconception, and possibly irritation lie in wait. People from different cultures make decisions in different ways: they have dissimilar considerations and weigh interests differently when making a decision. They form teams in a different way, attach importance to different procedures and rules, and communicate differently about the (lack of) progress of a project.

We discuss two aspects of culture in more detail: the fact that cultural stereotypes exist only in our heads and not in the workplace, and the fact that people are generally inclined to see their own culture as superior.

5.1.1 Cultural Stereotypes Only Exist in Your Head

Distinct behaviors can be identified within a certain culture, but there is not one person who actually possesses all of these characteristics. Moreover, national culture is not necessarily the dominant force within a person's behavior. Business culture, professional culture, or personal

TIP 38: UNDERSTAND NATIONAL CULTURES

I often start intercultural workshops with short presentations by each participant about his cultural background. I ask people to bring some symbols, discuss some habits, and list some of the points with which others may have difficulty when interacting with their culture. Not only is this great fun, but also there are three serious benefits to doing this exercise with a group of people:

1. People are proud to talk about their own culture. Seeing people's pride when speaking about their home country leads to appreciation.
2. Culture becomes relative. When seeing the huge differences between cultures, people inevitably realize that everybody is different, and that there is no right or wrong.
3. Cultural differences provide us with a common language. Regardless of how big the differences between cultures may be, people usually share a physical language (often English) as well as a common experience (feeling oneself a stranger/observer) that enables them to open their minds to other cultures.

Do this exercise with your team!

culture also plays a part, and often even a bigger part. As a result, individual interactions in the workplace cannot be predicted on a basis of cultural stereotypes.

Figure 5.1 shows—for two different groups—the distribution of a certain cultural trait over the people in a group (Trompenaars 1997). This can be, for example, the distribution of the importance that people attach to power distance, one of the dimensions that we discuss in the next chapter. The graph indicates how many people demonstrate a certain trait to an observed extent. This trait has a normal distribution: you can determine an average, and moving to the edges, there is more deviation from the average occurrence of this trait. This means that two individuals A and B, belonging to the same culture, will demonstrate quite a disparate orientation toward the acceptance of an unequal distribution of power: person A scores average on this scale and can be described as typically belonging to this group—his behavior fits the norm for the group. Person B, on the

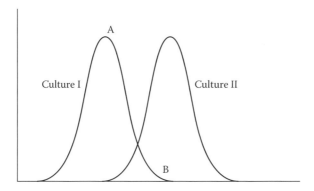

FIGURE 5.1
The distribution of a cultural trait over the people in two different groups (culture I and culture II). The vertical axis represents the number of people showing a specific behavior. The degree of acceptance of a specific cultural trait is shown on the horizontal axis. (From Trompenaars, *Riding the Waves of Culture: Understanding Diversity in Global Business*, London: Nicholas Brealey, 1997.)

other hand, demonstrates deviant behavior compared to the norm of culture I. Nevertheless, the acceptance of an unequal distribution of power is lower in culture I than in culture II, while the behavior demonstrated by person B is actually more typical for culture II than for the culture he belongs to, culture I.

This illustrates that cultural stereotyping bears a big risk. Generalizing about culture is fine ("The Dutch are blunt"), but you will always find many exceptions to the rule. Toward the edges of the "bluntness curve," you will find people who are very modest, indirect, and subtle. I know some of them, and believe it or not, they are very nice people. Still, outsiders have the impression that Dutch people are direct, to the point, and sometimes outright blunt in their expression. Remember this when you generalize. You can assume that a group of people will act according to a certain set of rules typical for that culture, but you need to verify this assumption: most, but not all, members of the group share culture. Furthermore, we always have to be aware that individuals can demonstrate behavior that is quite different from the average, and that these people add a lot of color to intercultural business. For instance, you could find yourself bowing deeply and correctly handing your business card to the Japanese with two hands, while they are already engaged in a heated discussion about business matters, in which direct accusations and confrontations already abound.

TIP 39: STUDY AND FORGET

Before interacting with other cultures, study the culture of the country carefully and make sure you are aware of norms, values, etc. After studying these characteristics, forget these again in the actual interaction with individuals. No individual behaves exactly as the cultural models predict. Be prepared, but when meeting real people face-to-face, you should treat everybody as a unique human being with unique characteristics.

5.1.2 Our Culture Is Superior

We are inclined—when working with people from other cultures—to see our own culture as superior: this is called cultural ethnocentrism. Since culture is acquired, taught, and internalized throughout the years, the behavior of that culture becomes normal to us. Consequentially, deviant behavior is perceived as different or abnormal. Even though we may conceptually understand that everyone has his own, unique construct of his own culture and that tolerance and respect for people who are different is the proper thing, we often react differently emotionally. In the heat of the moment, we may lose our tolerance and are inclined to rate a strange culture negatively. "The department in India is a complete chaos, they aren't in the least bothered by the fact that project milestones are not met." With such a statement, the Western speaker presumes his own culture's superiority over the Indian culture: if only everybody in this world—Indians too—would adhere to the way we organize projects here in the West, the milestones would surely be reached in time.

It is known that an ethnocentric attitude of management has a direct, negative effect on the success of expatriate managers in that culture (Tung 1987; Whitney and Yaprak 1991). When managers believe that the cultural norms and values of the parent company (headquarters) are superior, expatriates come to the local sites with the wrong attitude: instead of being focused on understanding and contributing, they are programmed to locally enforce compliance with the "superior" processes set at headquarters. They consequently lose local trust and can accomplish very little.

TIP 40: AVOID CULTURAL ETHNOCENTRISM

In meetings with your team, avoid any displays of cultural ethnocentrism. Without realizing it, you may be presuming that your way of working is the best, regardless of the working practices in other places. There is ultimately nothing wrong with enforcing a certain organization-wide way of working, but only after you have ensured that you have listened to all possible inputs and have understood remarks and concerns at all the sites, etc. Only then should you make your decision and do what you think is best, not what your culture tells you is best.

5.2 INTERCULTURAL COOPERATION

In order to establish successful international cooperation and prevent cultural differences leading to business fiascos, we can take some important precautions:

1. Formulate the business goals objectively. Ensure—before you start working together—that the goals of the cooperation are clear. These goals should be objective, irrespective of interests, and recognized by all parties.
2. Create trust. This usually takes more time than we anticipate. It also takes more time than we often actually have. Establishing trust does not have to be a soft issue, involving meditation, horse whispering, or building life rafts—although the effect of such group activities can be tremendous. Trust can be built in a very personal but professional manner. For practical tips on building trust within cross-cultural teams, see Section 9.2.
3. Discuss every culture's unique approach. At the start of your cooperation, spend time on the approaches the participants would use in their respective cultures. Have them explain their culture and their way of working in detail. It is advisable to ask someone with experience in working with different cultures to facilitate such a session.
4. Discuss the way in which you are going to cooperate. Use the lessons learned in the previous session in order to formulate clear agreements on how you will work together on this project. In terms of

the model of the four levels of communication (Figure 2.1), you are agreeing on the process, the way of interaction, and the way in which climate and feelings will be dealt with.

5. Implement the agreed approach, involve everybody in the initiation of the cooperation, and ensure that—not only at the start but throughout—the cooperation is evaluated and the approach monitored. Trust should be maintained always, allowing mutual feedback on the progress throughout the project.

In this way, the Dutch and the Indian team will have committed themselves to the same—objective—goal, and they will be jointly responsible for the success of the cooperation and the accomplishment of results. And the Indians will meet deadlines. For sure.

In this chapter, we have discussed the impact of culture on management and communication. Above all, we have concluded that problems in intercultural business settings generally have their roots in poor interpersonal communication, and that advances can be established by breaching fixed communication patterns. We have also argued that a solid understanding of cultural differences is essential to establishing effective communication. That is what Chapters 6 and 7 are about.

TIP 41: THE COMMON GOAL

When you find yourself in a cross-cultural cooperation that is not going well, go back to step 1 of the above plan for dealing with intercultural cooperation. Problems on the workfloor can often be understood by going back to the early stages of the cooperation. Find the common goals that were defined for this cooperation, and make sure you understand the details of the initial agreement. The problems of today can often be traced back to the incomplete or false expectations produced yesterday. Redo the work on setting a shared objective for the cooperation, and ensure all involved parties understand exactly what is expected of them. All your people need to know how they can contribute to this goal, regardless of the culture they belong to.

REFERENCES

Andreas, S. (2002). *Transforming the Self: Becoming Who You Want to Be*. Moab, UT: Real People Press.

Hofstede, G. (1980). *Culture's Consequences: International Differences in Work-Related Values*. Beverly Hills, CA: Sage Publications.

Hofstede, G., Hofstede, G.J., and Minkov, M. (2010). *Cultures and Organizations: Software of the Mind: International Cooperation and Its Importance for Survival*. New York: McGraw-Hill.

Trompenaars, F. (1994). *Riding the Waves of Culture: Understanding Diversity in Global Business*. London: Nicholas Brealey.

Tung, R.L. (1987). Expatriate Assignments: Enhancing Success and Minimizing Failure. *Academy of Management Executive*, 1, 117–25.

Whitney, K.R., and Yaprak, A. (1991). Expatriate and Host Country Cultural Fit: A Conceptual Framework. In *Proceedings of the Academy of International Business Southeast Asian Conference*, Singapore, June 20–22, 24–29.

6

Country Cultures: A Classification

Mister multicultural sees all that one can see, he's living proof of someone very different to me.

—**Amy Macdonald**[*]

6.1 THE HOFSTEDE DIMENSIONS OF CULTURE

One of the most frequently used models to explain cultural differences was developed by Dutchman Geert Hofstede. His books *Cultures and Organizations: Software of the Mind* (Hofstede et al. 2010) and *Culture's Consequences* (Hofstede 2001) contain many insights founded on academic research into culture. Hofstede developed his model on the basis of research within IBM, and identified five dimensions of national culture. This chapter defines these dimensions and describes their implications for the business environment.

The Hofstede model of culture is based on value surveys in many countries of the world: the values people hold (the beliefs they have about how things should take place) determine their attitudes and behavior, and hence the characteristic conduct that you come to associate with a particular culture.

---

[*] Lyrics from Mr. Rock & Roll by Amy McDonald, 2007.

6.2 POWER DISTANCE

Inequality is everywhere. Some people have more status and are more respected than other people. Countries differ in the way they accept and deal with such inequalities. In countries with a high Power Distance Index (PDI), people with less power expect and accept the fact that power, expressed in inequality in status and fortune, is unequally distributed. Countries with a lower PDI assume that people are equal: there is less acceptance of an unequal distribution of power. In general, many countries strive for equality, but do not realize that to the extent they might wish.

Geert Hofstede's research classifies countries on a scale from 0 to 100, indicating the degree to which inequality is accepted in a particular country. Western European countries (Germany, Austria, the Netherlands, Scandinavia), in particular, have low PDI scores (low acceptance of inequality). Most countries in the world have higher PDI scores. In Europe these are France, the French-speaking parts of Belgium and Switzerland, and all Eastern and Southern European countries. Worldwide, they include Latin America, Asia, and the Middle East, where an unequal distribution of power is the norm (Figure 6.1).

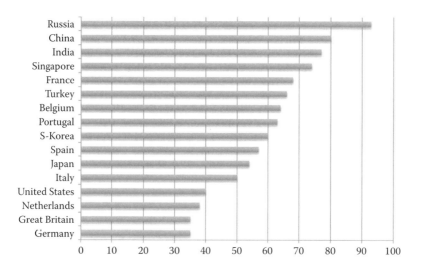

FIGURE 6.1

The power distance in certain countries of the world. (From Hofstede et al., *Cultures and Organizations: Software of the Mind: International Cooperation and Its Importance for Survival*, New York: McGraw-Hill, 2010.)

In countries with a high PDI, much importance is attached to status and education, and because often only the higher social classes have access to education and thus to well-paid jobs, the gap in prosperity between the classes increases. Power distance is directly related to the wealth of a country: in general, the wealthiest countries (Western Europe and North America) have a low PDI. In contrast, many inhabitants of countries with a high PDI live below the poverty line and have a low GDP.

Power distance is also expressed in the typical interaction between children and their parents or between students and their teachers. Children in countries with low PDI scores are allowed to speak up to their parents, and they are often encouraged to be independent and choose their own path. The other way around, a high PDI is frequently expressed through more respect for people who are older: young people ask older people for advice. In many countries it is not appropriate for students to make direct eye contact with their teachers. Respect is shown by looking down, unless you want to indicate that you understood what has been said.

A natural respect for teachers, doctors, and bosses is limited in low-PDI cultures like the Netherlands: people are allowed to indicate that they do not agree with a person higher up the hierarchy, and they can even openly criticize them. The latter also relates to other aspects of culture, but the fact remains that the power distance is low, and the Dutch, for example, can openly criticize their bosses. This is inconceivable to people from many other countries with which the Dutch work. What the Dutch perceive as open and honest (they tell it like it is, which is clear and honest) is perceived as irreverent and blunt by people from other cultures.

6.2.1 Power Distance in Interpersonal Communication

In business environments, power distance manifests itself in the relationship between people higher up the hierarchy and people of lower rank, and also in the degree to which power is concentrated among a limited number of people in the organization.

In countries with a high PDI, superiors and subordinates are fundamentally unequal: they have different salaries, enjoy different privileges, and have different degrees of influence within the company. They not only treat each other differently, but also are fundamentally different. Power is absolute and depends on the formal authority (based on family background, caste, or group) someone has. The people with positional power control the people who do not have it: they determine salary raises, control information, and make important decisions. Contacts between the boss and the employee in these cultures can only be initiated by the boss, who is always in control. The subordinate's future is in his hands. The power in businesses in countries with a high PDI is concentrated at the top, and a hierarchy is maintained in which the higher ranks check and instruct those of lower rank. Subordinates expect to receive clear instructions from their boss about what they should be doing. If the boss refrains from doing so, he is not a good boss. Employees in such circumstances will not respond by showing more initiative themselves. After all, this is not their role.

How different it is in countries like, for example, the Netherlands, where the power distance is low and bosses and subordinates see each other as equals. The formal hierarchy is pretty flat, and is merely seen as functional. Power can be earned on the basis of accomplishment, effort, and hard work. Power in this system provides structure and transparency. A switch in job or position is possible: someone can be the boss at a certain moment, and later be the subordinate, or the other way around. The barrier to stepping into the boss's office and talking to him about something is relatively small. Symbols that indicate high status (big cars, private parking spaces, and all sorts of privileges) are distrusted: anyone can park their car anywhere in the car park. Subordinates in such cultures are less dependent on their manager: they work more autonomously.

The difference between high and low power distance becomes clear when we talk about the concept of abuse of power or corruption—a typical term for egalitarian countries with low power distance. When someone is used to differences in power and acknowledges these differences, he will not be likely to use the term *abuse of power*, since using power is self-evident. It is only natural that a person of higher rank can afford to be directive toward an employee. This makes perfect sense in the light of this cultural background. Becoming a victim of what we might call abuse of power in such countries is more a question of bad luck: it does not have the same negative connotation as in low-PDI countries. Codifying procedures in order to prevent abuse of power—as is often done in Western cultures—is something that is difficult to understand for people from countries with a high power distance.

There is also a difference in the importance attached to certain job positions. In countries where formal status is important (high PDI), people are inclined to assign a very different status to different job positions, such as seller and purchaser. In low-power-distance countries, people consider one another as equals: the power of the market determines who is the most important party. In the book *International Business Negotiations* (Ghauri and Usinier 2008), S.H. Kale states that in Japan, "the seller has been considered little more than a beggar."

In business settings power distance plays a role in terms of:

Decision making: No matter how individualistic the culture (see Section 6.3) may be, in a country with a high PDI a subordinate will hardly ever make a decision when his boss is present as well. This means that in business discussions, the top-ranking person will do the talking. Even when the roles have been explicitly assigned and the boss is not the formal spokesperson, he will still be the person making the final decisions. And even when the superior is not present, his say will still be decisive. Once, I (Dutch by origin, so low PDI) was confronted with a canceled deal, only a day after our negotiations with a French client had resulted in a fair agreement between both parties. The highest manager of the business—who was not present at the meeting—did not agree with the final result. This can be tactics (see Section 11.8 on tactics of power play), but it can equally be an honest reflection of the hierarchy within the other party's organization. This example also exposes the poor negotiation preparation on our side: negotiators from a culture with a low power distance are prone to forgetting to map the decision-making unit (DMU), the person or group that makes the decisions, beforehand. Such things ought to be taken into account when determining strategy.

Forming of opinions: In low-power-distance cultures, a superior will generally take the opinions of his subordinates into account. If he does not, people will think he is a poor manager or at least a manager who does not know how to manage his people adequately. In order to form his opinion, the superior will rely on both his own point of view and the input of his subordinates. In contrast, an employee in a country with a high PDI will be dependent on the opinion of his boss in order to formulate his own assessment, and will refer to formal rules more often than forming an independent opinion. Whenever you put a direct question to project team members from a culture with a high PDI, they will not answer it but look at their boss, waiting for the moment he expresses his opinion. People from low-PDI cultures find this strange: Surely every person is able to answer for himself? Not really. In a country with a high power distance, it is quite inappropriate to state your own opinion as a subordinate when your superior is present.

Status and balance in teams: In countries with a high power distance, status and a person's education are important. Whenever dealing with a team from such a country, it is important to find out in advance the social status and roles of the other people you are dealing with. It is advisable to understand the relationships within the other team, so that you know whom to address and whom to treat with special regard. In hierarchical societies, attention should also be paid to the good balance of two teams that wish to discuss business: when one delegation sends its highest executives, it will not appreciate the other delegation consisting of only an account manager and two of his employees. Low-PDI countries would accept this small delegation, provided the delegation has sufficient mandate, and the right competence and knowledge are present at the negotiation table. If you are from a low-PDI culture and are doing business with a high-PDI culture, it is important to assess the authority of the other party carefully, and to evaluate whether or not your counterparts have the authority to make certain decisions. If not, help the other party to

TIP 42: POWER DISTANCE SCORES

When steering a cross-cultural team, assess the power distance scores of your team members' countries of origin (use Table A.1 in Appendix A or refer to the original Hofstede scores (Hofstede et al. 2010)). When your PDI score is significantly lower than that of your team members, realize that they will look to you for guidance and authority when working on tasks. The degree of self-reliance and proactiveness that you expect from them does not come naturally. Realize, too, that people will rely heavily on your opinion in decision making (or on the opinion they expect you to have). If you want honest feedback and input from your team members, you will have to ask them explicitly. The other way around, if your PDI score is significantly higher than that of your team members, realize that people expect to be consulted for their opinion and that they expect to work independently and not be controlled or supervised too much. Also, expect open feedback and criticism, and much less respect for authority than you are used to.

involve their higher echelons that are authorized to make such decisions: exercising the social hierarchy is considered normal in cultures with high power distance.

Finally, purposefully using or deploying power is much more customary in countries with a high PDI: simulations by J.M. Brett (2007) have shown that in business discussions, the Japanese resort much more often to the use of references to superiors, threats, ultimatums, and accusations to frustrate the other party. Americans—who are used to a much lower power distance—do this less frequently. In negotiations with parties that deliberately use hierarchy and send a top manager to reinforce their arguments, most low-PDI managers on the other side of the table will not be impressed. They will play down the display of power and even wave it aside as "melodrama."

6.3 GROUP ORIENTATION (INDIVIDUALISM VS. COLLECTIVISM)

Every person is an individual. However, individuals in so-called collectivistic cultures (low score on individualism (low IND)) feel strongly connected to a group and draw their identity from that group (family, organization, tribe, society). The interest of the group is more important than the interest of the individual: people are loyal to the group to which they belong, and in return, the group provides protection and members of the group will always stand up for one another. People identify with the group rather than profiling themselves as independent and autonomous.

In contrast, in individualistic countries (cultures scoring high on individualism (high IND)), individual interest overshadows the interest of the collective: the ties between the individuals are loose and everybody takes care of himself. Task prevails over relationship. Of course, people also work in teams and are sometimes part of a group within these cultures. However, this always serves some other perceived self-benefit. Freedom of choice and independence are important concepts in such cultures. Individualists in general will look to differentiate themselves from the others in the group, underlining their uniqueness. Collectivistic cultures tend to see this as self-centered and competitive behavior that conflicts with the loyalty to and conformity with the group that they value so much. It is hard for collectivists to really understand that individualists have such low need for dependence on others—just as hard as it is for individualists to understand why people put their own interests aside for the benefit of the collective. People from individualistic cultures tend to see collectivist behavior as the absence of a personal opinion: this is far from the truth, but perception rules!

The least group-oriented cultures (thus, the individualistic ones (see Figure 6.2)) are the Anglo-Saxon cultures, such as the UK and Australia, the Netherlands, and the Scandinavian countries. The United States is regarded as the most individualistic country (91): to Americans it is important to realize that they belong to the top 3% of most individualistic countries in a predominantly collectivistic world. They are the exception to the rule.

The standard of living in countries strongly correlates to the degree of individualism: poor countries are generally strongly focused on groups, whereas in rich countries people tend to be more self-oriented and focused on personal gain. Hofstede et al. (2009) argued that collectivism in that sense could be considered as adjustment to poverty and famine, whereas individualism is an adjustment to prosperity and abundance. Japan, however, is an exception to that rule.

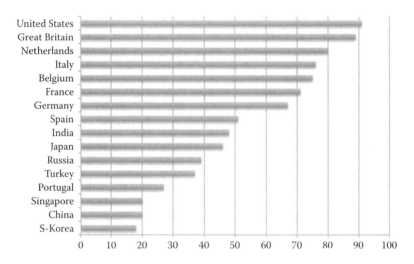

FIGURE 6.2
Degree of individualism (IND) in certain countries of the world. (From Hofstede et al., *Cultures and Organizations: Software of the Mind: International Cooperation and Its Importance for Survival*, New York: McGraw-Hill, 2010.) Please note: In this chapter we use the term *group orientation* or *collectivism*, which is the opposite of individualism. A low score represents a collectivistic culture.

The role and objective of education is dependent on group orientation: in an individualistic society, education prepares an individual to assume an independent role in a society of individuals. In collectivistic cultures, though, the education is geared to you acquiring the necessary skills to be and remain a fully loyal and committed member of the group.

The role of family is also quite different. In collectivistic countries, extensive families—including parents, grandparents, cousins, aunts, and uncles—live together or very close to each other. In individualistic cultures, the core of the family is the father, the mother, and their children. The ties with the rest of the family are weaker.

The following—loosely translated—quote came from a Portuguese colleague of mine. Having lived in the Netherlands for a few years, she is still wondering about Dutch culture. "What I appreciate about Portuguese culture is that parents help their children with taking care of the grandchildren. It is quite natural that they do so. Here I often hear about grandparents who live their own lives: they are not always there for their children and grandchildren. Similarly, children in Portugal take care of their parents when they get old or ill. They live in your house or, when they cannot, they come by every day. Here in the Netherlands, when you get old you have to go to one of these homes for the elderly, right?"

With a score of 27, Portugal is strongly collectivistic. The Netherlands scores 80 and is very individualistic.

The intense social contact, which is typical of collectivistic cultures, is consolidated when people act to maintain harmony in the group. People in these cultures try to avoid direct confrontation: they save others from "losing face" (this would disrupt the social order). For this reason, their communication is indirect. Consequently, they have an indirect way of indicating whether they mean yes or no: a direct no would be too offensive. This can lead to confusion, as individualistic cultures see indirect communication as dishonest: "Why don't you just say what you think? Then we all know where we stand."

The way people relate to the group to which they belong is important in all collectivistic cultures. The group can either be a small entity (the inner family or a small tribe) or extend to the whole nation (the Koreans strongly feel that they are part of the group of Koreans when dealing with people from different cultures). In China too, people learn from a young age onward that serving the country and its people should always be a priority. In collectivistic China, individuals cannot live a peaceful life without the larger group of Chinese (the nation) doing well.

There is a negative correlation between power distance and group orientation: strong dependence on the group, which is characteristic of collectivistic countries, usually comes with major hierarchical differences between people and more dependence on people with power.

Managers working with typical collectivistic cultures (Korea, Malaysia) often point out that in their interaction with businesspeople from these cultures, more individualistic characteristics can be observed nowadays (assertiveness, direct communication, individual opinions). There are several reasons for this. Countries that are characterized by rapid economical development often show collectivistic tendencies toward their in-crowd, but present themselves in a much more individualistic way to the outside world (Noordin 2009). In addition, the culture of rapidly expanding businesses often has organizational characteristics that are related to individualism more than to collectivism (competition, can-do attitude, managers taking personal responsibility).

6.3.1 Group Orientation in Business Communication

The most striking difference between the two ends of the spectrum in group orientation occurs in the way decisions are made. Whereas it is normal to come to a decision and choose the appropriate next steps yourself in individualistic cultures, a decision is usually a collective process in collectivistic countries. The whole group is involved in the decision making, and it is therefore crucial to ensure that everyone is informed and approves. This modus operandi is well demonstrated in the way a question is answered when two teams discuss. This is illustrated in Figure 6.3.

On the left, we see the two phases that represent a communication situation in an individualistic culture: a question is put to one of the people across the table. Either the response can be direct or someone else can answer directly. At most, the people in the team will exchange some information. External people may be informed about what is happening, but it is unlikely that they will be involved in giving an answer (unless it is a culture with high power distance and the external person is the superior).

In the collectivistic case (on the right) the question is discussed within the group to which the question is put. All members of the group are involved in the discussion, in order to prepare a group answer. While doing so, members often base their opinion on what others in the group have said. Personal opinions are less important: the idea is to come to consensus as a group. Here, it is very likely that external people will be consulted since

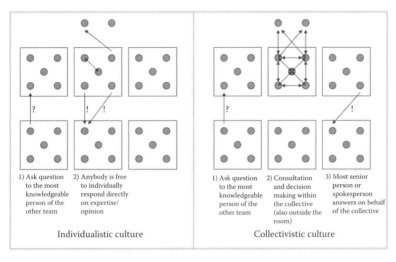

1) Ask question to the most knowledgeable person of the other team
2) Anybody is free to individually respond directly on expertise/ opinion

Individualistic culture

1) Ask question to the most knowledgeable person of the other team
2) Consultation and decision making within the collective (also outside the room)
3) Most senior person or spokesperson answers on behalf of the collective

Collectivistic culture

FIGURE 6.3
How individualistic and collectivistic cultures respond when a question is asked.

they, as a part of the in-crowd, will need to agree to the decision. When the group has come to consensus, the leader of the delegation answers on behalf of the group. Usually, this is the most senior person.

From the perspective of collectivistic cultures, the way people come to decisions in individualistic cultures is hard to understand: collective cultures see nonhomogeneous cultures as dangerous. The fact that different people communicate different points of view to them seems chaotic and detrimental to the group process.

In a collectivistic culture, not meeting targets usually causes a feeling of shame within the group: people are not so much ashamed of their personal failure, but of the fact that this is an embarrassment to the group they belong to. The effect will be that individuals start working harder in order to ensure that the group improves its performance: this abrogates the feeling of shame. In individualistic cultures, such feelings are much more personal: "I have failed and so I will have to perform better next time in order to prove my professionalism and competence."

The phenomenon of losing face follows the same mechanism. In collectivistic cultures, behavior that is not in accordance with the social norm causes a feeling of embarrassment and shame to the group: you are embarrassing the whole group. You will therefore do everything in your power to prevent this from happening: you give face to the group. To most Europeans and Americans, this concept of losing face is hard to understand. In our individualistic cultures, we give a personal explanation: when we do something that does not meet expectations, this can be perceived as a personal weakness or lack of professionalism. The oriental loss of face, however, occurs in a social context and brings shame upon the collective of which you are part: you prevent this by giving respect to the group. An example of this is apologizing: this is done a lot in Asian cultures, in situations where Westerners would not find it necessary at all. In these cultures, people will ensure they are cautious in their social intercourse: after all, you don't want to discredit anyone. To Westerners, this seems like a tricky and complex affair, as if people are continuously "treading on eggs." And indeed, Japanese, Chinese, and Koreans have to—it is an essential part of their culture.

In business discussions, group orientation is important where it comes to:

Taking position: As explained in Figure 6.3, decisions in collectivistic cultures arise through group processes in which all members of the group jointly work toward a shared opinion. This can lead to a situation where a Westerner who is negotiating with Koreans, for example, may not get an answer to his question and feels as if he is having to move heaven and earth to get one. This is a total waste of energy. It is best not to get too unsettled while the collective is busy coming to a joint point of view: silence is a much more effective response. Wait calmly, and use your time to carefully observe what is happening on the other side of the table. You can learn a lot! When you work and partner up with people from a collectivistic culture, make sure you allow the other party time to go through the group processes.

Harmony or conflict: In collectivistic cultures, it is very important to maintain harmony in the group. Shared goals are more important than individual goals that serve a person's own interest. This means that businesspeople from collectivistic cultures are naturally more inclined to feel sorry for the other party: they seem to have an antenna for the social processes, feelings, and opinions around the table. This also relates to the fact that in conflicts, American managers tend to focus on the tasks and the content (think of the four levels of communication; Section 2.3), while Chinese managers are much more focused on the social and relational aspects of the conflict (interaction and feelings in the four levels of communication).

It is well known, for example, that people in individualistic cultures tend not to opt for an avoidance style of behavior in conflicts (see Section 4.3), preferring to adopt a dominating style. People from collectivistic cultures see the avoidance style as a fully legitimate style when dealing with differences of opinion or difficult conflicts. They try to avoid the dominating style, as this harms relationships and trust (Wei et al. 2001).

Relation of trust: In order to be able to do business with collective cultures, it is of paramount importance to establish a relation of trust. Only when there is trust can you belong to the in-crowd: you have deserved the trust. This process takes time, lots of time, and time is what managers from Western cultures often lack. Investing in becoming better acquainted with the other party is of great importance. While doing so, you don't talk about business: people only communicate on the basis of genuine interest in the other person. For Westerners, their "slow progress" in South America, Africa, and Asia is often perceived as problematic: it takes such a long time and it never seems to go anywhere they want to be. Westerners tend to be efficient, stick to schedules, and see all these socializing activities as forms of procrastination rather than as necessary conditions to be met before business can be done (Martin and Nakayama 2007).

The fact is that the majority of cultures on this earth do it that way: on the basis of a valuable and personal relationship. The task-driven business manager, focused on his goal, may score high marks in Western performance systems, but in the majority of countries in which he does business, he will not establish any sustainable relationships and consequentially not acquire any long-term business. That is because his goal in terms of content has more priority to him than his relational goal. The more modest person, investing in relationships and establishing trust, will receive little respect in the short-term, individualistic cultures in the West, but in the long run, he will be more successful in building up and maintaining a successful business when working with the predominantly collectivistic cultures in the world.

The elements mentioned above lead to big differences between oriental and Western cultures, differences with many consequences that reach further than merely the way groups and individuals make decisions. Their impact is often underestimated, but business results can certainly suffer. Many management models are cast in an American mold and are applied worldwide, often unconsciously or against better judgment: in *Cultures and Organizations*, Hofstede et al. (2010) argues that "management by objectives" is a purely individualistic concept that will not be understood in a collectivistic culture. Only, they will never tell you this directly, and we frequently forget to ask. The same holds for annual performance appraisals and addressing underperformance: these are part of the standard set of management tools in Western cultures, but they often do not work in the collectivistic world because they easily lead to confrontation and loss of face when not used properly.

In collectivistic cultures, it is quite normal to treat people who belong to the collective (in-crowd) in a way that differs from the way people who don't belong to the collective (out-crowd) are treated. Thus, treating one customer differently from another is normal, and the doubts and discussion Westerners tend to have about such practices do not occur in collectivistic countries. In these countries, offering gifts in exchange for favors is common, and often an integral aspect of a business transaction. European companies, however, publish procedures on how to deal with gifts in order to prevent employees enjoying any privileges. This is a nightmare situation for salespeople who operate in Russia and African and Asian countries:

TIP 43: INDIVIDUALISM SCORES

When steering a cross-cultural team, assess the individualism scores of the countries of origin of your team members (use Table A.2 in Appendix A or refer to the original Hofstede scores (Hofstede et al. 2010)). When your IND score is significantly lower than that of your team members, realize that your team members see themselves as individual, independent professionals. You may be surprised by what you perceive as a lack of loyalty from your team members, and you may have difficulty with their direct, low-context form of communication. The other way around, if your IND score is significantly higher than that of your team members, realize that your people behave according to collectivistic values. People are very sensitive to their role in the group: they will avoid direct confrontation and make sure that nobody (also you) loses face. Your team members are unlikely to publicly express a different opinion than yours: only in a private setting will they—when stimulated to do so—open up to you. Realize that information sharing is very important for the members of your team, and that public praise or criticism is difficult for them to handle.

they have to constantly maneuver between the strict rules specified by their Western head office and the reality of the countries that they visit, where presents and payments in order to get things done are common practice. There are some striking examples of high executives who undeniably broke the rules on gifts and bribery. These managers, however, were responsible for a global business at the time, and simply adapted to local cultural norms. Nonetheless, they were judged on the basis of the rules that prevailed in the culture of the country accommodating the head office.

6.4 MASCULINITY

Men and women anywhere around the world can be either tough and goal-oriented (often focused on material success) or rather modest and caring. Gender-appropriate behavior differs per society. In some cultures, the roles of the sexes (tough, assertive, and focused on material gain for men, and caring, modest, and focused on the quality of life for women) are very different. But they may tend to overlap in other cultures. We refer to the former cultures as masculine (high MAS score), and to the latter as feminine (low MAS score).

The consequence is that in masculine cultures, aspects such as income and promotion are important to people, whereas in feminine cultures, things such as the working relationship with the manager or the cooperation with others tend to have pride of place (Figure 6.4).

The most masculine countries in the world are Austria, Slovakia, Hungary, Japan, and Venezuela. Interestingly enough, all continents host extremes on the MAS scale, in contrast to the previous dimensions we covered. In Asia, China and Japan represent the more masculine societies, whereas South Korea, Vietnam, and Thailand are more feminine cultures (although the Korean culture is perceived by most foreigners to be very masculine). Similarly, in Central and South America, Chile and Costa Rica belong to the softer countries, and Colombia, Mexico, and Venezuela have a much tougher, masculine culture.

In general, fighting in order to achieve something is much more accepted in masculine countries: advancement, success, and high earnings are what people strive for. The focus is on excellent school results, the culture is more aggressive, and you have to make sure you are heard in order to get anywhere. In more feminine countries, this is avoided: average school

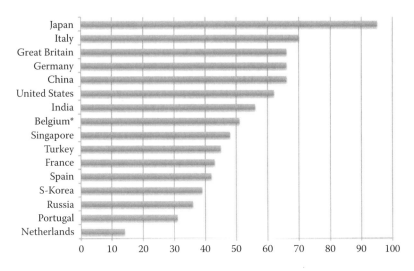

FIGURE 6.4

Masculinity (MAS) in certain countries of the world. (From Hofstede et al., *Cultures and Organizations: Software of the Mind: International Cooperation and Its Importance for Survival*, New York: McGraw-Hill, 2010.)

results are the norm and problems are addressed less aggressively and in a gentler manner: things are dealt with on the basis of equality and equal opportunities. In these cultures, cooperation and a friendly work atmosphere are more important.

The principle is well illustrated by the role of sports in American high schools: the competitive character in which the best wins is praised in the United States and there is nothing better than someone fighting his way to the top from a hopeless position, from rags to riches, from newspaper boy to president. Children are taught to strive to be the best: *the winner takes it all.* People from feminine countries have difficulty in identifying with this passion for achievement: they also enjoy sports, but rather in terms of a social and recreational pastime, where sports are practiced outside of school, and where they contribute to the quality of life. In feminine countries, losing a sports match often comes with the words: "It was a good match. Although we didn't win, it still was a good match, and that's the most important." You will not hear this on the sports fields in masculine cultures.

In both kinds of societies, men and women can have a career and rise to higher positions. However, whereas this is a free choice in feminine cultures, men have no choice in masculine cultures. It is imperative that they build a career and generate the family income. To women, the choice to have a career tends to be optional, and not quite as imperative. Whereas in the feminine Scandinavian countries men are appreciated for turning to more caring roles at home and working less when the children are small, this kind of choice is inconceivable to a Japanese man. Japan is the most masculine country in the world. The role of women in the business environment also differs. Western women representing their company in Asia as the head of a business team will experience a warmer reception in feminine Taiwan than in masculine Japan. Obviously, the business culture in Japan is becoming more global these days, but I have experienced several encounters where the presence of a Western woman in the negotiating team initially caused quite some unease on the Japanese side.

The role of work differs from society to society. The masculine culture is characterized by the motto "live to work": work and professional growth are key, and the lives of men in particular revolve around work. A man will more readily accept that his private life has to yield to his career. Take Japan, for instance, where people sometimes die from working too hard (*karoshi*), and where cheap hotels have been opened near business centers so that men can sleep in something that looks like a box in the wall (capsule hotels). This offers an affordable alternative to traveling the usual 1.5 to 2 hours home from work. After a long night at the office, you allow yourself to be shoved into a wall as if you were the contents of a coffin, in order to be able to start work early the next day. In feminine cultures, people have a hard time understanding such a society: "Why don't you quit your job?" is what people would ask you in a situation like this. People from feminine cultures find the quality of life and the work-life balance more important.

6.4.1 Masculinity in Business Communication

Meetings are daily ingredients of the agenda of many professionals. In feminine cultures, conducting meetings is typically a way to discuss issues, to keep everybody informed of what is going on, and to jointly find solutions. People appreciate decisions being made on a basis of consensus. In masculine cultures, consensus is not required: decisions are made anyhow, not merely during meetings, but in restaurants, in the hall, or in the office of the boss. It is not required to have everybody feel good about the final decision: a decision is made after an exchange of standpoints and often after a debate. In this phase, everybody battles for his ideas to be accepted, and the final decision made afterwards is supposed to be the best possible decision. Masculine Japan forms the exception to this rule: consensus is very important here, but the process of arriving at consensus is dictated by the group orientation in the Japanese culture, and not by its masculinity.

In masculine countries, meetings are more about presenting yourself and demonstrating your professional contribution. The latter aspect is also determined by the degree of group orientation: in individualistic cultures, people will appreciate this kind of masculine meeting culture, whereas in collectivistic cultures, the individual is not visible in meetings, but is more committed to serving the collective result. Assertive and competitive (masculine) behavior during a meeting in collectivistic cultures is seen as a threat to harmony and is a sign of limited loyalty to the group.

The role of conflicts greatly differs in masculine and feminine cultures. In the face of a border conflict or potential source of geopolitical stress, a masculine nation will easily send a couple of aircraft carriers and warships to the scene. Feminine cultures will put that down to an expensive and unnecessary display of power, and they will resort to solving the issues through peace talks and negotiation.

The same applies to conflicts at work. In Section 4.2 we discussed the Thomas-Kilmann model (Figure 4.1), in which we presented five different ways of dealing with conflict, all of which were governed by a combination of acknowledgment of either one's own interests or the other person's interests. In this model, we can interpret the vertical axis (focus on own benefit) as the masculine axis, while the horizontal axis is the feminine one (focus on the other). In practice, this means that competition and collaboration as conflict styles will be accepted in all societies, but avoidance, compromise, and accommodation are typically feminine concepts that will often be frowned upon in masculine societies. "You don't flee from a proper business fight and compromise is for cowards." In feminine cultures, however, people solve conflicts by negotiating (cooperatively) and making compromises. In many countries, the latter in particular is something that is quite incomprehensible as a means to deal with conflicts of interest. The typical Dutch polder model—where all parties are satisfied with the outcome—is the norm in the feminine Netherlands. In many other countries, however, you choose to go for the benefit of one of the parties or both, but a situation where both win some and lose some is seen as a weak solution.

6.4.2 Discussion Style

The atmosphere in which discussions occur differs in masculine and feminine societies: the representative of a masculine culture will often practice a style that may seem tough, aggressive, and undesirable to a person from a feminine culture, even though collectivistic tendencies such as maintaining consensus can also be present here. Similarly, the masculine side will be surprised by the acquiescence of the other party and the fact that the other party is constructively seeking solutions instead of fighting for their position. Confrontation fits the masculine style, whereas consensus is much more valued by teams from feminine cultures. We can identify the difference between masculine and feminine in terms of the four levels of communication (Figure 2.1). In masculine environments, content will be formulated sharply and in terms of extremes (polarization), the process will be configured so that a fight can be fought, the interaction will be more aggressive and feisty, and the climate tough and cool. In feminine cultures, the content will generally be more objectively formulated, the process will allow both parties to present and defend their positions, interaction will be calm and collected, and the climate constructive and harmonious.

6.4.3 Power Display

A display of power in a business discussion, with the aim of making the other party change its mind, is normal practice for masculine cultures seeking the best result. Of course, this aspect relates to power distance (respect for the more powerful person), but also to masculinity. The party bringing in a higher-level manager who underlines the position of his team with a display of power intends to gain advantage by doing so. Moreover, it is self-evident that everything that may contribute to a good outcome is allowed. The feminine team on the other side of the table most likely has some difficulty with this approach. Often heard responses are: "Can't you handle it yourself?" "What an act!" or even "Okay, can we move on now?" The latter team is aiming for a good atmosphere and a satisfactory result for both parties and the theatrical intermezzo by the angry top manager is quickly forgotten. When the feminine culture also has a low power distance, as is the case in the Netherlands, the angry manager's act may be ridiculed, and the Dutch will not be impressed at all.

6.4.4 Compensation

Another example of the cultural expression of masculinity-femininity in the workplace can be expressed in financial compensation—the remuneration and rewards for the work done (see also Section 8.2). People in feminine cultures are generally more concerned with equality and mutual solidarity, and pursue clear guidelines to benefits, remuneration, and fair processes. In these cultures, there is more concern for the weaker links: some people have to be helped and they should have an equal opportunity to put in a good performance and reap the associated rewards. In masculine cultures, the business atmosphere is tougher: people who work the hardest and achieve the most are compensated most, so there is a much more direct correlation between performance and remuneration. People have to strive to be the best, and when they succeed they are rewarded.

TIP 44: MASCULINITY SCORES

When steering a cross-cultural team, assess the masculinity scores of the countries of origin of your team members (use Table A.3 in Appendix A or refer to the original Hofstede qualifications (Hofstede et al. 2010)). When your MAS score is significantly lower than that of your team members, you should realize that your people value an open and assertive debate a lot more than you do. They expect a good scrap about individual opinions, and expect the strongest in the discussion to win. Your people are used to a tough and competitive work environment, and may have difficulty with your style, which they will classify as soft and sometimes even unprofessional. Your people expect strong opinions from you, even when it comes to their individual performance and behavior. The other way around, if your MAS score is significantly higher than that of your team members, realize that your people value interpersonal relationships much more than you do, and that the atmosphere in which the work is done is very important to them (and sometimes even more important than the factual results that are achieved). People have difficulty with a tough, impersonal, and competitive work environment, and achieve better results in a caring and pleasant work environment.

Sharing Experiences

Lekha Susan Philip, Process Manager, Bridge Global IT Staffing, India
LinkedIn: http://in.linkedin.com/in/lekhabridge

Lekha Susan Philip *process manager at Bridge Global IT Staffing, is responsible for client cooperation in India and Europe. The company provides staffing solutions and helps create a dedicated team of remote colleagues. In this aspect the role of a process manager is to ensure a smooth working process between European clients and Indian developers. The role involves having a clear idea on all ongoing projects and maintaining a weekly meeting rhythm to discuss and improve the cooperation.*

Working as a process manager in an IT firm in India, with its head office in the Netherlands and clients spread over Europe, dealing with an entirely different culture and trying to understand their work processes, is something I do day in and day out. And it has been a very humbling process.

We were recently approached by a Dutch client, who owned a website and wanted our help in rebuilding the same. Her experience with outsourcing had not been very good before. They were confronted with late deliveries and disappointing quality, which required rework of almost all features. The client was still stuck with an Indian freelancer who just did not keep up with the deadlines. In spite of these bad experiences, the company decided still to retain him. Her reasons for this were (1) the price and (2) he knew the website well and it was difficult to transfer this knowledge to a completely new team.

The first thing we tried to do was take over the project and bring in a scrum model to help get the work transferred. It is in our culture to pick things up, take ownership, and get the work done. We spent hours discussing the plan, and we were confident that she would agree with the approach.

A day before the work was to start, the client disagreed on the plan and wanted to bring in other tasks for us and wanted to have the freelancer stick with his set of current tasks. We took another week to try and get the client accustomed to our process, but eventually had to settle for a plan where the client decided the tasks, we put in estimations, and started after her approval. It turned out that we had assumed too easily that we could take control over the project, and our client had assumed too easily that she could hand over the work with minimum involvement.

The approach we agreed on proved to be a good plan: she defined the tasks, and estimations and plannings were left to us. The cooperation went smoothly after that. And an often underestimated aspect of outsourcing once again became visible: clear agreements in the early phase of the project are essential to be successful in the end.

Practical advice for the international manager:

- Avoid making assumptions about how people in another culture work. Avoid making assumptions about the history of a client's outsourcing experience. In this case, avoid making the assumption that she wanted to give us control: she didn't. Check your assumptions by asking loads of questions.
- Make early agreements in a (outsourcing) project about ownership. Define who decides on the specifications, who decides on changes, what process to follow to deal with proposed changes, how to communicate about progress, etc. Solving these issues while doing the work is hard, and will lead to more misunderstandings.
- Be flexible. Come up with different work models, as clients will differ in the way they can adapt. We had a clear-cut process that required clients to stick to a quite rigid meeting rhythm. Our client was running her own business with irregular working hours and could not stick to rigid timings. So we brought in another model than what we usually followed, where she could spend a few hours analyzing the estimations and then schedule a talk with the developer in a time frame of five hours (working hours that matched the client's business hours).

6.5 AVOIDANCE OF UNCERTAINTY

What the future holds remains a mystery: nobody knows exactly what is in store for us, or the issues we may face next week. Societies differ in the manner in which they deal with such uncertainties. Countries that seek to avoid uncertainty (high Uncertainty Avoidance Index (UAI)) go to great lengths to protect their way of life, through legislation and regulations, but also through engineering, or by dictating specific behavior through religion or civil structures. Countries that score low on UAI are tolerant of unpredictability, and can handle ambiguity quite well: they do not see this as a threat, but rather as an opportunity. They accept the uncertainty that is inherent in our being (Figure 6.5).

UAI can be considered the degree to which people feel threatened by uncertain or unfamiliar situations: in society, this is expressed in the form of stress and the need to reduce uncertainty.

In general, European countries display a considerable tolerance of uncertainty. However, there is a difference between South and East European countries, which have a tendency to avoid uncertainty, and the rest of the continent. The exceptions are Portugal and Belgium, which score very high. Asian countries generally have a low UAI, especially Southeast

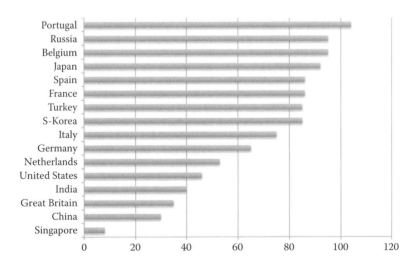

FIGURE 6.5
Uncertainty Avoidance Index (UAI) in certain countries of the world. (From Hofstede et al., *Cultures and Organizations: Software of the Mind: International Cooperation and Its Importance for Survival*, New York: McGraw-Hill, 2010.)

Asia; Korea, Taiwan, and Japan, on the other hand, score much higher. The image of Central and South America varies and the U.S. scores rather average.

It is remarkable that countries with high UAI display high stress rates: apparently fear and emotional instability come with the urge to avoid uncertainty. As a result, life in these countries looks busy, nervous, and somewhat paranoid, and it is striking that a correlation can be found between UAI and the number of suicides in a certain country. Uncertainty avoidance has a strong positive correlation with the personal characteristic of neuroticism (see Chapter 4) and a negative correlation with acquiescence. To uncertainty-avoidant cultures, life in more relaxed countries may seem boring, slow, or lazy.

An ex-colleague living in the Netherlands (UAI 53), reflecting upon her life in Portugal (UAI 104), once said: "In my home country, it is as if everyone is always ready to fight. It is unbelievable; it is as if everybody is nervous all the time. Everything is geared to how quickly you can do things. I think everybody is stressed. It results in everybody wanting to measure everything, and personally this leads to tiredness, frustration, and depression. It also leads to too many car accidents; I believe it is related to lifestyle."

The stress that seems inherent to life in countries with a high UAI can be expressed in public. It is a fact that in the most uncertainty-avoidant countries, aggression and emotions can be and are ventilated, whereas low-UAI countries are more reserved. There, people apparently prefer to keep their emotions to themselves.

The ways people avoid uncertainty in countries with high UAI differ, but there are usually strict rules for everything. Uncertainty avoidance is expressed in language, where many vocative cases exist, and in the importance attached to objectives, tasks, and timetables that indicate who should be doing what and when. Take the timetable of the Shinkansen train in Japan, for example. The train leaves every few minutes and all passengers have been assigned a specific seat. A Japanese person knows exactly where to stand at the platform in order to board the train at the nearest point to his seat. Japan is among the highest-scoring UAI countries in the world.

6.5.1 Uncertainty Avoidance in Business Communication

Countries with high and low uncertainty avoidance differ with regard to the way people behave in the office. As explained above, the climate in countries with a high UAI will usually be busy and stressful: people work hard, time is money, and the more work you have finished, the more you are in control of your life and your environment. In business discussions, this will manifest itself in a high stress level, the need to be busy all the time, pushing for progress, and generally a more aggressive way of selling (mistakenly assuming that this will increase the chance of getting what you want). In countries that are more tolerant toward uncertainty, the business climate is more relaxed: there is no need for constant activity. In these countries, the atmosphere is generally more informal and convivial, and people resort to aggressive (sales) techniques less frequently.

Companies often have matrix structures, where people report to both their line manager (direct boss, vertically) and their functional manager (professional, line of business, product or project, horizontally). This is typically a structure that the less uncertainty-avoidant countries can appreciate. There is no need to organize everything right down to the finest detail, and any confusion because of dual reporting lines can be dealt with. This is unpleasant to highly uncertainty-avoidant countries: having one person report to two bosses is asking for trouble. To these cultures, the ambiguity inherent in a matrix structure is undesirable, and people will have difficulty adapting to such a structure.

In a business framework, uncertainty avoidance is relevant in terms of:

Role of laws and rules: Businessmen from uncertainty-avoidant countries will frequently refer to laws and rules. Even when they are not obeyed, they are still of great importance. In contrast, a person from a country with a low UAI will be more comfortable in a less structured environment: he will accept the rules that his colleague presents, but expects them to only be applicable when functional. And that is exactly what a high-UAI person will never do: he always lives by the rules. In business interactions, the rules will not always be clear: in collectivistic cultures, where much communication occurs indirectly, rules are often implicit and rooted in traditions (think of South Korea, Japan, Russia, and many Latin American countries). However, this does not mean they are less valid. In fact, they are so firmly rooted in people's patterns of behavior that recording them in documents is hardly necessary.

Content or process: Uncertainty-avoidant countries focus on the content of the debate or discussion: it seems as if they are continuously searching for the ultimate truth, as that will reduce uncertainty. In the context of Figure 2.1, the focus is on the top—only on the content and the process—and much less on the deeper layers. However, this focus is determined not only by uncertainty avoidance, but also by other dimensions of culture, such as group orientation. On the other hand, countries with a low UAI devote more attention to the process. In business discussions, it is wise to take this into account: the more one party is focused on a certain level, the better the chances of breaking through the impasse by switching to another level. In uncertainty-avoidant countries, it is easy to keep talking about the content level, but the biggest breakthrough will most likely be made when a switch to other levels can be made.

Trust in specialists: Highly uncertainty-avoidant countries generally place much trust in specialists, whom they gladly bring into play to solve complicated situations. In contrast, countries with a low UAI rely more on general competences and skills: generalists with brains are very capable of making business decisions. This is definitely an aspect to take into account when putting together your project team. If you are dealing with strongly uncertainty-avoidant counterparts, it is wise to include the right specialists in your team. This aspect

TIP 45: UNCERTAINTY AVOIDANCE SCORES

When steering a cross-cultural team, assess the uncertainty avoidance scores of the countries of origin of your team members (use Table A.4 in Appendix A or refer to the original Hofstede qualifications (Hofstede et al. 2010)). When your UAI score is significantly lower than that of your team members, you should realize that your people value clear work processes and role descriptions. They may perceive your pragmatic attitude as dangerous. Your people expect clear instructions and clear responsibilities: provide these. Whereas you may see mistakes as good learning opportunities, they are ashamed of their mistakes. If your UAI score is significantly higher than that of your team members, realize that your people do not understand your eye for detail and your efforts to reduce risk. You come across as very formal, inflexible, and rigid to them. Do not, however, interpret their behavior as reckless or unprofessional: stimulate their pragmatism instead, as this is complementary to your preciseness and eye for detail.

manifests itself in recruitment of new personnel: the French (UAI 86), for instance, attach importance to expertise and specialization, whereas the Dutch (UAI 53) are more inclined to look for general competence and personal traits.

Result: The impact of uncertainty avoidance ultimately becomes evident in the closing stages of business meetings. Cultures with high UAI value precise formulations of agreements, and always want to discuss many details and risks. At that moment, people from less uncertainty-avoidant countries are already packing up to get to the airport. They are much more comfortable with filling in the details at a later date. The outline of the deal has been determined, and that is what counts.

6.6 LONG-TERM ORIENTATION

To non-Asians, this last dimension of culture is the hardest to understand, as it is a mostly Asian dimension whose underlying cultural values have their roots in the teachings of the Chinese philosopher Confucius (500 bc). This dimension comprises the concept of time and how people deal with this concept. In a culture with a long-term orientation (high long-term orientation (LTO)), people focus on what life will bring them in the long term, through virtues such as endurance, thriftiness, and frugality. With the choices they make today, they strive for a better long-term future, accepting present discomfort if necessary. Short-term orientation (low LTO) lies at the other end of the spectrum, where people focus on what is now or what was before: this is often related to respect for traditions and satisfying expectations.

As this dimension was later added to the four on which Hofstede had conducted extensive research, there is no measured score for some countries in the world.

The original Hofstede dimension of long-term orientation is based on the so-called Chinese Value Survey (CVS), for which data from only 23 countries in the world are available. The World Values Survey (WVS) is based on an American selection of human values and includes data from many more countries. Michael Minkov analyzed the WVS data in 2007 (Minkov 2007). One dimension shows a strong correlation with Hofstede's original CVS data, although the underlying values are slightly different.

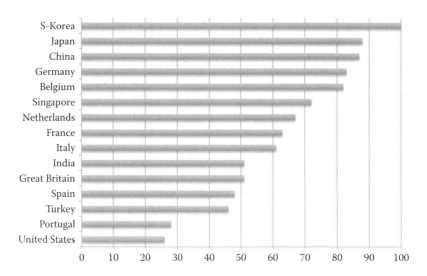

FIGURE 6.6

The long-term orientation (LTO) in certain countries of the world. (From Hofstede et al., *Cultures and Organizations: Software of the Mind: International Cooperation and Its Importance for Survival*, New York: McGraw-Hill, 2010.)

The data for the dimension of long-term orientation shown in Figure 6.6 are based on these WVS data.

As previously stated, this new cultural dimension is also referred to as the Asian dimension, and it is not surprising that the countries that have been most influenced by the philosophy of Confucius have the highest scores on LTO (China, Japan, Taiwan, South Korea). The Southeastern Asian countries of Malaysia, Thailand, and the Philippines score low on this scale, just as the European Mediterranean countries do. Most Western European countries form a cluster that scores moderately to relatively high on this dimension, while Latin American, African, and Middle Eastern countries score low on LTO. The United States, with a score of 26, is clearly short-term-oriented.

The dimension of long-term orientation is expressed in people's attitude toward life: when their focus is long-term, they will be frugal and they will stick to their goals and attempt to realize them step-by-step. In doing so, they take short-term or temporary discomfort in their stride. In Asian countries such as China and Korea, the government used to set up long-term campaigns for achieving certain goals. An example is "The Great Leap Forward" under Mao in China, which started in 1958. Everybody was expected to participate, for the benefit of the country in the long run: short-term hardship was to be taken for granted. Our Western frame of reference highlights the negative aspects of such campaigns (suppression, famine, and miserable working conditions). However, this principle not only demonstrates the suppression that is or was typical of such campaigns, but also the willingness of leaders and citizens to work on long-term results, despite the lack of prosperity in the present.

In short-term-oriented countries, efforts are expected to yield results quickly: companies focus on the bottom line. Traditions and aspects from the past are certainly taken into account, and people pursue stability and balance, instead of relying on their own capacity to adapt to new circumstances.

6.6.1 Long-Term Orientation in Business

A short- or long-term orientation is relevant to business in terms of:

Business objectives: Inherent in the definition of this dimension, business objectives need to be achieved in the long run for countries with a high LTO, whereas countries with a low LTO score have short-term goals. Europeans and Americans generally focus on reaching a deal, getting the order, agreeing on next year's prices, and formulating the terms of cooperation of the joint venture for the coming year. The Asian orientation toward the long term implies that people are much more inclined to focus on the relationship that will determine whether or not the cooperation will be successful in the long run—setting the conditions in order to jointly be successful. These do contain short-term goals as well, but the overall focus is on mutual gain in the long run (Table 6.1).

These differing goals often become obvious when Americans and Japanese do business. When Americans get on the plane to Tokyo, they have clear ideas on what they want to take home (in two days). They are expecting to achieve quick results—after some prework by some of their local people—and so they have brought along their legal experts who can draft the contracts on the spot. Across the table they find a delegation of Japanese who are looking to assess whether they want to do business with this party in the long run. For that reason, the relationship that is to be built up is of great importance, and this can mean that several face-to-face meetings and visits are needed to establish trust. The fact that the legal experts are present at the table is not fully understood by the Japanese. Moreover, it is seen as a sign of distrust.

TABLE 6.1

Examples of Various Goals in Business Discussions for Low-LTO and High-LTO Countries

Short-Term Orientation	Long-Term Orientation
Obtaining the order	Establishing a business relationship for the future (the order is only the consequence of such a relationship)
Setting next year's product prices with the client	Evaluation of the cooperation in terms of the initial goals: a review of the price levels is only a part of the total evaluation
Agreement on the cooperation within the joint venture (JV) for the coming year, based on experience so far	Agreement on the cooperation within the joint venture, such that the JV will be successful: the cooperation in the coming year is important, but is only part of the complete venture

Personal relations: In countries with long-term orientation, personal networks are very important: these are established throughout your entire working life. If they are solid, you will always be able to count on them. Asians structure their network of relations, and they respect the order or ranking systems that exist within these networks. To Westerners, such complex networks of business relations are opaque. Inquiring about the relationships between people only sometimes evokes a willing answer. The network that Asians rely on consists of both family and business contacts, and a person's entire network can be perceived as one big in-crowd (see group orientation; Section 6.3) that serves as a basis of continuous support.

Pragmatism vs. abstraction: Long-term orientation usually comes with a pragmatic approach: using common sense to solve issues. The Chinese are known for dealing with situations quite flexibly and pragmatically, and this may look messy or unstructured to a Westerner. However, to Chinese people, this is the way to progress: you have to be tolerant of the circumstances that arise and be flexible enough to find a solution quickly. Businesspeople who are oriented to the short term often display a more analytical style: abstract rationality reigns whenever Westerners explain their arguments. This means that Asians are more inclined to think integratively, and practice shows that Asians tend to seek the long-term, integrative potential of cooperation.

> ### TIP 46: LONG-TERM ORIENTATION SCORES
>
> When working with external partners, assess the long-term orientation scores of the countries of origin of your partners (use Table A.5 in Appendix A or refer to the original Hofstede qualifications (Hofstede et al. 2010)). When your LTO score is significantly lower than that of your partners, realize that they need time to test the relationship, build up interpersonal trust, and work out the finest details of your partnership in such a way that both of you gain significant benefit in the long run. Your partners are not in for quick deals. Do not display too much eagerness; avoid pushing your partners for quick results, as this will not be appreciated. The other way around, if your LTO score is significantly higher than that of your partners, realize that they are under pressure. They did come to visit you, and expect to get home with tangible results. Even when it is impossible or unwanted for you to realize this, express your understanding and appreciation of their energy and drive, and be willing to make clear agreements about next steps. Although it is perfectly fine for you to "just see what next time will bring," this may be too open for your counterparts and they may lose interest in working with you.

In the context of long-term orientation and in individualism vs. collectivism, we argued that building up a good relationship takes time and that most Western cultures have a time orientation that differs from that in many other cultures. In general, the advice to Westerners would be to take more time than initially anticipated when entering any business venture.

6.7 OTHER CLASSIFICATIONS OF CULTURE

Besides Hofstede's model, there are also other classifications of culture. Some can be partly traced back to the Hofstede dimensions.

6.7.1 Orientation to Content or Context

As described in previous chapters, different countries communicate differently: in low-context communication, it is about clear language and explicit communication, whereas in high-context communication, the context of the words is important (Hall 1976). The communication is implicit and a lot of meaning is conveyed through nonverbal communication.

Swedes, Germans, Dutch, Israelis, and Americans clearly communicate low context: people appreciate "telling it like it is." The phrases they use are unambiguous, specific, and clear. Recognize the positive association these terms raise when you are a Western reader: we see this communication style as something positive.

High-context communication finds such direct language very disturbing, a threat to harmony, and often leading to unnecessary loss of face. In countries where this is common, communication only has meaning in context. So there are various unwritten rules that stipulate how to talk to someone, who can say what to whom, how something should be said, which words can or cannot be used, and even which intonation should be used. The purely verbal component of language is incomprehensible to outsiders and can lead to irritation among down-to-earth Americans or Dutch: "Why don't you just say what you mean?" In countries such as Japan, China—to a lesser extent, but to Westerners still high context—and in the Middle East and many Mediterranean countries, there is quite a lot of nuance and subtlety in communication, which is not expressed through words but rather through context. In these countries, people do not need to speak volumes, since the context says it all (Figure 6.7).

An Indian participant in one of my training courses recently said that he observes that Westerners usually ignore the double meaning and indirect statements that they (the Indians) include in their communication. I had to disappoint him and explained that Westerners don't just ignore the statements (which would mean that they have detected the signal but have decided not to act on it), but don't even pick them up. Westerners lack an antenna for detecting most of the high-context communication.

This is illustrated by the way a person indicates that he does not want something or that he does not agree. When Western people do business with the Japanese they can be annoyed by the obscurity of expression: "Whenever I ask something they are silent for a while, and when they finally say something I have no clue what they mean exactly." A well-known example of this is the fact that Japanese will hardly ever say no to a proposal. Instead, they say, "Very interesting" (but not now), "Maybe" (but maybe not), or "Let's look at practical details" (we believe that it is unfeasible). Westerners tend to classify this way of speaking as cumbersome and even dishonest. They have no problem saying no to a proposal. And when

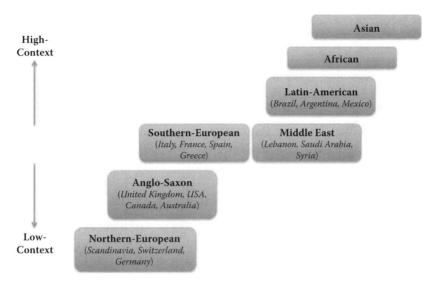

FIGURE 6.7
Low-context and high-context communication in several geographical regions/countries of the world, derived from various studies by Edward Hall (Hall, 1976; Hall and Hall 1990).

TIP 47: PRACTICE HIGH-CONTEXT COMMUNICATION

If you yourself come from a culture (low context) that values directness and frankness, familiarize yourself with high-context communication. First of all, in your interaction with people from high-context cultures, you should study how they construct their sentences and how they package their message in nice words. Doing this frequently raises your attention to the details of communication and increases your sensitivity to the context of communication. As a second step, you should train yourself in high-context communication. Think about statements that you want to make at work, and first make them very explicit, direct, and clear (low context). Next, try to formulate the same statements in a high-context way. Find a couple of alternative descriptions for what you want to say. As a check, ask yourself: Could any of the listeners to this message possibly feel embarrassed or insulted by what I say? If so, reformulate.

the other party replies yes, then they immediately interpret this as yes (at the same time they may miss the nonverbal context which expresses hesitation and reservation).

It is sometimes stated that low-context cultures share a vocabulary, while high-context cultures share the social context. Take note that there is quite some similarity with communication in individualistic and collectivistic cultures: low-context cultures are mainly individualistic, while high-context cultures are primarily collectivistic.

6.7.2 Orientation to Task or Relationship

Some cultures are focused on the task; others are focused on the relationship between parties. This distinction has already been explained in the context of long-term orientation. Where the focus is on the task, the relationship is merely a means to reach a goal: the relationship between the two business partners needs to be such that they can jointly come to a decent agreement. Task-oriented businessmen like coming to clear agreements, not only in terms of content, but also in terms of process (see Figure 2.1): they will aim for a contract with clear formulation of the agreement. In extreme cases they are prepared to harm the relationship for a better outcome and so-called dirty tricks are primarily used in task-oriented cultures. In relationship-oriented cultures, the relationship is most important: a relationship will first have to be established before two parties can actually do business. This means many meetings, networking, personal connections, and social activities: precisely the things many Westerners feel they do not have the time for.

6.7.3 Orientation to Harmony or Conflict

In many cultures, such as the African cultures, but also China and the Philippines, maintaining harmony is of great importance: feelings of discord and tension are suppressed. In these countries, discussions will generally focus on reaching consensus, while the interpersonal relationship must be maintained, no matter what. In other cultures, discord can be an incentive: it allows a good discussion, in which both parties have a chance to understand one another better and know "what they are in for." A person from a harmony-seeking culture will not understand this type of setup: How can you know what is real when there is a continuous atmosphere of conflict and discord? In a conflict-oriented culture, people are prepared for conflicts of opinion and are reasonably comfortable in addressing them; think of the United States, the Netherlands, Germany, Italy, but also India.

6.7.4 Orientation to Time

Finally, there are various ways to deal with the concept of time. In certain cultures, time is limited—there is always too little of it. This is the case in many European countries and in the United States. The ubiquitous question "How are you doing?" is generally answered, "Fine, uh busy." In Asia you will not often get that answer: time is continuous, it is infinite, there is enough of it. In Arab countries everybody expects delays. The term *mañana* is often used in Latin America to indicate something will be done somewhere in the future, when all conditions are right.

We distinguish so-called monochrone from polychrone cultures. In monochrone cultures (such as Germany, the Nordic countries, and the United States) the concept of time involves linearity and punctuality: schedules and milestones are of great importance. Time passes in a straight line and people are often engaged with one task at a time (think about all Western time management training). The limited availability of time often leads to restlessness and stress, and the linear perception of time leads to overestimation of rationality and logic (Trompenaars and Voerman 2009).

In contrast, in polychrone countries (such as Mediterranean countries, the Arab world, but also France) time is a broad concept, tasks can be performed parallel to each other, and appointments are not fixed—they are more an intention. Breaks are normal, and deadlines are flexible. People are accustomed to frequently switching activities, and they divide their attention over many things at the same time. When a plan is not feasible, you adjust the plan.

This aspect causes much irritation between West European or U.S. companies and local entities in India or Mexico, for example. Time is valuable to Westerners, and agreements on timing must be strictly followed. People in India have a whole different sense of time: a delay is less serious, they are flexible, and they have a more fatalistic attitude—when something occurs causing the deadline to be missed, that's just how it goes. This is a nightmare for American and European project managers: How can they ever fulfill their commitments to clients and partners when others are "frivolous" about time? Westerners mistakenly interpret this way of dealing with

TIP 48: CLARIFY TIME EXPECTATIONS

When meeting people from polychronic cultures (or other cultures where time is less fixed), discuss explicitly your time constraints and your expectations with regard to the use of time. Explain that you have limited time, express good reasons for your stance, and state a clear request: many people will be willing to adjust their planning schedules and make sure you can leave in time, even though their own orientation on time is different.

time as a lack of planning and project management skills on the Indian side. For example, examine the long periods the Indians devote to planning a wedding—including all the little details. You must conclude that there is no problem with the planning and project management skills of your colleagues from India. Time is just less of an issue (Verluyten 2010).

The answer to this dichotomy is to invest time (yes, time) up front, in order to clarify what both parties can expect of each other, and particularly to establish the best way to communicate if agreements are not met. When you explain clearly to people in India what you mean by deadlines and what the consequences of not meeting them are, and you subsequently ask them how they would like to work in order to prevent delays, a lot can be won. However, the usual pattern is that we do not take the time to do so when we are under pressure in large international projects and we want to deliver on time, no matter what. As a project manager, you will have to breach this pattern by spending less time running around, stressing, and putting out fires here and there. You need to invest time up front on managing intercultural cooperation in your project.

REFERENCES

Brett, J.M. (2007). *Negotiating Globally: How to Negotiate Deals, Resolve Disputes, and Make Decisions across Cultural Boundaries*. San Francisco: Jossey-Bass.

Ghauri, P.N., and Usinier, J.C. (2008). *International Business Negotiations*. 2nd ed. Bingley, UK: Emerald Group.

Hall, E.T. (1976). *Beyond Culture*. New York: Doubleday Anchor Books.

Hall, E.T., and Hall, M.R. (1990). *Understanding Cultural Differences: Germans, French and Americans*. London: Nicolas Brealey.

Hofstede, G. (2001). *Culture's Consequences: Comparing Values, Behaviors, Institutions and Organizations across Nations*. Thousand Oaks, CA: Sage Publications.

Hofstede, G., Hofstede, G.J., and Minkov, M. (2010). *Cultures and Organizations: Software of the Mind: International Cooperation and Its Importance for Survival.* New York: McGraw-Hill.

Hofstede, G.J., Pedersen, P.B., and Hofstede, G. (2009). *Werken met cultuurverschillen.* Amsterdam, The Netherlands: Business Contact.

Martin, J.N., and Nakayama, T.K. (2007). *Intercultural Communication in Contexts.* New York: McGraw-Hill.

Minkov, M. (2007). *What Makes Us Different and Similar: A New Interpretation of the World Values Survey and Other Cross-Cultural Data.* Sofia, Bulgaria: Klasika i Stil Publishing House.

Noordin, F. (2009). Individualism-Collectivism: A Tale of Two Countries. *Problems and Perspectives in Management*, 7(2), 36–45.

Trompenaars, F., and Voerman, E. (2009). *Servant-Leadership across Cultures: Harnessing the Strength of the World's Most Powerful Management Philosophy.* Oxford, UK: Infinite Ideas Limited.

Verluyten, P.S. (2010). *Intercultural Skills for International Business and International Relations: A Practical Introduction with Exercises.* Louvain, Belgium/The Hague, The Netherlands: Acco.

Wei, W., Yen, E., and Zhu, J.J. (2001). Individualism-Collectivism and Conflict Resolution Styles: A Cross-Cultural Study of Managers in Singapore. Online source (http://www.adr.gov/events/2009/nov19-2009-materials-article.pdf).

7

Business Culture in Various Countries

It's like people who ask each other where they come from ... everyone comes from somewhere, but so what?

—Richard P. Feynman[*]

This chapter provides an overview of the (business) cultures of many countries in the world. Generalization is inevitable in an overview of this sort. When you yourself do business with these cultures, you will recognize the generalizations. And just as with any generalization, the picture presented can always be countered with examples that do not correspond to that general image. A country culture is merely a generalization, and certainly in business practice, organizational cultures and personal preferences are extremely important factors too. In addition, the world is opening up and specific country cultures may be less pronounced in business interactions between two global companies. Whatever the case, the information in this chapter will not be sufficient for a proper preparation of complex intercultural business deals. Anyone wishing to do business with a specific culture should consult literature on that particular culture, or organize workshops with country experts in preparation for his tasks. Nevertheless, the concise descriptions in this chapter will be useful to understand the manifestation of cultural differences in a business context.

The list of countries is not complete, and I have selected those countries with which international companies do most business. It is inevitable that this overview will inadvertently omit countries that may be of great importance in a specific industry. This chapter is mainly based on my own experience, supplemented by conclusions from literature on intercultural management (Morrison and Conaway 2006; Lewis 2006).

---

[*] Feynman, Richard P. (1999). *The Pleasure of Finding Things Out*. Cambridge, MA: Perseus Books.

7.1 ASIA

In this book we frequently talk about the Asian culture, which obviously does not exist. Korea and the Philippines are totally different in terms of culture, yet both are Asian. And within Korea and on the various islands of the Philippines very different subcultures exist. In spite of this, there are some patterns that hold for most or all Asian countries, which are very different from the cultural characteristics of the Anglo-Saxon world, for example. For this reason, it is still useful to generalize and talk about the Asian culture in this context.

Western cultures (Europe, America) and Asian cultures (in the context of this section, I am mainly referring to China, Korea, and Japan) have developed very different philosophies and frames of reference down through the centuries. Where Westerners assume that all behavior can be explained by clear rules and logic, Asians see objects more holistically: the relation and the interaction with their environment are relevant. The Asian frame of reference regards the world as a whole instead of as a sum of the parts. This also means that from an Asian perspective, the world is too complex to capture in rules, models, and categorizations. Things happen, events are often volatile and unpredictable, and not all problems can be solved by logic. Which certainly does not mean that Asians have a problem with logic: however, they rely on it less often than Westerners do.

Europeans and Americans do not understand the ambiguous descriptions that are typical of oriental culture: Westerners like to categorize everything around them, refer to structure and logic, and believe that they are in control when they understand the rules and the logic behind things.

These differences can be explained historically. The idea of individuality goes back to ancient Greece: people had freedom of choice and were responsible for their own lives. They developed individually, visited theaters and recited poems, debated, and competed in large-scale sports tournaments. How different this was in the East, where people—in the tradition of the philosopher Confucius (551–479 bce)—lived in complex systems of social commitment and hierarchy. The stability of society was based on the inequality of people. The collective, consisting of the family, community philosophy, and nationality, was more important than the individual. Harmony would always be preferable to the open dissemination of dissonant opinions. In this structure, antagonistic parts are supposed to be two parts of a whole, where one part would not be able to exist without the other. The symbol of yin and yang visualizes this principle.

In oriental cultures, seeking harmony emphasizes the value attached to relationships. In his book *The Geography of Thought: How Asians and Westerners Think Differently ... and Why*, Nisbett (2003) explains how the basis of this idea is formed during childhood. When playing with their children, Japanese mothers already raise matters of relationships and feelings: "The farmer feels bad if you don't eat everything your mom cooked for you" or "The toy is crying because you tossed it away." Awareness of other people's feelings and emotions manifests itself in basic communication: it is the responsibility of the receiver to understand what the sender is saying. This orientation is at odds with the Western orientation that tells us the sender must speak clearly and ensure that the receiver can understand him. In oriental cultures, feelings, wishes, and needs are taken into account more often, and behavior relating to the we-dimension, as described in Section 1.5, comes more naturally to Asians than to Westerners.

In business interactions, Asians will generally try to avoid heated debates and arguments, due to their orientation toward harmony. Western people find this very difficult: How can you jointly achieve a certain result when you are not open and clear about where you stand? Westerners see it as a sign of honesty to openly discuss any differences of opinion, in that process, they tend to forget any hierarchical relationships or status. A Japanese negotiator, however, will discuss any differences of opinion before the meeting, enabling the group to act as a unanimous collective in the formal meeting. His high-context language ensures that any differences of opinion that may possibly arise will not escalate: so the most explicit response you may expect in public is a thoughtful nod or a statement such as "I see" or "That's interesting."

7.1.1 China

The influence of China, which we call a country, but in fact covers more than 10 million square kilometers and five time zones, reaches much farther than the country borders: many countries use the Chinese character system, for example. Also, Chinese philosophies, such as Confucianism and Taoism, are famous and very influential outside China.

The rules of Confucianism (Confucius, 551–479 bce), in particular, still determine the way the Chinese do business these days. Confucius attributed little importance to power, and much more to being a caring ruler, living in harmony with the people. A good life meant cultivating virtues and serving the state with your qualities. The assumption is that a leader is wise and good, and that citizens are loyal to him. The man rules over the woman, just like a leader rules over his people, and the children obey their parents without any complaints and will take care of them when they get old. Parents deserve respect, as age brings wisdom.

Nowadays, many Westerners do business in China: some are successful, some less so. China—despite major changes over the last 10 years—is still quite bureaucratic and is mainly controlled from Beijing. Contacts at many different levels—central and local—are vital to doing business successfully in China. Since many companies are partly or entirely state-owned, they have direct links to the ministries. This sometimes means that there are strict instructions on what the government thinks should be the outcome of a big business deal, or what the basis should be for a new joint venture. Even though you might be dealing with the highest-ranking person in the company, the president, his mandate may very well be limited by nonnegotiable instructions from the government.

From this perspective, you can understand that management in state-owned Chinese companies is a concept that differs greatly from its counterpart in the free-market Western world. The appointment of high-level managers is often subject to heavy interference by the government, and criteria that go far beyond technical competences and skills are applied. Once a manager, your responsibilities are extensive: in addition to your direct job-related responsibilities (which are often unclear by Western standards), the manager is expected to take care of the welfare of workers and their housing. He also may have serious responsibilities to fulfill in society in general. Performance management according to Western configuration breaks down, as managers are evaluated not only on business results but also on their degree of loyalty, their commitment to society, and the network they build up and maintain.

In collectivistic cultures, consensus within the group is of paramount importance. Even though decisions are made at the top, the top takes the time to hear the input of those who can contribute and those who might be affected. After all, it is important that the whole group benefits from the decisions, and managers will spend quite some time on face-to-face meetings with their people. Nonetheless, it is clear who is in charge and makes the decisions: there is a strong hierarchy in Chinese companies. The boss is the absolute leader. You will never see a Chinese employee contradicting his boss in public. In business meetings, it is wise to address the person with the highest rank: it will be quicker, it creates clarity for the subordinates, and it is also a sign of respect, which will be appreciated. Do not ask employees for their opinion when their boss is present: this puts them in a tricky position.

Communication in China is predominantly indirect. The Chinese perceive strongly assertive behavior as aggressive and irreverent, and they have much more appreciation for qualities such as modesty and subservience. Consequently, in the eyes of many Chinese, Western people often are rude and insensitive and—untroubled by any sense of subtlety or relationship—tend to upset the group harmony that the Chinese are so eager to maintain.

Networks are very important in China: the culture revolves around relationships, both between people and between groups. Without help, it is quite impossible for foreigners to build up a network (*guanxi*), and existing networks are hard to fathom. Networking in China is much more than shaking hands and linking with as many people as possible on LinkedIn. Instead, it is an art that the Chinese have completely mastered. In order to establish an adequate network and meet the right people, a local intermediary who knows the ins and outs of social intercourse and is well respected is very valuable. Coming to a fruitful cooperation is a long road, and to the Chinese, the road to get there is just as valuable as the result.

TIP 49: ASK THE CHINESE

When discussions with Chinese counterparts do not proceed well, take a time-out and try to find locals who can help you understand why. Western logic will not provide you with the answers. Take a time-out and ask your Chinese counterparts—on a one-to-one basis—for advice. "If you were me, what would you do next?" or "What would you advise me to do now?" will bring you further than continuing to push for your goals. When you have asked for help, listen attentively to the answer. Do not apply logic to the verbals, but read and interpret the context and the nonverbals. Your Chinese counterparts will certainly give you hints on how to proceed: it is up to you to pay attention to the hints and interpret them correctly. Remember that hierarchy, company rules, and government regulations can very well get in the way of doing business, and you will need the help of your Chinese friends to get over (or around) these barriers.

In China many companies are still (primarily) owned by the state and individuals have no sense of ownership. Westerners may find this annoying, but in the light of China's recent history, it is not surprising. In companies and organizations, it is very important to ensure people have a job and are kept busy. This can lead to hilarious situations in our eyes. During my first visit to Qingdao in 1998, we had lunch in a restaurant where three employees were in charge of "fly swatting": their job was to chase away any flies buzzing around our table. By the way, all windows and doors in the restaurant were open wide.

Another aspect with which many non-Chinese have a problem is the concept of time: to the Chinese, time is not scarce; there is plenty of it, and as a result, they can hold out for a long time on many fronts. It took the Dutch from 1653 to 1749 to obtain approval to open an office in China: that's when the Dutch learned to forget quick results. They came to understand that in a country where everything is organized from the top, getting things done can take a long time and bureaucracy and delay are the order of the day. Therefore, in business cooperation, you should not try to convince the Chinese by speaking of implementation periods or other time-related concepts. Instead, you should talk of potential financial gain or the number of people benefiting from this deal. When confronted with slow processes, there is only one correct reaction: acceptance.

Those who do business with Chinese need to know the status of their Chinese counterparts and the relations between the people on the other side of the table. You will need to take the time to work this out, and directly inquiring about such things will not always get you a satisfying answer. You will have to ask many indirect questions and interpret the answers carefully. After a while, the relations on the other side of the table will become clear. In order to understand how decisions come about, you will also have to find out about the positions of your counterparts, their education, and especially their position within the party: after all, establishing a network with the right influential officials is very important.

Finally, here are some rules that are important for doing business with Chinese partners:

- In meetings, you will generally find quite a large number of Chinese on the other side of the table. Make sure you know who is who, and what their relative positions are. Invest some time in doing so, ask for support, and if necessary, put your questions directly to the person with whom you have already established a relationship. If you do not invest this time, your deal will fail: you need to know whom to address and who makes the final decisions.

- The Chinese are comfortable with silences during business discussions, and will not feel the need—as most Westerners do—to break the silence with small talk or, worse, by making a concession. The Chinese are not inclined to react to anything you say, although they will definitely have heard you.
- The Chinese are famous for disclosing very little information during negotiations, while asking plenty of questions. You will need to be firm on this: don't be unsettled by this "unfairness"; make sure you get the information you need. And take into account that the many questions are also part of the process to get to know you and your company, and are not only for gathering information for their own benefit.
- The Chinese enjoy the game of negotiation—much more than we do. Moreover, the game is more important than the outcome. In this game, patience is a virtue. The Chinese know that Westerners are impatient, but they are not inclined to adjust to that. They have all the time in the world. So, you better make sure that you are not bound by time, and if you are, don't show it.

Contracts serve a different purpose in China than they do in the West. In China, a contract is only the beginning of cooperation. Generally, Chinese will not have a problem with canceling a recently signed contract if that suits them. It happened to me that a Chinese client reopened the negotiations only five weeks after we had signed a contract, because the conditions no longer suited them: market conditions had changed. *Would we be kind enough to lower our prices?* In Western cultures, this is not a proper way of doing business. To the Chinese, however, it is normal to ask a trusted partner to help him when he needs it. Accepting this will strengthen the relation of trust that is so important in China in the long run.

Finally, anyone negotiating with Sinopec, Ping An Insurances, Baoshan Steel, China National Petroleum, or other large Chinese companies (Fortune's yearly list of the 500 largest companies currently contains around 10% Chinese companies) should take into account the fact that large deals are often struck in the karaoke bar or nightclub. This is the place where the issues that seemed insurmountable during the day can vanish into thin air due to the considerable amount of free-flowing alcohol.

7.1.2 Hong Kong

Many of the rules for China are applicable to Hong Kong as well. In addition, there are some things you should know when dealing with China Mobile, Cathay Pacific, or Bank of Eastern China:

- Punctuality is generally much more important here than on the mainland of China.
- Negotiations will—just like in China—proceed slowly: details are important in Hong Kong, and this should be taken into account when preparing a presentation for an important business meeting.
- It is important to consistently work with the same team when frequently visiting Hong Kong. Changes in your team will disturb the relationship, and the Hong Kong Chinese negotiator likes to know his counterpart personally.
- If you give a presentation, it is wise to be modest and reserved: Hong Kong Chinese appreciate that and perceive it as a sign of respect and willingness to build up a long-term relationship.

7.1.3 Taiwan

The Taiwanese live to work, not the other way around. The role of family in Taiwan is important, and the colleagues you meet during the day in the chic Taiwanese office will return to their small flats in the evening, where several generations of one family live together. Whatever the Taiwanese earns goes to the family. The Taiwanese are generally cheerful: public areas will therefore be livelier than on Mainland China, for instance. In Taiwan, people generally speak less English than in some other Asian countries. Take this into account, because they will not tell you that they don't understand what you are saying; you will have to detect this yourself.

In Taiwan too, business is done on a basis of mutual respect and trust, so it is important to invest time in building up a good relationship. Frequent face-to-face contact is key: telephone conferences will not be enough to establish such a relationship. Email alone is out of the question. The Taiwanese, too, have great reverence for older people: in business meetings, the most senior manager will be seated at the center. That makes it easier: the hierarchy is more evident than in Korea or Japan, for instance. Hierarchy is important in Taiwan, and you should CC the higher-level managers in many of the emails you send. This is a proper way of doing

TIP 50: DON'T PUSH THE TAIWANESE

If you ask a question to a Taiwanese counterpart and you do not get an answer immediately, do not respond by pushing him harder. It will not help. He has certainly not forgotten your request, but there is a reason why he cannot provide an answer right now. Your question may have caused difficulty: he cannot answer without first getting the buy-in from management, for example. Ask him gently for advice on how to move on, and trust him to get back to you as soon as he can. Offer your help to get barriers removed.

business: it keeps everybody informed so the bosses know what is going on, and moreover, it is simply a quick way to get things done. Copying in high-level managers does not have the European association with improper escalation.

The Taiwanese enjoy eating and drinking: during the day, business partners will be invited to some of the countless small restaurants in Taipei, which may look somewhat chaotic and seedy to us. Many topics will be discussed during dinner: people are very interested in exchanging ideas on everything but business. Moreover, it is wise not to touch upon any controversial subjects, such as the relationship with Mainland China, certainly not when you are just becoming acquainted with your business partners. Entertainment at night is a fixed part of doing business, so it is advisable to participate in the long nights of booze, karaoke, and fun.

7.1.4 Japan

The Japanese are proud of their beautiful but—to foreigners—highly mind-boggling country. Japan is often mentioned by Westerners as the most difficult country to do business with, and even people who have lived and worked there for many years will tell you that you will never be one of them, however hard you try.

Traditionally, Japan is collectivistic, but less so than other Asian cultures: people are part of a group and are focused on the goals and interests of the group. However, in Japan everybody is encouraged to form his individual opinion about things and to express this opinion (obviously always in a respectful way that does not harm the group process). Individual job descriptions are rare: the individual and his role are subservient to the group to which he belongs. When you are cooperating with a team of Japanese, you will always be confronted with a collective. When you ask a direct question, you will never get a direct answer from one person. Instead, your question generates a process (led by the most senior person) in which the group comes to consensus (see Figure 6.3). He will then answer on behalf of the group. The Japanese seek such consensus in everything they do. When an important decision is to be made, they will "spiral around the issue," never stating possibilities and opinions too clearly, but gradually moving closer to a decision by taking all inputs and ideas into careful consideration. This process is considered more important than the decision itself. It is inevitable that the process of receiving input from many people and consulting many layers in the company will be very time-consuming.

Just like any other culture, however, Japanese culture is not static, and Japanese values have changed substantially over the last few decades. Japanese business culture has been strongly influenced by Western culture. The younger generations appear to be more individualistic than previous generations, and the expression of individual opinions—although always indirect—has become more common (Oyama 1990).

The Japanese generally come across as friendly but reserved, and will always avoid direct confrontation with you. You are advised to do the same, because direct confrontation will harm solidarity and will embarrass the whole group. A Japanese negotiator will never say no when you propose something, but will always utter something like "Very interesting" or "We need to check how realistic this is." This all means no. Since loss of face is such an important factor in a complicated network of social relations, it seems as if a Japanese person has a built-in antenna that allows him to intuitively detect what is expected of him and how he should behave. He submits to many unwritten rules that are hard for Westerners to fathom, and this complex protocol of doing things (offering drinks, speaking first or last, paying respect openly, greeting) will never be fully understood by an outsider. This holds also for any communication in Japan: the special language of politeness (*keigo*) has different words (verbal) and music and dance (nonverbal) for communicating with superiors or with subordinates. Where upward communication is always very polite and indirect, the Japanese manager can be very tough and direct when speaking to subordinates in his own in-crowd.

The Japanese are very hierarchical, and it is important to know the status and position of your counterpart. They are masters in using power in an indirect way. In a harmonious, calm, and usually inconspicuous manner, they will influence their environment in such a way that all relations are properly treated. For this, they abide by a complex array of unwritten rules that reflect the business culture and internal relations: a Japanese person operates in a straitjacket of social conventions. The gradual internalization of such conventions starts at a young age, and by the time a Japanese person starts his working life, all aspects of this behavior have become self-evident.

The Japanese have a long-term orientation, too, in which the establishment of a long-term relationship is of great importance. The Japanese will endlessly bombard you with questions about the product you are offering, your quality assurance system, and other things that are relevant to the deal. Apart from the fact that this information is important to them (Japan has a high score on uncertainty avoidance), this is predominantly in order to test the relationship, and to assess whether or not you will be a reliable business partner to them in the long run. The impatience that is typical of Western companies is not useful here: doing business in Japan takes a long time.

Most business deals are made informally in the evening in a karaoke bar. Of course, you don't talk about this afterwards, but you feel the effect of it. Deals in Japan are primarily arranged outside of the official meeting: they have many meetings before the real meeting takes place. That is why it is important to give the Japanese all the information they request in advance and not wait until the meeting itself. A timely provision of that information helps the process. After all, the Japanese need time to determine the conditions of the business meeting and to arrange consensus on what they can offer and what they want to get out of the meeting. When you want to make a strong point during business discussions, or if you want to express your disapproval, make sure you address the group instead of an individual; in that way you minimize loss of face.

People from other cultures often describe the Japanese as expressionless: you can never tell from their face what they are thinking or feeling, and the rest of their behavior (nonverbal) does not tell us anything either. This does not mean we can conclude that the Japanese have no emotions or even that they do not express them. Stating that we are just not able to read their emotions is somewhat closer to the truth. Lab experiments with cameras in simulated negotiations (Graham 1993) have shown that the number of facial expressions such as smiles and frowns is precisely the same as in other cultures: so the facial expressions *are* there. Graham concludes that the so-called Japanese poker face is not expressionless: it expresses just as much as our faces do, but apparently we are not able to read the expressions.

And if you ever find you have forgotten to comply with the socially accepted conventions in practice, do not be surprised if the Japanese start laughing. They are not laughing because they think it is funny, they are laughing to hide their embarrassment or discord.

Sharing Experiences

Dorit Grueber, Vice President, Marketing, Asia, at GROHE Pacific Pte. Ltd., Singapore
LinkedIn: http://sg.linkedin.com/pub/dorit-grueber/0/272/348

Dorit Grueber *is a passionate international marketing leader with significant experience in Asia in strategic marketing, brand building, and innovation. She has worked for over 20 years on the client side. Driven by her belief that strategic marketing is applicable across all industries, she gained a wide range of business experience in both B2C and B2B. Dorit started with Kraft Foods in Germany and moved on to Asia with a focus on the coffee and confectionary categories. From there she worked in the personal care (Sara Lee), alcoholic beverages (Asia Pacific Brewery), aviation (JetStar Asia), and publishing (LexisNexis) industries. She joined the consultancy side as a director for EffectiveBrands, a*

global marketing consulting firm, with focus on building global brands, before she joined GROHE Pacific as head of marketing for APAC.

I was working for a multinational company in Germany when a job opened in the Hong Kong office. I was adventurous and attracted to Asia, and this was my opportunity for an overseas assignment. I interviewed and was the favorite candidate, but there was one problem: I'm a woman. My potential boss doubted a woman could do the job because the role dealt frequently with Japanese and Korean businesses. Despite my qualifications, my gender was a significant issue in Asian cultures that, 20 years ago, were dominated by males with gray hair. Nevertheless, to their credit, my boss and others put their doubts aside and offered me the job. I accepted eagerly if naively, unaware of the challenges I would soon face.

We conducted our business in Japan and Korea through joint ventures, neither of which we controlled. My brief was to bring best international marketing practices to the ventures. The local partners were skeptical, to say the least, of this outside "wisdom" being delivered by a woman. During one of my early visits to Korea one of my counterparts asked me, in complete seriousness, if I was there "as a friend or enemy." Welcome to business in Asia, Ms. Grueber.

The early business meetings were frustrating and demeaning. I would be greeted nicely, but served coffee after all the males had been served. Worse, after the meetings began, I was treated as if I did not exist. I was never asked for my opinion, and when I gave one nobody really paid attention. My words had no weight. Socially everyone was nice, but no one listened to my professional contributions.

Would my boss's initial doubts be confirmed? Unless something changed, I was doomed to become another example of a woman failing at business in Japan and Korea. I was determined not to let that happen. Yet simply being more assertive was likely to make the situation worse, not better. I decided the keys would be a positive attitude and clearly communicating I am here to help and I am here to stay.

I set about helping in every way I could. I soon learned that my ideas were not the problem. When a man vocally supported my proposals, they were readily accepted by other men. What I lacked was the credibility to present them myself. Male peers had the credibility of being male; I was starting from a lower level. So I enlisted help from males with whom I had established credibility. Sometimes I just asked for vocal support. With more difficult groups I sometimes asked a male colleague to present my proposals on my behalf. And sometimes I sought backup from senior male managers in my own company, where I had already established my reputation as a respected marketing professional. A breakthrough came during annual budget reviews when our CEO asked the venture teams: "Has Dorit approved this proposal?" From that point, I was taken more seriously.

Sometimes credibility is established in unexpected ways. One night after work in Japan I joined the team at a German Bierhaus at the Ginza. Most people outside Germany assume all Germans are good beer drinkers, so expectations among my Japanese colleagues were high and I would be tested. The alcohol flowed freely, as it tends to at office gatherings in Asia. The next morning the whole team was late to arrive, except for me. Suffice to say I passed the test. It seems trivial, but that moment of social bonding and respect carried over to our working relationships as well.

I learned that an essential part of Asian cultures is to show persistence and to gradually work toward what you want to achieve in the long run. When my venture colleagues realized I was not just a one-year expat who would soon be gone, but that I was dedicated to their success and backed it up with solid work, things slowly changed: my proposals were listened to, I was asked for advice, and my opinions counted.

I've now been working in Asia for more than 20 years. The early frustrations are past and most of my challenges arise from the business—as they should. I have experience, credibility, and seniority, and my reputation precedes me. I am proud that I did not give in despite all the difficulties: I remained true to myself and my values, I knew what I wanted, and I worked hard to get it. In the end I earned the respect that any businesswoman deserves.

I recently visited my old team in Korea. When they heard I was coming the whole senior management team gathered in the lobby and bowed when I entered. The president took me for lunch and told me they are successful because of my help. Surely that is an overstatement, but I must admit I felt all my hard work was fruitful in the end. When I left, they all bowed again. Ms. Grueber felt truly welcomed to business in Asia.

Practical advice for the international manager:

- Respect other cultures, but stay true to yourself. Pursue your ambitions persistently and with determination, but always from a position of respect for other cultures.
- Seek support from those with credibility. In my case, being a woman was an impediment with many males until they saw that other males supported and respected me. I had to leverage the credibility of others to establish my own.
- Build your own brand. Leverage your network by mentioning people and your relationship to them. Tell people how long you are with the company. Get credit for your contributions. Build a reputation that deserves respect.

7.1.5 South Korea

South Korea occupies a special place in Asia, and is characterized by years of interference from and domination by surrounding countries such as Russia, China, and especially Japan. Do not classify South Koreans as Asians, as they take pride in their independence. They protect their own language and culture and their status as a worldwide example of a fast-growing nation. The relations with Japan in particular are a sensitive topic of discussion, as is their relation with the stalinistic North Korea, with which they are still officially at war. These issues are not comfortable subjects of discussion when meeting your business partners from Samsung, Hyundai, or LG. And when visiting Korea as part of an Asian "tour," do not place too much emphasis on where you have just come from or what your next destination is. South Koreans want to hear that you are investing time and energy in the important country of Korea, and treating them as "just another Asian country" will not be appreciated.

It pays to invest time in researching the history and culture of this fascinating country. A businessperson with a lot of experience dealing with China and Japan will still encounter many surprises in Korea. Of course, many general cultural characteristics (collectivism, long-term orientation) are similar to those in other Asian countries, but there are big differences as well. South Korea is much more nationalistic, and in business you will notice that—regardless of which company you are dealing with in Korea—the interests of Korea come first. The way of coping with conflict is also distinctly different: where the Japanese are famous for their sensitivity and indirect way of addressing important topics, the Korean will deal with business conflicts in a very direct way, and fight for his own interests and those of his country. This style comes across to many Westerners as extremely aggressive at times. The Korean businessman will come across as very friendly in interpersonal contact, but when it comes to accomplishing his objectives, he will be very determined and outspoken. Korea is perceived as much more masculine than the Hofstede score on this dimension would suggest: South Korea scores 39 (which would classify the country as feminine compared to masculine Japan, with a score of 95).

Korea is very collectivistic. The inhabitants are clearly focused on their in-crowd, which can be their family, their company, or even the total country. Koreans do not like individualistic behavior, and their first allegiance is always to the pride and interests of their own country when dealing with other countries. Doing something beneficial for the country of Korea will be appreciated and remembered.

Koreans know what they are aiming for when doing business, and are very result-oriented. They always make sure to return to their country with what they aimed for, and if that is not possible, they will do all they can to return to their superiors without losing face. In commercial interactions with Koreans this is important to know: put yourself in their position and ask yourself: "What do they need to take home to their superiors, and how can I help them show that they have achieved a lot?" Korean businessmen usually receive a very limited mandate from their management, which partially explains why Koreans can come across as very tough and rigid. The word *compromise* seems not to exist in the Korean wordbook. Rigidity is a sign of a tough business culture: it regularly happens that somebody in a Korean *chaebol* loses his job (or is "promoted" to another division) because he did not meet his targets and therefore could not avoid loss of face for his company and his superiors.

Western sales and purchasing people learn to go for win-win solutions and try to increase the pie before sharing it. They become frustrated in Korea, because the Korean negotiators often simply do not have the mandate to negotiate elements other than price or delivery time. They will not be able to accept your efforts to achieve win-win, although they understand very well that this is what you are doing. This element also makes Westerners perceive Koreans as aggressive and tough: they seem to go only for their own interests and continue to ask for concessions from you without doing many concessions (if any) themselves. To Koreans it is normal to take extreme positions in negotiations, although they know that they will have to succumb later in the process. Your job is to make sure that they can do this without losing face.

Koreans go far to get what they want: a long negotiation on Saturday in a very cold building without food and warm drinks is no fun. The most extreme case I witnessed was when one of our engineers was locked in a room with the apparatus that she was supposed to repair. The Koreans expected her to phone when the problem was solved, and only then would they reopen the door. At moments like this you have to become crystal clear on what you will and will not tolerate from your Korean business partners. Drawing a line by walking away or closing the discussions will ultimately be accepted by the Koreans, and even appreciated.

Doing business in Korea can be much more of an emotional process than in many other Asian countries. Trust and respect always form the basis of your professional relationship, but Koreans can adopt aggressive positions at times. They can express anger and frustration in a very direct and emotional way at such moments. It is very important for you to stay calm and collected and remain in control: your professionalism will be appreciated.

When dealing with Korea, you always have to remember to deal with the country more than with an individual company. I frequently found that the prices I had offered one company one day were known to the competitor the next day. It is not uncommon for your own local people to promote this process: they work primarily in the interest of their country and less in the interests of an individual company they may represent.

Here I give a good example of tactics in Korea. One day the Korean business partners of a large multinational treated the Dutch team of negotiators to a nice evening out. In accordance with good Korean tradition, this involved much karaoke singing and excessive drinking. No surprises there. When the negotiators finally returned to their hotel in Seoul, they were not looking forward to the start of their negotiations at 8 o'clock the next morning, although they realized that the Korean delegation would have the same disadvantage. The next morning they were shocked when they arrived at the negotiation table, tired after only a few hours of sleep and still under the influence of the large quantity of alcohol. A fresh and well-prepared negotiation team entered the room to represent the Korean side: the Koreans who had been "on duty" the previous night were not present. The Dutch team clearly was at a disadvantage that day.

7.1.6 India

From all corners of the world, more and more activities in the field of IT, technology, and services are being outsourced to India. Large Indian companies (Reliance, Tata, Bharat Oil) and many international IT companies are attracting numerous foreign representatives, all of whom know that working with Indian organizations can frequently cause misunderstandings. Just as in many other countries, it is worthwhile hiring an expert in the field of doing business in India before starting your venture. India is a complex society with many different religions, languages, and cultures. The famous caste system (four traditional castes and thousands of subcastes), which has its roots in Hinduism, has many social norms. The dynamics of this system are hard for outsiders to understand, and help from people who know the society and business ethics is advisable.

The citizens of India are proud of their country, and contributing to the prestige and prosperity of the country is an important motivation for its inhabitants. Make sure that you inquire into the habits of the country before you do business. The contacts you build up this way will be needed later, for business is a very personal affair, which is conducted through networking and frequent face-to-face meetings. Before any business cooperation, invest time in building up a good relationship: inquiring after family and friends contributes greatly, especially since decisions need to be in harmony with the family and the social structures to which you belong.

Hierarchy also plays a significant role in doing business in India: seniors are respected for their wisdom, and as a rule, the eldest person will do the talking. Out of respect, the others remain silent. When discussions with Indian counterparts come to a deadlock, help from a higher level (supervisor) can provide a breakthrough: make sure you go about this carefully, since you do not want to pass by the colleagues you are already working with.

While in most Asian countries calm conversation and modesty are virtues, Indians love heated debates and emotions can be expressed freely. Respectful assertiveness is expected and appreciated. Meetings are competitive and contain extensive argumentations in order to come to conclusions. Negotiation is in their blood: it is daily practice and they enjoy several rounds of negotiations in which they really give their all.

India has a considerably fatalistic mentality: the reasons for success or failure are found in nature and in the environment. A person's influence on his own fate is limited. This means that in international business, Indians can come across as passive, despite the fact that they work very hard. From our frame of reference, it often looks as though they are working hard but not very efficiently.

Time is never a restriction in India: there is plenty of it. Expect to run into delays in business; they are inevitable. Making a big fuss about that is not appreciated, and it can even be held against you. A wiser option is open acceptance of the delay and an offer to help minimize the impact of the delay in other ways in the meantime. Project managers whose team is partly in India are wise not to count too much on the Indian planning. Instead, it is better to train yourself to identify the risks and the resources that you need: this does not mean that Indians are incapable of planning; it is just that their attitude toward risks and schedules is very different from ours. If the Indian team tells you "We need more time," it is not a question of tactics—it is sincere. Usually this has to do with the fact that decisions come about much more slowly than planned: many people are involved and the bureaucracy does not help either. This is different from the way things work in Japan or China, where decisions take time as well, but that time is actually spent on reaching consensus in the group. In India, time is consumed by bureaucracy: waiting for people to approve, with or without the necessary stamps, seals, and signatures.

TIP 51: DEADLINES IN INDIA

When your Indian counterparts do not deliver the required results (software updates, paperwork, design documents, or subassemblies) in time, do not get frustrated about the fact that they did not tell you up front. Their pride got in the way, and the Indians take pride in working very hard and doing all they can to achieve the best possible results. However difficult and unnatural this sounds to you, take personal responsibility for all the deadlines of the Indian team. Praise them for their hard and dedicated work, identify the problem that got in the way of timely delivery, ask them for advice on how to solve this problem, and offer any help you can in realizing the deadline.

7.1.7 Singapore

City-state Singapore is very multicultural. It looks very Western, but appearances are deceptive: underneath the surface you find a captivating country, which largely corresponds with the general picture that we have already sketched for Asia, and particularly China: 75% of Singaporeans are Chinese.

People in Singapore are very loyal to their country and their company. Here too, consensus within the group and hierarchy are important factors. The eldest person is generally the leader of the delegation. Before you have established a business relationship with Singapore Telecom or Olan International, you will need to have established a personal relationship with a Singaporean employee. As in many other Asian countries, loss of face is avoided and aggressive behavior is not appreciated. On the contrary, they like people who speak calmly and in a friendly manner, and who act modestly. Long silences in a conversation or meeting are customary and are seen as polite.

7.1.8 Thailand

Thailand stands out from many other Asian countries because of the friendliness of the people: they always seem to smile and they come across as being very relaxed. This is in their culture: direct confrontation—as in many other places—is avoided. A Thai believes in a gradual and nonassertive way of getting things done and in taking other people's feelings into account.

Another difference is the pragmatism that characterizes Thailand. Where many other Asian countries have a long-term orientation that they apply to every decision they need to make, the Thai (like Singaporeans and Filipinos) are pragmatic. Their fatalism plays a big role: a human being cannot determine his own fate; luck and fate determine how you end up.

7.1.9 Philippines

The Philippines are not long-term-oriented either: planning for things that lie in the far future is unrealistic anyhow, and short-term pragmatism typifies Filipino attitudes. The Filipinos have a rich and diverse culture, with many Chinese, Spanish, and American influences. This country is collectivistic as well: family is the most important in-crowd to which a person can belong, and consensus in that group is needed to make decisions.

In the Philippines, you have to make a big effort to gather the right people around the table. The real decision makers will only join the table after a long period of relationship building. Personal relationships are of great importance: the Filipinos need to get to know you as a person and to trust you before they can partner up in something as important as business. Business meetings in the Philippines are conducted professionally and formally. No matter how tough the business conflict, harmony is maintained and direct confrontations are avoided. Recent years have seen large groups of young Filipino professionals who are quite extravert, outspoken, and direct: they act self-confidently and assertively where needed, although always in a respectful way.

Hierarchy is important in the Philippines but is not immediately visible to a visitor: find out who is the highest in rank and who is the most senior and respected person. This person will be very influential in decision making, and major difficulties in your interaction with Filipinos can often be resolved through the proper involvement of this person.

7.2 EUROPE

7.2.1 France

France occupies a central position in Europe: the French are conscious of their worldwide influence and power and are keen to be appreciated and admired for it. They are proud of their country. Numerous world-renowned French artists, composers, and authors support this French sense of pride. In the corporate world, France has brought forth imposing names such as Christian Dior, GDF Suez, and BNP Paribas. France is a country of class and status.

It is striking that the people in a country that is such a strong player at the global level refuse to speak English, and are at an utter loss when asked to express themselves in English. Fortunately this is becoming less and less the case: nowadays many French are learning English in school and work in international companies where English is the official language. The fact that French are reluctant to switch to English reveals an underlying value: the wish to be second to none. The French are often well aware—even more than necessary—of their lack of proficiency in other languages, and that is why they are not comfortable expressing themselves in English, since that will only confirm their ineptness. I have experienced on many occasions that when you confirm that you understand them quite well, they suddenly are more free and comfortable in speaking English.

The French work with strictly defined positions and tasks. Companies are very hierarchical and centrally organized, power is concentrated at the top, and the director enjoys a high status based on his position. Doing business with the French means that you will have to be conscious of the high degree of hierarchy. You will only seldom meet a Frenchman who openly criticizes his boss, and he will never directly oppose him. At least, that is what it looks like. He will counter his boss and express his discord, but in a very correct and indirect way. In the French hierarchy, the decisions are made at the highest level and the higher echelon can easily revoke a decision that is made at a lower level. When Americans think they have a deal, the French can easily perceive it as conditional: we have a deal, with the condition that our management needs to agree as well. In business agreements, it is therefore important to know the positions your counterparts hold and what you can expect from each person: Are they authorized to make a decision or are they merely informers of the real decision makers, who hide out somewhere at headquarters?

Meetings in France often are chaotic and unstructured. The French are mostly polychronic, which means they can engage in more than one thing at a time. Communication is based on reasoning and arguing. This can be seen in many a conversation between French people; even if you don't speak the language, you will notice that people are debating. It can also be found in the way that presentations on a certain topic are structured. The kickoff of a business meeting can be a presentation that is larded with

---

TIP 52: THE FRENCH BOSS

Build up a good relationship with the French boss (national manager, department head, etc.). This person can make or break any proposal, and not having a good relationship with high-level people can stand in the way of getting things done. The lower levels will not help you achieve results when their boss does not support your project or your goals: getting the boss to buy in is essential. Showing respect for their authority is a first step to get along well with the French cadres.

facts, arguments, and background information, which are shared in a convincing and often emotional way. This finds its origin in the French education, where the skills of conceptual thinking and logical reasoning are valued greatly.

In France, personal relationships with business partners are important. These relationships are not built over lunch; it is a question of time. Those who are working with the same people for some time will find that trust grows. The French are more open in their opinions and feelings and more willing to help you reach your goals. The reader who thinks that is the case in every country is correct, but this effect is stronger in France. Initially, the French may come across as formal or inaccessible; later they will share information and cooperate more easily.

The French negotiation style is characterized as aggressive. Fortunately they seem to forget that determination over a good meal and a glass of wine: French wine.

7.2.2 Germany

Germany is a country of hierarchy and status: in this hierarchy, titles are very important and so are status symbols. Status is predominantly derived from an academic education or a high position. Communication in German companies flows from top to bottom and does not meet any resistance on its way down. In Germany, there is much respect for superiors, and employees will not openly challenge new initiatives. It is interesting that this hierarchical country has a relatively low Power Distance Index. The hierarchy is not rooted in the dimension of power distance and does not assume fundamental inequality between humans. On the contrary, Germans generally maintain the principle that everyone is equal. The reliance on hierarchy finds its base in the dimension of uncertainty avoidance: clear reporting lines and hierarchical processes provide structure, and structure reduces uncertainty.

Meetings are orderly in Germany. Time is a much more sharply defined phenomenon than it is in North America, Latin America, or Mediterranean countries. People are punctual, work efficiently, and generally meet all deadlines and stipulations. In the BMW, BASF, and Siemens offices— where things are formal and punctual—the daily workload is determined by the agenda. This is also a consequence of its high—for West European countries—uncertainty avoidance (see Section 6.5).

Just like the French, the Germans dislike generalists: expert knowledge is sought when resolving complex issues in the office, and people gain authority according to the skills they possess and their accomplishments. Managers in German companies are chosen for their technical skills and their previous experiences with similar work.

Germans love well-thought-out plans and precisely defined procedures. In many countries, when you are told during meetings "That is not how things work around here" or "Follow guideline such and such," you know those are negotiation tactics. The negotiator attributes power to the rules and procedures in order to suggest that he himself cannot do anything about it. In Germany, however, this kind of comment is not a form of tactical negotiation: it indeed is a true reflection of German culture: "These are the rules here and we have to abide by them." For this reason it can be very confusing for a German to be asked to step off the beaten track: your proposal to adjust the German provider's terms and conditions can be met with utter disbelief and the German can be genuinely surprised by your lack of sense of reality.

Business meetings are efficient: facts and solid data are presented. Arranging precise data in a logical way is much appreciated. Germans attach great importance to clarity and the stabilizing effect of rules. In your business interactions with Germans it can be quite relevant to have some knowledge of German rules and laws: studying them is time well spent. This can help you when confronted with external bodies (government, unions, workers' committees, etc.). German companies are very aware of the interdependent relationships they have with other entities, such as the workers' unions, and they take these relations very seriously. As a manager with part of your team in Germany, you cannot avoid being confronted with the many rules and processes that the unions have negotiated with

TIP 53: GERMAN EFFICIENCY

When in Germany, communicate clearly and get to the point quickly. Germany is one of the countries where you do not first have to build up personal relationships before being able to do business (although good personal contacts will obviously help you). Germans value clear and fact-based communication and like you to get to the point in a respectful, but direct way.

the company. A good understanding of these agreements will help you when running a partially German business.

7.2.3 United Kingdom

Inhabitants of the United Kingdom (UK) initially come across as somewhat distant, but when you get to know them better, they are often open and friendly. However, they do not appreciate an overjovial attitude. Work and private life are separate things, and the British are generally somewhat traditional and reserved in their manner: in what they wear, but also in their interest in your private life. To us this may seem distant, but it is not meant as a rejection.

The British use indirect language, larded with civilities: nonverbally they express restraint and they tend to keep up appearances (with a sense of humor). Emotions are seldom displayed openly, but the choice of words and intonation add a lot of nuance. You will seldom come across a British person bragging about his success or achievements. And don't expect a Brit to suddenly switch to a new way of doing business or to new technology: they generally are rather conservative and are quite attached to their long-standing traditions.

Status is important in the UK. These days, status and standing are based on the school or university that you attended and less on ancestry. Those with status and standing are bound to reach the higher ranks in businesses and other organizations. And in the UK, all authority is concentrated at the top. Employees are dedicated and loyal and respectful toward management and its decisions.

Nevertheless, meetings in the UK tend to take long. This is not a result of seeking consensus with many people, but because of politeness: everyone can contribute to the discussion and is given the time to do so. This happens in a courteous and harmonious atmosphere.

In business meetings, participants can act rather individualistically, as long as they respect the hierarchy and the rules and do not harm the interests of the organization. The employees of the Royal Bank of Scotland, BP, and Legal & General attach value to careful preparation and an excellent presentation at the start of business meetings. During the meetings, the British are not very creative: they tend to seek traditional solutions to familiar problems.

7.2.4 The Netherlands

The Dutch are famous for their lack of sensitivity to formal hierarchy, their directness (often referred to as bluntness), and their typical decision-making style (that comes across as indecisive).

As a Dutch author, I often find myself explaining in training courses and workshops that the Dutch are the exception rather than the rule when it comes to culture. On four out of five of the Hofstede dimensions (see Chapter 6), the Dutch take rather extreme positions: most countries in the world are more sensitive to hierarchy, more collectivistic, certainly more masculine, and more uncertainty avoidant.

Dutch like to treat everybody equally, and dislike public displays of status and authority. Hierarchy in companies serves a purely functional purpose: without organizing the company through organization charts and reporting lines, the organization would not function. It is solely for this reason that the internal division of power is tolerated. Power distance, however, is low: the position somebody occupies is not at all determined by birth, and status is achieved rather than given. The Dutch believe that everybody can be the boss provided he achieves the right standards and fits into the organization. And once somebody has achieved a position of power and authority, he is not expected to use this to get things done: influencing without using your authority is the standard method in a Dutch business environment.

Foreign guests in the Netherlands immediately notice the directness of communication: the Dutch say what they think, and do not hesitate to be clear and outspoken. Where most other cultures carefully choose their words to maintain harmony and avoid loss of face for others, the Dutch

---

TIP 54: THE BLUNT DUTCH

Be prepared for the Dutch directness. Do not interpret their direct communication as disrespectful or insensitive. The directness really reflects a no-nonsense attitude: it is clearer and more efficient if I tell you clearly how it is. You should be very direct with the Dutch as well—regardless of position and status—and tell them what you think. They will appreciate your honesty and will hardly ever feel insulted by statements made in a business context. Being short, concise, and to the point is much respected in the Netherlands.

take pride in what they describe as honesty. They will vividly defend the notion that saying what you think without hesitation is a sign of honesty, and for the same reason, they qualify indirect forms of communication as dishonest. Although appreciated by some, the directness of the Dutch is more often perceived as blunt.

The other main characteristic of the Netherlands is the low score on the masculinity/femininity scale: only a few countries in the world score more feminine than the Netherlands. People are treated equal, and the distinctly different roles of men and women in society are something of the past. The motto in the Netherlands is "Work to live," which is typical of feminine countries. People in the Netherlands value their private time, so do not ask your Dutch workers to work late in the evening or to come in over the weekend: this is private time to be spent with the family. The same holds for the summer period when you may experience difficulty scheduling a company visit in June, July, or August. The collective holiday period may last several weeks and will not be compromised. Decision making in the Netherlands also follows feminine characteristics: consensus is achieved by finding compromises between the positions of all parties involved. The Dutch have a special word for this: *polderen*. Where the Dutch will explain compromising as a clear manifestation of going for win-win, other—more masculine—cultures will see the compromise as a lost opportunity to optimize the outcome for one (and hopefully more) parties involved.

7.2.5 Belgium

Although often compared to the Netherlands, the cultural differences between the two small neighboring countries could hardly be greater. Companies like Dexia, Fortis, and Delhaize have company cultures that are characteristic of their home country, where hierarchy is an important factor in daily business. The Belgian culture can also be characterized as uncertainty avoidant and relatively masculine.

The boss is the boss: once he has given his vision he will not be publicly criticized for it. In addition, he does not expect people to disagree with him in the open. The boss is expected to give clear instructions to his people.

Belgians speak and act quietly and reservedly, and from this perspective, they perceive other cultures as loud. Adjusting to this style and rhythm will be appreciated by Belgian hosts, who prefer a quiet and thoughtful exchange of opinions above a direct and assertive communication style. Modesty is appreciated and indirect communication valued. Belgians are used to thinking in terms of networks and social relationships.

7.2.6 Spain

Spain is an independent and proud country, where authority is respected. Spain is hierarchical and the position and status of counterparts should be carefully checked in order to know how to do business. Spain scores average on the dimension of group orientation: everyone makes his own decisions, but will also take into account the interests of the group to which he belongs. Often this will be family, from which the Spaniard derives his personal identity.

Spaniards are very dedicated and very personal in everything they do: this means that they will not be inclined to refer to impersonal things such as rules and procedures. However, they do seek structure and stability. Spain is very uncertainty avoidant, so where rules and procedures can help to mitigate uncertainty, they will use them. Uncertainty avoidance can also be seen in the role of religion: it provides structure and stability.

When doing business with Spaniards at Santander or Telefónica, for instance, establishing personal contact is of great importance. Show empathy and show who you are, even though your Spanish counterpart may not come across as very inviting. His reserved attitude reveals that he is still establishing the relationship and needs to get to know you better. Good food and good wine are welcome aids in building up a relationship: your hosts appreciate talking about food and drink, and a dinner offers great opportunities to become better acquainted.

7.2.7 Italy

In Italy negotiation is part of life: Italians enjoy it and they will not be at all surprised when you too are looking for the best possible deal. Italians negotiate with flair: it is an elegant game played with passion. Nonverbal communication is an important aspect of communication in Italy. The words only determine a fraction of the impact of the message: the nonverbal behavior is conclusive.

Italian employees at Generali, Fiat, or Banco Populare, for example, do business with people, not with companies: they always want to get to know you personally, and you will therefore have to present yourself in order to establish a worthwhile business relation. Even the most commercial transaction is a purely personal deal for the Italian. If you fail to invest in a personal relationship, you will quickly be excluded, although you may not immediately notice this has happened. Italians will always remain polite and use friendly wording. Building up a relationship takes time and Italians take their time. Where many cultures may perceive time as something scarce that we should use cautiously, the most worthwhile use of time to Italians is investing in a personal relationship.

Traditional gender stereotyping is still quite strong. Italy is very masculine, and this is expressed in the way women take part in business meetings. A female business partner will be treated gallantly, but she will have to work twice as hard as the men to establish her position. Traditionally, Italians will expect the woman to take a more caring role in society and the man to seek a career and financial gain. Doing business with a woman who has a strong opinion and an assertive attitude will be something that Italian managers will not be used to.

Italian employees generally like to interact with colleagues and partners: they prefer open-plan offices and discussions can be highly personal even in this professional environment. Being together and discussing issues is of key importance to Italians, and this will override a strict business agenda or formal discussion points.

TIP 55: ITALIAN DRESS

Make sure you dress well for your face-to-face meeting with Italians. Italians like to assess whom they are working with (your age, family background, education, etc.), and their first reference is the way you dress. Style comes before comfort: a suit, a perfectly fitting shirt (preferably of a well-known brand), and shoes and belt that match (Veeger 2011). Forget the American, relaxed style: sneakers or sports shoes with a suit will be frowned upon, and it is better to leave your jeans at home. You cannot be overdressed in Italy, and your effort to dress well will be appreciated enormously.

7.2.8 Scandinavia

The Scandinavian countries are famous for their hospitality and quality of life, which is something that Scandinavians themselves greatly appreciate. In contrast to most other countries, Scandinavians make a strict distinction between business and private life, and people will not take their work home. Only the most feminine cultures understand this focus on work-life balance. The Scandinavian countries are among the least masculine countries in the world, along with the Netherlands.

Scandinavians generally come across as informal and relaxed. This can give the wrong impression: the relaxed attitude is too easily interpreted as a somewhat naive business culture where people do not fight for their interests, but seek to maintain harmony. This is true, but behind the friendly mask there is usually a well-prepared person who knows exactly what he wants: he will fight for it—in a friendly but firm manner. There is a reason that companies such as Ericsson, Volvo, StatOil, and Nokia are world famous. Scandinavians can be very direct (low context), but they remain friendly. This directness reflects the Scandinavian appreciation of clarity and honesty, and it is best to state your opinion as clearly as possible as well.

The tough businessmen who have made Saab, Wärtsilä, and Maersk famous all radiate an inner peace. Scandinavians—especially the Finnish—use few words to get their message across. After they have stated their message, they are silent. Such long silences can make other cultures quite desperate. The Finns know this and use it to their advantage, knowing that a long silence will force the other party into concessions. The Finns themselves are perfectly comfortable with long silences.

In business meetings with Scandinavians, it is wise to come very well prepared (they will certainly be) and present your position and point of view with many objective facts. Refrain from criticizing someone else openly, whether it is a colleague or another relation. The tolerant nature of Scandinavians, as well as their high acceptance of people with a different opinion, entails that criticizing others is neither understood nor accepted.

In efficient Scandinavia, no small talk is required to start building up a relationship. It is okay to get down to business immediately, and during the meals you will enjoy together, it is fine to keep on talking about business. Many other cultures will understand little of such impersonal and goal-oriented behavior, but Americans certainly appreciate it.

All the Scandinavian countries—Norway, Sweden, Denmark, and Finland—have low power distance: people are considered equal and the hierarchy in companies serves a purely functional need. Scandinavian companies generally are built on a strong base of cooperation and full participation. The combination of strong individualism and low masculinity leads to Scandinavians having a great concern for fairness and the well-being of others. The way of working is not prescribed: management by objectives suits the nonhierarchical Scandinavians, and as long as the results are good, managers will not tend to interfere with the work of their employees.

7.2.9 Russia

Again the focus is on a country that is so big that it includes multiple time zones, and a variety of different local cultures that all have their own specific characteristics. Here too, we cannot avoid generalizing.

Western cultures generally do not have a very lively and vivid image of Russia, but in the hearts of the Russian people you find much warmth, emotion, and friendliness. Russians are proud of their country, its position in the world, and the economic improvements that have come about since *Glasnost* (openness) and *Perestroika* (state and economic restructuring) of the end of the 1980s. They live up to the expectations of being included in the four BRIC countries (Brazil, Russia, India, and China) that boast a strong emerging economy and global presence.

Doing business in Russia does not necessarily require strong personal relationships with your counterparts, but Russians are ultimately people-oriented and trust is important. Although initially hard to establish, once personal contact has been realized, doors will open and business problems can melt away quickly. In major partnerships and large economic cooperations, the Russians certainly need to trust their counterparts, and this trust is more important than the economic value of the transaction. Not much gets done in Russia without a strong network of people you know and trust: it is all about connections and influence. You will need local help to establish these contacts and to be introduced to the right people.

Russia, with an individualism score of 39, should be considered collectivistic. However, group thinking and loyalty to the in-crowd are of a different nature than in most Asian countries. Russians have been conditioned by many years of communist rule, where the individual opinions of citizens could not be heard and people were used to orders coming from the higher ranks of the political party. The decision-making style in Russian corporations reminds one of this era. Decisions are made by the highest in rank and people expect "the system" to drive decisions: Russians are not known for their proactiveness and eagerness to take personal initiatives.

For a manager supervising a (global) team with Russian team members, it is important to realize that hierarchy is very important to Russians: they respect age and position, and expect you to act in a way that matches your position. Russians do not easily understand the philosophies of participative leadership and servant leadership: they expect their leaders to be firm, visible, and directive. As a manager, do not expect to get feedback from your Russian team members. Any feedback they would give would clash with your authority and, for that reason, is rejected. When you want the input of your employees, you will have to demand this in a very direct and clear way.

You need patience to conduct business with Russians. Things take time and always take longer than expected. That does not bother the Russians themselves. Your pressure for efficiency and your desire to reach quick conclusions will not be picked up, and will more likely work against you. Be prepared for long waiting times, changing deadlines, and deliveries that are postponed.

When conducting business do not make concessions too quickly. Russians have a tendency to demand very big concessions from your side, while not giving in themselves. Quickly abandoning your position and making a concession will be interpreted as a sign of weakness: you will win appreciation by playing tough and not giving in easily. And if you do make a concession, ask what's in it for you and what the Russians themselves are prepared to surrender: make your moves conditional. Preparing yourself for what we call dirty tricks and tactics is necessary, and some training on how to counter these tactics can be a good investment to get the best out of your commercial adventures in Russia.

7.2.10 Central and Eastern Europe

We present countries such as Poland, Bulgaria, Romania, Hungary, and the Czech Republic as if they are the same, although anybody who has traveled frequently in these regions will know that this does not do justice to the unique culture of each country. These countries have in common the fact that they have a history of many years under communist regime, which has left its mark on modern business environments. The change from collective to competitive, from maintaining to growing, has been a substantial one. It is not common for people to take ownership, be proactive, and realize personal growth without being rewarded for this by a higher instance. Bureaucracy and the absence of individual responsibility and customer orientation regularly frustrate Western people dealing with Eastern Europeans. Visitors to such regions frequently say: "With that kind of attitude you'll never make it." However, this is changing rapidly.

The consequence is that Westerners doing business in this region will themselves need to take ownership of the process and the progress. You will need to be proactive in setting the agenda, deciding on whom you expect to meet, and to supervise the continuity of progress. When you have gained their trust, most Eastern Europeans will readily accept this division of roles.

Hierarchy is generally strong in these countries: decisions are made at the top and communication flows downward through strictly defined lines of reporting. Senior people are treated with much respect. Meetings serve to inform people of decisions that have already been made outside the meeting room. The exchange of information that Westerners expect is often absent. Most business meetings have a quite formal character, and only once people get to know you do they become more casual, although meetings always maintain a formal character.

Agreements made—including deadlines, deliverables, and milestones— will need to be administered well and in detail. Most Central and Eastern European countries are uncertainty avoidant, and like to be very precise on even the smallest details. You will need to take the initiative in making sure that previous commitments are kept: people in the region pay less attention to strict deadlines and planning schedules, as these shift when the inevitable happens (like power cuts, new laws and regulations that suddenly need to be followed, or new directives from the top).

7.2.11 Turkey

Doing business with people from a Turkish background requires investment in building up a relationship. Cooperation will fail if you do not first establish a personal connection. Without a relation of trust, it will feel as if you are working "with the brake on." Trust is very important in the Turkish culture: it cannot be taken for granted. Where we assume trust is a given until proven otherwise, to Turks it is the other way around: trust— which is a given within families and among intimate friends—must be earned. Turkish people will therefore gather a lot of information about your status and background, and will want to get to know you personally.

Where Western cultures are future-oriented, the Turk will base his attitudes on the present and the past: traditions are important in Turkish society. Compared to Western cultures, Turkey is collectivistic: the individual is secondary to the group of which you are part. This group—consisting of family, friends, and good relations—is very important: the Turks enjoy spending time in the group and deepening their valuable relationships.

When negotiating with Turkish partners, take into account the fact that they are sensitive and proud: compliments about their country or their merits are appreciated. Criticism is hard to digest. If you want to make a strong point in negotiations, never become accusatory, but focus on the person and explain your reservations in a respectful way. Emotions may be expressed in negotiations, and Turks will appreciate an assertive attitude. Traditional men-women roles are strong in Turkey; expect the Turkish negotiation delegation to consist mainly (but not exclusively) of men and the masculine leader to make all the major decisions.

7.3 UNITED STATES OF AMERICA

Much has been written about American business habits. This is partly because American culture is clearly different from other cultures, but also because Americans like to promote themselves. They are very visible, and confidently draw attention. So much attention is paid to how Americans behave in social settings. Whereas a Vietnamese or African businessman may be just as colorful or unique, he is less noticeable in the presence of Americans.

The most striking dimension is the strongly individualistic culture in the United States: Americans are taught early to see themselves as independent. And even though American employees at Best Buy, Citigroup, or Motorola are very capable of cooperating with each other, this is more a functional relation than a social one: it could improve their ideas, and they will need other people's buy-in, so they'd better cooperate. Although strongly individualistic, collectivist influences are present: in California, where one-third of the population is Hispanic, the typical American culture is less pronounced. The same holds for downtown Manhattan, where we see more characteristics of a global business culture than of a typical American culture.

Everything in the United States seems to revolve around competition: at work, in sports, and socially, achievement is what counts. Some Americans seem to be stuck in a permanent race, where only winning counts. This comes with a self-assured style, which looks overconfident and aggressive to many other cultures. In her book *The New Rules of International Negotiation*, Catherine Lee (2007) states: "A perceived offensive attitude of superiority and arrogance often accompanies a US businessperson into cross-cultural meetings." Colleagues from Latin American countries—who were part of my negotiation team when we were negotiating with an American partner—described the Americans as "bossy, like they always try to push me down." The Chinese often regard the Americans as irreverent, especially when an American tells a Chinese person what to do on the basis of his own American frame of reference. The lesson for Americans is that even though they may come a long way with their air of superiority within their own country, this style impedes an equal relationship with others outside U.S. borders. And in many countries, it is exactly such a relationship that forms the basis for successful business.

An assertive and self-assured style, unjustly labeled as arrogant, is an elementary part of the American culture. Americans come to the point quickly and spend little time on exchanging pleasantries or informalities about the weather. "How are you doing?" should be enough, and while you are still formulating your answer to that question, they will have started the business discussion. Speed is important, time is money, and so business meetings over breakfast or lunch are very common in the United States. But speed can be an advantage. As they are often prepared to take risks, energetic and determined Americans can ensure that a lot is achieved in a relatively short time. However, speed also means that Americans are not used to silences, and they get nervous when Japanese or Finnish partners are silent for long periods.

The United States has a relatively low score on power distance (40), suggesting that people treat each other as equals and that positional power is used only as a last resort. Nevertheless, American companies are perceived as hierarchical. However, employees are not submissive to the boss: as a human being he is an equal, but he serves a different (and more important) role in the company. The word of the boss is not sacred; people can challenge the opinion of their boss, and strict rules and regulations about employer-employee codes of conduct do apply. Fairness is an important criterion: the performance appraisal of the American employee must be objective and fair. More subjective arguments—although these inevitably play a role—will not be mentioned.

The communication in America is direct and you will know exactly when Americans don't agree: a clear no. To Americans, avoiding loss of face is not an important element of business. There is a reason for the clarity provided by their low-context communication: by being clear and transparent, uncertainty and ambiguity are reduced, which clears the way to the goal. That is why Americans like to finish things: it provides certainty. They have difficulty with cultures that keep decisions open, or which wish to reopen discussions once a decision has been made. This is inconceivable in America: a decision has been made and so we stick to it. Hence, striking a deal or signing a contract is a big deal: legal advisors will join your table in the early stages in order to note down meticulously the terms of agreement.

Give the Americans on your team a lot of freedom. Define their objectives clearly and then give them the freedom to perform. Americans work in a goal-oriented way, like to simplify things (when things get too complicated it will often be the American who says, "Why don't we just …?"), and pursue their goals with determination and much proactiveness and drive.

7.4 CENTRAL AND SOUTH AMERICA

Several aspects of doing business in Central and South America are generic and are discussed here, before zooming in specifically on Brazil and Argentina.

Doing business with companies such as Petrobas, JBS, and Carso in Central and South America takes time, time that many Western businesspeople lack. This plays up in many decision-making processes in South American business, which take place at the absolute top of the company. But lower levels all need to be informed of, and involved in, this process, even though their final say in the decision is only token. Also, countries in Central and South America are more bureaucratic than what we are used to. Hence, the advice is to reserve lots of time for business interaction in this region, and when you don't have that time, don't start. Progress will be slow, and getting visibly frustrated will only work against you.

All transactions that Western businessmen regard as business transactions are seen by South Americans as personal interactions. Personal relationships of mutual trust need to be built up, which again takes time. Because trust is obviously strictly personal, the composition of the team or delegation that is dealing with the South Americans should not change. When changes occur, trust will need to be built up again, which again takes time. So the habit of bringing experts into meetings at the moment you think this is appropriate often works to your disadvantage in South America. When starting to do business, it is good to openly discuss the mutual trust and to emphasize how much you value the relationship with your partners. Although openly discussing this feels uncomfortable to many Western businesspeople, on the other side of the table it clearly indicates that you have good intentions.

Smooth interpersonal relationships are important in this region, so keep your communication polite and pleasant, even when there is no real reason to do so in your view.

The most important countries in the region obviously have their own specific characteristics as well.

TIP 56: REPLACE IMPERSONAL LOGIC WITH PERSONAL EMOTIONS

In Central and South America you can invest a lot of time showing beautiful presentations, supported by facts, graphs, and tables covering all-important details. Your counterparts will politely listen and ask the right questions about your presentation. But decisions will not be made based on these facts and data alone. Feelings are more important than facts, and emotions are more important than logic. When composing your team to deal with Central and South Americans, you will need to pay attention to this aspect. A highly emotional and extraverted person who is focused on relationships and personal contacts may not get the highest marks in the annual performance appraisals in Western Europe or the United States, but he may be exactly the person you need in South America.

7.4.1 Brazil

Brazil is known for its colorful society, where people are emotional and express their moods and feelings. It is important not only to enjoy this aspect of society, but also to make use of it when doing business in Brazil. The most difficult business discussions that are deadlocked can be revitalized after expressing your emotions or frustration, disappointment, or eagerness. This obviously should be done in a correct, respectful but also visible way. Feigning this is hard and your nonverbal behavior will always betray your true emotions to the other party, so don't fake it. But you should certainly not bury your emotions and pretend that they are not there. Showing that you care can work in your advantage and give you the personal trust that Brazilians value so much when doing business.

In spite of a moderate score on masculinity, Brazil is nevertheless perceived as masculine. The traditional picture of the macho man is strong, and men expect women to take a subordinate position: large inequalities between men and women are still the norm.

Lack of punctuality is characteristic of Brazil, and business is perceived as chaotic by many Western visitors. Although this is not the same in every organization, people deal differently with time than in our part of the world. Brazilians do several things at the same time and lack the orderly notion of time that many Westerners have. In discussions, you will hardly find moments of silence as people talk profusely. This is accompanied by nonverbal gestures, increased vocal volume, and frequent interruptions. We tend to call this chaos in other parts of the world, but Brazilians feel good about it and are used to nothing else.

Brazil is a group culture where loss of face should be avoided at all times. It is your responsibility not to embarrass a Brazilian, so avoid direct expressions of criticism and avoid confrontational statements. For this reason, communication is high context, although at times very direct and honest. You will have to be sensitive and feel what is required in the situation you are in. The same rules cannot be applied to every situation, and flexibility is expected of you.

In business, it is vital to build up personal trust with your counterparts. Brazilians need to know who you are before they want to work with you. Building up trust takes time, and you should expect to return to Brazil often if you want to build up a long-term business. This is also a necessity for practical reasons. In many meetings with Brazilian companies, the highest representatives of the company—who make all the decisions—will often not attend the meetings. Come back often, enter into personal relationships, and build up trust, so that you get to know the real decision makers well.

7.4.2 Argentina

Argentina often seems more European than many other Central and Latin American countries. The Argentinians appear to be more open, and can communicate very directly at times. A formal and serious way of doing business is the norm, but do not take this as a sign of coldness. On the contrary, Argentinians are warm people with a lot of passion, and they will occasionally display this. The formal atmosphere will be broken when trust has been established: once they trust you as a person and get to know you well, conversations will become more casual. In this relationship-driven culture, you will need to build up networks and use these to your advantage: local agents who bring you in contact with the right decision makers are of great help—without them everything will take longer and prove to be more difficult.

7.5 MIDDLE EAST

In his studies of culture, Hofstede collected value scores from a few countries in the Middle East, such as Egypt, Iraq, Kuwait, Libya, United Arab Emirates (UAE), and Lebanon. He then generalized his findings to all other Arab countries, including Jordan, for example. And although some similarities can be found between these countries, many Middle East experts have criticized this generalization and concluded that—in spite of the similarities—most of these countries cannot be compared and treated as if they belong to the same cultural group (Al-Nashmi and Syd Zin 2011; Alkailani et al. 2012).

In the case of Jordan, for example, Alkailani et al. (2012) argued that society there has changed, and that the thirst for knowledge and the level of education in this country is higher than average in the region. Also, this country has the highest number of skilled workers, and all these factors are known to correlate with low power distance. Indeed, studies by Alkailani et al. revealed that the power distance you would derive today from the same value surveys would be very low, rather than the high score

(80) that Hofstede found. In Jordan today, young employees are not afraid of disagreeing with their bosses, and expect to be consulted and involved in decisions about their work.

Also, before generalizing about the region, we should be aware that people from all over the world are employed in this region (take Saudi Arabia as an example): you will find many Europeans, Americans, and Australians in supervisory and management roles, while you find employees from India, Pakistan, the African subcontinent, etc., in unskilled labor. The presence of all these nationalities obviously reduces the visibility of the local country culture. Working with these countries, you cannot rely on thorough knowledge about local culture alone: flexibility, tolerance, and respect for anything that is different will bring you further here.

Nevertheless, we present some general characteristics of the whole of the Middle East here, before zooming in on some special cases, such as Saudi Arabia and Israel.

The Arabs do not expect Westerners to know a lot about their culture, history, and habits, and certainly do not insist on Westerners speaking the local language (Arabic in most countries). This makes the appreciation all the greater when you have invested time up front. Spending effort to understand the way of life and understand the basics of Islam (which reaches much farther than exclusively a religion) is very much appreciated, and will make your stay in the Middle East easier and much more interesting at the same time. But even when well prepared, do not engage in conversation about the local political and religious conflicts too easily: talk about this only when your hosts steer the discussion in this direction.

Doing business in the Middle East takes time, and many Western people will need to slow down and leave their watch at home when doing business here. Showing that you are under pressure works directly in your disadvantage. Public displays of frustration should be avoided, as it can break down any previously established business relationship. People like arguing and negotiating in this part of the world, and they do so frequently. Orientation toward time is different: punctuality is an unknown concept, and you should not be surprised to have to wait an hour before the right people have assembled to meet you. This is not tactics but a normal way of doing business in the Middle East.

Individuals in the Middle East can speak up and express their opinions, but always in such a way that the group to which they belong is not brought into discredit. Individualism scores are average: the cultures can be classified as individualistic, but with a strong sense of awareness for the collective with which you are associated. The unspoken rules for communication resemble those of most collectivistic countries: respect and harmony are of great importance, and loss of face should be avoided at all times. So when in disagreement with your counterparts in the Middle East, always make sure that you treat the other party fairly and with respect. Losing your temper (raising your voice, pointing with your finger) is not appreciated. Training yourself to speak politely and express your opinion in a nonconfrontational way is a strong basis for trust and long-lasting relationships in the Middle East.

The above rules do not apply to your counterparts from the Middle East: Arabs frequently use public displays of emotion, enhanced volume of speech, and rhetoric, certainly when they want to emphasize something is important to them. This gives Westerners the impression they are angry and aggressive, which is not the case. Open displays about how you feel are normal here: expressive and exuberant, but always with modesty and respect.

Power distance in the Middle East is large: people with status are highly esteemed and people with power are treated respectfully. Family bonds and ties to the royal family or other powerful families in the region give somebody power, and are guarantees for preferential treatment in society and at work. Whereas achievement is important in the West, in the Middle East it is status, which is derived from your links to people with power. Within companies, this means that the achievement-based management of the West (performance management processes; see Section 8.3) is not understood and does not apply.

Time-keeping standards in the Middle East cannot be compared to those in the West. The general belief is that time cannot be controlled, and when you still try to do this you will not be taken seriously. Only God

---

TIP 57: PREPARE FOR CHAOS

Meetings, negotiations, and work conversations are chaotic in the view of the Western visitor to the Middle East. People will walk in and out of meetings, may answer phones in the middle of a conversation with you, and are often engaged in several conversations at the same time. Do not interpret this as a sign of disrespect or disinterest: it is just the local habit and an orientation toward time that is very different from what you are used to. Go with the flow and accept that everything takes more time than you perhaps scheduled.

controls the future, and nobody else should try to influence the way things go. This aspect of business life in the Gulf is beautifully described in the book *Don't They Know It's Friday* by Jeremy Williams (2012). Williams states that time is not important in the region, but the right time is what is relevant here: not the absolute time your clock indicates. And for everything there comes a right time, whenever that may be.

Personal relationships count in the Middle East, and are more important than the company you represent. Arab people need to get to know you as a person, and only once trust has been established will they work with you. Business teams who change a member of the team are often surprised to see all discussions come to a stop: whereas in individualistic cultures you can change a member of the team, introduce the new person, and continue, this means that trust needs to be built up with another person in the Middle East, starting from scratch. People in the Middle East are event-driven more than time-driven: the event of getting together and getting to know each other is much more important than the time it takes to do this.

Most countries in this region are masculine: traditional differences between the sexes are large, and society is arranged in such a way that men do business and make decisions, while women run the household and have the "caring" jobs.

7.5.1 Saudi Arabia

This country hosts workers from all parts of the world: oil plants are run by Pakistani, Turkish, African workers, etc., while there are many technicians and expats from Asia (Japan), Europe, and the United States. Unlike most other Middle East countries, the collective is more important than the individual here, and people feel part of the family. Communication is high context, full of metaphors and stories, and you need to interpret this context to fully understand what your counterparts wish to say. The body language in this part of the world is uncomfortable to most Westerners: close proximity, frequent touching, many gestures, and occasionally loud voices.

Confrontation and unpleasant discussions should be avoided, although you should not be surprised if the Saudis unexpectedly have an angry outburst, before returning to a more controlled and sympathetic style again.

Male leaders, usually connected to the right family, make the decisions. When decisions have been made (and most likely have been agreed within the family that is in power), they will not be changed and are no longer subject to public discussion.

In Saudi Arabia, you should always arrange business appointments through locals. You will need local help in ensuring the right decision makers are there, and working through locals facilitates getting things done. Another reason to work with locals is that you cannot plan appointments here on the basis of your own calendar: the Islamic calendar knows many special days on which no meetings can be planned, and workweeks in Saudi do not include Fridays.

The traditional difference between the sexes is extremely large in Saudi, where women are not expected to participate in business interaction at all. In public life, they act separately from the men, sit in special sections of restaurants, and do not drive cars.

7.5.2 Israel

In many aspects Israel is comparable to other Middle Eastern countries: things tend to go slowly and take a lot of time, so you will need to display patience and accept that the right time will come. Meetings are never private in Israel, and like in other countries in the region, people will walk in and out of meetings, take phone calls, invite others to join, etc. Western people tend to get irritated by this lack of structure and apparent chaos.

At this point the similarities between Israel and other Middle East countries stop: Israelis are frequently compared to Americans in terms of individualism. They are known for loud and informal encounters and their directness. Individuals make decisions in Israel, and although they do operate in groups, consensus in the group is of less importance here: individuals can speak for themselves.

Israelis like to argue: business meetings contain much debate in a confrontational and emotional style. Israelis can be surprisingly direct, put their demands on the table, and tell you openly what they do not like about your proposal. When making decisions, social aspects and feelings play a large role, more than objective facts and rationality do. When confronted with the directness of the Israelis, it is important to stay calm and professional, to ensure you continue to be taken seriously.

Power distance is low in Israel: in principle everybody is equal. The low power distance and high individualism scores are visible in the direct style, and the fact that confrontations and emotions are not avoided. Loss of face is not something that the Israeli businessman worries about much:

he is certainly sensitive to interpersonal relations, but values frankness and openness as well.

7.6 AFRICA

Talking about the culture of Africa is much of a generalization: you cannot compare the extremes of Morocco and Mozambique, or those of Sudan and Gabon. The colorful variety and wide range of subcultures on the continent justifies a book in itself. Still, we look here for general characteristics, which differentiate the African continent from other parts of the world.

In some African countries, the influences of European colonialism are still very visible (Namibia, Togo, Rwanda, Burundi, Ethiopia), whereas in other countries, Arabic and Islamic influences dominate (Tunisia, Egypt, Morocco, Sudan). But that is just the beginning. In many countries people belong to tribes, and every tribe has its own rules, habits, and values—its own culture.

All African countries, with a very few exceptions, are collectivistic, and individual interests are subservient to group (family or tribe) interests. Mutual respect between African tribes is large: although the image we have in the Western world is dominated by tribalism, conflicts between countries and civil wars, most of the subcultures have a deep respect for the culture of other people.

African countries are all short-term-oriented, with the exception of South Africa, which scores equal to some European countries on this dimension. In short-term-oriented countries, people attribute success and failure to luck (and not to personal effort), people have a small amount of savings for the future, traditions are important, and people take pride in their country. Enjoy today, as tomorrow may bring new challenges. People accept life as it comes and feel they have little influence on the course of events. This attitude is reflected in the way in which people respond to the frequent breakdowns of public transport: time will pass anyway, so we will be patient and wait for better times.

Most countries are collectivistic and hierarchical: status traditionally belongs to tribal leaders who protect the tribe (the in-crowd) and are in charge of the tribe. And although tribe culture rapidly disappears in urban areas of quickly developing countries such as Ethiopia, Mozambique, and Congo, the characteristics remain. People have much respect for elderly

> **TIP 58: DISAGREEMENTS IN AFRICA**
>
> Do not bring disagreements out into the open: Africans take pride in dealing with differences of opinion privately. When disagreements come up, it is wise to isolate the elderly person from the group and ask for his advice. Building a rapport with this person will gain you major advantages when dealing with African businesspeople. Africans value spending time building up trust, and will strongly prefer cooperation above competition. Disagreements and conflict break the harmony that they value so much, and reduce trust. Rely on face-to-face contact for your business interactions in Africa: do not think that a few video conferences will do the trick.

people (who generally lead) and spend much time building trust and maintaining harmony. Within the groups, decisions are made by consensus, although the voice of the elderly person represents multiple votes. Elderly people enjoy respect, and when trying to convince a group of Africans to work with you, your main job will be to positively influence the elderly and thus acquire more weight in the group.

Other things that set African countries apart from other cultures in the world are their relaxed, laid-back mentality (while still working very hard), their strong belief in spirits, magic, and the worship of ancestors, and their indirect communication in the form of stories, poetry, and references to similar situations. In Africa, it is common to facilitate business with personal gifts and payments: do not call this bribery or corruption but train yourself to accept this as a normal, highly valued standard of personal relationships in business. Applying Western logic to this process does not help you much.

7.6.1 North Africa (Libya, Morocco, Tunisia, Algeria, Sudan, Egypt)

These countries are characterized by the nonconfrontational character of interpersonal relationships: on a personal basis, people will avoid disagreement and conflict when doing business. Personal relationships prevail and are reinforced with gifts, social events, and drinks. A network is important, and your success in business depends on whom you know, not on what you know.

In general, expect to go with the flow and cast aside your own habits temporarily. Society is built on honor that is linked to the good name of the family and to personal reputation. Honor is expressed through invitations to events, social gatherings, and drinks. If you want to do business, do not turn down these invitations, as you will be breaking the code of honor.

Time is polychronic in this part of the world (see Section 6.7): time does not pass by in a sequential order and there is plenty of it. Deadlines are negotiable and can shift due to all kinds of circumstances: when dealing with time, you must abandon your Western logic. Never expect quick decisions and rapid business deals. A great deal of discussion, relationship building, and establishing trust will be needed before you are in business in North Africa.

7.6.2 West Africa (Ghana, Gabon, Gambia, Nigeria, Senegal, Sierra Leone)

The population of these countries is often characterized as outgoing and friendly: people are proud of their country (especially when it is rich in terms of history, natural resources, or modern advancement). Family relationships are important, and opening discussions with questions about the family of your hosts will be very much appreciated. This introduction phase takes a lot of time that Westerners often feel they do not have: to be successful in this part of the world, however, you will need to invest much time in building up personal relationships. Expect lots of talk and references to family: every individual feels part of a family and is recognized on the basis of his family background. The family provides security, a social structure, as well as financial resources and any type of guidance for business and life. Establishing a strong personal relationship is key.

Communication in these countries is indirect, as in most collectivistic countries. People avoid putting one another into difficult positions, and thus will avoid conflict or any discussion that sounds confrontational. Silence is respected, so if you find yourself doubting what to say, it is better not to say too much. The other person's facial expression will not betray any traces of discomfort: smiling is an effective way to mask discomfort.

7.6.3 East Africa (Kenya, Uganda, Tanzania, Somalia)

Here people belong to groups, too, and their focus on the group can be even stronger than in other parts of Africa. To do business in East Africa you first need to be trusted by the group and accepted as one of them. The relationship building needed for this requires patience: lots of time will be used up in small talk that cannot be rushed. Asking people many questions about their personal life and their family helps greatly in becoming quickly respected, and all this is done in a harmonious and pleasant environment.

Protecting face is important, so criticism should not be shared. If shared, this should be done in private and in an indirect way. Avoid expressing strong opinions, as you will almost certainly lack the sensitivity needed to feel what can and cannot be openly discussed. Talk in a low voice as they do, and take a humble and modest approach. You will gain a lot of respect with this attitude, and this will pay off later when you do business.

7.6.4 Southern Africa (Namibia, South Africa, Botswana, Angola, Mozambique, Zambia)

Here also, the rule is not to rush any business process and certainly not the phase in which you get to know each other. Ask lots of questions and show genuine curiosity. Being interested in other people's personal and business life will help you win trust. Although business here can be more formal than in most parts of Africa, this does not mean that personal relationships are not important. They are, and you will need to be trusted first before being accepted as a potential business partner.

South Africa occupies a special position on this continent. This country cannot be characterized as a collectivistic but rather as an individualistic society. People come up for their own rights and strive to make the best of their life. People value the quality of life, and use the weekends to enjoy and relax in the beauty of their countryside. Hierarchy is of importance here as well: not only during the apartheid regime, but also today there is still much respect for people in high positions and the status they gained through commitment and hard work. The inequalities that are present in the country are accepted, although not as much as in the past.

Western businesspeople have less difficulty dealing with South Africa than with most other countries in Africa. The South Africans are ready to talk business quickly, and do not spend too much time getting to know each other and building very personal relationships. Western people feel at home visiting companies like Sasol, Tiger, and Telkom. In South Africa, personal relationships are still valued a lot and taken very seriously, but they can be built up in the course of doing business.

TIP 59: SENIORITY IN SOUTH AFRICA

When business discussions with South Africans don't proceed well or as well as you would like, and you want to make significant changes to the way you are dealing with each other, make sure to find out who is the most influential person on the other side of the table. This is not necessarily the person with the highest formal position: age and seniority determine somebody's real status. Speak to the elder person about your worries and be respectful and understanding of his wise words. The most senior person is generally very influential in realizing a breakthrough in difficult business discussions.

7.7 AUSTRALIA AND NEW ZEALAND

The business culture in Australia and New Zealand is relaxed. Here you will not find employees running around offices nervously, having hurried conversations. People down under take their time. So do not expect a quick deal, but accept that things take time.

In communication, people are clear, honest, and direct. Saying no is something that Ozzies and Kiwis have no trouble with, and they will not be surprised if you do so as well. Society is egalitarian: classes or differences in status do not exist and everybody is equal.

In negotiations—no matter how relaxed they seem—Australians know very well what they want. Also keep in mind that an Australian—no matter how friendly—will always represent the company he works for, whether it is BHP Billiton, National Australia Bank, or Rio Tinto. Make sure your

---

TIP 60: ARROGANCE IN AUSTRALIA

In your interaction with business contacts down under, avoid any reference to your status, the hierarchy, or your education level: they will not be impressed. Avoid every form of boasting or bragging: it will be held against you. Rather, behave as one of them, roll up your sleeves, and get to work in an amicable and friendly way. Anything that smells of arrogance can put Australians off, and limit your chances of successfully doing business with them.

kickoff presentation for the meeting is short and businesslike. Limit yourself to objective facts and avoid going into much detail.

Sharing Experiences

Brian Musson, Import and Export Marketing and Promotion Manager at DENBRI Shanghai International Trading Co., Ltd.
LinkedIn: https://www.linkedin.com/in/brianmusson

Brian Musson *is import and export marketing and promotion manager at DENBRI International Trading Co., Ltd., in Shanghai, China. He has held this position since the company was established in 2009. In a very rich and varied job he finds himself serving a wide variety of international clients dealing with China. His experiences involve many cases where he is surprised to see the lengths that they, as suppliers, go to to help clients when problems come up—as they often do in China.*

Our trading company in 2010 had a client called Mr. T who was running his business in Sydney, Australia. One day—after he had ordered 1,000 T-shirts from a supplier in China—through either carelessness or tiredness, a tragic error occurred. Mr. T overpaid a supplier!

At this time in 2010 the client normally paid a 30% deposit first and later the final payment of 70% to us, and we would later send the funds, once checking had occurred, to the manufacturer. In this case, however, because it was only a small job, Mr. T decided to work directly with the supplier in China. This didn't matter to us, as Mr. T was an excellent client and we were prepared to move heaven and earth to help him.

Because it was such a small payment, Mr. T paid the supplier the full amount in advance! Only he inserted one extra 0 into the bank payment instruction sheet. He paid the supplier US$40,000 instead of $4,000. The next day, when the error became clear, Mr. T had a difficult day. After three days of emails and phone calls to Ningbo, China, requesting to correct the mistake, the answer came by email: "Mr. T. This was clearly a gift from you as no one sends China an overpayment of $36,000. Thank you, and you are our friend for life!"

We were called to help out, and as this was our number 1 client, we were determined to help him out. Denise, my Chinese-speaking coworker, and I went into our car and made the five-hour drive to Ningbo the next day. What we thought was going to be a day's work over there ended up being three days and two nights. When we finally arrived at the company we were told that the people we were looking for did not work there, and that they only used this company name. But as the Chinese manufacturer knew who they were, he called them, only to hear that yes, they had received this wonderful gift, and no, they were not inclined to return it. Could we please go away and stop bothering them!

We didn't. We had to go outside for some fresh air and cool down. While we did, the people we were looking for showed up, and we took some pictures of them and their car. This ended up in a fight over the camera, and the police coming in to clear the situation. The final outcome was that the police asked me whether I wanted to file charges against the couple, to which I declined, but only if Mr. T's money was repaid. The police took the position that the supplier couldn't keep the money as it was international theft, and this did the trick. All the money was finally returned through the manufacturer, and a very happy Mr. T had learned an important lesson.

It's another reason that no matter how small your order is, you should *always* use a trusted and legal supplier! It avoids these types of situations from spiraling out of control.

Practical tips:

- Only work in China with qualified, legal, and trustworthy suppliers. In case of doubt, accept a delay and first find out full details about the party you work with. Mistakes are too costly.

- Remember that in intercultural encounters, things are not always what they seem to be. If a deal looks too good to be true, it probably is not worth pursuing. Again, mistakes are too costly.
- When negotiating with another international party that plays hardball and takes a very tough position, you sometimes have to return the favor and take a very tough position as well (as I did with taking pictures and getting police involved). You have to show you are on equal level with your negotiation partner.

REFERENCES

Alkailani, M., Azzam, I.A., and Athamneh, A.B. (2012). Replicating Hofstede in Jordan: Ungeneralized, Reevaluating the Jordanian Culture. *International Business Research*, 5(4), 71–80.

Al-Nashmi, M.M., and Syd Zin, S.A.R. (2011). Variation in Communication Satisfaction of Academic Staff in Universities in Yemen Depending on National Culture. *Cross Cultural Management: An International Journal*, 18(1), 87–105.

Graham, J. (1993). Japanese Negotiating Style: Characteristics of a Distinct Approach. *Negotiation Journal*, 9(2), 123–40.

Lee, C. (2007). *The New Rules of International Negotiation: Building Relationships, Earning Trust, and Creating Influence around the World*. Franklin Lakes, NJ: Career Press.

Lewis, R.D. (2006). *When Cultures Collide: Leading across Cultures*. London: Nicolas Brealey International.

Morrison, T., and Conaway, W.A. (2006). *Kiss, Bow or Shake Hands: The Bestselling Guide to Doing Business in More than 60 Countries*. Avon, MA: Adams Media.

Nisbett, R.E. (2003). *The Geography of Thought: How Asians and Westerners Think Differently ... and Why*. New York: Free Press.

Oyama, N. (1990). Some Recent Trends in Japanese Values: Beyond the Individual–Collective Dimension. *International Sociology*, 5, 445–59.

Veeger, M. (2011). *Italiaanse zaken. Zakelijk success volgens Italiaans recept*. DSV Media.

Williams, J. (2012). *Don't They Know It's Friday? A Cross-Cultural Guide for Business and Life in the Gulf*. Dubai, UAE: Motivate Publishing.

8

Managing Performance

Your performance depends on your people. Select the best, train them and back them. When errors occur, give sharper guidance. If errors persist or if the fit feels wrong, help them move on. The country cannot afford amateur hour in the White House.

—Donald Rumsfeld*

Twenty-five managers gathered in the small auditorium where I had been asked to instruct them about the annual performance management process that was about to start. The organization knew that simply asking them to start the process again would not be enough: people needed a refresher course on the essentials of the process and the system in use. In addition, many new managers enter the organization each year and also need to learn about effective performance management reviews. The company had recently been taken over and had become reasonably accustomed to an American approach to performance: most managers would describe it as much tougher than it used to be.

Most of the managers in the room led virtual teams, with team members who resided at various places in the world. The matrix structure on which the organization was built maintained direct reporting lines in various countries, with indirect reporting lines to international project leaders or function managers. The training course went well, although many critical questions arose, all of which were related to the way the process would be run abroad. This aspect had not been given much attention in the training course, and managers were clearly worried about cultural aspects playing a leading role. Their three main objections against the rules of performance management were:

---

* www.brainyquote.com

- "I do not have any power to set the objectives of my people. This is done locally, although the local managers have no clue about the details of this project and what we aim to achieve." (Chinese manager)
- "I have underperformance issues in my team, and I know how to deal with that here in the U.S. But addressing the underperformance of somebody in Asia I think would be very rude, and who am I to deliver the bad news to some of these guys far away?" (German manager)
- "The process for performance management is overorganized and way too rigid. I mean, how can we set objectives this early and expect them to last for a year? Things can change tomorrow. Many things outside our influence can happen, and then the objectives and deadlines don't mean much anymore." (Indian manager)

These objections—although already meaningful within their own cultural context—will be recognized by many people working in a global environment. These are the barriers that prevent us from doing what needs to be done: in this case, managing performance, which is a key task of every manager. Calling these barriers excuses would not be fair: none of the managers was trying to make up excuses for not having to tackle the hard work. And do the managers have a point in raising them as potential barriers to doing what needs to be done? No. If I were the manager of these managers I would have a response to each of them:

- "Why not? Objectives are objectives, regardless of whichever country you are working in or whatever structures you are operating in. You do not need formal authority to set objectives. You need to influence the situation and get results without authority, all of which depends on how you use your interpersonal skills to communicate the objectives to your people, whether you are their formal boss or not."
- "Why not? Underperformance is underperformance: it is your responsibility to address it. Tolerating it is harming the company you work for: bite the bullet and do it."
- "Why not? Deadlines are deadlines. We need to stick to these; otherwise, the project will be delayed. That's what deadlines are for. The unexpected is not a reason to not meet your targets. Don't find excuses: make it work."

The training course was partially successful in the end. I could give clear answers to all the questions raised by the managers (see above), and the basic principles of performance management had once again been explained to all. But later I asked myself: Will they now really lead the performance discussions differently from the way they would have done without this training? Unfortunately, I had to conclude this was not the case. The barriers were still there. And although we spoke about them and I told them what to do in each of these cases, I answered their questions from my own cultural perspectives. Headquarters language. I went to speak with all three managers afterwards and found out that indeed they did not change their approach, as this would not work within their culture.

Headquarters in Europe had defined the process, heavily influenced by the American style of management to which they were still becoming accustomed themselves. Nobody at headquarters had spent time thinking about how to deal with performance management in different countries of the world. Of course you can define objectives, address underperformance, and make people meet deadlines; this is not a difficult task at all. But you will need to do this in a different way in every region or culture: if you want performance management to contribute successfully to the organization's objectives, it will need to work locally.

Goals are set along lines of hierarchy. The mixed lines of command in matrix organizations are confusing to Chinese: Who is the boss and therefore sets the targets? How can employees accept targets from somebody who is not their formal boss? How can double lines of reporting exist? This leads only to confusion and obscurity, and that should be avoided. How can you exert influence when you do not have any form of authority? The Chinese are used to a clear line of command in which they often find a more senior person above them. This person is the one who sets the objectives.

Addressing underperformance in a direct and confrontational way disrupts harmony and causes loss of face, which should be avoided in collectivistic cultures at almost any cost. How can a person continue to function well within the group when underperformance is dealt with in such a direct and aggressive way? And why do we try to pinpoint which person is responsible for the underperformance: this is a group effort and we all share the responsibility for his failure. In such a framework, the German manager is right to be cautious about the way he brings the message: he knows he will have to do it, but to address underperformance in a collectivistic culture is a delicate process involving an exertion of influence on the group, using the local lines of hierarchy, and always ensuring that the problem is resolved without the person losing face.

Deadlines are important and we all work extremely hard to achieve them. We work day and night and do all we can to be successful. But things can happen. Locally other priorities can be set, the customer frequently changes software requirements, and resources that were initially assigned to the project are no longer available. This happens, so we better try to make the best out of the changing circumstances rather than stick to unrealistic deadlines ("… which we could have told you in advance were unrealistic, but you didn't ask …"). This way of arguing would be typical of the Indian project leader. External forces may impact deadlines, and we cannot individually control whether we meet the deadlines or not. Muslim managers believe something happens because God wants it to happen, and many West Asian cultures (India, Pakistan, and also Hong Kong) believe that luck always plays a role in all events. You cannot control that, so it is advisable to be less rigid and accept that deadlines are flexible.

When deploying performance management processes across the world, culture needs to be taken into account: not to change the essence of the process, but to determine the way you execute the various steps in different cultural contexts.

8.1 GOAL SETTING: SETTING OBJECTIVES AND COMMUNICATING THEM

Any success depends on clear goals. This is why the performance management process—and on a higher level every strategic process in a company—starts with setting clear goals. Without these, the daily activities in the company will not contribute to the things the organization wants to achieve. But many managers live by the day rather than by their objectives, and are much less effective than they could be. Individual goal setting also provides great rewards in personal life. The person with clear and ambitious goals achieves much more than the person who does not have goals. Success author Brian Tracy uses a simple but very effective seven-step plan for achieving success in any undertaking (Tracy 2005):

1. Decide exactly what you want. (You need to be very specific and clear: visualize your goal.)
2. Write it down. (Written goals have a higher chance of being executed and realized.)
3. Set a deadline. (Without this, a goal is a dream. A real goal is a dream with a deadline.)
4. Make a list of everything you need to do to achieve the goal. (Break down the goal into small chunks.)
5. Organize the list into a plan. (Put the chunks of work in the right order, prioritize, and arrange the flow of activities.)
6. Take action. (As soon as the plan has been formulated, start the first activities immediately: many people who strive for success stop after they have made the plan.)
7. Do something every day that brings you closer to your goal. (A journey of a thousand miles....)

And, in fact, the same method can be used for making a success of company goals, where steps 1–5 are quite often executed in a continuous strategic cycle, and where steps 6 and 7 (the execution phase) often receive insufficient attention.

It is well known in the literature that people commit to goals they perceive as desirable and feasible (Locke and Latham 1990; Oettingen and

TIP 61: DESIRABILITY AND FEASIBILITY OF GOALS

Make a list of three major personal achievements in your life (like running a marathon, playing saxophone, or learning a lot about wine) and three things that you always wanted to do but never did (write an English book, run a mountain trail, or learn to speak Korean). Now assess each of these against the criteria for desirability and feasibility. How much did you really want it, and how realistic is the idea of achieving these goals in the near future? The things you want to do someday but have not yet done are either not feasible or not really desirable, or both. Now take the list of goals you have defined for your team, and judge these against the same criteria. Do this also from the point of view of your people. (How desirable is this for them? How feasible is that for them?) With these insights, how can you now assure that these goals will be met?

Gollwitzer 2001). Desirability is reflected in the attractiveness of achieving the goal, and what the consequences of achieving the goal will be. Feasibility is more about individual reflection on your own capabilities to achieve the goal and your belief in a positive outcome. These studies also made it clear that the two factors of desirability and feasibility determine the intensity of the endeavor people put into achieving their goals: in other words, the more attractive and the more realistic the goals, the more committed people are in working toward their goals.

People in different cultures are attracted to working to achieve different kinds of goals. From previous discussions on the dimensions of culture (Section 6.3) you can expect people in individualistic cultures to prefer to pursue goals that are related to achieving personal success and seeking social independence of others. On the other hand, people in collectivistic cultures look for success within their group, and seek the social interdependence of their group members. As such, there are many criteria that determine which goals people pursue, which obviously not only depend on culture but also on other factors, like personality, living circumstances, and general expectations from life.

Conceptually it seems easy to understand how people work in groups in collectivistic cultures. We can accept that people in these cultures first think about the group and only later about themselves. However, culture goes much deeper. Just replacing individual goals by group targets is not enough to adapt your approach to collectivistic cultures. The manager of an international team will need to go through four steps for effective goal setting:

1. Translate organization objectives into group objectives.
2. Understand what kind of goals motivate people in each of the cultures involved.
3. Decide to translate these into individual objectives (or not).
4. Communicate the objectives to all people involved.

The American approach to goal setting is very individualistic, as you may expect in American culture. Superiors make decisions and communicate these to the people who execute them. Individuals may disagree on the decisions being taken, and in discussions they will raise their voice and express dissent. However, once the decision has been taken and the direction is clear, they will execute it and make sure the targets are met. Individuals have personal responsibility for achieving their goals and objectives, and when they need others to reach their objectives, they are expected to organize this. You own your goals and targets, and success or failure is in your own hands.

The American goal-setting process is very present in the management by objectives (MBO) approach: top management in a company sets the strategy, and this strategy is delegated to the lower levels in the organization, where people are expected to make it happen. The basics of this style of management mean that tasks are assigned to individuals, and that the sum of all these tasks will result in the strategic outcome that was foreseen. Indian people, however, believe that you cannot break down your end objective into a set of individual goals, as there are many more factors beyond your control that determine whether the end result will be attained or not. They find it unrealistic to assume that individuals can influence desired outcomes, and they find evidence on a daily basis for this when projects run late and targets are not met. At the same point, somebody from Korea will point out that it is not the sum of individual effort that reaches a specific objective: individualism leads to selfishness, and therefore to a focus on the wrong objectives.

The international manager needs to understand the kind of goals that motivate his people, and whether or not people expect to be involved in the definition of the objectives. Here, we give some practical tips for goal setting when different dimensions of culture play up.

8.1.1 Power Distance

In countries with a high power distance (high PDI) goal setting is done at the top, and this does not require input from people at lower levels. Goal setting should be in the hands of the ones who have status and power. In these cultures, decision making happens strictly according to hierarchical structures, where there is sometimes an exact definition of the level at which a certain kind of decision can be taken before higher levels get involved. A disadvantage of high-PDI decision-making processes is that valuable input from ground workers and experts can be ignored, and people do not feel committed to the goals that have been specified higher up in the organization. Superiors take operational decisions daily, and assign tasks to subordinates. This should not be seen as a form of micromanagement, but rather as the normal way of working in high-PDI cultures. In high-PDI countries, this top-down decision making is fully accepted by subordinates: they expect it and will be confused if they are asked to contribute to such tasks themselves.

In countries with low power distance (low PDI), everybody is equal in principle, and for this reason, everybody is also capable of contributing to the goal setting. Goals are negotiated. This is believed to be a better approach than top-down goal setting, as all valuable inputs are taken into account in the process. In a country such as the Netherlands, people openly question the validity of goals set by the highest levels of hierarchy: "What do they know about our jobs?" Employees in the Netherlands expect to participate in decision making, certainly when they have expert knowledge that is important. A good manager in such cultures is a people manager who involves his people in setting the strategy, defining goals, and deciding how to execute the process. The motivation of employees is directly correlated to this view: employees will only be motivated to perform tasks when they themselves have been involved in defining these tasks.

The effect of participation has been studied by Erez and Earley (1987) in a study comparing American and Israeli approaches to goal setting. Erez looked at the influence of culture on participation in goal setting, and the resulting effect on performance. Israeli culture is characterized by a very low power distance (PDI 13) compared to the United States (PDI 40). In practice, the role of power distance in the United States is actually much larger than this figure suggests, as large companies are generally managed along a clear hierarchical structure. Erez found that when others assigned them goals, the Israelis performed significantly poorer than they did when they participated in setting the goals themselves. For Americans, however, their performance was higher when goals were assigned to them: Americans could deal much better with goals set by others. When people were personally involved in setting goals, the Americans and Israelis suddenly showed similar performances. It is known that in low-PDI countries people react adversely to nonparticipative goals (think of Scandinavia, Israel, the Netherlands), whereas in high-PDI countries people expect (and even demand) nonparticipative goal setting (Erez et al. 1985; Latham et al. 1988).

8.1.1.1 Checklist for the International Manager: Setting Goals

- Think of your own role, and of what people of different cultures expect from you in specifying goals. In hierarchical settings, specify the goals and explain what you expect of your people. An authoritarian style is expected. In less hierarchical cultures, you should involve people in defining their goals: even when you know what you want them to do, make them feel they have contributed to defining their own objectives. This is not just "window dressing": you have to be open to being influenced by alternative suggestions, and be truly receptive to the contribution of employees in setting their objectives.

• When you manage a mixed team of high-PDI and low-PDI cultures, involve some people (those from less hierarchical backgrounds) in the goals to be set. When these inputs have been collected and used, define the final objectives and communicate these—clearly and without hesitation—to the whole team.

• Realize that when discussing goals with employees, people from high-PDI cultures expect power distance: your role is different from theirs, and they will feel uncomfortable when you put yourself at the same level as them and adopt a participative style. On the other hand, your people from low-PDI cultures expect you to treat them as equals.

8.1.2 Individualism/Collectivism

As discussed previously, goal setting in individualistic cultures is about defining how each individual contributes to the overall company objectives: people will organize themselves to achieve these goals, and they will be individually rewarded when they succeed. In collectivistic cultures, group goals take precedence over individual goals. Here, individuals primarily serve the group they belong to, and their personal goals are of less importance when working on a collective mission.

Goal setting on a personal level happens in every culture. In individualistic cultures, these are the objectives that count, and these are placed in the context of the overall company objective. Personal goals are also defined in collectivistic cultures, but here the aim is to see them in the context of what the whole group is trying to achieve.

8.1.2.1 Checklist for the International Manager: Setting Goals

• For people from individualistic cultures in your team, you will need to focus on how they individually contribute to the overall goal. Concentrate on what you expect of them, and how they will be rewarded for success. Remember, these employees will ask themselves: "What is expected of me, and what's in it for me when I succeed?"

- For team members from collectivistic countries, you will need to set the overall objectives and explain to individuals about their contribution to the group. Give the group time to digest the group objectives: they will need to share the goals and organize themselves in the proper way. Expect this to take time. Then follow up in group meetings, and review how the group is doing. Inquire about the problems they are encountering, rather than ask everybody individually to share what they have done.
- With team members from individualistic cultures, you should regularly review how they are doing and how their work is advancing toward their individual targets. These do not have to be long face-to-face encounters, but can be quick catch-up meetings of 10 minutes. The theme is: "How are you doing and what do you need from me?" Act immediately to any early signs of underperformance: never wait for more evidence to pile up.

8.1.3 Masculinity

People in masculine cultures, especially when these are individualistic as well, expect ambitious goals: these should be stretching, but achievable. These people are motivated by challenge and competition.

People in feminine cultures also expect different targets. Besides the hard, measurable tasks, they are driven by the quality of their cooperation with others, their happiness at work, etc. Individual targets will be more focused on giving the employee satisfaction with the job he is doing, and contributing to the overall work environment. In these cultures, people appreciate goals such as "Motivate the team and make sure that they work energetically on cooperating with sales." Even though this goal is not formulated in a SMART way (not measurable and time-bound; see Section 8.3), people in feminine cultures will find motivation in goals like these. People from masculine countries will reject this kind of goal, and will focus on the result of better cooperation: higher sales figures or more innovative R&D product designs will be the essence of their goals.

The validity of goals is subject to culture as well. In masculine cultures, goals that have been defined constitute the target all should pursue: such targets should be ambitious and should not be adjusted during the year. In feminine societies, it is acceptable to adjust targets when insight changes. When circumstances alter, this is a good reason to agree with the employee on new goals. As a manager it is wise to familiarize yourself with company guidelines on this: in some companies goals are goals (no matter how circumstances have changed), and in some companies the manager is expected to adjust the goals when changing circumstances require it.

8.1.3.1 Checklist for the International Manager: Setting Goals

- For people from masculine cultures, make sure that targets are content-driven. Make sure you describe the target according to the SMART principle, where the A of ambitious is important. Stretch your people; they expect it and will be motivated by it.
- For people from feminine cultures, you should also define targets that focus more on the work environment and the working method than on hard and measurable targets. Emphasize how people are expected to cooperate, and think about what your people need in order to be happy at work, as this will directly influence their level of motivation.
- Make sure that individuals in masculine countries understand how they will benefit from achieving challenging targets (especially in individualistic cultures). A split bonus scheme (how much do people receive when on target and how much when they exceed target) will motivate going that extra mile. The aspect of career advancement is also very motivating. Make sure that individuals in feminine countries understand the value of their contribution to overall goals: their role in the team and their cooperation with others are key. Discuss issues like team atmosphere and work-life balance (the soft aspects) in relation to people's goals.

TIP 62: LOCAL BUY-IN FOR PERFORMANCE GOALS

Set goals for all members of your cross-cultural team, even when there is no direct reporting line to you and they reside in other countries. Ensure that performance goals are set by the local manager in consultation with you or set the goals yourself and discuss them with the local manager. Make sure that goals are specific: this is the only way to initiate the discussion about reporting lines and work agreements with local organizations. Regardless of culture, every professional wants to know what is expected of him. Provide this clarity: it is essential to ensure that goals are achieved.

8.2 MOTIVATION AND EMPOWERMENT

One of the topics with which managers—especially of virtual and remote teams—often struggle is the motivation of employees from different cultures. Motivating people from your own culture can be challenging enough at times, but when culture plays a role the challenge increases. What motivates an individual in India, Argentina, or France? What motivates employees in general in such countries? Before we consider the role of culture, we must first look into motivation itself: What is it and how can you ensure your people become and stay motivated?

The central question in motivation is: What drives people to behave in a certain way? In the context of a company, we rephrase this question: What urges employees to behave in such a way that they (like to) contribute to the organizational goals? Phrasing it like this (steering individual behavior in such a way that your objectives are met) sounds like manipulation, but that would be a too negative description of the subtle influence you have as a company on what people do. As a company, you can influence the way your people behave. This can be done by making sure the expected behavior is displayed by role models at the top of the company. The top should communicate the benefits of such behavior to employees. They ought to reward certain behavior. The desired conduct should be stimulated through praise and feedback. And although the way a person behaves is a rather personal thing, as a company you can—and should—influence the collective, and make a conscious choice regarding the specific behavior that suits the company brand and ethics. Do you want your people to be innovative, out of the box, and optimally creative, or do you want them to serve every customer in the customer's best interest?

TIP 63: WHAT'S IN IT FOR ME?

Motivation of people all comes down to the question: "What's in it for me?" When motivating your team members for activities in the office, always make sure you ask this question first and answer it from the perspective of your people. Your people need to know how they will benefit from working on the goals you set them. Make sure you know this up front, and make people see what's in it for them when you tell them to work on certain tasks.

As Hofstede et al. (2010) argue in their book *Cultures and Organizations*: "Culture as collective programming of the mind plays an obvious role in motivation. Culture influences not only our behaviors but also the explanations we give for our behaviors. As a result, an American may explain putting in extra effort on the job by the money received, a French person by personal honor, a Chinese person by mutual obligations, and a Dane by collegiality."

The factors that drive motivation are culturally determined, as culture itself is about values, attitudes, and beliefs: these are the determining factors of motivation and demotivation.

Herzberg et al. (1959) make a distinction between two important motivators on the job: intrinsic motivators (the extent to which a job is interesting, challenging, and rewarding in itself) and extrinsic motivators (physical conditions, money received, relationship with coworkers). The intrinsic motivators are often overlooked: it is so much easier to motivate and reward a person with money (all you need to do is send a mail to HR to arrange this) than it is to really examine the motives that will make someone perform better. Intrinsic motivation is not hard to influence, but often we just do not know how to do this. Nobody told us when we became a manager. The challenge is to find out—on an individual level—what brings people pleasure: What do they find important and what knowledge is significant to them?

To the organization the challenge is to design jobs that are intrinsically motivating: the heart of Herzberg's theory is that intrinsic elements of the job directly motivate the employee, while extrinsic elements of the job should always be fulfilled; otherwise, they will harm motivation.

The most famous theory behind human motivation is that of Maslow (1970). Maslow argues that motivation is determined by need rather than performance. In other words, people become motivated by the needs they have, and will always seek to fulfill these needs. But different people have different needs. Maslow introduced a hierarchy in the human needs, varying from the need for food, water, sex, and sleep at the very lowest level up to the need for self-actualization and personal development at the highest level. The assumption is that only when the needs of the lower levels have been met will the needs of the next level drive motivation and behavior. When basic needs are met, higher-level needs become the focus of action.

Another way to look at the Maslow pyramid is to realize that all human beings will value the higher-level needs of esteem and self-actualization,

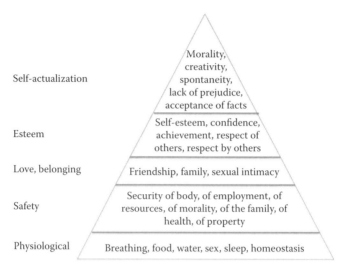

FIGURE 8.1

The Maslow hierarchy of human needs. (From Maslow, *Motivation and Personality*, 2nd ed., New York: Harper & Row, 1970.)

but that many people in poorer regions see most of their energy consumed by having to satisfy lower-level needs first (Figure 8.1).

Applying this to organizations means you need to ensure that the lower levels of motivation are already being met: people need food, water, security etc. Most managers will not have to worry about this: even in countries that are poor and where food distribution and water supply are problematic, managers generally work in environments where this has been dealt with. The better office locations in the capital are not representative of what is going on in the rest of the country. In India I have worked in fantastic office locations in Mumbai where all basic human needs are fulfilled, but looking out of the window, I could see those areas of town where people were struggling for survival. Many office workers are motivated by the wish to supply the basic human needs (lower levels in Maslow's pyramid) to their families. Managers should be aware of these motivators: not all family members being cared for by your employees are receiving their most basic human needs. It can safely be assumed that every reader of this book will have his needs met at the lowest two Maslow levels, but this cannot be extrapolated to other people in your company. Your people in Taiwan may have the responsibility to devote their entire income to their family to ensure that they can provide the medical help their elders need and the security their children need.

The international manager here should realize that the group of lower-level employees (often unskilled factory workers) is generally motivated by things that differ from those that appeal to the higher-level employees (professionals, managers). Every manager should understand which needs are of importance to his employees, and how the employees prefer to satisfy these needs.

Motivation is directly linked to rewards: companies tend to stimulate the behavior they desire of their employees by offering the right rewards, and to reduce any unwanted behavior by the appropriate punishments. In this way, companies steer the conduct of their employees and allow them to make a better contribution to the goals of the organization. The underlying assumption is: when you are rewarded, you behave the same way later in order to be rewarded again. This is the carrot-and-stick principle, where the carrot is the same as the bone is to the dog and the fish to the dolphin: these are believed to stimulate more of the desired behavior. Direct rewards motivate when tasks are routine, require control, and do not involve too much challenge.

Recent insights (Pink 2009) have made people realize that this reward-and-punishment principle is outdated: it only works under limited circumstances, when the work is repetitive and the performance is measured primarily on efficiency alone. In recent times, however, more and more work in organizations has come to rely on creativity rather than repetitiveness, and on effectiveness rather than efficiency. More complex and self-directed jobs require a different approach. When creativity and autonomy are important aspects of employee behavior, the carrot-and-stick principle breaks down. This is vividly described in the book *The Surprising Truth about What Motivates Us* by Daniel Pink (2009). He calls the principle Motivation 3.0, which addresses the engagement of employees rather than the pure motivation. Engagement goes one step further and addresses the degree to which employees are involved in their job and are enthusiastic about it, thus helping the organization to reach its objectives.

Pink (2009) describes three factors that motivate and engage skilled workers in the 3.0 era:

Autonomy: The urge to direct our own lives. This is the freedom and autonomy to work and perform in the way that we value most. Pink uses Google as an example of a company where autonomy is stimulated: employees are given 20% of their time to work on whatever they want, which is expected to promote creativity and, with that, better ideas and results.

Mastery: The desire to get progressively better at something that matters. The idea here is that getting better and developing your skills at something you find important (tasks that are neither overly difficult nor overly simple) is stimulating. This requires an environment that promotes learning and development.

Purpose: The possibility to do what we do at the service of something that is bigger and better than ourselves. It connects to our purpose in life: Do you want to do the job and be appreciated for that, or is your purpose bigger than this, and do you aim to realize ambitious dreams that enrich yourself and your company?

The international manager must understand which needs are important at various locations, and he should think about how to satisfy these needs in the most stimulating way. This requires comprehending the local culture and understanding the people who are working for you within that culture.

Maslow's hierarchy of needs (Figure 8.1) is believed to be universal. However, it is likely that different cultures will put these human needs in a different order. Whereas self-actualization is the highest motivator in the individualistic United States, it is the need for security that is more of a motivating force to people in France and Germany, and it is security and affiliation (belonging, esteem) that are important to people in Latin America.

In fact, the Western view that takes self-actualization as the highest human need should not be extrapolated too easily to other parts of the world. In individualistic societies indeed, people value their own individual development and realizing their own creative potential to the full. However, in a collectivistic society, self-actualization might be seen more as a matter of serving the group and society. In these cultures, esteem and belonging are basic human needs, and being part of a group is a need that ought to be served first before energy is spent on physiological needs and safety. From low to high, the needs in these cultures are expected to be esteem and belonging, physiological needs, safety, and then self-actualization. The latter, however, focuses on the group: the self is the group, and the highest motivator is to optimize your own contribution to the honor and harmony of the in-crowd. This is a thought that dovetails with the virtue that humans must possess in long-term-oriented societies: the willingness to subordinate oneself to a purpose.

Hofstede uses the dimensions of masculinity and uncertainty avoidance to determine which of the Maslow factors are main motivators among self-actualization: in strongly uncertainty-avoidant countries, safety will be a primary motivator, while in feminine cultures, a sense of belonging takes pride of place. Clustering these two dimensions leads to different possibilities of dominant Maslow factors:

Country	Uncertainty Avoidance (UAI)	Masculinity (MAS)	Dominant Maslow Factors
Thailand, Portugal, Costa Rica, France	High	Low	Security, belonging
Japan, Germany, Italy, Arab region, Argentina	High	High	Security, esteem
Sweden, African countries, the Netherlands, Scandinavia	Low	Low	Achievement, belonging
United States, Australia, Ireland, Hong Kong	Low	High	Achievement, esteem

The above discussion on the Maslow hierarchy across different cultures raises the question as to whether the Motivation 3.0 factors of autonomy, mastery, and purpose are universal, or will they also work out differently across cultures? Gallo (2008) argues that in poorer countries, people are happier with jobs with little variety and autonomy, and that remuneration, supervision, and working conditions (extrinsic motivators) are more important. To them, these extrinsic motivators are weightier than the autonomy, mastery, and purpose that drive employees in Western countries. Pay is an important motivator in Taiwan, for example: people change employer and go to work for the factory across the street for just a little bit more money. In many companies, this brings a problem with knowledge workers, in particular, who bring and take valuable knowledge and experience with them. Here it is important to understand that it is not money itself that motivates, but it is what people can do with the money that makes the difference. In the West, money provides the means to satisfy higher-level needs (do a course, develop yourself, etc.), whereas in Africa (most African cultures) and Asia (Taiwan in this case) it means you can contribute more to the needs of the collective in which you live. Here, the whole family benefits from the money you bring in, and people may feel it is their obligation to contribute to the family by accepting the other job across the street.

The conclusion here should be that choosing the way to motivate employees requires sensitivity to the cultural context in which the employees work. The extrapolation of Western motivators, such as personal advancement and self-actualization, to other cultures should be avoided. The international manager will need to understand what drives his people in different parts of the world, and he should act sensitively to the local cultural context when deciding how to address these needs. Western concepts cannot simply be applied to other cultural contexts: management practices such as participative management, empowerment, job enrichment, knowledge management, and total quality management, for example, all require a high degree of intrinsic motivation for them to be effective. This fits the Western Motivation 3.0 environment very well, but may not be valid in a call center in New Delhi, India, or a manufacturing plant in Juarez, Mexico, where short-term monetary rewards may be highly valued.

8.2.1 Checklist for the International Manager: Motivation

- Realize that in high-PDI cultures employees do not question the tasks delegated to them or their role in the company, so their motivation to perform seems a given fact. People follow orders, whether they are personally motivated or not. In high-PDI countries, the manager should give clear mandates and orders, and he should motivate by rewarding along the hierarchical lines in the company (boss praises or rewards the employee). In low-PDI countries, delegation and participation are important management concepts: the Pink factors of autonomy, mastery, and purpose contribute to motivation.
- Ask yourself whether your people feel themselves to be autonomous individuals or perhaps feel strongly connected and loyal to an in-crowd (individualism vs. collectivism). In individualistic countries, people will be motivated by publicly receiving individual signs of appreciation, such as promotion or bonuses. In collectivistic cultures, you should avoid praising the individual, and work with collective incentives and motivators.
- Realize that in masculine countries monetary rewards, honor, and symbols of power can be individual motivators, whereas in feminine cultures people will be more motivated by a good working climate,

pleasant colleagues, and high-quality working conditions. In feminine cultures people value solidarity and equality and, for this reason, will avoid extreme forms of remuneration for individual performance. In masculine countries, people like to be rewarded well for individual achievement and performance.

- Uncertainty avoidance should also be taken into account when thinking about job motivators. Expect people in high-UAI countries to be motivated by clear job descriptions, tasks, and responsibilities, as well as a secure pension. People in cultures that emphasize uncertainty avoidance (Belgium, Peru) have a stronger need for security than people in cultures that are less concerned about avoiding uncertainty (Singapore, Ireland).

As a general rule of thumb, the international manager should reward U.S. and Western European employees by giving additional remuneration for good individual performance. These rewards should be allocated on a short-term basis (directly related to recent contributions) related to specific activities, and announced in public (worker of the month, etc.). In other, more collectivistic cultures, you should give enough remuneration to all, and punish and criticize unwanted results and behaviors. But you must do this in an indirect way and address the group rather than the individual. Keep the long-term focus of these cultures in mind. Rewards need to be matched to local expectations. Many companies struggle with their remuneration and benefits system when guidelines from global headquarters are incompatible with local reward systems and processes. Always work with local experts to define remuneration and reward policies in other cultures.

TIP 64: MOTIVATING YOUR TEAM MEMBERS

When working with people from various cultures, it helps to understand what motivates them. You ought to reread the motivators mentioned in this chapter (Maslow, Pink, etc.) and determine what motivates all your individual team members. Take their cultural background and programming on the five cultural dimensions into account. Understanding what drives people is the key to effective interpersonal relationships, and these are vital to achieving results across cultures.

8.3 PERFORMANCE MANAGEMENT

Performance management ensures that employees serve the overall company objectives: it defines and administers their goals, judges how well they contribute, and often rates them in comparison to their peers. The process of performance management in most companies consists of a continuous cycle of four phases: planning (translating company objectives into lower-level objectives), monitoring (evaluating progress against target, stimulating and motivating, defining corrective actions where needed), and reviewing and evaluating (annual performance discussion, the sign-off of the final performance rating, start of the new cycle). The process runs continuously, although it is at a peak in the phase of the year when all individual performance discussions are held.

Variations on the standard process do exist. Some companies have more frequent interactive moments to evaluate performance: this occurs in the form of a mid-year review or even a quarterly review. Some companies couple the performance management process and the learning and development process in such a way that learning serves to build up the competences required to realize individual targets in an optimum way. And some companies compare individual performance ratings with those of their peers, and include some form of a "guided distribution" to ensure that the right mix of expected performance, above-target performance, and below-target performance is realized. Subsequent pay raises and bonuses are granted accordingly.

In recent years, we have seen the trend that companies focus not only on the what in the performance management process (the hard objectives), but also on the how (the way in which the results have been obtained, the so-called soft criteria). The final performance rating then consists of two distinct components: To what extent did the employee meet the expectations (targets), and how did the employee behave while working on these targets (behaviors)? The SMART objectives form the criteria for the what measurements, as these have been defined at the start of the performance cycle. The criteria for the how measurement are generally derived from the company values, and hence from the underlying behavior that the company expects to see from its employees. In this system, it is possible to end up with a low performance rating when an employee meets all targets but does not display the behavior expected of him. Equally well, somebody can receive a positive performance rating when not all targets have been met but when the attitude and behavior of the employee are above expectation.

In this standard description of a performance management process, a few assumptions have been made:

- Goals should be defined in terms of SMART (specific, measurable, actionable, realistic, and time-bound).
- The performance appraisal meeting is a two-way dialogue between manager and employee.
- Employee and manager should mutually agree on objectives and on the rating of the performance outcome.
- Both manager and employee agree and sign off the document.

Culture also plays a role here. Each of the above assumptions has been defined in a specific cultural setting: the American and Western European cultural values are visible in these assumptions. Rewriting these guidelines and using the words we generally use to describe the dimensions of culture leads to:

- Goals having to be defined very specifically to avoid ambiguity: there should be no uncertainty about the interpretation of the goals.
- The performance appraisal meeting being a two-way dialogue between two people who have different power and status: just as the superior speaks frankly to the employee, the employee also speaks openly to his superior.
- Objectives not being specified top-down by the person with highest hierarchical authority but, instead, defined in a mutual talk between manager and employee: the employee has a say in the decision on his performance rating.
- Two people with unequal power and status needing to decide together on the performance appraisal outcome, and jointly sign off the document.

A few other assumptions have been made in the process, which are also culturally relevant:

- The performance of the individual is relevant: goals and objectives are defined for each individual employee.
- Underperformance of the individual should preferably be dealt with in a direct and open way, confronting the person with the gap between his performance and the expectations of the company.

- Not only hard objectives count in the evaluation of individual performance, but also the way in which the results are achieved.

The above descriptions are characteristic of individualistic cultures with low power distance, and indeed most processes for performance management (and even the term *performance management*) originated in the United States. Also characteristic of this culture is the fact that the performance appraisal needs to be a fair and objective process based on quantifiable data: more subjective factors should be ruled out of the process that affects the position and payment of the individual.

The above-described performance management process is followed by many companies worldwide, also in countries that have a quite different cultural profile. The international manager should realize that—although the process is being followed—people locally may have difficulty with some of the process elements. For this reason, we look more closely at three dimensions that impact the way people deal with the performance management process in their company.

8.3.1 Power Distance

In high-PDI countries, inequality between the boss and subordinates is a fact: there is a natural difference in status between those who have the power and those who do not. Inequality of power is accepted. Subordinates respect their managers and will hardly ever question their opinion. People in these countries expect the manager to be firm and to set goals, and they will take these goals as a given. Performance evaluations by superiors in these countries will rarely be contradicted or criticized. The performance meeting is a one-way discussion where the manager informs the employee of his opinion on the performance.

In these countries, people also accept—much more easily than in the United States—that subjective factors play a role in evaluating the performance of an employee. The person with the power evaluates the contribution of the person who lacks the power, and this process is subjective by definition. Whereas in Western countries people would point out this is unfair and that the process should be fully objective (even when in reality this is hardly ever the case), in Asian, Latin American, and East European countries (generally high power distance), people expect inequality and subjective evaluations of their performance.

8.3.2 Individualism/Collectivism

In collectivistic countries people are concerned with group targets and department goals rather than with their own personal targets. A consequence is that
people in collectivistic cultures expect to be recognized as a group for their
contribution. And although everybody knows that some group members
contribute more than others, this is not considered particularly relevant. The
rewards are not meant to make some people of the group more valued than
others. On the contrary, it is the total outcome that counts, and everybody
should be valued equally to maintain the harmony in the group. Individual
recognition would only break the harmony. The manager in these cultures
is expected to reward the group collectively, and public recognition for the
contribution of the group is an important aspect of this.

This is not to say that individual monetary rewards are not valued or
appropriate in collectivistic countries: they definitely are. Management
will still reward individual effort and the contribution of the individual
to the overall company objectives. However, this is something between
the manager and the employee, and this incentive system is confidential
in its nature. When no one knows how others are rewarded for their good
contributions it does not disturb the group harmony: there is no jealousy
and no one stands out publicly from the group.

8.3.3 Masculinity/Femininity

The trend to base a performance rating on both the what and the how (did
somebody meet the targets, and in which way did a person work toward his
targets?) could be seen as a more feminine approach to performance management. The extreme masculine view would be to define very ambitious
targets and have individuals strive to meet—or preferably exceed—these
targets and be rewarded for this. People live to work and should do all they
can to ensure that they achieve the maximum possible at work. The more
feminine view would be not only to judge whether or not the person has
met his targets, but also to look at the social context in which this happens.
The way the results are met in the context of the social collective (the company) is important. The competition and ambition that are characteristic
of very masculine societies are absent from very feminine societies: here
people work hard, but not so hard that it detracts from their life outside
work. In these cultures, somebody who tries to be much better than the

others is frowned upon: in fact, it is necessary to avoid outperforming others in some countries (Thailand, for example).

In masculine societies people live to work: they will always finish work first, and in such cultures, it is common—if not expected—to work after office hours or over the weekend. People may not take up the full number of holidays they have a right to take, as there is still valuable and important work to be done. This contrasts with more feminine cultures where people work hard but limit this to office hours. Masculine cultures (like the United States) frown upon this, and may interpret an adherence to business hours alone as being not fully committed to work. People from feminine countries—such as those in Northern Europe—respond to these cultural differences by putting in long hours of work, simply because they may feel the pressure to do so from the dominant, more masculine company culture.

Performance evaluation in masculine countries is usually a simple and direct comparison between the target that was set and the achievement. A black-and-white evaluation tells you whether or not the target has been met. In feminine societies, managers tend to take the circumstances into account: "What was the outcome of the work?" and "Did things move in the right direction?" are more important than whether or not the absolute target was met.

8.3.4 Checklist for the International Manager: Performance Management

- Ask yourself whether people in your team originate from high-PDI or low-PDI countries. Employees from high-PDI cultures expect you to define objectives and communicate these one-way. It is your task to set targets and, in a later stage, evaluate whether or not these have been met. People from low-PDI cultures expect a dialogue and want to be consulted when setting their targets.
- In multicultural teams, make sure to start setting departmental and team objectives first and then translate these into personal objectives. Make sure your team members—certainly when they originate from collectivistic countries—see the big picture and know what they are responsible for as a group. As a next step, make agreements about personal objectives, but present them nonetheless in the context of the big picture. When rewarding the team for a good performance, praise the team in public (nonmonetary rewards) and ensure that the

team as a whole gets the credits. Personal incentives (salary raises, bonuses) should be discussed in private.

- Keep in mind that not all members of your team are motivated by the same thing (see Section 8.2). In masculine cultures, people are generally ambitious and will give priority to work objectives above immediate personal interests. People gain satisfaction from their job on the basis of hard results, and it may be difficult to explain that their ultimate performance rating also depends on the way they do their job. Invest time in explaining about the how of working and the behaviors that are expected of them. If acceptance of the how as a criterion for performance rating remains low, close the discussion and state it as fact: you will be judged on the basis of your personal targets and on the way you reach these targets. Period.

- Finally, you should train yourself in really understanding the other person. Can you—from his perspective and his unique vision of the world—understand his performance? From that same perspective, can you understand how he feels about the performance evaluation process that you implement? This understanding will help you to motivate your employees, address gaps in performance (Section 8.4), and discuss further the learning and development processes of the people (Section 8.5).

TIP 65: DURING THE PERFORMANCE MANAGEMENT DISCUSSION

Before carrying out a performance management discussion with an employee, examine which characteristics of his culture are relevant for the upcoming discussion. Once you know the (culturally driven) expectations of the employee, you can refer to them during the discussion ("I know in your culture you are more used to a one-way discussion, but I really value your input about the goals that we have set, and I want to know what I can do to help you reach your targets"). Show that you are aware of the different cultural expectations, while simultaneously sticking to the performance management process as defined in your company.

Sharing Experiences

Geof Cox, International Management and Organization Development Consultant, New Directions Ltd., UK
LinkedIn: uk.linkedin.com/pub/geof-cox/0/28a/324

Geof Cox *is an international management and organization develop-*
ment consultant, the principal of his own company New Directions Ltd.,
which aims to help individuals and organizations reach their potential.
He works with public, private, and not-for-profit organizations and
specializes in workshop design and delivery, appreciative inquiry, and
large group facilitation. In his more than 30 years experience, he has
worked with managers from over 90 nationalities in 34 different coun-
tries. He has authored a number of books and contributed numerous
chapters, study guides, and articles on management. His most recent
books include Getting Results without Authority *(BookShaker)*, Ready-
Aim-Fire Problem Solving *(Oak Tree Press)*, 50 Activities for Creativity
and Problem Solving, *and* 25 Role Plays for Interview Training *(both*
Gower).

An example from my own consulting experience: A major multinational energy company based in the UK found that their agreement to
offshore a great deal of their financial back office operation to India
was fraught with problems between the UK managers and the local

managers in India. The details of how the arrangement would work, where responsibilities lay, quality standards on accuracy and timing, and communication processes were all agreed, when the deal with the Indian outsourcing company, which was one of the largest operations of its type in India, was negotiated. Cultural differences were taken into account and built into the processes and procedures. Systems were designed and tested to support the detailed agreement. These were piloted in the UK with a team of managers from the Indian company working with the UK managers who would be overseeing the operation to test and check the systems and processes. All worked well, and a number of changes were made to improve the processes.

However, when the system went live in India, the problems started to emerge. The processes did not work as well as during the pilot, communications started to break down, responses from India were not as expected, and accuracy and timeliness of data started to decline. On the surface, the Indian-based operation was the same as the pilot operation when everything was tested in the UK. The difference was tracked down to cultural differences between the Indian managers who negotiated the deal and conducted the pilot, and the local managers who operated the process in India.

They appeared the same—they had the same education, the same level of qualifications, came from the same culture, had experience of the same type of work, were of the same age and gender mix, etc. The difference was that the managers who set up and ran the pilot operation from India were used to an international environment—they had negotiated and set up a number of similar operations across the world. In doing so they had adapted to a more Western way of operating and communicating. The local managers in India had not had the same exposure on the international circuit and reacted with the more traditional stronger hierarchical mindset and were less prepared to question requests and say no than their international colleagues. Despite the company doing its best to be culturally sensitive in its setup, it was caught out by not recognizing that there were different subcultures at work in its partner organization.

Practical advice for the international manager:

- Don't generalize from a few examples. Make sure that you understand the culture and differences with all the people that you are dealing with, especially if some have different life and work experiences than others. Nationality is not the only cultural difference; there is language, religion, education, gender, race, class, experience, and expertise, all of which go to make up the individual cultural mix of the person you are negotiating with, and could be significant.

- When you are relying on remote communication, remember that the local culture is likely to be expressed more strongly (on both sides), as the environment will reinforce cultural norms.
- Spend longer communicating when in remote situations. The potential for misunderstanding the other party is enormous. Summarize more and check understanding more—research suggests we ask 10 times fewer clarification questions in a remote environment. And it takes up to five times the amount of time and effort to build rapport in a remote working relationship as it does in a face-to-face environment.

8.4 DEALING WITH UNDERPERFORMANCE

Every manager will need to deal with employees who do not deliver the amount or quality of work that is expected of them. To most managers, dealing with underperformance is perceived as one of the most difficult things they have to do, and because it is difficult, it often gets forgotten, delayed, or the message is softened so much that the employee does not even notice that he is being held accountable for the quality of his work. The first and most important step as a manager is to realize that this is not just a difficult aspect of your job: it is your job. The job of the manager is to deal with underperformance, just as his job is to hire people, motivate them, meet targets, and such. When performance is not up to standard, this needs to be rectified, and companies expect the managers in the company to do so. This sounds tough, and it is. To alleviate this hard tone a little, we must also state that the way to deal with underperformance varies per culture.

There are many cultural—as well as personal—reasons why a manager does not like to deal with underperformance. On the cultural side, a low power distance may lead to an avoidance of dealing purposefully with the performance of equals ("Who am I to tell the person that he is not doing well?"). In collectivistic countries, the risk of losing face and disrupting harmony is considerable, and for this reason, dealing with underperformance is simply avoided. When dealing with underperformance, it helps to come from a more masculine culture, where people strive to be the best and have a competitive attitude.

I believe that underperformance should and can be dealt with in every culture: the way in which the manager should address the issue is culture dependent, and it is important for every international manager to have an understanding of the cultural factors that affect the way underperformance can be dealt with.

8.4.1 Power Distance

A manager should regularly see the world from the position of the employee—in this case, an employee from a high-PDI culture such as the Philippines, Russia, Serbia, Mexico, or China. This employee will take the word of the manager as the absolute truth, and consider the performance evaluation of the manager as final: it is not open to debate. The manager's statement about shortcomings and his negative feedback will be interpreted in absolute terms: this is reality and my performance is not up to standard. In low-PDI cultures, where the relationship between manager and employee is more equal, people tend to interpret the message as more personal. In countries such as the Netherlands, Israel, Australia, and Sweden (low PDI), the opinion of the manager is just one opinion, and although an important one, it does not represent the absolute truth. In these cultures, employees expect the opinion of the manager to be open to influence, and this will often be the case when employees face negative evaluations and criticism.

When dealing with employees from high-PDI cultures, the above-mentioned elements might form a reason to soften the message: the employee will get the implication anyway, but delivering the message in a softer way may have less impact on the motivation of the person. Especially when the culture is a combination of high PDI and low IND (collectivistic, hierarchical, such as Guatemala, China, and several Eastern European countries), there is a risk of being too clear: loss of face and permanent disruption of harmony can be a consequence. On the other hand, when addressing an employee from a low-PDI culture, the manager needs to be prepared for pushback and discussion. In this case, you will need to decide up front whether or not you are open for discussion.

8.4.2 Individualism/Collectivism

In collectivistic cultures (Asia, Arab countries, and Latin American countries) the manager will need to understand the impact of a very direct performance message. The manager should not criticize too much, or at least do this indirectly and cautiously. You should deliver the message factually. Place the focus on the job tasks, and certainly avoid the message getting too personal ("You are not good at …"). Personal pride and honor can be damaged, and the person may quietly decide to leave the company rather than face the humiliation of such criticism.

Loss of face is an important aspect of (business) life in collectivistic cultures; when you address underperformance and give negative feedback, the person will lose face, certainly when this is done in public or becomes public knowledge. When heard privately from a boss, the message will be absorbed and dealt with. A public display of dealing with underperformance will lead to loss of face for the employee, and is a terrible thing for him in the context of the group in which he operates. Moreover, publicly talking about underperformance of an individual will also undermine your status and authority as a manager: it is your responsibility to avoid somebody losing face, and failure in this respect means you are not a good manager. Managers from individualistic and masculine cultures in particular (cultures focused on individual performance, such as the United States, the UK, Italy, and Hungary) will need to adjust their style when dealing with underperformance in collectivistic cultures. In such frameworks, it is much better to pack criticism in the form of a suggestion, padded with many positive observations about the job as well: employees will be sensitive enough to pick up your message very well and deal with it.

Keeping harmony could even be more important than reaching the exact targets that have been set, although keeping harmony was not included in your personal objectives for this year. A manager from individualistic, Western countries should realize that there are many unwritten rules in collectivist countries, and employees may even expect you to tolerate underperformance for the sake of the collective. On several occasions, I have witnessed very obvious cases of personal underperformance in Taiwan or Korea, where the manager deliberately decided not to deal with this, or only very indirectly. The harmony within the group was of greater importance to this manager than the individual performance of an employee, and as long as the group delivers the expected results, there is no need to risk disrupting the harmony in the team.

So what should the manager do to deal well with underperformance? The following five steps provide a good guideline, and most of these steps (except the details of steps 3 and 4) are culture independent:

1. Identify the problem
2. Analyze the problem
3. Discuss with the employee
4. Define a course of action
5. Monitor and follow up

Identify the problem: Ensure you understand the real issue you are dealing with. Go for the real problem, and not the superficial (most visible) problem. When an employee behaves arrogantly, this may be a problem to you, but this is not the real problem. The real problem is that when this employee meets with customers, they tend to back off and interact with the competition instead. Your real problem is loss of revenue and customer dissatisfaction, while the attitude and communication style of the employee is one of the factors causing the real problem.

Analyze the problem: The essence of this step is to understand why an individual displays undesired behavior. You will need to get to the bottom of the question and really understand it. When it is hard to get to the root cause, the next step is easy: ask. Sit down with the employee and find out. This will help you gather valuable information that will help you define a solution in a later stage. Part of the analysis is also to ask yourself whether the employee could reasonably have been expected to perform well: Did you set the right performance objectives last year? Did you clearly discuss with the employee what you expected of him? Did you ever inform him that you were not satisfied with his progress? The only way to correct the situation is to address the root cause, even when this involves adjusting the way you work yourself rather than the way the employee works.

Sit back and analyze the underperformance situation in detail. Remember the Chinese proverb: "For every hundred men hacking away at the branches of a diseased tree, only one will stop to inspect the roots." Be that man.

Don't get me wrong. All this understanding does not mean that we accept the underperformance—on the contrary. But understanding is a necessary element of being able to address the underperformance in such a way that the organization benefits from it. As a manager you have to deal with underperformance, and your decision whether to deal with it or not should not include any cultural factor. The *way* you deal with it should.

Discuss with the employee: Meet the employee, share your conclusions from steps 1 and 2, and check your understanding. Focus on the task, not the person. Offer your help and ventilate your optimism about being able to solve this issue. The most important aspect of this step is to make sure you check your assumptions. In steps 1 and 2 you have made many assumptions, such as "The employee knows what I expect of him" and "In his culture following up on actions is accepted, even with superiors." As is the case with any assumption, these should be checked in order to help understand the employee. A good manager will be firm in his statements, but open to the possibility that his assumptions could be wrong.

In collectivistic cultures that are sensitive to losing face and disrupting group harmony, any message concerning underperformance should be packaged in a wrapping that softens the sharp edges. It is important to communicate positive aspects as well. Even in a one-to-one setting, you ought to give your message in an indirect way: "I see that it is difficult for you to get everybody's commitment to the project. I can understand that, as it is a complicated project. I think you need help on this. I've looked into some training courses and...." Their sensitivity to high-context communication is such that they will understand your message immediately, but you save them the humiliation of losing face, in relation to you or the group.

Define a course of action: You now will need to decide what should be done to improve the performance. This step expects you to describe exactly which actions will be taken. Take power distance into account: in high-PDI cultures you will need to be directive and express your expectations of the employee, whereas in low-PDI cultures your general guidelines will be sufficient (the employee has the freedom and responsibility to work toward his targets individually without your specific guidance). Make sure you keep track of all agreed actions, and that you check whether or not these actions truly

> ### TIP 66: LOCAL INVOLVEMENT IN GLOBAL PERFORMANCE EVALUATIONS
>
> When addressing underperformance with an employee in a different country, ensure you involve local managers (even if they are not the formal line manager) to advise you, to be present at the performance discussion, or even to hold the discussion with the employee on your behalf. Involving locals has the added value of giving weight to your performance evaluation: your strong opinion may otherwise just be taken as typical of your culture ("These Americans are always so harsh and direct ...").

rid the organization of the problem. You should avoid quick fixes, as the problem will inevitably return in a later stage.

Monitor and follow up: Performance problems would not have occurred if they could easily have been prevented. For this reason, you cannot expect that taking one single action will be sufficient to solve them. You will need to stay with the issue, monitor whether or not improvement is visible, and take corrective action where needed. If you notice that performance is not improving, you will need to return to steps 2 and 3 above, until the right actions—that remove the problem—have finally been taken (step 4).

8.4.3 Checklist for the International Manager: Dealing with Underperformance

- Remember that different cultures assign different weight to your statements about underperformance. Anticipate the reaction from the employee when addressing the issue. In high-PDI cultures, employees will take your verdict as the absolute truth, and you will need to soften your message to make it effective. In low-PDI cultures, you should expect pushback from the employee and you will have to decide beforehand whether or not you are in for discussion. Act as though you have to defend your case against the employee in court: gather facts, know the context, and choose your words carefully.
- Whatever the culture, the message you deliver when dealing with underperformance is a very sensitive one. Prepare very well.

Understand the culture of the employee you are dealing with, in such a way that you find the most effective manner to address the issue.

- Focus on the task, not the person. Especially when dealing with people from or in collectivistic cultures, people expect indirect communication, to maintain harmony and avoid loss of face. Feedback should be given indirectly in order to avoid irreparable damage in collectivistic cultures; there are many ways to express that you are not satisfied. In such cultures, you can decide to discuss the issue with the whole team or group: in collectivistic cultures you can then expect the group to deal with the issue themselves in a harmonious yet effective way.

8.5 LEARNING AND DEVELOPMENT

The learning and development of employees is a key responsibility of any manager. The central question any manager should ask himself is: "Are my people able to do what needs to be done?" When people lack some specific competencies, the knowledge or skill gaps need to be addressed. In some companies, the process of identifying and addressing skill gaps is integrated in the annual performance cycle, whereas in many other companies, the responsibility for identifying gaps lies with the employee or the direct manager.

The aim of this section is not to discuss the proper setup of the learning and development function in a company; neither do we want to introduce the full process of teaching and training employees. However, it is important to understand some of the implications of country culture for the process of learning.

8.5.1 Power Distance

In many countries, identifying an employee's learning needs is the responsibility of the manager. In other countries, managers expect employees to take personal responsibility for their development. This will determine whether the manager is actively or passively involved in identifying a learning need. In hierarchical cultures with high power distance, the manager is expected to pick up this role actively and tell his employees what they need to learn. In these cultures, the manager is even expected

TIP 67: EFFECTIVE LEARNING

When you identify the learning needs of one of your employees, do not refer them to HR "to find a nice training course." Stay involved until you are absolutely sure that the person will go to the right program. "I want to learn to exert more influence" sounds very legitimate, but this does not mean the course entitled "Effective Influencing" is the right medicine. Why is the person not good at exerting influence? Is he a bad listener who is preoccupied with his own agenda, or is he convinced that his opinion is less valuable than that of others? In each case, the person should attend a different training course. Question, reflect, and analyze. The help of HR is valuable, but they usually do not see the person at work. You do.

to organize this process in conjunction with HR, and often only informs the employee afterwards, when the decision has been made regarding the way the learning need will be addressed. Often this will be in the form of sending the employee to a training course.

In countries with low power distance, the employee himself is expected to take responsibility for the development of his skills. In these cultures, the manager needs to facilitate the learning process to a greater extent: he needs to make himself available in order to give feedback to the employee, and to advise the employee about his developmental requirements and the way to address these most effectively.

Power distance also plays a role in the way employees deal with learning new skills from a trainer or instructor. In typical high-PDI societies (like China), teachers expect to be treated with the respect normally afforded to elderly people, and there will be a clear power distance between student and teacher. The teacher tells the student how to do things: the student listens, does not interfere, and takes the teachings for granted. In low-PDI cultures, this will not be the case and teachers and students will treat each other as equals. This has very practical consequences for the level of inter-activity in a typical training setting. In high-PDI cultures, the interaction will be very limited, while in low-PDI cultures, there will be much more interaction: the teacher will frequently ask for the opinion of the learners, he will adapt the instruction format to what the participants need at that moment in time, and he will not be surprised when challenged. This often comes as a surprise to Asian participants in training courses in the

United States and Europe: Asians perceive Europeans and Americans as disrespectful if they challenge the trainer, and are critical of what they learn. Trainers from the Western world need to understand that the level of interaction they expect from a good student will be absent in countries with high power distance.

8.5.2 Individualism/Collectivism

In the Western world, learning is largely focused on competence development: Which knowledge, skills, and attitudes does the employee need to be able to do the job to his and our full satisfaction? HR processes concentrate on determining the critical competences for each job, assessing the competence level of employees against these requirements, and addressing the lacunas through training or other learning methods. This approach is typical of individualistic cultures where the focus lies on individual behavior and personal values. People have unique talents and abilities, and they are encouraged to develop their skills and behaviors to grow further as an individual within the company.

In collectivistic countries, people have different associations with the word *learning*. They interpret it as understanding how to contribute more to the success of the larger community: the team, department, or company. In this framework, learning is more informal and focuses more on the unwritten (social) rules that an employee needs to master. The code of conduct relating to contributing to the group effort is a very important subject of learning (although nowhere written down). In countries such as Korea and the Philippines, the unwritten rules reflect local wisdom: people learn "how we do things around here" and how they are expected to interact with each other within the group. In these cultures, people cannot be expected to take personal responsibility for learning the proper skills and competences for their job: this is the responsibility of the manager, while their main focus is to contribute as well as they can to the collective effort.

Another factor is the openness with which people speak of strengths and weaknesses. The Western ideal is that there should be open discussion in the office about people's individual strengths ("You gave a very good presentation to the board this morning: you were great!") and individual weaknesses ("You should not be so open and direct to your stakeholders! You should learn how to do this better and more tactfully"). An open discussion about strengths and weaknesses is not pursued easily in collectivistic societies: individual praise sets the person apart from the group, and this should be avoided in public. Pointing out individual weaknesses is an offense: this brings the person in discredit and makes him lose face in front of the group.

8.5.3 Masculinity/Femininity

The international manager will need to understand what motivates his people to learn new skills. When the employee comes from a masculine culture such as Italy, Hungary, or Mexico, he will value performance and status. In these cultures people are eager to learn continuously and to advance their careers: they nurture a desire to become better at their job and to excel, as that will benefit their career. When the manager wants his people to learn new skills, he will need to point out how this will benefit them in terms of employability, recognition, payment, and career advancement.

In more feminine countries, career advancement is not the main motivator for employees (see Section 8.2): people are more focused on the quality of life. They value their relationships with other people, and will be motivated if they are able to increase their pleasure in work, and improve their work-life balance. The manager will need to focus more on these aspects of a job when promoting training opportunities to his people.

8.5.4 Uncertainty Avoidance

The culture dimension of uncertainty avoidance also has a substantial effect on how companies deal with the development of their workforce. In high-UAI cultures (focused on reducing uncertainty), a manager will stick more strictly to job roles and job descriptions and will be more critical of whether or not people meet the requirements of the job in terms of competences and skills. An employee who does not meet all these strict criteria is a greater risk to operations. Learning new competences and skills is a way to directly reduce the uncertainty associated with making mistakes and working ineffectively. Mistakes should be avoided. In these cultures, the learning environment will also be more structured: people learn how to do things the "right" way and the focus lies on the employee's knowledge. The learning processes in these countries appear to others as overstructured and too detailed.

> ## TIP 68: LEARNING ON A TRAINING COURSE OR ON THE JOB
>
> When a learning need has been properly defined, the automatic next step in many cases is to find the right course. Before you start browsing the online training catalogues, ask yourself how the learning need could be addressed if there were no external courses. Creative solutions are often more effective than any standard training course. Learning on the job (extended assignments, mentoring, pairing with a more experienced specialist, remote group learning, interactive knowledge sharing, problem-solving sessions, peer learning) is powerful, and is usually only explored when there is no budget for external courses, unfortunately. Try to find internal learning solutions—with the help of HR and external specialists—before spending the learning and development budget on training by external providers.

In cultures that are more tolerant of uncertainty (low UAI) we see more open-ended learning environments: in the United States and Scandinavia the focus is on learning from mistakes (rather than avoiding mistakes). In open-ended learning environments, people learn to respond creatively to situations that come up: they receive feedback from others, have good discussions about the situation, and about what they could have done differently. Classroom learning in these cultures will be more focused on enhancing the person's individual ability to respond well to unexpected situations, rather than learning well-defined and specific competences and skills.

REFERENCES

Erez, M., and Earley, P.C. (1987). Comparative Analysis of Goal-Setting Strategies across Cultures. *Journal of Applied Psychology*, 72, 658–65.

Erez, M., Earley, P.C., and Hulin, C.L. (1985). The Impact of Participation on Goal Acceptance and Performance: A Two-Step Model. *Academy of Management Journal*, 28, 50–66.

Gallo, F. (2008). *Business Leadership in China*. New York: McGraw-Hill.

Herzberg, F., Mausner, B., and Snyderman, B.B. (1959). *The Motivation to Work*. New York: John Wiley & Sons.

Hofstede, G., Hofstede, G.J., and Minkov, M. (2010). *Cultures and Organizations: Software of the Mind: International Cooperation and Its Importance for Survival.* New York: McGraw-Hill.

Latham, G.P., Erez, M., and Locke, E.A. (1988). Resolving Scientific Disputes by the Joint Design of Crucial Experiments by the Antagonists: Application to the Erez-Latham Dispute regarding Participation in Goal Setting. *Journal of Applied Psychology* (Monograph), 73, 753–772.

Locke, E.A., and Latham, G.P. (1990). *A Theory of Goal Setting and Task Performance.* Englewood Cliffs, NJ: Prentice Hall.

Maslow, A.H. (1970). *Motivation and Personality,* 2nd ed. New York: Harper & Row.

Oettingen, G., and Gollwitzer, P.M. (2001). Goal Setting and Goal Striving. In *The Blackwell Handbook of Social Psychology,* ed. A. Tesser and N. Schwarz. Oxford, UK: Blackwell.

Pink, D.H. (2009). *Drive: The Surprising Truth about What Motivates Us.* New York: Riverhead Books.

Punnett, B.J. (2009). *International Perspectives on Organizational Behavior and Human Resource Management.* New York: M.E. Sharpe.

Tracy, B. (2005). *Focal Point: A Proven System to Simplify Your Life, Double Your Productivity and Achieve All Your Goals.* New York: Amacom, American Management Association.

9

Managing Teams

> We trained hard, but it seemed that every time we were beginning to form up into teams we would be reorganized. I was to learn later in life that, perhaps because we are so good at organizing, we tend to meet any new situation by reorganizing; and a wonderful method it can be for creating the illusion of progress while producing confusion, inefficiency, and demoralization.
>
> **—Charlton Ogburn**[*]

"I called you to discuss an intercultural awareness training for my team. The team consists of five people from India and five from the Netherlands. They are all located here in Eindhoven and are in charge of the software development for the Leonardo project. There's trouble in the team and some awareness of culture—especially focused on Western Europe vs. India—should help." The week after the call, I talked to the manager of the team about this training and I was not sure whether intercultural awareness would have any effect within his team. He told me about the very abrasive emails that were written by the Dutch as soon as the Indians had completed a piece of work, the disrespectful way in which the India team members failed to show up for team meetings, and the escalations in the direction of the highest-level managers in India. After hearing these observations, I was sure there was more to be learned. I proposed what I often do in cases like this: hold a day of interviews with individuals from both teams.

It was a nice day. I met Dutch engineers who were very passionate about, and had very outspoken opinions on, the way software should be written by the Indians. These people were truly concerned about the lack of progress the team was making. I also succeeded in quickly winning the trust of the Indians by talking to them about their country, the region they came

---

[*] Ogburn, C. Jr. (2002). *The Marauders.* New York: Overlook Press.

from (I had put a map on the wall where we put flags of their homes), and the kind of jobs they had done before coming to Holland. I met Indian people who felt lonely, disrespected, and unable to live up to expectations. More importantly, I met 10 people, all of whom had pride in their jobs—despite the bad working atmosphere—and who were all committed to producing the best possible result for the company. They somehow did not manage to work together productively.

What was the problem? The heart of the issue was a poorly defined project charter, complete lack of trust between the people, with the consequence that communication in the team had broken down. In other words, the objective of the team was not clear, and the team did not function as a team, but rather as a disorganized group of frustrated individuals. It was striking that, whereas the Dutch and Indians were sitting at workbenches in the same open-plan office, their communication took place through toxic emails. And when I asked one of the Dutch engineers about the background of the Indian project leader, he said: "What the hell does that matter? I don't know where he comes from and whether he is here with his family or alone. That's not relevant!"

The discussion with the manager of the team was short. I recommended that he should save the money spent on hiring me for an intercultural awareness training, and that he should (1) redefine the project charter and first get a buy-in from management in both countries, (2) get the team together to introduce themselves on a personal basis and have a nice meal in a good (Indian!) restaurant one evening, and (3) regularly organize a get-together of the Indian and Dutch engineers to build trust, discuss progress, and see where they could help each other. Three months later the team was doing much better: trust had increased, communication was more respectful, and they achieved more timely results than ever before.

Managing a team is much more complicated than managing yourself, certainly when the team includes different nationalities and cultures that have to cooperate flawlessly to achieve results. Research has proven that heterogeneous teams (multiple cultures, no subgroups within the team) outperform homogeneous teams in the long term, although homogeneous teams tend to do better in the early stages of team formation (Earley and Mosakowski 2000).

A well-known experiment in Atlanta in the 1990s concluded that on complex projects, the results of international teams were better than when the teams were homogeneously composed of people from one national background. It was the other way around for routine tasks: here homogeneously composed teams of people from one cultural background did better. For complex assignments, diversity is a major contributor to high performance, and the associated difficulties in communication and building trust should be tackled.

How this ought to be done is the subject of this chapter.

9.1 BUILDING UP THE TEAM

Assembling a team to work on a specific task is usually a hurried process: the pressure is on in the office, and the reason to suddenly assemble a team is generally the result of a crisis of some sort. With the best of intentions, management takes its responsibility, and ticks off this action point by calling together the specialists who best understand the problem. But collecting a group of smart individuals with the right expert knowledge is certainly not enough to build a great team. The assumption we often—and unconsciously—make is that highly educated and specialized people will be smart enough to understand what to do, and how to work together. Look, however, at this quote by Gratton and Erickson (2007) in their *Harvard Business Review* contribution of November 2007: "The higher the educational level of the team members is, the more challenging collaboration appears to be for them. We found the greater the proportion of experts the team had, the more likely it was to disintegrate into nonproductive conflict or stalemate." Work for the team leader or manager!

In my experience, four steps need to be taken to form an effective team and make it work. If steps 1 and 2 are omitted, there will still be a team, but it certainly will not be effective.

1. Decide on the objective
2. Prepare the environment
3. Select for diversity
4. Make it work

9.1.1 Decide on the Objective

A clear objective is essential for the team. In their research among 58 executives from multinationals, Govindarajan and Gupta (2001) found that establishing a clear objective is one of the top three most important tasks for a global business team, yet it often scores low in terms of realization. Apparently, a clear team goal is hard to define. We always find reasons to avoid defining the goal very specifically, because we think the team will do more when we do not restrict them too much. Some innovation teams even avoid setting goals at the start of a project because the range of possible outcomes of the project is so diverse that they cannot predict what to go for. Some project teams are formed before all stakeholders have agreed to start the project, and for this reason the scope of the team is defined very broadly, to accommodate the different opinions of all possible stakeholders at a later stage. And some teams that have been instructed to drive change will start to work immediately because there is urgency: they will not delay their important mission with sluggish administrative tasks like goal setting. All of these reasons—however understandable—should not be excuses for not setting a clear and specific goal. In the middle of a crisis, step back and first oversee the situation, and carefully decide on your objective.

In the Indian-Dutch collaboration mentioned at the start of this chapter, the goal was vaguely defined. They were to build the software of the Leonardo project together, with the Dutch doing high-level design and testing, and the Indians structuring the software, making the functional designs, and doing the integration. Only the high-level functionality of the final software stack was specified, but a clear functional specification was not in place. The manager indicated that "the team was expected to apply their creativity and be proactive in doing what needed to be done." This is a recipe for failure. Not only did this indicate a limited understanding of Indian culture (where creativity and proactivity cannot be expected from individuals without creating the right boundary conditions), but it also would have failed in the Netherlands just as quickly. Without a clear objective (in this case a full specification of required functionality and boundary conditions, such as the software stack to be used to start up the project, etc.), the team is wasting its time.

I like the analogy that success author Brian Tracy (2008) uses in his book *Flight Plan*: "A plane flying from A to B is most of the time off-track. Although it has a clear target (the airfield that is the destination marked 'B' on the 'flight plan'), all kind of unforeseen circumstances force the pilots to continuously make adjustments: other traffic, wind streams that make it more economic for the plane to fly at a different altitude, bad weather on the way etc. The point is that although the plane is most of the time off-track, it will arrive exactly at its destination and sharply on-time. This is the result of up-front target setting: you need to have a clear and specific goal (in this case 'B' on the map)."

The team goal should be specific: the team goal is not to work on a new product for customer X or to find a solution for problem Y. You need to be much more specific. The challenge is to do this without overdoing the SMART target setting and losing yourself in metrics and definitions. Rather, you should focus on the fundamental questions that help you define where you want to go:

- What is it we are after? What is the vision of how the office will look once the team has been successful with this task? Visualizing the desired state (or the ideal state) helps a lot in thinking without constraints, and realizing the best possible future for the team and the company.

TIP 69: WHAT'S THE GOAL?

Define the goal for each new project team, communicate it to the members, and then ask them to comment honestly on it and give feedback. In this phase, you should listen, and not (yet) defend the goal you have specified. Listening to the objections of the people who will later execute the work not only pinpoints the weak spots in your plan (there will certainly be several), but in many cultures, it will also add to the motivation of your people by giving them the opportunity to speak up. Your goal was that they bring the new product Alpha S3 to market. They point out the product is expected to be customized for four clients but that there is no capacity for doing so, and that they fear many unforeseen customization cycles. So does the goal of the project include having Alpha S3 run successfully at all four customers? Is it the team's responsibility to solve capacity constraints? Is it the team's responsibility to decide on the specification of each customer release, or does marketing have the final say in this matter? The objections of your team are valuable. Now ask the team how they propose to deal with this. When you have gone through this process, the goal is usually crystal clear, and the team members now know what is expected of them.

- How will the company benefit from what we do? This is deep thinking but fundamental to being effective as a company: Which company objectives are realized when this team is successful? If this link is not clear, do not start. Get back to deep thinking, ask advice from others, but always make sure you understand exactly why we are doing this. How does the company get better when we perform this task outstandingly?
- What is the consequence of not doing it? There should be a clear and unambiguous answer to this question, one that shows that this goal is important. If the consequences of not doing this task are mild or hard to specify, there is usually a good reason not to start the project at all.

The answers to the above questions should be shared with the team and with the environment (see the next step in Section 9.1.2).

9.1.2 Prepare the Environment

What will change for the environment once the team has accomplished the goal? The environment refers to all stakeholders, whether they are customers, suppliers, management, executives, public interest groups, or whatever. Everybody who has an interest in the outcome of the project will need an answer to the question "What's in it for me?"

The team can only be successful in the context of its environment. It cannot invent a new product when corporate R&D does not support its work. It cannot optimize production lines when production planning is

---

**TIP 70: CONTENT, PROCESS, AND
INTERACTION IN PROJECT PLANNING**

When you assemble a team to work on a new project, plan the project using the upper three levels defined in Figure 2.1 (the four levels of communication). This way, you force yourself to think about the content of the project (what is to be delivered), the processes (how exactly the team will work), and interaction (how the team members will interact and cooperate). The more specific you force yourself to be on these aspects, the more effective the project team will be in reaching the required results.

not aware of what the product is doing and why. It cannot implement a new IT system when not all stakeholders in the company have reached consensus on the specification. It is important that all involved parties (the environment) know what is coming, and that eventual bottlenecks are removed so that the team can make a good start. This works two ways: it benefits the environment as they are stakeholders and have an interest in the success of the project, and it also benefits the team: it makes a flying start as everybody is aware of what it has been set up to do.

9.1.3 Select for Diversity

The essence lies in the word *diversity*: it is much harder to assemble a diverse team than just assemble a team. However, diversity is crucial in bringing creativity and problem-solving capability to the team. The tension that emanates from diverse points of view is required to create breakthroughs (Comstock 2012). As we see in Section 9.5, productive conflict and constructive tension are critical elements for a highly functioning team, while artificial harmony and conflict avoidance can kill creativity instantly.

It requires energy to deal with the tension that is inherent to diversity, and we all have an unconscious tendency to save effort and invest energy in other things (like discussion on the content). Individuals have an intrinsic preference for working with people who resemble them, people with whom they share common qualities and who have similar cultural beliefs, mores, and traditions (Andaya 2009; Neal 1998). The manager's task when assembling a diverse team is to accept that it will take energy to make the team work.

A few guidelines for the manager when assembling a diverse team:

- Select the right people. This is much more than just gathering the most relevant experts for the task. It can only be done by carefully thinking through the responsibilities and tasks of the team: Which activities do they need to execute in order to be successful? Once you know these critical activities, you can determine which behaviors you expect from the people who will perform these tasks. And only once you know these critical behaviors can you know what kind of people to look for. I often apply the high impact learning method (Brinkerhoff and Apking 2001) to this process: (1) look at the organization objectives, (2) derive from these the critical tasks, (3) derive from these the behaviors you expect from people, and (4) fill in the behavioral/competence gaps. Do this well, but don't overdo it: a piece of paper to sketch the necessities is enough.

- Select the right mixture of people. Make sure there is a good blend of creative vs. analytical people, a good mixture of task-focused and people-focused individuals, a good mixture of detail-oriented and big-picture-oriented thinkers, etc. When you have selected the right people for the project team, assess every individual against a few nonnegotiable criteria you specify up front. These can be hierarchical equality within the team, external focus and connections, or whatever else you consider critical to success.

- Select people who can effectively play at all four levels of communication (see Section 2.1): you certainly want good content people (specialists), but you also want people who can address the procedure of working on the tasks, and people who are comfortable addressing interaction and climate issues when they come up. The team will need this when going through the inevitable difficult phases of teamwork (storming).

- Select people who are familiar with teamwork across cultures. These should not be the people who have only done cross-cultural awareness training courses and know Hofstede's theoretical framework, but people who have experience in a complex international setting. They can bring practical insight into how cultural differences play out on the workfloor.

- Select the leader of the team. This is certainly not the person with the most technical experience or the most expert knowledge. This is a person known for his team leading and people skills. The analogy applies again: the pilot of a huge aircraft needs to be a good pilot, but on top of that he needs to work impeccably with his co-pilot, flight engineer, and navigator, and should be capable of giving clear instructions to the rest of the crew. With regard to the Thomas-Kilmann model on conflict management (Thomas and Kilmann 1974), it is best to look for people with a natural preference for the collaborative (win-win) style, rather than people who score extremely high on domination or accommodation. They should be able to appreciate and manage diversity.

9.1.4 Make It Work

Once the team has been assembled and they start up their activities, stay with them, especially in the early phases of teamwork. Make sure that the people on the team are really on board: invest a few hours on getting the team together and talk through all environmental aspects, the objective, and the tasks at hand. Spend an equal amount of time on the questions and doubts they nurture. As long as you feel some people on the team are not on board (not committed, not capable, or not willing), this is still the phase in which you can and should make early adjustments to the team.

Encourage the team members to get to know each other on a personal basis, and help them develop an attitude of acceptance of one another. Do not underestimate this aspect and certainly do not put it aside as one of these soft issues you need to deal with. There is nothing soft about molding a team and making it work! My experience with project leaders in charge of complex projects is that when they get to an evaluation of a finished project, this is often one of the first things they point out. "Instead of just starting work immediately, we should have spent time on getting to know each other, building trust, agreeing on how we communicate, and organizing ourselves into a high-performance team."

9.1.4.1 Culture

A few aspects of culture are of importance when building up a diverse team. Three of the cultural dimensions play a role here.

Power distance: When assembling a project team, power distance—and the consequences for internal hierarchy—will need to be taken into account. Check the following items:

- Team members from high-PDI countries will expect clear guidelines and direction from the leader of the team, whereas the leader in low-PDI countries (like the Netherlands, Germany, UK) may take up a more supporting role and is himself one of the contributing team members. He will be expected to be more directive in assigning tasks in high-PDI countries (Russia, India, China).
- Does the team have a responsibility to represent the company externally? If so, the team leader should be visible as a person with status and power when working with high-PDI countries.

- Make agreements on decision making within the team. In high-PDI cultures, the person with the highest status within the team will be expected to make decisions (or at least make sure these are made on the basis of the input he receives from others), whereas in low-PDI cultures, team members will expect autonomy in making decisions, or at least expect to be consulted when a decision is to be made.

Individualism/collectivism:

- Ensure people are committed to team success, and that they value being successful together rather than being successful alone. In collectivistic cultures, people are used to acting in the interest of the group they belong to. They will naturally have more loyalty toward the team, and they will strive to make the team successful at all costs. People in individualistic cultures are not used to this way of thinking: they see themselves as individual contributors to the team. This attitude requires more effort from your side to shape the team into a close and committed group.
- How should you share information and make decisions on the team? In collectivistic countries, people will be more inclined to ensure that all team members have all the relevant information, and that everybody is involved in the decision-making process. In individualistic countries, it is also important to share information, but it comes less naturally to most team members (information is power). Organize this aspect of work in the early stages of collaboration.

It is important to note that the antithesis between individualistic and collectivistic is not black-white, and that the above-described extremes may not be so visible in reality. For example, Japanese project teams will clearly exhibit collectivistic behavior (especially when looked at from a Western perspective). However, internally, the individual contribution of team members to the project will take precedence (Andaya 2009).

Uncertainty avoidance:

- Do people expect a clear task description? In cultures with high uncertainty avoidance (high UAI), uncertainty is reduced by carefully organizing the work structures. One aspect of this is to make sure everybody knows exactly what is expected of him within the team. In low-UAI cultures, people will be more open to just taking the work as it comes, and they avoid overorganizing their environment.

- Does the team need to be full of experts? In high-UAI countries, it is expected that the team will contain several or many experts. It ought to be plainly visible to the outside world that the team has been chosen to accommodate the right experts. In low-UAI countries, the status of the team will not suffer from not having the right experts on board. Here, the team can be assembled on the basis of other criteria, such as individual personality traits.

9.2 BUILDING TRUST

"I don't trust him," "I have little trust in the idea this is the right decision at this point in time," "I trust you will be here at 4:00 p.m. sharp." These are all sentences in which the word *trust* is used. And in all these sentences the meaning of the word *trust* is slightly different. In this chapter, we base our discussion on trust on work done by Nico Swaan and Erik Boers (described in their book *Making Connections* (2012)), and articles the author has written in conjunction with Nico Swaan about trust in the (virtual) workplace (Garten and Swaan 2012).

According to Solomon and Flores in *Building Trust in Business, Politics, Relationships and Life* (2003) we can discern three types of trust:

1. Simple trust: Trust given without thinking about and reflecting on the consequences, in the way a child gives his or her trust to someone who approaches him or her with a smile.
2. Blind trust: Trust given to someone uncritically and without questions or reservations.
3. Authentic trust: Trust as a choice you make: a choice to be open and give your trust while being fully aware of the risks involved.

In the work environment, simple trust and blind trust are seldom relevant. This is an important observation: what we mean by trust in the personal world of friends and family usually has a different meaning from that of trust in the work environment. Whereas in private life trust is about all three forms of trust described above, we generally refer to the category of authentic trust in the office: I give you trust in the sense that I accept the eventual consequences of being vulnerable and frank with you. The definition implies that you give trust to another person and thereby earn the privilege of receiving it yourself.

Authentic trust is close to the definition of trust advanced by Rousseau et al. (1998) and Mayer et al. (1995): trust is the willingness of the trustor to accept the risk of relying on the trustee, even if the trustor is unable to monitor or control the trustee.

In this sense trusting someone means that we have confidence in his character and abilities, and we assume that we share similar values. You believe you share basic values, and only when you discover that this is not the case is trust broken. From this definition it follows that important aspects of building trust involve sharing your own values and listening to and respecting someone else's values. As Swaan and Boers describe this: "Trust cannot be built or maintained on the basis of assumptions. Fundamental to building and maintaining trust is the willingness and ability to share your own thoughts and feelings, and to enquire after and listen to the thoughts and feelings of others. Trust is built on openness— openness about oneself and openness towards the other. Closing oneself off and basing actions on assumptions about what someone else may think or feel destroys trust, damages relationships and hurts individuals, sometimes deeply."

Building trust is key. In previously mentioned research by Govindarajan and Gupta (2001) building trust was found to be the most important task any global business team faces.

How do we create authentic trust? You cannot design trust into an organization, or tell people to trust each other from now on: trust needs to be built step-by-step. Building up a high level of trust takes time and is difficult. That is because it requires vulnerability, openness, and courage to truly connect with others. Such traits are not present in the workplace by default. Also, you yourself are the first one who must build up trust, and only when you have consistently demonstrated that you are willing to adopt a vulnerable position and build up a true connection with the other person can you expect the other person to do the same.

It is more difficult to develop trust in a diverse team, because there are different work practices around, and different perspectives on, the same thing. A team member from a different background may find it difficult to identify with your work practices. And even though the people in the team have the same common goal, their diversity may already harbor different personal objectives, to say nothing of different functional reporting lines,

> ### TIP 71: DO YOU TRUST THEM?
>
> Consider some of the colleagues and partners you work with, and ask yourself whether you trust them or not. This will force you to reflect on "What makes you trust them?" or "What happened in the past that made you lose trust?" Now go through the rest of this chapter and decide for yourself which form of trust you look for in people. The latter part of this chapter will then tell you which cultures work with the same definition of trust, and which cultures are home to people with different expectations when they talk about trust.

different priorities and agendas (Jassawalla and Sashi 1999), etc. The same holds for geographically dispersed teams in which team members often experience more conflict than collocated teams because of the challenges of sharing information, the limited time to communicate, and not seeing each other when communicating (Zhang 2011).

9.2.1 What to Do to Build Trust

There are certainly many things a manager can do to promote a culture of trust and to ensure that his team starts to act on a firm basis of personal trust. But before we give a toolbox to the manager so that he can start to build trust, we challenge the manager to look in the mirror and engage in some introspection first. Are you really willing to build up trust?

According to Solomon and Flores, people "develop trust through interaction and conversation, in relationship *with* each other." Trust can be built by actively deploying four categories of behavior (Swaan 2012) in the course of interaction and conversation:

- Category 1: Receptivity. The extent to which you are open to others. Examples: Inviting others to express their views fully and openly, listening empathically, looking at issues from other people's perspectives.
- Category 2: Transparency. The degree to which you are open about yourself, your ideas, and the information at your disposal. Examples: Speaking unambiguously, avoiding hidden agendas, being honest about your own motives.

- Category 3: Positivity. The degree to which you avoid negativity and remain positive about yourself, others, and various situations. Examples: Focusing on the good in people and situations, demonstrating realistic optimism, expressing appreciation for the contributions of others, avoiding blaming others, and making negative judgments.
- Category 4: Other-directedness. The degree to which you reach out to and put yourself out for others. Examples: Offering help or assistance, keeping others actively involved, adhering to promises and commitments made.

These four categories of behavior are essential to the creation of authentic trust. You may not score high on all four categories at the moment (honestly, I don't). However, if you want to be known for your capability to build up trust in teams, you should aim to develop yourself in each of these four categories.

Now what should you be prepared to do as a manager if you want to be a role model in the above four categories? This requires:

- Courage
- Openness about yourself (vulnerability)
- Time and patience
- Switching off your assumptions about the other person and his motives
- An open, inquiring frame of mind
- Self-confidence, and an ability to trust yourself (Swaan and Boers 2012)

On a very practical note, what you want to start working on as a manager right now is to:

- Accept that we are all different. This sounds easy but is hard to accept under pressure of work. We often say that we really value people who are different, but still we expect them to behave in the way we prefer. This is where (cultural) ethnocentricity kicks in: our way of doing things is obviously better and superior to the way the other person does them. Force yourself to accept that people are indeed different, step back in difficult situations, and try to understand the situation from their point of view. Practice this by focusing your mind on three people at work whom you really don't like or trust. Now force yourself to think of these people in a positive and respectful way, and continue practicing this until it is automatic and feels right.

- Pay attention to sensitive issues and do not avoid them. Before the tension-generating issue escalates, you need to have the courage to bring it out in the open. A manager is regularly required to get out of his comfort zone, and enter the arena of tension, disagreement, and conflict. Bringing sensitive issues out into the open requires cross-cultural competence: the way to bring sensitive issues to the table in Serbia or Russia is very different from the way it should be done in Thailand or Malaysia.

- Talk, talk, talk. Keep talking to all people involved on the team. Continuous, constructive, and open communication is the best medicine against a lack of trust. This involves informal communication, setting the right example, being present and accessible, frequently taking the initiative to ask people if there is anything they need help with, etc. It also involves formal communication in the more conservative forms of team meetings, as well as scheduled one-to-one discussions, etc. Stimulate people from different cultures and backgrounds to interact and communicate. If you don't organize this, similar cultures will stick together in the workplace, as that is the most comfortable situation for them. If you want diversity to work positively and trust to accumulate, organize the mutual communication well.

- Break down language barriers. Keep it simple.

TIP 72: ENGLISH: KEEP IT SIMPLE

While English is usually the common language, it is not the mother tongue of most employees. Language difficulties can create many misunderstandings in multicultural teams, and impede the communication that is so essential to building up trust. Avoid using too much English or American vernacular: nonnative speakers may not understand many expressions and typical slang. Keep it simple. English and American people generally find it hard to adjust, as they have the idea that everybody understands them. Slow down, articulate your words clearly, use simple words, repeat what you say, and check for understanding.

9.2.2 Building Trust across Cultures

We started this chapter by defining *trust*, and arguing that authentic trust is the kind of trust we refer to when building up trust in project teams. This requires explanation, as most Anglo-Saxon countries start with a different definition of trust: you can be trusted if you do what you say you will do. This definition of trust is very close to the concept of reliability, and it is well known that in most Northern European countries (such as the Netherlands, UK) and the United States this definition of trust is unconsciously used by most people. It is often stated in Stephen Covey's books on leadership, for example, that trust is all about making and keeping commitments: he argues that when you make a commitment, this builds hope, and when you keep hope, this builds trust.

This form of trust is, however, not what we mean here when speaking about the "glue" that holds teams together. When talking about trust in the context of team effectiveness, we refer to authentic trust as introduced earlier in this chapter.

Different cultures mean different things when they talk about trust (Lewis 2006). Figure 9.1 plots several regions of the world, where—generally speaking—different meanings are given to the word *trust*. In the region indicated I (Anglo-Saxon countries like the United States, Western Europe, and Australia) trust mainly has to do with reliability and consistency. In the rest of the world (regions II and III) trust is a much more

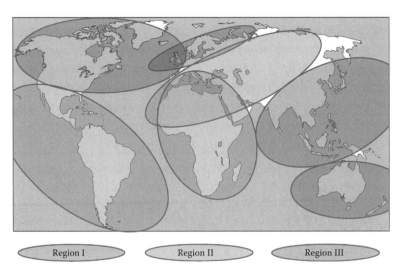

FIGURE 9.1

Different regions of the world, and the meaning they associate with the word *trust*.

personal thing, not dealing so much with reliability but more with authentic trust, as described above.

We zoom into these regions a bit more:

Region I: Here people will trust you if you do what you say you will do, and if you are consistent (reliability). The truth here is an absolute truth. Whether you trust someone or not is a rational choice, indicating whether you think you can rely on the person or not. For this reason, building up trust is not a long-term process but gets done while working together. Before starting to do business, no extensive relationship building is required, and the no-nonsense attitude in these cultures is that small talk is often a waste of time. The little relationship building that is done can be done virtually: although not ideal, the belief is that when phone conferences and other virtual meetings are well organized, people can get to know each other and work together well. Swedes, Americans, Dutch, and Germans like to be efficient, and usually get to work as soon as they can. Long dinners and intensive talk about the well-being of family members are avoided, and family life is seen as something different than business life. These two different worlds are kept separate, and work-life balance is an often discussed subject in these cultures.

Region II: In this region trust is a much more personal thing, that does not come from the head, but from the heart. People can trust each other when they get to know each other personally. And personal relationships are built over time, sometimes during years. These personal relations go beyond the individual: in these—mostly collectivistic—cultures trust involves the in-group to which you belong, like the family. Business meetings in Latin America, the Middle East, and Africa may involve long discussions about the well-being of family members: this process is not hurried, and not joining these discussions or not opening up can be seen as a sign that you cannot be trusted. Trust is a very personal thing, and involves many hours of socializing and really getting to know each other. Trust in these regions often comes with preferred treatment: when people trust you, it is easier to get things done. This long-term trust-building process cannot be done through virtual meetings: seeing each other face-to-face is required, and there is no low-cost substitute for this. Trust is not for sale.

Region III: Trust in this region is similar to that in region II, with one addition. In this part of the world trust is a reciprocal concept, involving returning favors and helping each other. When a person can be trusted, this includes an obligation on the person to take good care of you. If I do well for you, you have an obligation to return the favor and treat me well also. This extends over longer periods, and sometimes up to a lifetime. (In the Philippines, the concept of *utang-no-loob* involves debt of gratitude: I should pay you back for a favor you did to me. This is a deep value and does not involve a quick return of favor: people take this very seriously and take pride in the obligation to take care of each other.)

Traveling from region I to region II or III to do business, you should be prepared for a much more personal way of building trust than you are used to. Here trust is all about your willingness as a person to become one of the in-crowd, and opening yourself up in such a way that business partners can get to know you on a very personal basis. This is much closer to the concept of authentic trust rather than reliability. In Italy, building trust is a very personal process, and only once people get to know each other on a very personal level and open up can they establish a relationship of trust. In Asian cultures, trust is a different concept once again: you build trust in a mutual relationship, where you both give and take to make the collective stronger. Trust in these cultures can only be built up in an environment of harmony, where indirect communication prevails.

Let us look again at a few of the Hofstede dimensions of culture, and see how these impact trust building:

Power distance: In Western cultures (region I) building trust has little to do with status and hierarchy. Whether a person can be trusted or not has to do with reliability and predictability, and these criteria hold for bosses as well as subordinates. How different this is in region II and region III cultures, where the default setting is always by definition to trust people higher up in the hierarchy. A boss can be trusted; otherwise, he would not be a boss. This again opposes multiactive cultures where trust is a very personal thing, something that has to be earned personally within the group, especially when you have power and status. Once you are a trusted person, trust will stay and is not easily broken.

Individualism: Where the cultures in region I of Figure 9.1 are individualistic, all countries in regions II and III are collectivistic. In the latter category, trust is mainly something that is defined in the context of the in-crowd you belong to: collectivistic cultures personalize interactions and see these less as information exchanges. In region I cultures, trust is a more individual and more of a black-and-white concept: you can or cannot be trusted. It is known that in collectivist countries, people may place little trust in those outside their in-crowd, and that higher levels of trust will always be assigned to people you know. This is particularly valid for countries that score high on uncertainty avoidance, with Hofstede arguing that anything that differs from the norm within the group is suspicious and unwanted: a protective culture can form in the group, believing "what is different is dangerous" (Hofstede 2001).

In strongly collectivistic cultures, people will also need to meet face-to-face on many occasions in order to build up high levels of trust, while the North European and Anglo-Saxon cultures are inclined to trust others using modern communication links (phone, video, email, net meeting) with less need to meet in person. It is important for a Western manager responsible for a multicultural team to realize this: you cannot build trust by having a two-hour conference call where you all introduce yourselves on an individual basis. People will need to get to know each other personally and face-to-face, in order to be able to trust each other. Although inconvenient at times of travel restrictions and cost-saving measures, it is important for international managers to realize that reserving a travel budget for building trust is inherent to working globally.

Long-term orientation: Another factor where the region I cultures differ from the others is the time it takes to build up trust. As already argued in Chapter 6, building trust is a long-term process in most countries where personal relationships and long-term commitment to common interests are key. This is the reason why building up a business relationship in Africa or Asia takes very long and requires many face-to-face meetings: people need to get to know each other on a personal basis, and need to test the relationship in various circumstances in order to know whether or not the other party can be trusted in the long run.

The international manager has to dissociate himself from the meaning of trust that is the norm in his own culture, as the behaviors that come with building trust differ across the world. While being reliable and engaging in direct forms of communication help build up interpersonal trust in the United States, respect for hierarchy and authority and the willingness to enter into debate contribute to trust in France, for example. And while a German person needs data and facts to trust you and your story, Indian people tend to place more trust in the person who respects and appreciates them and values a personal relationship.

Sharing Experiences

Jeff Wilcox, Managing Director at ROCKWOOL Asia, Singapore
LinkedIn: https://www.linkedin.com/pub/jeff-wilcox/8/8a6/487

Jeff Wilcox *is managing director of ROCKWOOL Asia, which manufactures and markets a range of stone wool-based insulation materials for energy-saving, fire-safe solutions in industrial, marine, and building applications. ROCKWOOL is a publically listed Danish company and world leader in stone wool insulation with operations across Europe, North America, Russia, China, India, and Southeast Asia. Jeff has lived and worked in Asia for over 20 years in marketing, business development, and general management roles. He now lives in Southeast Asia after some 15 years of living and working in China.*

One of my early assignments in China gave me my first taste of cultural misunderstandings based on quite different concepts of trust. We often say we trust someone when we can predict how they will act in a given situation. But then they act differently.

We had established a large green-field business with over 50 imported Mercedes mixer trucks and state-of-the-art high-capacity batching plants. We had a centralized maintenance department led by an experienced expatriate and had recruited many locals to build the team. On reviewing the costs of tools after a few months of operation it was noted that there was an unusually high cost for hammers. In fact, we were buying a lot of hammers on a weekly basis. Suspecting fraud the expat manager dug deeper, only to find that there was indeed a large pile of broken hammers hidden within the maintenance compound. On inquiring with the maintenance supervisor as to why, the expat maintenance manager was informed by his local staff that the hammers keep breaking due to poor quality. On comparing the cost of the poor quality hammers with that of a better quality hammer the expat was told that they did not buy the better quality hammer because that was too expensive.

With my Western mindset I assumed people would take responsibility, and that it was better to buy 1 good hammer than 10 hammers that easily break. The locals, however, had been instructed to reduce spending, and they were not used to making decisions on matters like this themselves.

Similarly, one day the CEO visited our start-up operation, and the expat managing director (MD) requested his assistant buy a backup bulb for the overhead projector. Halfway through his presentation to the CEO, of course the projector bulb blew, and when he asked his assistant for the replacement, she simply informed her boss that she didn't buy it because it cost too much! End of presentation!

I often encountered situations where people were reluctant to offer their ideas, less they be blamed or persecuted if they were wrong! They were not ready to take responsibility, to be empowered (as we call it), even though we trust their skills and experience to do so! Once I got the comment that "bosses are meant to solve problems, not team members; bosses are paid to take responsibility, not us, so don't blame us!"

Practical advice for the international manager:

- In hierarchical cultures like the Chinese, do not rely on your assumption that people will take a critical attitude themselves: when you want them to take responsibility and make their own decisions (buy more expensive hammers), you should spend a lot of time explaining the overall objective, and tell them that you expect them to work on best ways to realize that objective.

- Do not assume too easily that people from different parts of the world have the same meaning when they talk about empowerment, responsibility, or trust. Communicate openly about the different meanings, and make sure locals understand your expectations in detail ("I want you to take responsibility" is very unclear in this respect).
- Be very explicit on your expectations of people. When you want your local staff to brainstorm or come up with creative solutions to existing problems, make sure there is no hierarchy involved in their discussions and that they can come up as a group with proposals (rather than run the risk as an individual to be wrong).

9.3 TEAM COOPERATION AND COMMUNICATION

Whatever the exact definition of *trust* and regardless of where you are in the world, trust cannot be built up without communication. The subject of communication within teams is so wide and has been so well studied that we focus only on the true need for good communication within teams. One essential ingredient of good in-team communication is the use of international English.

To start with, you have to make sure that people within teams do actually communicate. This is not as easy to realize as you may think: when specialists set to work they may often exchange technical facts and figures, but communication is more than just an exchange of factual information: communication serves to deepen understanding of issues and create breakthroughs that individuals may not be capable of realizing. As the example at the start of this chapter showed, a very one-sided use of communication channels (email in this case) demonstrates that if the interpersonal communication that forms the basis for cooperation and trust is lacking, trust will not materialize. A manager of a cross-cultural team—especially when partially remote—will have to be prepared to spend half of his time on basic communication within the team.

Various studies (McKinney et al. 2004; Tomas and Drury 1988) have emphasized that effective communication is key to team effectiveness. In their work, the authors argue that project team success can only be achieved once the communication within the team is good (read: frequent and of high quality), and when the team discusses its composition and way of working as well as the content. This underlines the need for a project manager or team leader to invest time in setting up the communication structures within the team, which involves much more than only setting up a weekly Monday morning call to update each other on the work at hand. It involves thinking about the communication media that are used within the team, the protocols of exchanging information and keeping each other updated, the frequency of knowledge sharing and project updates, the way communication flows from point to point within the team (formal/informal, central/decentralized, individual ad hoc or organized for the group), and the way in which the team communicates with the external world.

The cross-cultural aspects of communication are of key importance. For a mixed project team of Japanese and European engineers, for example, Western colleagues will need to be aware of the difference between talking to the leader of the team and talking to peers. Although there is certainly a difference between these groups in American or European culture, nowhere is this aspect so well organized and sensitive as it is in Japan. When seniority or higher status and position are involved (such as teacher-student relationships, referred to as *sempai kohai*), the communication is very formal, very polite language and words are used, and it is essential to show respect to the person with higher position. But not

TIP 73: AIM OF THE MEETING: INFORMATION EXCHANGE OR DECISION MAKING?

When you set up a meeting with people from different cultures, think up front about the aim of the meeting. Is it to exchange information (project updates, hear what all the others are working on, department news, news from the management), or is the aim to divide tasks and make decisions? When both are relevant for your team, it is better to separate these two issues into separate meetings: one for information exchange, and the other (probably with a significantly smaller group) for task assignment and decision making. Much confusion about the purpose of meetings is removed by simply separating different kinds of purposes into separate, short, and focused meetings.

all communication in Japan is formal and uses such respectful language. When talking to equal-status colleagues or friends, the *tomodachi* type of communication favors a very flexible structure, is highly informal, and can be much more direct than we are accustomed to from the Japanese (Andaya 2009).

So what should a manager do to set up the communication within a cross-cultural project team?

First of all, communication starts with the language used. In the previous section (9.2), we argued that native English speakers often have a disadvantage when working in cross-cultural teams: they speak too quickly and with too many difficult words, so that many other cultures have difficulty understanding them. Think of the well-structured and very polite forms of English that native English speakers use and of the slang Americans use when building up their sentences. A few tips for breaking down the communication barriers are:

- Simplify. It is better for native English speakers to forget 80% of their vocabulary, and use words that are simple and easy to understand. Complex grammatical structures will be impossible to follow for nonnative speakers. Words like *complacency, mediocrity, impeccable,* and *thoroughly* should be avoided if you want all team members to understand you.
- Avoid synonyms. Using many different words for the same thing is highly confusing for someone who has difficulty with the language. When something is difficult, say so, and do not replace the word *difficult* with *complicated, complex, challenging, demanding,* and *troublesome* (just to name a few).
- Speak slowly. This is the most difficult one, as we all tend to speak at the rate at which we are comfortable. Time and again, cross-cultural work reminds you that your English is usually better than the English of most people you are dealing with. The slower you speak, the more people will understand you.

So which communication recommendations are relevant for managers of cross-cultural teams?

- Install a culture of feedback within the team. It should become natural for people in the team to speak about their communication, and to tell each other whether or not they are expressing themselves clearly. Even in cultures where feedback is not part of the norm (as aspects of harmony and politeness play a role), feedback mechanisms can still be installed among team members to ensure they inform one another that they are speaking too rapidly, using words that are too difficult, or are composing sentences that are too complex. When doing business in Asia, I frequently point out to UK managers it is impossible for their Thai or Malaysian counterparts to understand them: people are usually very grateful when you communicate this in a constructive way. Giving clear feedback can be learned quickly, also by people from cultures that are not familiar with it.

- Talk with the team about the way you communicate. Again, step back regularly from the content and evaluate the communication with the team. This does not have to result in a long and soft touchy-feely session, but can very well be covered in the last five minutes of the team meeting. "How well do you think we communicate, and what can we do better?"
- Spend time on structuring the communication. This is your job as a team manager. Hiding behind the assumption "This is everybody's responsibility" will not be effective. It is your role to help others improve their communication, and only once you have played this role consistently for some time will it become part of the group culture.

TIP 74: FEEDBACK IS A PRESENT

To install a feedback culture within your team, you will first need to set an example: train yourself in giving adequate feedback. Do this by giving completely factual and nonjudgmental descriptions of the behavior you observe ("I notice you interrupt me frequently while I speak") and then describe the impact this has on you: "I feel as if people are not listening to me. But I really want others to know what I think." This becomes most powerful when followed by a clear request: "Shall we first explain our views separately and really listen to each other, before we argue and try to reach a conclusion?"

9.4 DECISION MAKING IN TEAMS

Every team faces decisions that need to be made on a daily basis. And although this process can be challenging enough in a homogeneous team, decision making becomes exponentially more complicated when the team is dispersed over various locations and consists of members from different cultures.

The decision-making process can vary per country. Coming from a cultural background where everybody is expected to be consulted before any decision is made (the Netherlands), I had to get used to situations where one person makes the decision, or where a small group of people have the power to do that. To me, the fact that sometimes not everybody has to be heard was an eye-opener. In the ideal situation in Southeast Asia, for example, the person in charge has assembled critical information from experts and has given his people the opportunity to contribute. The decision-making body then proceeds. This can be the family in a family company, the highest boss in a very hierarchical society, etc. To me, the process after a decision has been made is even more fascinating: whereas in the Netherlands you can publicly disagree with a decision made, in other countries you would not even consider disagreeing once the top man has spoken. In some countries, you act completely in agreement with the decision when you are in public, while continuing to argue and debate heavily behind the scenes (France), whereas in some other countries you accept a decision made as simple reality, whether you like it or not (Austria).

It is beyond the scope of this book to go into an analysis of decision-making models here, but we do address the influence of the most important cultural dimensions on the decision-making process.

Power distance (PDI):
- In countries with a high power distance, the voice of some people weighs more heavily than the voice of other people. This means that, as a manager, you first need to be aware of your own status in such a situation. Without knowing it, you may be the manager with most power (in some countries an expatriate manager already has this status because he comes from headquarters and is therefore considered to be highest in power). People listen to anything you say, and while you are just thinking out loud, others take your ideas for a given, and start implementing them.

When you are from a low-PDI culture yourself, be aware of the status and position that people from high-PDI cultures give you.

- In high-PDI countries, it is the role of the person with most status or wisdom to make the decision. So you will need to find out who this person is. When not sure, ask your local counterparts.
- When decisions are made in high-PDI cultures, these decisions are respected and followed up. It is not done to argue about these in public and certainly not to criticize, as this would undermine the authority of the highest power (while also ruining the group process where harmony is key).
- In some countries (certainly collectivistic, high-PDI countries like Japan) you must expect decision making to be a complicated process. After one layer in the company has made a decision, the issue is then moved upward to the next level of decision making (this is called the *ringi* system: every layer in the company goes through its own level of consensus forming and decision making). In this complex yet very powerful system, everybody contributes opinions and suggestions to the decision-making process: after the decision has been made, it will no longer be questioned internally.

Individualism/collectivism (IND):

- In collectivistic countries, it is important to involve everyone in the decision-making process, as this benefits the group cohesion that is so very important. Although most collectivistic countries have a high power distance, and decision making will be left to the highest levels in the organization, everybody will need to be aware of the issues, as this creates collective buy-in. For this

---

TIP 75: DECIDE HOW TO MAKE DECISIONS

When seeking cooperation between individualistic and collectivistic cultures, make sure that you establish agreements about how decisions are to be made. Working methods can differ considerably on this aspect of culture. In the early stages of cooperation, clarify the processes, specify the decision makers of each party involved, and above all, determine the process to be used to come to decisions. Finally, you should also agree on the way decisions are to be documented so that they are well tracked and clear to everybody.

reason, Western people should leave cc lists on emails from collectivistic countries as they are: there usually is a very good reason for sharing the mail with many people who should be aware of what is going on, even though you may not know who these people are and what they have to do with the decision.

- Once a decision is made, everybody in a collectivistic culture will defend the decision publicly and speak with one voice. This is important, as not doing so would disrupt harmony in the group and work counterproductively.
- Decision making takes time—much more so in collectivistic than in individualistic countries. This has to do with involving many people in the process, reaching group consensus in various stages of the decision-making process, and sharing all relevant knowledge.

TIP 76: USE EMAIL WISELY

1. As soon as you start typing an email or typing a reply to an email, ask yourself whether or not your mail really adds value. Is it necessary to send the mail, and does the company benefit from you sending this mail? If so, proceed. If not, don't clutter somebody else's mailbox: pick up the phone or find other ways.
2. Choose your cc list wisely: decide who needs to be informed and whose help is valuable. In high-PDI cultures, involve the hierarchy when this helps. In collectivistic cultures, make sure the right people in the group are informed. In high-UAI cultures, ensure you involve the right experts and write a structured message.
3. Do not modify the cc list that somebody else made. Many Western people have the tendency to remove names of the people they don't know from cc lists. Remember that in collectivistic cultures, the group needs to be informed of important matters, so trust the choice of your colleague to involve the right people (he usually has a very good reason for involving the people that you don't know yet).
4. Always close your mail with a conclusion, an action, or an agreement. If you can't, go back to step 1, and ask yourself whether your mail really adds value.

Masculinity/femininity (MAS):

- In masculine countries decision making is generally a more competitive and sometimes even aggressive process. The discussion preceding a decision needs to be such that all views have been aired, and an assertive fight over standpoints helps to ensure that the best decision gets made. A manager facilitating decision making on his team should allow room for this debate. This is different in feminine countries, where disagreements are gently steered toward compromise in such a way that all parties have won something in the process.
- In a masculine country where arguments are exchanged and the strongest argument wins, the group manager needs to facilitate this exchange of arguments and add to it. While tempted probably to jump in and join the debate, your role also is to facilitate the process.

Uncertainty avoidance (UAI):

- The decision-making process in high-UAI countries gets more attention than in low-UAI countries: by running the process in a proper and well-thought-out way, the quality of the decision increases and uncertainty is more efficiently excluded from the process. In Japan, for example, decision making is a very serious and formal process. Many memos are shared between all people involved, to ensure that all opinions are heard and reviewed. When everyone is in the loop, the risks are effectively mitigated.
- In high-UAI countries, the opinion of the experts generally counts more than the opinions of other contributors to the decision-making process: relying on experts reduces risk. This is in contrast to the situation in low-UAI countries, where everyone involved can add to the process and contribute, whether they are experts or not.

General advice for managers driving decision making in their cross-cultural teams:

- Be process-oriented and sensitive: the manager plays a critical role in decision making. Even when not making the decision yourself as a manager, you manage the process well, and thus ensure that the best possible decision is made.

- Reflect on the decision-making body in each culture: for each cultural environment you work in, ensure that you understand who makes decisions and how the process works. Local agents are key in this process, as it is often impossible for foreigners to figure out exactly how decision making runs in another environment. Get help.
- Reflect on all the input you need before a decision is made. This involves questions such as: Are the right people involved in the decision making? Who are the experts who need to be heard? Should everybody be consulted, or only a small group of people?
- Reflect on how to get acceptance for a decision made. Do the majority of people automatically support the decision, or are they expected to disagree and need to be heard?

9.5 THE FIVE DYSFUNCTIONS OF A TEAM

More often than not, teams do not function effectively, or at least not as effectively as they could. Even when there is trust among the team members, communication is good, and decisions are made efficiently, there are still many factors that can cause a team to dysfunction. Patrick Lencioni (2002) created a simple yet tremendously powerful model that deals with the causes of ineffective teamwork. The model has been used worldwide to assess teams and work on one of the five so-called dysfunctions, with the aim of making the team achieve better results. Without exception, my experiences of working with the model have been very positive, as people recognize in the model what they so often struggle with at workfloor level. However, the Lencioni model was built in the United States, and American culture is very visible in the description of each of the model levels. In this chapter, we describe the five dysfunctions in the context of culture, and make suggestions about how to use the model to make your cross-cultural team more effective.

9.5.1 The Five Dysfunctions of a Team

The model describes five dysfunctions, starting with *trust* at the base of the pyramid, and ending with *results* at the top. The five dysfunctions can be addressed in isolation, yet they are interrelated: failing to operate

FIGURE 9.2
The five dysfunctions of a team, the Lencioni model. (From Lencioni, *The Five Dysfunctions of a Team*, San Francisco: Jossey-Bass, 2002.)

effectively at one of the lower levels will inevitably lead to failure at a higher level, resulting in nonoptimal team results (Figure 9.2).

9.5.1.1 Trust

Trust is the lowest layer in the Lencioni model. We devoted Section 9.2 to the notion of trust in teams, and there we introduced three different concepts of trust in different regions of the world. The American culture is representative for the entire region I cluster. In this culture, trust is considered to be equivalent to reliability: if you do what you say you will do, I can trust you. We extrapolated this to what we called authentic trust, to describe the kind of trust that requires vulnerability and openness about oneself. This is the kind of trust that Lencioni refers to.

Lencioni describes trust as the confidence among team members that their peers' intentions are good, and that there is no reason to be particularly protective or careful in and around the group. This means that teammates must become comfortable with the idea of being vulnerable in relation to one another, and be confident that this vulnerability will not be used against them. Lencioni says: "As soft as all of this might sound, it is only when team members are truly comfortable being exposed to one another that they begin to act without concern for protecting themselves. As a result, they can focus their energy and attention completely on the job at hand, rather than on being strategically disingenuous or political with one another."

The behaviors that underpin this form of trust are:

- Willingness to be vulnerable
- Openly admitting mistakes and weaknesses
- Asking for help
- Quickly and genuinely apologizing to each other
- Knowing about each other's personal lives and being open to discussing them
- The leader having to show vulnerability first, and thus risking losing face in front of the team

It is here that the American footprint of the model becomes obvious. Putting yourself in a vulnerable position—although perceived as a positive step in most feminine or moderately masculine cultures—will not be easily accepted in a very masculine culture, where people do not openly admit mistakes and weaknesses, or ask one another for help. In most masculine countries, putting yourself in a vulnerable position is perceived as weak: in these cultures, the masculine values of competitiveness, personal strength, and assertiveness rule.

We have already given much advice on building trust in Section 9.2. In Table 9.1, we add specific recommendations for the team manager in charge of a cross-cultural team, when operating in a more masculine, less individualistic (therefore less American) culture.

9.5.1.2 Conflict

Lencioni continues: only once trust has been established and team members have opened up to each other can they engage in "unfiltered and passionate debate." Here Lencioni takes the position that (productive) conflict is essential for the team to grow, and that only when people speak openly about what they think can they commit themselves to the team goal. Lencioni declares that although he does not support destructive fighting and mean-spirited attacks, "the conflict can have many of the same external qualities of interpersonal conflict—passion, emotion, frustration—so much that an outside observer might easily mistake it for unproductive discord." Another important citation from the book: "When team members do not openly debate and disagree about important ideas, they often turn to back-channel personal attacks, which are far nastier and more harmful than any heated argument over issues."

TABLE 9.1

Building Trust in the Context of an American Culture and an Alternative Formulation for Other Cultures

Lencioni Behaviors to Build Trust in Context of the American Culture (Low PDI, High IND, Moderately MAS)	Alternative Formulation of Attention Areas When Building Trust in Other Cultures (High PDI, Low IND, High MAS)
Willingness to be vulnerable, and openly admit mistakes and weaknesses	Willingness to neutrally observe and reflect on the functioning of the team and of oneself: this to be done in a nonpublic setting such as in very small workgroups or one-to-one situations. Reserve time to allow team members to open up without risk. Do not emphasize mistakes and weaknesses, but focus more on improvement points and development areas that will ultimately make the team better and more effective (these formulations avoid breaking harmony and group adhesion).
Quickly and genuinely apologize to each other	Offer support and help to each other in order to continuously improve the quality of the output of the team, and learn from each other to become better as a team.
Leader has to show vulnerability first, and risk losing face in front of the group	In high-PDI cultures, it is not done to have an open discussion about the functioning of the team in the presence of the leader, as this would be seen as criticism to the leader. Act as a role model showing vulnerable behavior and openness, and demonstrate over time that openness is encouraged and stimulated. Losing face in front of the group should be avoided: the functioning of individual team members is a sensitive issue, and is better dealt with in very small (two or three people) workgroups and addressed indirectly.
Trust building involves open discussion among the group members	Trust building involves getting to know each other on a personal level, having fun outside working hours, and supporting each other in continuously learning and improving during working hours.

Source: After Lencioni, *The Five Dysfunctions of a Team*, San Francisco: Jossey-Bass, 2002.

The behaviors that underpin this form of positive conflict are:

- Engaging in unfiltered and passionate debate about ideas and issues
- Putting difficult issues on the table to be resolved
- Arranging gripping team meetings, not boring ones
- Having passionate and unguarded debate
- Extracting and exploiting the ideas of all team members

Here too, it becomes clear that the model finds its roots in the United States, where it is a virtue to speak your mind openly, where everybody's unfiltered opinion counts, and where individual freedom to express your thoughts and opinions is the basis of democracy. We see here the cultural dimension of individualism (and a bit of masculinity), which drives the way people deal with conflict: it is OK (and even expected) to speak your mind and publicly say what you think, as the final decisions the team makes will be better when all can contribute without hesitation. The masculine element is recognized in the statement that conflict brings out the best in people, and that confrontation is healthy.

In many cultures, however, the collectivistic notion of maintaining harmony within the group and avoiding loss of face outweighs the open expression of opinions: opinion forming and consensus building are not done in public, and involve a careful process of reaching consensus. In these cultures, the open debate with unfiltered personal opinions will be avoided, as this can hurt feelings and disrupt group harmony. In the collectivistic context, open conflict is a sign of social failure that should be avoided.

Research into the factors that help a team to be successful in the United States revealed four main team characteristics related to dealing with conflict (Cutcher-Gershenfeld and Kochan 1997). The manager should:

- Be comfortable in dealing with conflict
- Be committed to resolving disputes close to the source
- Resolve disputes on a basis of interests before rights and power
- Learn from experience with conflicts

In such behavior we recognize the Western, individualistic ideal of dealing with conflict in a direct and active way, openly expressing opinions, and emphasizing the values of autonomy, competitiveness, and need for personal control. Preferred conflict handling styles are competing and cooperating. This is in contrast to the collectivistic association with indi-rect and passive communication, such as the avoiding and obliging styles of handling conflict, emphasizing the values of passive compliance and of maintaining relational harmony (Wei et al. 2001).

Advice for managers on how to stimulate the open exchange of ideas (Lencioni: healthy conflict) in a less individualistic, less masculine society is shown in Table 9.2.

TABLE 9.2

Stimulating Constructive Conflict in the Context of an American Culture and an Alternative Formulation for Other Cultures

Lencioni Behaviors to Stimulate Constructive Conflict in Context of the American Culture (High IND, Moderately MAS)	Alternative Formulation of Areas of Concern When Stimulating Constructive Conflict in Other Cultures (Low IND, Low MAS)
Compelling team meetings where difficult issues are openly put on the table	Organize meetings for the open exchange of ideas (not opinions), emphasizing that this leads to increased quality of the final decision. Create safe environments for expressing oneself. Advance an idea and invite people to write down pros and cons. Ask people face-to-face for their advice instead of opinion.
Unguarded debate, extracting and exploiting the contribution of all team members	Explain that you are looking for the best possible solution in the interest of the group (company). Explain that this is about as many opinions as possible, not about judging the opinions of others. At the beginning, engage in anonymous brainstorming techniques. When facilitating the meeting, do not impose your personal opinions on the group, and rephrase the contributions of others in completely neutral terms. Invite people personally during lunch or coffee to say what they think.
Passionate, active, and outgoing style of exchanging opinions	Stimulate a safe environment where people speak in a low tone of voice and behave calmly and show self-discipline. The unguarded element of Lencioni makes collectivist cultures nervous about losing control and making personal mistakes. A safe environment is one where people speak face-to-face and not at the same moment, listen carefully to each other, are not judgmental but use neutral language, and show respect for each other's contribution.

Source: After Lencioni, *The Five Dysfunctions of a Team*, San Francisco: Jossey-Bass, 2002.

9.5.1.3 Commitment

Only when people can engage in passionate and unguarded debate will they be committed to the decisions made by the team. In this definition, commitment is driven by clarity and buy-in. The clarity of decisions is a result of unguarded debate, in which all opinions are openly put on the table. The buy-in results from people having had the opportunity to ventilate all opinions, doubts, and arguments: Lencioni states that once people have had this opportunity, they will buy into the collective team decision (even though their original opinion was different). This avoids sabotaging behavior, and team members not being fully committed.

Lencioni sees consensus as a danger to commitment: when quick consensus is reached, this may leave some of the team members with unexpressed doubts and different opinions. In the end, however, a bold decision—which was originally not supported by team members—is fine as long as people know their opinions have been heard and considered. Lencioni further makes a case for creating certainty by making bold decisions: "Great teams understand that it is better to make a decision boldly and wrong—and then change direction with equal boldness—than it is to waffle." The latter option is stated negatively, but refers to situations where the team has doubts and continues to collect more data in order to feel more certain about making the right decision.

The behaviors that underpin commitment are:

- Knowing what your peers are working on and how they contribute to the collective goal
- Leaving meetings confident that your peers are committed to decisions (even where there was initial disagreement)
- Ending discussions with clear and specific resolutions, decisions, and calls to action
- Buying in and committing to decisions
- Participating in a culture in which you learn from mistakes

The cultural elements we see in the above-mentioned behaviors and the explanation of commitment are characteristic of low-uncertainty-avoidance cultures (it is OK to make a bold decision when not yet in the possession of enough data; this is better than taking no decision at all) and high individualism (people will not buy in when their personal opinion has not been heard). The latter assumption does not pose a problem in the opposing culture of collectivism, where people are supportive of any group decision by definition: they will prioritize the harmony and consensus in the group over their individual need to be heard. However, cultures that score high on uncertainty avoidance will not understand the Lencioni argument of bold decision making and stimulating a culture of mistakes: mistakes ought to be avoided in these cultures, and clear decisions are supported as long as the decision making has been thorough and detailed.

Advice for managers who wish to stimulate the commitment of all team members in a more uncertainty-avoidant culture is shown in Table 9.3.

TABLE 9.3

Stimulating Commitment in the Context of an American Culture and an Alternative Formulation for Other Cultures

Lencioni Behaviors to Stimulate Commitment in Context of the American Culture (Low UAI, High IND)	Alternative Formulation of Areas of Concern When Stimulating Commitment in Other Cultures (High UAI, Low IND)
Buy in and commit to decisions (but feign agreement)	The concept of feigning agreement does not exist in collectivistic cultures, and is not the opposite of openly giving your opinion. The possibility to ventilate opinions has passed, a decision has been made, and we are, by definition, now in agreement with that decision as a group. The team leader needs to ensure the decision-making process is clear to all. He does this by communicating frequently, and clarifying everybody's role in the execution of the decision.
Learn from mistakes; change direction without hesitation or guilt	Mistakes—especially in high-UAI cultures— are to be avoided: in these cultures, it is better to follow a very thorough and detailed decision-making process that avoids mistakes. When quick decisions are made, these should be underpinned with data and rational arguments. For buy-in, people need to know the objective, and need to know that a good process has been followed in which expert opinions have been heard and where all alternatives have been well researched.

Source: After Lencioni, *The Five Dysfunctions of a Team*, San Francisco: Jossey-Bass, 2002.

9.5.1.4 Accountability

Accountability in the context of teamwork is the willingness of the team members to speak to peers about behavior that might damage the team. Doing this requires a person to tolerate interpersonal discomfort and engage in a difficult conversation, activities that most people tend to avoid. Holding each other to account in this sense is helping the team, as it is a sign of respect for each other and of having high expectations of one another's performance. Peer pressure is seen by Lencioni as the most effective way to maintain high standards of performance, as "it avoids excessive bureaucracy around performance management and corrective action."

The behaviors to stimulate accountability are:

- Calling upon peers to adjust actions and behaviors that seem counterproductive to the good of the team
- Drawing attention to each other's deficiencies and unproductive behaviors
- Challenging each other about plans and approaches
- Ensuring poor performers feel pressure to improve
- Identifying potential problems by unhesitatingly questioning one another's approaches

The most pronounced cultural dimensions that impact the way a manager deals with accountability are individualism and masculinity: it is no surprise that these are the same dimensions that determine the way in which somebody deals with conflict. Accountability itself has a different meaning in different cultures: whereas people in individualistic cultures are personally accountable for achieving their targets, people in collectivistic cultures are—by definition—accountable to the group. Holding one another accountable is less necessary in collectivistic cultures, and individual underperformance is sometimes not even dealt with in order to avoid discord in the group and a person losing face. When underperformance is dealt with, it should be done in a very indirect and delicate way (certainly not quick and to the point as the American culture would favor), in order to avoid the person losing face.

Advice for managers to stimulate accountability in a more collectivistic and low-masculine culture is shown in Table 9.4.

TABLE 9.4

Stimulate Accountability in the Context of an American Culture and an Alternative Formulation for Other Cultures

Lencioni Behaviors to Stimulate Accountability in Context of the American Culture (High IND, Moderate MAS, Often Perceived as High MAS)	Alternative Formulation of Attention Areas When Stimulating Accountability in Other Cultures (Low IND, Low MAS)
Call out unproductive behaviors and actions that seem counterproductive to the team	A manager deals with the unproductive behavior of his team members, also in collectivistic, more feminine cultures. Address unproductive behaviors one-to-one rather than publicly. Also, the manager can rely on other members to point out unproductive behavior to each other, but in such a way that the person on the receiving end of the feedback retains face. Deal with sensitive issues one-to-one, gently pointing out what you would like to see, rather than criticizing the behavior you no longer want to see.
Challenge each other unhesitatingly on plans and approaches	In collectivistic, less masculine cultures, people challenge each other in the framework of a friendly exchange of ideas, rather than a hostile debate on opinions. A less directive and gentle approach will be respected more in these cultures, and an indirect way of realizing improvements will be sought. Keep in mind that your aim is to increase accountability, which is realized in an indirect, harmonious manner here.
Ensure underperformance will feel pressure to improve, and that underperformance is dealt with	Performance issues in collectivistic cultures are sensitive issues, as dealing too directly with underperformance leads to loss of face for the person and for the group. The manager is expected to point out indirectly which behavior he wants to see in the future, rather than emphasize what is wrong today. The feedback is directed to the group, not to an individual, even when it is clear who is meant. The group will have their own mechanism for self-correction, without damaging the individual and disrupting harmony. Deal with underperformance sensitively and carefully, and seek advice from locals on how to address it. I have seen many examples where asking locals for advice resulted in the disappearance of the underperformance problem, without this ever being addressed publicly.

Source: After Lencioni, *The Five Dysfunctions of a Team*, San Francisco: Jossey-Bass, 2002.

> ### TIP 77: HOLDING EACH OTHER ACCOUNTABLE
>
> Openly discuss the value of holding each other accountable within the team. Even people coming from a culture where it is not done to publicly express observations about the other person usually see the benefit of doing so, and they are prepared to do it, but in a different (nonpublic, indirect) way. As a manager, you should invest in creating a culture of open communication about performance. A short workshop on feedback and coaching skills can help: holding each other accountable by asking questions rather than by stating opinions is a powerful means of interaction. Stimulate a feedback culture and continuously set the right example.

9.5.1.5 Results

The final—and ultimate—dysfunction of a team is the inattention to results caused by members of the team who care more about things other than the collective goals of the group. This happens when team status and individual status get in the way. Team status is a situation where belonging to the team is more important than the specific results the team achieves: being associated with an organization can often be enough (especially when the organization or group is considered very special due to its mission or the results achieved in the past). Individual status is what takes over when people go for their own personal (career) goals rather than the collective goals of the team.

The behaviors and attitudes that reinforce attention to results are:

- Collective goals having priority over individual needs (or needs of divisions)
- Making sacrifices in the department for the good of the team
- Morale being affected by failure to meet team goals
- Being slow to seek credit for one's own contributions and quick to point out those of others
- Championing a culture of achievement orientation
- Minimizing individualistic behavior
- Instantly enjoying success and suffering from failure

The cultural elements for attention to results are less significant, as any culture will recognize the need to steer toward the best team results and to give higher priority to team results than to any individual interest. Every manager will need to find a way to address this in his team. The more individualistic the culture, the more effort that needs to be put into this element of effective teams.

In spite of some reservations we have about the Lencioni model in a cross-cultural context, the model is extremely powerful in making teams reflect on their effectiveness and working on improvements. Working your way through the book with your team and having an open discussion about the five dysfunctions will help any team to become (even) more effective than they already are.

9.6 REMOTE AND VIRTUAL TEAMS

The preceding chapters dealt with assembling and managing teams in the workplace, and the cultural factors that a manager should take into account when running his team(s). Many teams these days are so-called virtual teams, referring to physically dispersed teams of which the members reside in various places (and time zones) worldwide. Although unavoidable these days, working together from different locations is not ideal for the quality of teamwork. For example, Straus and McGrath (1994) observed that distributed teams (we use this term interchangeably with virtual teams) experienced more conflict than collocated ones. This was mainly attributed to the challenges of sharing complex information between the various team members.

Building up trust is certainly negatively affected by the physical distance between team members. It is known that the amount of personal communication between so-called trustor and trustee determines the trustworthiness for that trustee. Section 9.2 already indicated that building up trust is one of the most difficult tasks for a manager running a (virtual) team, while at the same time building up trust is also essential to forming a successful team (Zaheer et al. 1998). The positive relationship between trust in a team and the presence of creativity and critical thinking has been highlighted by Reina and Reina (1999).

On the other hand, trust can be built by means of a few simple steps, and there is good evidence that building trust within a virtual team can be done just as well as in traditional teams: it just takes more time (Bos et al. 2002). The remainder of this chapter will make it evident that a manager can do a great deal to ensure that virtual teams can also be very effective. For example, initial team building is more important in distributed teams than in traditional, collocated teams (Staggers et al. 2008). It can be done very effectively by ensuring that there is a so-called discussion arena right from the outset, where team members can discuss their way of working and their expectations of each other (Platt 1999).

There is a lot that can be done by the manager to build up trust and improve team effectiveness. We list eight practical recommendations for the manager of a virtual, cross-cultural team:

1. Install a culture of respect in which diversity is valued. Differences between people should be a source of creativity and enjoyment within a team. However, diversity is so often perceived as something difficult, something that you must accept and deal with, rather than embrace. This diversity not only refers to cultural background, but also and equally to age, background, specific experiences, the interests of team members, and the capabilities they bring. A manager has to set the right example by inviting input from all different backgrounds and showing respect for different points of view. Every human being wants to be recognized for his unique contribution as a person.

2. Set the rules for communication. In the early stages of teamwork it is important for the manager to establish plain rules for the way team members communicate with each other. Certainly when there are no spontaneous face-to-face meetings due to the multisite character of the projects, the manager should provide clarity to all team members about what is expected of them, and how they are expected to communicate. This involves answering questions (sometimes in conjunction with the team), such as:

   • Which media do we use for communication?
   • Is everybody willing and able to install these media on PCs?
   • Can everybody use these media, or is training required?
   • How much formal communication do we set up, and how much of the communication do we leave informal and open (spontaneous)?
   • What are the rules for replying to emails, returning phone calls, etc?

   I once hosted a discussion where we asked all team members of a virtual team to list all the aspects of communication that annoyed them: sharing this list led to many very direct improvements, with a big impact on the overall success of the team.

3. Make trust a topic of discussion on the team. The issue of trust can and should be discussed within teams. The early stages of team formation (preferably face-to-face) are ideal for this. Discuss the various forms of trust described in Section 9.2. But, more importantly: ask team members what they expect of others in order to be able to trust them. Explain the culturally different views people can have on building trust. What do people need in order to create an atmosphere of trust? Ask people to write down the five things that they remember most about a team in which people really trusted each other: share these items and discuss how you will ensure this will really happen.

In later meetings with the team, put the topic back on the agenda. This should not be a long session where everybody rambles on about trust. It is much more effective to tell people up front that you will ask them at the end of the session what should be done to increase interpersonal trust (saying that you will ask the question up front will give some more reactive cultures the opportunity to prepare). And then ask. Spend the last few minutes of your group meeting on the topic of trust and start by asking: "What can I do to make sure we work together openly and trustfully?" Set the example.

4. Pay more attention to procedures and way of working. In a virtual work environment you will need to spend more time on setting the right procedures and explaining to people what you expect of them. Explain what is on the agenda, how we should discuss and communicate during a teleconference, etc. Clarifying this up front saves a lot of difficulty later. Everybody who has phone conferences with people from various countries will know that when the conference leader asks a question, there can be this awkward silence, followed by a lot of confusion, people not understanding the question, and long monologues started by the most assertive team member. Avoid all of this. When you tell people up front what you want to discuss and exactly what questions you will be asking them, most cultures will feel the obligation to prepare, will understand the question when you ask it, and therefore will be more confident about answering. This recipe works very well, especially in phone conferences with people from collectivistic cultures.

5. Make it personal. As a manager you have to make the choice between task-focus and people-focus all of the time. Building trust requires people-focus. You will have to get personal and build on the relationship with and between your people first, before any meaningful work can be successful at the task level. Trust will not build up in the team if people do not open up, reveal themselves, and adopt a vulnerable position. You will have to show your people how to do this, by sharing your own feelings of happiness, disappointment, uncertainty, or fear.

   Again, this does not mean that your discussions with the team from now on will be about soft people issues. On the contrary, your team meetings are about results and how to achieve them. Your other contacts with the team—formally and informally—are geared to building up trust, getting personal, and developing meaningful relationships with and among your team members.

6. Involve people. More than face-to-face meetings, virtual meetings run the risk of becoming one-man shows, or at least involve only a few of the attendees, while the others do their emails in the background or mute the phone while getting another coffee. In the first three minutes of the call, we are usually concerned with the person calling, but after this we tend to get so engaged in the content of the discussion that we forget to involve others.

   The team leader of a virtual team invites all people to join the conversation, by limiting the speaking time of the most vocal team members, and by inviting the more taciturn individuals to speak up. This is certainly beneficial to the introverts who find it difficult to jump in and claim their space: they need to be invited to contribute. This also holds for cultures where modesty is a virtue and where people learn to contribute by listening (most Asian cultures). Invite them to contribute. Prepare them up front for what you expect of them, and then mention their name in the meeting and give them the floor. Praise them for their contribution and respectfully deal with whatever they bring in, in such a way that they want to be heard next time as well. Preparing people for the fact that you will invite them to contribute will avoid the embarrassment of being put on the spot, and gives an opportunity to prepare well.

7. Don't overorganize. In spite of all previous recommendations to prepare and make sure people know up front what is expected of them, you should maintain a degree of flexibility to allow for disruptions

and unexpected topics that people want to discuss. Especially in virtual team meetings—where it is hard to convey feelings such as enthusiasm, happiness, or pride—you will need to provide a platform for this, and this cannot be planned for.

8. Engage in real conversation, and give 100%. To build up authentic trust on a personal level (which most cultures want; see Section 9.2), personal contact will be required in an open and vulnerable setting. You have to reserve time to engage in genuine and open conversation, which does not directly deal with the task at hand but with the people involved: the two of you. The informal exchange of ideas offers emotional advantages: in real conversation we create an interpersonal bond that connects people. This aspect is described very well by Stephen Miller in *Conversation: A History of a Declining Art* (2007; Swaan and Boers 2012).

   This also means you will have to concentrate for the full 100% on your conversation: do not get sidetracked by emails that arrive on your screen while taking a phone call, reading articles while speaking during web meetings etc. When you concentrate for the full 100% on the conversation, people will notice this, feel heard, and feel connected to you. Similarly, when you are not there for the full 100%, people will pick this up as well, and although your conversation may sound OK if they listen to the words only, the music and the dance (see Chapter 3) will reveal that you are not really engaged. Avoid this at all costs. Listen attentively and search for nuances in what is being said: this will give you clues about what is really going on. As a golden rule, reduce the amount of time you spend in the I-dimension (Section 1.3), and shift your focus to the you- and we-dimensions entirely.

Finally we discuss a few very practical tips for the manager who works with his remote team while having contact through video conferencing, web meeting, or phone conferences. Too many phone conferences with remote team members start off this way:

- "Who's online?"
- "Marc, are you there?"
- "Marc is not there, we need him."
- "Hello, who just joined?"
- "Can you mute the line please? Who is driving his car?"

- "I need to step out in five minutes. Sorry."
- "Jane, are you there? Yes, hello, Suzan just joined. Who's online?"
- "The line is bad. Shall we all dial in again?"
- "We just lost Marc. Should we wait for him?"
- "Who just joined? Is that you, Eric?"

This pattern tends to repeat itself for the first 10 minutes of many phone conferences, and recurs every subsequent meeting. If you allow this to happen, you are stealing the time of all who are on the call. Your job is to set the rules: be firm on this aspect and take responsibility for the effectiveness of your meetings. Invest time explaining these rules very clearly, and each time that somebody does not obey the rules, speak to that person immediately. Indeed, they may initially experience this as painful, but they will also appreciate the effective meetings you will have in the future.

A few tips are applicable to phone conferences and video meetings. These tips sound very obvious, yet applying these can make a world of difference to the quality of your virtual meeting:

1. Ensure a professional setting. Your professional meetings should be done from a professional environment. Virtual meetings offer the possibility to do them from anywhere, but make sure that people who see the video image perceive you as a professional. It may be fine in your culture to be casual and work from home, but for your team

---

TIP 78: WHO'S ONLINE

Set rules for phone conferences and demand participants to stick to these rules:

- Everybody joins one to two minutes before the official start of the call.
- Everybody states his name and mutes the line when in an environment with background noise.
- Everybody ensures a quiet environment, or alternatively does not join the call.
- Everybody is available for the whole length of the call.
- When people drop out or come back in, ignore the signals indicating this and continue as normally.

members or business partners elsewhere this is most likely not the case. Configure the background carefully and test the video image that people will see later on.

This also applies to the way you dress: keep it professional. Although you are at home and nobody can see you in the phone conference, your attitude is different when you are in pajamas than when you are dressed as you would be in the office. Your Mickey Mouse shirt is for later!

2. Look at the other person as if he is there with you. This tip makes all the difference. When using video conferencing or a web cam for communication, keep your eyes on the camera. Do not get distracted by anything else, and make sure you center the video image of the other person just under the camera on your PC screen. Not doing so will constantly give the impression that you are looking at something else, and although you are not, your image will be that of a person who is not really there. Maintain eye contact with the camera, pretending the camera is the person you are speaking with.

Do not open other windows on your PC, and switch off other communication media such as Twitter, Facebook, Chat, etc. Your time is now reserved for the other person. Sounds easy, I know. But honestly, do you do it? Aha, I thought so.

Learn to do this by recording your next video call: there are free apps that enable you to record the conversation. Play it back and just look at the screen: this is confronting of course, but this is how you come across!

3. Keep it quiet around you. Do not go to a bar, noisy canteen, or airport lounge for your video call: it really pays off to pay a bit extra for a quiet place. Do not allow distractions, whether these are people walking by in the background, you pressing the button of the coffee machine, or hearing last-call announcements at the gate. Make your overseas contacts really feel connected to you. It is an investment in the professional relationship when you ensure that distractions are kept for later.

I hear you thinking: this advice will not work for me. I am busy and need to use my time optimally, so I need to take these calls on the go. Not doing so will make me less productive. I challenge you to try out the advice above for the next three virtual team calls; then you can decide. The quality of your meetings and respect for your role in the team will change instantly when applying these tips.

4. Switch it off. With the single exception of having a family member in critical condition in the hospital, mute the sounds of your cell phone

TIP 79: SUMMARIZE AND TRACK ACTIONS

Phone conferences with people from various locations are generally less structured than face-to-face meetings, and not all participants manage to follow the entire conversation and the decisions made. When the call is finished, summarize the meeting immediately and list the actions while assigning action holders.

or better: make sure that it is not even within reach during the conversation. Looking at the phone screen already gives a signal to the other person: this call might be more important than you are to me right now. It takes courage to put away the phone, I know. But when not doing so you indicate something else is more important than the person you are speaking to. It is unprofessional and detracts from real contact with the other person.

Believe me, I found this terribly hard to do in the beginning, but forcing myself to give my cell phone second priority—and the conversation with you first—has taught me a lot: the value of true contact, the building block of any team.

Sharing Experiences

Yip Je Choong, Business Development Director for an international sugar trading company, Singapore

Yip Je Choong *is a business development professional for an inter-national sugar trading company. His key responsibility is to grow his portfolio through establishing product presence in new markets through partnerships with local distributors who have access to supermarket and retail chains. To achieve this, he often has to engage in face-to-face nego-tiations with potential distributors or agents on long-term commercial terms. In most cases, these potential distributors or agents, especially in developing countries, are family-run businesses with a large footprint in the country or region.*

One memorable negotiation was with a certain agent in the Kingdom of Saudi Arabia. This agent is a large family-run conglomerate who has distribution rights to many big brands in Saudi Arabia, ranging from luxury vehicles to tobacco products, coffee, cheese, and many more Fast Moving Consumer Goods (FMCG) products. The head of this conglomerate is a wealthy sheikh who inherited the business from his father and would usually get involved himself in negotiations for distributing new products. We had scheduled a three-day visit to meet him and his team in Jeddah during the fasting month of Ramadan. The plan was to do a site visit on day 1 so that we could observe the consumer buying behavior in supermarkets during Ramadan where shopping is done between the hours of 8:00 p.m. and 6:00 a.m.

During the day, most businesses are closed due to the fasting month. Days 2 and 3 are for negotiations. We had prepared an agreement document with many clauses that we were planning to discuss. Day 1 went as planned; however, days 2 and 3 were not according to our expectations.

The sheikh had invited us to his home on day 2 to "breakfast" and have dinner in the evening. We were told that there would be no meet-ings planned during business hours. We arrived at his mansion and had to wait in an adjacent room while the sheikh and his team performed their prayers before dinner. During dinner, we were served with deli-cious food and discussions were centered on everything from family to hobbies and the weather in Singapore, nothing about business. At the end of dinner, the sheikh took us on a tour of his mansion, show-ing us his collection of expensive cars, watches, and antiques. On day 3, he invited us to his office and again spoke to us about general topics, totally avoiding the negotiation topics of our commercial agreements.

We were getting impatient but decided not to broach the subject as we did not want to appear impolite. About two hours before our car was scheduled to take us to the airport to catch our flight home, and we were resigned to the fact that we may have to schedule a second trip for negotiations, the sheikh suddenly said that he was agreeable to our pricing proposal and would like to make an initial order! Stunned, we thanked him for his order and promised to complete the necessary paperwork and expedite his order. We later found out that the sheikh had thought our commercial proposal was acceptable but had wanted to gauge our personalities before deciding if he wanted to do business with us or not.

Practical advice for the international manager:

- Do your homework to understand business culture in countries that you are not familiar and be sensitive to it. Sometimes taking a direct approach by "getting down to business" from the onset is not necessarily the best option.
- Be prepared to be flexible. Look at the situation from the other party's point of view or culture. Keep in mind the importance of building good rapport quickly, and one way to achieve this is to take a cue from the old adage of "When in Rome, do as the Romans do."
- In some cultures, a simple agreement with the key points is all that is needed. Thick agreement documents with many legal clauses are not held in high importance. Be prepared to accept this if you want to do business in that culture.

REFERENCES

Andaya, A. (2009). Influence of Culture and Communication Practices in Team Functioning: Case Studies on Japanese and Philippine Financial Project Teams. Master thesis, Umea School of Business. Online source (http://www.diva-portal.org/smash/get/diva2:291149/FULLTEXT01.pdf)

Bos, N., Olsen, J., Gergel, D., Olsen, G., and Wright, S. (2002). Confidence and Trust: Effects of Four Computer Mediated Communications Channels on Trust Development. Presented at Proceedings of the SIGCHI Conference on Human Factors in Computing Systems: Changing Our World, Changing Ourselves, Minneapolis, MN, April 20–25.

Brinkerhoff, R.O., and Apking, A.M. (2001). *High Impact Learning: Strategies for Leveraging Business Results from Training.* New York: Basic Books.

Comstock, B. (2012). Want a Team to Be Creative? Make It Diverse. *Harvard Business Review Blog Network.* http://blogs.hbr.org/cs/2012/05/want_a_team_to_be_creative_mak.html.

Cutcher-Gershenfeld, J., and Kochan, T.A. (1997). Dispute Resolution and Team-Based Work Systems. In *Workplace Dispute Resolution,* ed. Sandra Gleason. East Lansing, MI: Michigan State University Press.

Early, C.P., and Mosakowski, E. (2000). Creating Hybrid Team Cultures: An Empirical Test of Transnational Team Functioning. *Academy of Management Journal,* 43(1), 26–49.

Garten, F., and Swaan, N. (2012). Vertrouwen in een virtuele werkomgeving deel I en II. Het Nieuwe Werken Blog.

Govindarajan, V., and Gupta, A.K. (2001). Building an Effective Global Business Team. *MIT Sloan Management Review,* 42(4).

Gratton, L., and Erickson, T.J. (2007). Eight Ways to Build Collaborative Teams. *Harvard Business Review.* 11 (https://hbr.org/2007/11/eight-ways-to-build-collaborative-teams/).

Hofstede, G. (2001). *Culture's Consequences: Comparing Values, Behaviors, Institutions and Organizations across Nations.* Thousand Oaks, CA: Sage Publications.

Jassawalla, A.R., and Sashi, H.C. (1999). Building Collaborative, Cross-Functional New Product Teams. *Academy of Management Executive,* 13(3), 50–63.

Lencioni, P. (2002). *The Five Dysfunctions of a Team.* San Francisco: Jossey-Bass.

Lewis, R.D. (2006). *When Cultures Collide: Leading across Cultures.* London: Nicolas Brealey International.

Mayer, R.C., Davis, J.H., and Schoorman, F.D. (1995). An Integrative Model of Organizational Trust. *Academy of Management Review,* 20, 709–34.

McKinney, E., Jr., Barker, J., Smith, D., and Davis, K. (2004). The Role of Communication Values in Swift Starting Action Team. *Information and Management,* 41(8), 1043–56.

Miller, S. (2007). *Conversation: A History of a Declining Art.* New Haven, CT: Yale University Press.

Neal, M. (1998). *The Culture Factor Cross National Management and the Foreign Venture.* London: Palgrave Macmillan.

Platt, L. (1999). Virtual Teaming: Where Is Everyone? *Journal for Quality and Participation,* 22(5), 41–43.

Reina, D.S., and Reina, M.L. (1999). *Trust and Betrayal in the Workplace: Building Effective Relationships in Your Organization.* San Francisco: Berrett-Koehler.

Rousseau, D.M., Sitkin, S.B., Burt, R.S., and Camerer, C. (1998). Not So Different After All: A Cross-Discipline View of Trust. *Academy of Management Review,* 23, 393–404.

Solomon, R.C., and Flores, F. (2003). *Building Trust in Business, Politics, Relationships and Life.* Oxford, UK: Oxford University Press.

Staggers, J., Garcia, S., and Nagelhout, E. (2008). Teamwork through Team Building: Face-to-Face to Online. *Business Communication Quarterly,* 71(4).

Straus, S.G., and McGrath, J.E. (1994). Does the Medium Matter? The Interaction of Task Type and Technology on Group Performance and Member Reactions. *Journal of Applied Psychology,* 79(1), 87–97.

Swaan, N., and Boers, E. (2012). *Making Connections: Getting Things Done with Other People.* Great Yarmouth, UK: Bookshaker.

Thomas, K.W., and Kilmann, R.H. (1974). *Kilmann Conflict Mode Instrument.* Mountain View, CA: Xicom, a subsidiary of CPP, Inc.

Tomas, R., and Drury, T. (1988). Team Communication in Complex Projects. *Engineering Management International*, 4, 287–97.

Tracy, B. (2008). *Flight Plan: The Real Secret of Success*. San Francisco: Berrett-Koehler Publishers.

Wei, W., Yuen, E., and Zhu, J.J. (2001). Individualism-Collectivism and Conflict Resolution Styles: A Cross-Cultural Study of Managers in Singapore. www.justice.gov/adr/events/Materials.Nov19.0106.pdf.

Zaheer, A., McEvily, B., and Perrone, V. (1998). Does Trust Matter? Exploring the Effects of Interorganizational and Interpersonal Trust on Performance. *Organization Science*, 9(2), 141–59.

Zhang, X. (2011). Cultural Influences on Explicit and Implicit Knowledge Sharing Behaviour in Virtual Teams. *International Journal of Computer Science and Information Technology (IJCSIT)*, 3(4).

10

Managing Change

For the past 33 years, I have looked in the mirror every morning and asked myself: "If today were the last day of my life, would I want to do what I am about to do today?" And whenever the answer has been "no" for too many days in a row, I know I need to change something.

—Steve Jobs[*]

Change was in the air. All employees of the company in Vienna were gathered in the large auditorium, where the CEO and his team had a few announcements to make. The room filled up rapidly, and employees were in heavy debate about what might be the topic of announcement, and how many would have to leave the company as a consequence. The overall atmosphere could be described as tense: nervous managers and cynical employees.

At 4:00 p.m. sharp, a well-orchestrated event unfolded. The CEO made a short opening speech, and came to the point straight away. Sales had now been down for four quarters in a row, and without serious measures the company would not survive. The consequence was that several sites in other countries such as Denmark, Norway, and the UK would need to be shut down, and that Vienna headquarters operations would have to continue with 60% of the current staff. In total 4,000 employees were to leave the company in the next two years, the centralized marketing and sales operations would be decentralized to be closer to their customers in the field, and central services such as HR, finance, and quality would have to reinvent their workflows and do more with fewer people. The phrases "Lean and mean" and "Walk the talk" were heard a few times during the presentations, and the whole restructuring plan was announced as part of a new company culture, with new values such as honesty, customer-centric, and respectful.

---

[*] www.brainyquote.com

The Q&A session at the end was short: few questions were asked, and these were answered efficiently and firmly. And although surprised by the cynical tone in which the questions were asked, the management team answered all questions according to the script they had received up front. When the meeting was over, everybody quietly left the room. At the doors they were handed a questionnaire, asking about their opinion on the event. When the CEO saw the outcomes of the questionnaires three days later, he was surprised. Most people indicated that they had not understood the message, they criticized the management for not being open and clear, and said that it was a very high-level story without any details on what they could expect. The reactions were devastating: "This was not an example of honesty, on the contrary: I'm sure all plans have been cooked up already behind the scenes, but we are not allowed to know yet," or "If this is a new way of being respectful to each other, I'd rather go back to the old, apparently disrespectful culture."

What happened here? Managers in charge of the change process had made many classical mistakes. One of these was what William Bridges calls in his book *Managing Transitions, Making the Most of Change* (Bridges and Bridges 2009) "the marathon effect." At the start of the marathon, the fast runners (a remarkably high number of Kenyans and Ethiopians) line up at the starting line, and the rest of the runners are spread out for many blocks behind them, with the fun runners at the end. As the starting gun goes, the fastest runners begin. As these first runners take off, those behind them can start moving up to the "official starting line" and begin their race too. As this next group moves off the starting line, another group of runners approaches the official starting line and begins their race, and so on. While all of this moving and lining up is happening, the runners at the back of the pack are not moving at all. There is little room to start shuffling their feet, and they probably did not even hear the starting gun because of their position at the back of the pack. They eventually get to the official starting line, but much time has elapsed between that moment and the instant when the first runners took off.

We are reading a straightforward analogy of organizational change. The senior leaders of the organization who designed the change have had a chance to think through the change, talk about it, and get used to it. These leaders typically go through their individual transitions before they launch the changes. By the time they announce the change, they have already digested all the details of the new organization, and personal doubts and reservations about the change have been dealt with by that time. The next level of managers are probably just entering the transition stage, and even lower-level managers have heard about the change coming up but are too distant from the board to know any specifics. The workers have not even heard about the changes yet. In the case described above, the management are far ahead, and are convinced they have taken another big step in making this new plan reality. The workers in the audience hear it all for the first time, and need lots of time to digest the new reality and become part of it.

The Austrian company made more mistakes in the announcement of the change. These other mistakes have—as we see in this chapter—a cultural background: what one culture considers being good change practice is seen by a different culture as a highly unwanted way of handling change. We pick out three problems in this announcement of change that are—to a large extent—culturally determined:

- Where the CEO and his team were proud to have provided so much structure and detail, employees found the presentation messy and too generic. In their perception, there was no relevant detail included.
- Where the CEO and his team were part of a well-orchestrated event announcing all the changes, the employees felt that it all was one-way traffic: they were informed, rather than consulted. Why did management not include them in the creation of the new plans?
- Where the CEO and his team took the lead in the change, the employees felt that it was not wise to do so. "We are the experts, what does management know?" It seemed their knowledge of work processes did not really matter and that their professionalism was at stake, as it did not seem relevant to the changes coming up.

10.1 THE CHANGE PROCESS

For any manager in any kind of organization, change is a daily issue, and directing change is part of his everyday tasks. In a rapidly changing external environment where a company has to adjust instantly to market trends and competitor moves, it is inevitable that the regular way in which we do things will change frequently. "The way we do things around here" holds until a new way of doing things is needed, which is often sooner rather than later. Whether on the factory floor or in the boardroom, many people find it hard to cope with the dynamics of change, as it means letting go of what they are used to and entering the unknown. It is human nature to stay in our comfort zone where we know how to do things, rather than move into unknown territory. It is the manager's role to help others expand their comfort zone.

In this chapter, we deal with the intercultural processes that play a role when a manager is involved in changing his team's way of working. We do this by first looking at the role of the manager in a change process, which will be different in different cultures (Section 10.2). In the rest of the chapter, we follow three distinct stages of change: creating a climate for change (Section 10.3), implementing the change (Section 10.4), and ensuring the change will last (Section 10.5). We end the chapter looking at resistance to change (Section 10.6), which is all too frequently underestimated and inadequately dealt with by the management.

Change does not have to be radical. Quite often, change comes with statements that the previous work processes were wrong, and should be abandoned as quickly as possible. The current culture and the ideal culture are seen as two opposites of the cultural continuum. This might be enforced by the wisdom that change should start with having a "burning platform," a convincing and urgent reason behind the motivation for change. As Fons Trompenaars (Trompenaars and Woolliams 2003) argues, many change processes are dealt with too radically. While striving for a better way of working and while focused on the future, the past is labeled as wrong and needs to be forgotten as quickly as possible. The approach to change that Trompenaars proposes is more nuanced, aiming to change a few aspects of the current reality, while "keeping the continuity and unique cultural identity that an organization has."

Trompenaars also argues that our way of dealing with change is quite often dominated by our own cultural blueprint: "It is striking how the Anglo-Saxon model of change has dominated the world of change management. It is too often based on a task-oriented culture and the idea that traditions need to be forgotten as soon as possible" (Trompenaars and Woolliams 2003). For a manager in charge of a cross-cultural team, it is important to realize how his people are used to dealing with change, and which cultural beliefs they hold that could help them change or encourage them to resist. The manager needs to have the tools of change in his backpack, and needs to know how culture determines the way in which the tools should be used. We first look at the role of the manager in the change process.

10.2 THE ROLE OF THE MANAGER IN CHANGE

The assumption many management teams make about change is that it is their responsibility to define the change, and then spread it downward in the organization where others have to assimilate it. However, the definition of the desired change is not the most difficult part. It generally requires solid analysis of external and internal data, defining the "ist" (is/the present) and the "soll" (shall be/the future), and a strong vision as the guiding principle for the change. You can expect any management team to be able to come up with this analysis instantly. The implementation of change, however, is a different story, as this requires a much bigger group of people having to accept the new vision and change the way they work. The change that had been so well designed by the management team can fail when the organization is incapable of implementing it properly. The underlying thought seems to be: "We as management have defined the strategy and our task is completed; now you need to take it up and make it successful."

The description above is a very narrow view on change—although many people will recognize the principle from their own work experience. There are a few assumptions behind this model:

1. The management is in the best position to decide what the desired state will look like.
2. Deployment is a process that runs top-down.
3. The lower levels in the company are not involved in the definition of the desired state: they should merely execute what the top has decided to deploy.

As we see in this chapter, these three assumptions are largely influenced by culture. We discuss the cultural implications one-by-one below.

10.2.1 Management Is in the Best Position to Decide What the Desired State Will Look Like

In many cultures, being in the best position to do something is a matter of power and status, whereas in other cultures, your influence is largely defined by your personal capability to influence people, or by your technical competences and skills. In cultures where hierarchy in the workplace is taken very seriously (high PDI), it is obvious that you have to be high in the hierarchy to be able to define the direction of change. These are high-PDI countries (Russia, China, France) or countries with low to medium power distance in combination with high uncertainty avoidance (Germany, Austria, Switzerland). Employees from these countries will not use their personal influence to change the way of working when they do not have the formal power. In other countries—generally characterized by low power distance in combination with high individualism, such as the United States, Canada, and Australia—any person can decide what the desired state should look like. In these countries, the assumption is that you do not need a formal position to be able to influence the direction of the company, but that everybody can do so.

In high-PDI cultures (mostly collectivistic), the above discussion will be regarded as very Western and very theoretical: here it is normal that change is decided at the top. The ones who have formal power decide on the change, while the lower levels in the company automatically follow, by definition. These are countries such as China, India, Mexico, and Portugal, where important company decisions are made at the very top of the organization. The above-described situation, in particular, where any employee can drive change "as long as he has good ideas and makes these heard," is not understood in these cultures: it is simply not your role and not in your power to be involved in important major tasks like initiating change.

The above can be seen as the paradox of change: Should the change process be participative or should it be driven top-down? Participative change assumes that the workers in the organization collectively know more and have better vision on the effectiveness of work processes, and are therefore better to decide on the change. Top-down change assumes the top can best oversee the necessity for change, and therefore is in the best position to decide. As Dunphy argues in Section 2 of *Breaking the Code of Change* (Beer and Nohria 2000), the two views are not mutually exclusive, but should be complementary. Some organizational change is driven by external necessities that are not visible deeper down in the organization, and it requires senior management with a wider perspective to see the burning platform that makes change necessary. Such larger change processes may require change in cross-divisional work processes, and the initiative for such efforts is usually beyond what can be expected of individual contributors. Other change processes benefit from the collective knowledge on details of work processes and can only become successful when a large number of individual, relevant contributors participate in designing the change.

When multiple sites and divisions of the company—each with its own national and company culture—are involved in the change process, a mixture of the two styles of change is essential. The complexity of multi-site projects will require managers with sufficiently broad scope to oversee the total: individuals that serve the interest of one division or site will hardly ever be able to weigh all interests and choose optimal solutions, as this may mean compromising or giving up the interests of the organizational unit they represent. At the same time, once the required change has been defined and individual work processes need to be reengineered and optimized, the input of many skilled individual workers will be required to ensure success. The manager driving the change process should have the skill to manage his stakeholders and align top leadership on each of the steps of the change processes, as well as the capability to motivate specialists at lower levels of the organization to contribute to the change. Not every manager has these skills.

In the previously mentioned cluster of (collectivistic) high-power-distance countries, there is a true belief that formal position and power are simply more important than knowledge of details and work processes when it comes to defining company strategy. Knowledge converges at the top of the pyramid, and this top knows best what to do to set out the course. Also, in these countries, the people highest up in the company will be best aware of external trends, competitor moves, and customer wishes, so it is natural that they should define what needs to change.

In countries with high uncertainty avoidance, the opinion of experts is highly esteemed. Expert knowledge is a way to reduce uncertainty, and in these countries, the assumption will be that experts need to be involved in defining change. This does not interfere with the hierarchy that is very influential in some of these countries (Germany). There, people expect the hierarchy to be used to make sure all experts are heard, and that management will then formalize the decisions and set the course to be taken. Note that in these countries the direction set by the upper management will be implemented. However, the commitment to change will certainly increase when experts from lower levels in the company have been involved in defining the change.

Finally, there is a group of countries, such as the Netherlands and the Scandinavian countries, in which a low power distance is combined with an individualistic attitude and low masculinity. Here we see a reluctance (or even skepticism) to believe that management can define what is good for the company. Employees in these cultures will expect to be seriously involved in defining the change, and they will speak up clearly if they are not properly involved.

10.2.2 Deployment Is a Process That Runs Top-Down

Most management models on change originate in the United States: the Kotter model for change (Kotter 1996) is a good example (see later in this chapter). These models make the assumption that—once change has been defined—the deployment phase starts, the phase in which the whole organization needs to be convinced that it has to work in a different way. This model fits high-power-distance cultures, where it is natural that the highest layers in the company define the change, and the lower layers follow and implement (without questioning). The model also fits lower-power-distance cultures where hierarchy is still an important aspect of organizing a company: the United States forms the clearest example in this context. Here, change is deployed and implemented following a so-called tell-and-sell model: the management decide on the changes and drive the deployment, while the lower levels follow and adjust their working processes. In the United States, people ask, "What's in it for me?" when confronted with the changes. For management, this means they have to pay attention to organizing the right conditions for implementing the change, such as relating personal bonuses to an adoption of the new way of working, making sure everybody understands his career prospects, etc.

Collectivistic cultures generally have a high power distance: they accept that the highest management make the decisions on change and initiate the implementation process. However, making sure the new work processes are implemented at the lowest levels of the organization is a very collectivistic process, where much information is shared within the group and where people take collective responsibility to make sure that everybody in their group understands and accepts the new way of working.

10.2.3 The Lower Levels in the Company Are Not Involved in the Definition of the Desired State: They Simply Execute What the Top Has Decided to Deploy

This links closely to the previous assumptions, and relates to the way the new way of working is deployed. The decision-making step is either participative (for individuals in the company, as in the Netherlands and Scandinavia, or for experts in countries like Germany and Austria) or one-way (management decides, lower levels execute; this is more the case in—mostly collectivistic—high-power-distance countries). For a manager implementing change, it is important to realize the extent to which individuals expect to be involved in the change process:

- Involve them at a very early stage, solicit their input, and make them part of making decisions (the Netherlands, Scandinavia).
- Involve them in an early stage in order to get the right (expert-based) opinions, although management make the final decision and do not have to justify these decisions publicly (Germany, Austria, United States).
- Involve them in a later stage after all decisions have been made, and set a clear course and give instructions for deployment (Mexico, China, India).

The manager should decide which of these approaches fits the company culture best, and examine the expectations of the national cultures involved in the change process. It is clear that you cannot satisfy the cultural preferences of all, but it is good to go through the mental exercise of understanding cultural expectations before defining and deploying the change initiative.

Practical tips for the manager to decide on his role in the change process:

- Study your own assumptions about change: To what extent are these similar to the three assumptions stated above, and what are your personal expectations about the way change is to be organized? In particular, decide whether you will focus on the individual work processes or on the overall result. In the former case, you decide to be involved hands-on: then you will need sufficient knowledge to contribute to an optimal design of individual work processes. This approach works well in uncertainty-avoidant cultures, where the role of specialists is important, and where work processes need to be optimally designed to reduce the chances of error.
- Decide on your change strategy: Do you want compliance or do you want input from the organization to help design the optimal change? You should be very clear on this choice. Being really open for dialogue requires a modest mindset: you realize you do not have all the

answers and that your role is to orchestrate all parties contributing to change, rather than design the optimal change yourself. Only when you are really open to all these signals will the participative style of driving change be successful. However, when you have firmly decided on the required change and you are clear that this is the new way of working, do not pretend that you want everyone to participate and give his input, as this is simply not what you want. You have already decided, and now you want compliance. As long as you are aware of the potential dangers of this approach, it is perfectly fine to go for the compliance route and enforce new ways of working. In my experience, it is better to be directive in such a case: explain why the change is necessary and subsequently demand compliance. Do not pretend that you are looking for more input in the change process: you are not, and people will pick this up.

- What are the assumptions of the people in your team: Are these similar to or different from yours? Where different, you will need to understand the expectations of people who are affected by the change: you will need this understanding later when you have to decide how to guarantee buy-in from employees and how to deal with resistance to change.

10.3 CREATING A CLIMATE FOR CHANGE

Can you prepare for change, or should you just let it happen and deal with it once you are in the middle of it? This question almost has philosophical implications: Should humans try to control the unfolding of events in their environment, or should they let things happen and adjust to the new situation? I personally would promote the thoughtful, step-by-step approach, and I have good arguments for this. Any time spent on planning will be regained later when problems come up (after all, you are prepared now), and starting a change process too rapidly will result in acting without thinking, which is the reason why many change processes fail. This is my preference, in which my Dutch culture, as well as my own personal preferences, definitely plays a role. The Dutch are considered punctual, and like to plan before acting. And if it is not my culture, then it is my personality that drives my bias for the linear, step-by-step approach to change.

Different cultures value time differently, as we have already seen in Section 6.7. Whereas most Western cultures have a desire to control complexity and organize time by proper planning, Eastern cultures see time as a cyclic process: time comes and goes and cannot be controlled or measured. Everything is connected to everything else, and too much planning is simply effort wasted on trying to control something you cannot control. The two worlds do not understand each other's concepts well: Eastern people find the Westerners very rigid and unrealistic in their effort to try to control everything. They see the West as single-minded and impatient in this respect (Trompenaars and Hampden-Turner 1997). At the same time, Western cultures see Eastern people in general as slow, inefficient, and lacking structure.

The linear (Western) view of time and the synchronic (Eastern) view of time have an impact on the way people try to control their environment, and the way they want to deal with complex change. The tendency of the Western people will be to formulate a plan, starting at A, and move in an efficient way to B, specifying milestones, organizing project reviews, and

TIP 80: PLAN THE TIME OR TAKE THE TIME?

When implementing change at multiple sites, assess the predominant time orientation at these sites. Adjust your change management approach to this. In the case of monochronic time orientation, provide your people with a clear change plan, timeline, and implementation guideline, and organize the change process by providing detail and structure. Be clear about milestones and deliverables and explain how you will measure progress. While in the middle of the change process, you should keep people continuously informed of the current status and next steps. If you are dealing predominantly with polychronic cultures, realize that people have a more flexible attitude and do not look at things in a linear and rigid way, as you would in monochronic cultures. Here, your communication with people should mainly focus on the need for change, the various options available, and the overall vision (rather than the precise goal) that the change targets. Avoid detailed implementation plans and precise milestone reviews. It is better to provide people with the overall picture, their place in the change process, and the opportunities there are. Resist the temptation to close things down too early.

measuring progress with a change dashboard. Eastern people prefer to go with the flow, understand the need for change, and then start thinking in terms of people and relations in order to start the shift in the desired direction. Explore and learn along the way, and avoid driving the process to fixed decisions too quickly.

The above view is obviously very binary, and fortunately, the two extreme worlds are coming to understand the other pole more and more. Yet, a manager planning for change should know that cultures have different expectations of how you run the change process, and that many things that one person would perceive as resistance are ultimately nothing other than different perceptions of the role of time in a change process.

The most important implications for managing change are summarized in Table 10.1.

As stated already, splitting up the world into West and East is a generalization, and a lot of nuance should be brought into each generalization. Some Western countries follow a very pragmatic approach to change and are quite action-oriented: these are the countries low on uncertainty avoidance, such as the Netherlands, UK, and Sweden. In countries with high scores on uncertainty avoidance, such as Germany, Austria, and Belgium, a more thoughtful approach should be followed: here, people first want to understand the general philosophy behind the change, speak to experts, and understand the details and plan before getting into the action mode. When the management team consists of both opposites, it is important to talk about each other's expectations before organizing the change process.

Multiple models are used across the world to structure change processes (Lewin 1947; Kübler 1969; Hiatt 2006), one of the most famous being the Kotter model of change (Kotter 1996). Instead of following one of these

TABLE 10.1

Differences between the Monochronic and Polychronic Orientations to Time

Western View of Time (Monochronic)	Eastern View of Time (Polychronic)
Make a plan and stick to it.	Follow the flow and flexibly adjust to the unfolding of events.
Define the "ist" and the "soll" (present and future) state, and move there as quickly and efficiently as possible.	Allow for various possible outcomes and explore along the way to achieve the best result.
Install procedures and work with milestones and deadlines.	Focus on relationships and adjust and explore.

models and going through step-by-step, we choose in the next three sections to highlight several aspects of the change process.

One of these aspects is to ensure that you prepare your organization for change. Change in organizations generally is kicked off by the management that has come to new insights about the strategy or the (organization of) operations in the company. Which brings us immediately to one of the most made mistakes when planning for change: the assumption that when you explain the need for change, people will—sooner or later—buy into this.

What management often fails to see is that they have been thinking about the change already for months, if not years. They identified the need for change, they brainstormed about the possible options, they had to convince their peer managers about the need for change and the way to tackle it, they thought already about the several steps that need to be followed, they already spoke to external consultants about best practices elsewhere, they did a lot! While they were doing this, the rest of the organization quite likely was not aware and certainly not involved. There's a time lag between management and the rest of the organization that cannot be overcome by simply explaining the need for change once or twice. Management will have to realize that they are far ahead of the rest of the troops, and that it will take a lot of time to get the rest of the troops at the same level as they are themselves.

The starting point is to ensure that the organization feels the need to act and buys into the need for change. Explaining the need on a single occasion is by far not enough: several methods will need to be used to ensure that most people in the organization see the need to act boldly and quickly (often referred to as the burning platform).

The reason for change, however, can be missed in an organization that is complacent: a company with a monopoly in a market, or a company that has been growing aggressively for years and gained significant market share, can be very reluctant to acknowledge the need for change. Why change, when all is going well? Managers driving change should recognize this organization culture: they will need to deal with signs of complacency, after they have come to understand the (cultural) context in which the complacent attitude developed. For example, Caribbean cultures often give Westerners the impression that the inhabitants are lazy and complacent, which quite often they are not. Westerners driving change in such an environment will need to understand the cultural context in which they drive change, as sticking to their own paradigm ("They are lazy and will need to become more active") will not lead to success.

In contrast, organizations can also give the impression of being constantly on top of things and open to change, while in reality they are not. And some organizations are characterized by a lot of action, but actually do not focus properly on real, structural improvement of the business. Much energy is spent ineffectively. Some other organizations have a strong focus on improving the business every single day: these companies seem determined to act, move, and win. As we have seen before, these are characteristics of masculine cultures, while feminine cultures lack this continuous sense of striving to be the best. Which is not the same as missing a sense of urgency. For example, quality of life and good relationships are important aspects of the feminine Swedish culture: this culture can be wrongly interpreted by the masculine Americans as unwilling to move, resistant to change, and lacking a sense of urgency. In the end, however, the Swedish will adapt relatively quickly to changing circumstances once they see that the company will benefit from the change.

These examples all serve to point out that preparing the organization for change means understanding the organization culture, and from a thorough understanding of the organization culture, start to drive the point home that things will have to change. Talk the language of the people in the organization! Nothing worse than a very bright external consultant who can only describe the change process in abstract jargon; however bright his contributions, people will simply not understand him. A manager driving change—internal or external—will have to speak the language of the people in the organization, and he can only do so when he has really understood the national and organizational culture in which this language is spoken.

American change expert Kotter (1996) makes a convincing case for properly explaining the rationale behind change, in such a way that reason and logic "speak to the mind," while imaginative stories "aim for the heart." This is a wise approach to ensure acceptance of the change in multiple cultures: some cultures are much more open to objective reasoning, logic, and facts (Germany, Denmark, United States), while other cultures prefer to follow their heart when making decisions, involving subjective feelings and emotions rather than facts and figures (Italy, Colombia, China).

Part of preparing the organization for change also involves making sure that there is a group of people that will drive the change. In general, this

**TIP 81: LOGIC AND EMOTION
ON THE BURNING PLATFORM**

Describe the need for change (the burning platform) in such a way that the multiple cultures you want to address recognize the urgency of the present situation. To a mixed cultural audience, be sure to use objective facts and logic while also touching hearts by painting vivid images, talking about shared dreams, and addressing feelings and emotions. When addressing one particular culture, you should adjust your message. In Germany you should open your presentation with clearly summarized facts and logic. Do not rely on the facts too much when addressing Italian or Chinese people: here, it is better to rely on colorful images and to establish a personal connection with your audience, showing them your own conviction that change is needed.

will be a group of people who feel (and are) responsible for making the change successful. This is not necessarily the management of the organization: the team driving the change should be composed in such a way that they represent several disciplines and levels of the organization: the people in this group need to be trusted by all employees, and they should share a common objective. It is this group that—in the middle of confusion and uncertainty—will be able to drive the transformation process while keeping the end goal in mind.

American change expert Kotter (1996) has the view "that the team of people driving the change is clearly a team with enough positional power to ensure that the existing hierarchy in the company is well represented. This team needs to be able to act rapidly and decisively." Notice a few of the American cultural characteristics in this description, such as individualism (the right individuals need to be on the team), masculinity (make it successful), and short-term orientation (quick decision making, moving on).

In cultures that uphold more collectivistic values (as most countries in the world do) you also need a team driving the change, but this will usually consist of the senior managers who run the company. As long as management has validated the change and it is clear that the company as a whole benefits from the change in the long run, people will be loyal to the initiative and openly support it. Management is then expected to set clear directions for the deployment of the change, and people at lower levels will follow and organize the new work processes in line with this directive.

If the driving team behind the change is to have credibility and people have to trust its decisions, the cultural aspect of uncertainty avoidance plays a role. In uncertainty-avoidant cultures such as those of Spain, Belgium, Russia, and France, the team will have to contain experts with enough relevant knowledge and expertise; otherwise, the team cannot be trusted to make the right decisions. In that same culture, quick decision making (as Kotter describes it) is of less importance: it is more important that the right decisions are made, even when these take more time.

Finally, in individualistic, feminine cultures, people find it important to see themselves represented in the team, in such a way that their voice is heard. In low-power-distance countries in this cluster, people will even doubt the value of a special team to drive the change. When everybody has been involved in defining the new way of working, we can all individually contribute our expertise: there is no need to have a special authority for this. In high-power-distance countries with the same characteristics of femininity and individualism (France and Belgium), people will be more concerned about having the right people in the team, to the extent that all relevant stakeholders in the hierarchy are involved and can be reached. Without the proper involvement of individuals who are relevant in the hierarchy, change will not be successful.

After the urgency and need for change have been defined and a guiding coalition has been formed, a clear vision will need to be developed as part of preparing the organization for change. People not only need to understand the burning platform for change and have trust in the project team driving it, but also need to see the future and envisage how this will differ from the past. Kotter says about this: "A clear and powerful vision will do far more than an authoritarian decree of micromanagement can even hope to accomplish." Again, we clearly see the American assumptions behind the Kotter model of change (Kotter 1996): after all, the United States is characterized by an individualistic and low-power-distance culture.

Developing the change vision is an important aspect of preparation: to a large degree, winning the hearts and minds of people is about drawing a clear picture of what the future will look like, and making sure that this is a picture people can look forward to. They should recognize themselves in the future vision of the company, and really identify with this vision. It should be a realistic picture in which people identify their roles, and it should be clear and sufficiently focused to later provide guidance in daily decision making.

In countries where people feel part of a group and where hierarchy is important (most countries in the world), a clear and powerful vision alone will not be enough. Here people feel comfortable following the directions set by the leader(s) of the group. The American value is: "Once the goals are clear, individual professionals will do all they can to ensure they contribute to the goal." However, the vision in large parts of the world will be that making an organization successful has nothing to do with individuals doing the right thing efficiently, but has everything to do with clarity within the group, a clear division of tasks based on position and hierarchy, and building relationships that help the organization to reach the desired state.

Developing the vision behind the change is not something that can be outsourced to the internal communications department, in the hope they come up with a few nice slogans that people will like. Internal communications will often play a key role, and rightly so: their professionalism in structuring the communications within the company is vital. The responsibility, however, for having a vision in the first place, and knowing exactly how this change vision will support the company and business objectives, rests with the management. Developing the vision can partially be delegated to the group driving the change that we spoke about in this chapter; however, the responsibility for a clear change vision can only rest in one place.

Too many change processes failed in spite of the presence of a clear need for change and a determined group of people who picked up the task of driving it. When the vision behind the change is fuzzy and not well thought through, the organization will not close it into their hearts and minds and adopt the new future.

10.4 IMPLEMENTING THE CHANGE

Whereas the first phase we focused on was preparing the change (burning platform, driving team, and vision), the next phase is all about making sure that the organization buys into the plan.

In order for people to buy into the change initiative and support it, the vision behind the change will first need to be communicated to them. This step is crucial in making sure that the organization as a whole starts moving in the right direction. To stay with the marathon analogy at the start of this chapter, the communication must ensure that people who are behind the starting line when the gun goes off know when to start moving and what is expected of them. As they cannot see what is happening in the front of the line, they rely on clear communication from others in order to be aware of what is going on. A theoretical story about the impact of the starting gun, or the average speed at which the first runners took off, is not likely to inspire them: a vivid story about the fantastic race that they are about to start is.

The communication plan again cannot just be outsourced to the internal communications department: they can and should help in delivering the messages and choosing the communication channels to ensure maximum impact. However, the responsibility for the communication must remain with the change team. The topic is too important: it should not be outsourced or poorly managed, as the success of the change depends on it.

In individualistic cultures with low power distance and low masculinity (such as Sweden, the Netherlands), people expect to be heard and to be involved in the change process. One-way communication, which is the norm in very hierarchical organizations, will not engage them, and the consequence of one-way communication is generally that people disengage from the change. In these countries, people are reluctant and cautious if the communication comes from management only: people's feeling of autonomy is compromised and motivation decreases. A manager involved

---

TIP 82: ELEVATOR PITCH FOR CHANGE

In your communication about change, you should have a simple, vibrant, and focused key message. Too often managers have a lucid communication story in their own head, but that story is only clear to them. Asking them to describe the communication messages often results in a complete explanation of the why and the how of the change, with lots of logic and reasoning. The communication message, however, should be formulated up front in a few simple key statements that stick: train yourself to summarize the essence of the change in a few sentences.

in driving change should be aware of the dominant national cultures (and organization cultures) to ensure the right style of communication is set up and that it has the right tone for maximum audience acceptation.

Experience with international communication is key. When English headquarters communicate key messages of change to their production sites in Asia, you can be sure that the messages are announced in proper English and colored with the right intonation, structures, and nuance. The source of the communication will do his job well, but quite often he will forget about the receiver. At the Asian sites that receive the messages, the level of mastery of English is limited: people live in a different reality and will have difficulty connecting to the key messages. In the previous sentence, I said, "The level of mastery of English is limited," but in international communication this sentence should actually state: "Their English is not so good." Clear, simple messages win the hearts of most cultures, even when the underlying vision is complicated.

Part of the communication plan should be that you are able to answer for every individual employee "what is in it for him." People will only buy into your message when they see what your message implies to them. This aspect—although vital—is often forgotten by managers announcing, for example, a reduction of the workforce. Announcing that 10% of the people will have to go and focusing your talk on the reasons for taking these

---

TIP 83: BE ONE OF THEM

For any piece of communication to your (cross-cultural) team, make sure you spend some time on the way you will communicate. You will need to do three things when communicating change to your team:

1. Keep it focused: Focus on the essence of the change. Explain why it is needed, and what it consists of.
2. Keep it simple: Avoid any jargon or display of superior knowledge. Communicate your story in simple English that is understood even by people from sites where English is a major hurdle.
3. Be one of them: Avoid the image of the external consultant who uses his high-level knowledge to tell the people how they should work. Act as if you are one of them and that you—along with the workers—want to find a way to work better.

measures will not land: you will need to be able to tell everybody whether they individually belong to the 10% or not. Every individual listener will need to know what the message means for him. Quite often this is not known yet at the moment the message gets communicated: in that situation it is important to at least be crystal clear on when you will know exactly: "I regret today I cannot tell you who will have to go and who not, and I realize that is very dissatisfying for all of you. I will come back, however, with a total restructuring plan next Friday: on that day all of you will know whether you stay or go."

So even when you are not the initiator of change, you have responsibilities as a manager of a group of people to make sure your people can contribute optimally to the change goals. You will need to enable your people to perform as best they can. This means motivating them, while at the same moment removing the bottlenecks that prevent them from contributing to the change effectively.

One of your most important tasks in the change process is to ensure that your people know how they fit into the big picture: what is everybody's role and responsibility? Whereas these things are unclear in times of change, even to you as a manager, you still have the responsibility to clarify the situation to your people. As argued before, people from individualistic cultures will be quick to ask "What's in it for me?" in change processes. You should be able to answer this question.

As a manager, it is important to realize what your people need in this stage. In individualistic, masculine cultures (such as the United States), people like to work in an empowered way toward ambitious goals. In these cultures, you will need to be crisp and clear about overall goals and people's individual targets: once these are set, people will take individual responsibility to work toward these goals and contribute in the best possible way. Empowerment in this context is mostly about providing clarity on the vision and the goals: people will then aspire to reach the targets "whatever it takes." Your role as a manager then is to provide support.

This works differently in a culture that scores low on masculinity. Feminine cultures prefer to work in harmony, with good relationships between individuals in the team. They will typically strive for consensus about the next step to be taken. In these cultures, empowering your team and creating the right work environment involves people-focus rather than task-focus: removing barriers here is done by influencing people in such a way that they reach consensus about the right course of action.

The assertive clash-and-conflict style that is so characteristic of the individualistic and masculine United States will not yield results in most Latin American, African, and Asian countries, where harmony and consensus are important. Here the manager empowers his team by being clear on what he expects of them as a collective, and by then following up to ensure the group processes are clarified. He plays an active role here, using his power to ensure that everybody is allocated clear tasks and is aware of what has to be done.

Empowering people in very uncertainty-avoidant countries is nevertheless a different game: here it is all about providing clarity on how the new work processes should be carried out, who does what, etc. Restricted autonomy is no problem to people in these cultures, as the most important thing here is to provide clarity and, with that, reduce uncertainty. To influence his people in these countries, the manager will need to clarify work processes, clean up and adjust job descriptions, organize cross-departmental meetings to ensure that obscurities between different organizational units are resolved, etc. These cultures are often referred to as well-oiled machines: everything should run smoothly, and the more we are in control, the better it is for the company. Accordingly, the change process itself will also be well organized: nothing is left to chance.

Part of a successful change implementation is to generate signs of success that are clearly visible to the organization, so that people start to see that the change is working. This aspect of change management is largely culture independent: regardless of the location in the world, people benefit from seeing that the change process is paying off, and that it leads to success.

One of the aspects of culture that is visible here is the American short-term focus. In a country where individuals are ambitious and pursue ambitious targets, short-term results provide proof of progress and success: balanced scorecards with clear facts and figures will provide the information that managers need to ascertain they are on track.

Most Eastern cultures will have long-term orientation, and change processes in these environments will mostly be aimed at the long-term benefit of the company. Immediate success is of less relevance, as long as people are confident that the change will pay off in the long run. Less attention will be devoted to short-term facts and figures, and more time will be spent looking at trends, relationships, and the long-term result the company is pursuing.

10.5 ENSURING THAT THE CHANGE LASTS

The last phase in a successful change project concerns continuing to implement the change and making the new working methods stick. Management—obviously with all best intentions—often kills this part of the change process without realizing it. Once the change has been defined and the high-level changes have been made, they shift focus to new priorities, such as defining a next plan for doing things differently than before. Before the first change has been implemented, a new change plan gets defined.

The challenge in this phase is to keep momentum, especially now that the first wave of change enthusiasm has gone. When the early victories of the change process have been shared, the tendency is to celebrate and move on. At this point you should again recall the marathon analogy: management has finished the race in a time of 2 hours 10 minutes, while the majority of the organization needs at least double the time to get to results. After passing the finishing line, management should move to the workfloor to help the other runners become successful, rather than move on and enroll for a new race.

There is resistance to change in every organization. During change processes, the manager should stay focused on the end goal and deal effectively with resistance. To quote the words of Kotter (1996): "Whenever you let up before the job is done, critical momentum can be lost and regression may soon follow. The new behaviors and practices must be driven into the culture to ensure long-term success."

This stage of the change is characterized by increased momentum: more projects are added, more people get involved, more effort is spent in keeping urgency high, and proof of success becomes consistent rather than occasional. New processes need to be formalized and embedded in the organization, in such a way that the change is secured in the deepest levels of the organization. Leadership is required; otherwise, the change will stall, and the organization will gradually—but usually sooner rather than later—return to old behavior.

In countries with high power distance, management is expected to instruct the organization on what to do. In China and India, continuous commitment and drive from the top will be required in order to implement the new way of working. The higher the uncertainty avoidance, the clearer and more detailed these instructions need to be, and the more essential it is to record these procedures in clear documents (Mexico,

Portugal, Russia). Thus, in most cultures, management's responsibility in the change process does not cease after communicating the change; it only starts there. This is entirely different in low-power-distance, low-uncertainty-avoidant countries (United States), where management concentrates its efforts on the early stages of goal setting and communicating, while the workforce gets involved later when the changing work practices need to be implemented. There is obviously a supporting role for management here: they should stay actively involved in monitoring and adjusting activities, but part of the work of driving the change can be expected to come from the autonomous workforce.

In the cluster of countries where individualism, low power distance, and femininity are combined (Scandinavia, the Netherlands) a warning is appropriate with regard to this step of the change process: although it is important to be persistent in demanding the implementation of change, new insights ought to be taken seriously in these cultures. Emerging insight is a fact of life, and while implementing change, people will expect that decisions—once made—can be reconsidered at all times. Decision making in these countries is seen as an ongoing process rather than as a final step (the decision) that is taken at one point in time. For this reason, stakeholder management is a different activity in these countries: rather than merely informing the stakeholders, it is important to take all opinions of all important stakeholders into account, and to keep adjusting the course of action until everybody is on board. Action plans and procedures keep changing until everybody is satisfied with them. When arranging buy-in from stakeholders, the Dutch will frequently use the expression "It's a matter of give and take." You need to continuously make concessions to get others to buy into your plans.

In an attempt to drive change from its U.S. headquarters, the frustration of an American company in dealing with its European—especially Dutch—sites was more than obvious. The Americans became increasingly frustrated with the Dutch reopening every discussion they considered closed, and the fact that decisions were only temporary was hard for the action-oriented Americans to digest. The Dutch subsidiary kept coming with questions, and continued to oppose the proposed change. To the Dutch, the rigidity and drive of the Americans was frustrating: "They drive this through without making sure that everybody is on board; they don't understand what is important here to run a company successfully." The American company closed their Dutch subsidiary not much later, and ran their operations entirely from the United States.

Making change last means that a company needs to ensure that the new behaviors, norms, and values are adhered to in the long run. However, people in organizations build up a collective inertia that must not be underestimated. "The way we do things around here" is part of the organization and cannot be changed overnight: years will be needed, especially when behaviors and attitudes (company culture) need to change.

In collectivistic cultures employees will tend to collectively accept new working processes whether they individually agree or not. The higher the power distance, the less they will question the change, and the more they will accept the new way of working as the only right one. Losing people is unlikely to result from the new company culture, as people will form the new culture by adopting the behavior prescribed by the management. Monetary incentives will have less effect here, and certainly not at an individual level: personal incentives work counterproductively in traditionally collectivistic cultures, while rewarding the group and jointly celebrating success will have much more positive impact on the effectiveness of the change.

Sharing Experiences

Jennifer Wright, SVP Communication Operations and Learning and Development, Citi Bank, London, United Kingdom
LinkedIn: uk.linkedin.com/in/jenwrightconsulting

Jennifer Wright *is a Change Management Consultant who has more than 10 years experience of working on business transformation programs for BMW, Motorola, Chevron, Barclays, Barclays Capital, BDO, and Lloyd's Register. She has been the Change Manager for national and international programs including company mergers, large scale re-structuring, de-capitalization programs, global IT, and investment*

projects. Jennifer leads the London Chapter of the Change Management Institute, a not-for-profit organization promoting the change management profession internationally.

I remember a "root and branch transformation" I was involved in while in a support function some time ago. The transformation included strategy, people, and processes, and covered 70 countries. A major operation that was carefully planned and executed. Part of the deployment process was to launch a comprehensive communication plan, which aimed to reach all employees involved. The plan included global video conference town halls, newsletters, announcements, online "ask our leaders" live social media chat sessions, monthly team briefing packs, and regional leader conferences. Really any communications channel we could think of to reach the target audience convincingly was included. All these actions for sure drove up employee understanding of the transformation.

We found something interesting. We had assumed—unconsciously—that when we would provide good content, data, rationale, and logic, the buy-in for the transformation would increase. What we noticed however was that the biggest number of clicks on content occurred when something really personal was revealed.

This triggered us to create a new series of "meet the new leaders videos"(short talking heads) where leaders talked about the area they lead, but also about what they do in their spare time. To our enjoyment, the activities leaders readily mentioned were activities varying from base jumping, playing with their kids and growing asparagus. The more personal we made the stories, the higher the hit rates. Anytime an event was reported, photos were uploaded to a gallery and again the click through rate went up.

We proceeded with this approach, and while we grew in confidence, the leaders were encouraged to mix corporate strategy with showing their human side. This ultimately resulted in the leadership team being filmed taking the ice bucket challenge. Not something you would expect from a traditional bank's leadership team but a great signal of real change!

We had found a way—unplanned—to reach and engage a large group of employees by touching their hearts. Showing facts, data, and figures is one, but if you want engagement rather than understanding, you will have to include the human side of your business: personalize your leaders!

Practical advice for the international manager:

- Make it personal. So much business that is ran from Western headquarters is based on the local (Western) culture, but people unconsciously make the assumption that the rest of the world works like it does over here. In most countries of the world, however—as the author describes in this book—business is a personal matter between two people rather than a rational transaction between two organizations. Realize that in the majority of the world, you will have to touch the human aspects of doing business. Personalize your leaders!
- Global communications is not something you can do from the side of your desk. If a major change process you run deals with multiple foreign countries and cultures, you will need to spend full-time on the communications efforts. Learn how to touch the hearts of people in the countries you want to reach. Extrapolating your home country communications policy to the rest of the world is meaningless. Understand local cultures, and make sure they all get an answer to the question "What's in it for me?"
- Do not assume too easily that in logic, rational, driven cultures (task based, like most Western Europeans) the human side of business does not play a role. It does—it's just less visible to the outside world. Personal relationships are important everywhere. So make your interactions personal, whether you come from a culture where this is the habit or not.

10.6 DEALING WITH RESISTANCE

Resistance to change is natural; change requires people to work differently from the way they did before, and this moves them out of their comfort zone. People have a tendency to creep back to the comfortable status quo as quickly as they can.

To stay in their comfort zones, people show the following behaviors:

- Employees ask many "why" questions. (Why should we change? Why was the previous way no longer efficient?)

- Employees state why the idea behind the change is bad (applying all kind of logic to argue why the change will not work).
- Employees confirm the need for change, agreeing to the proposed changes while at the same moment maintaining the status quo at all costs.
- Employees display cynicism about the change.

You will quickly conclude that people resist change, but this is a conclusion drawn too quickly. More often than not, it is resistance to the way you treat people rather than resistance to changing the actual work processes (Lawrence and Ronken 1952). When confronted with a manager explaining why current work processes are inefficient and which changes are necessary, people rightly conclude somebody higher up is telling them they have done a poor job until now, and that this manager now knows how they should work differently. This message is not at all welcome, and in some (low-PDI) cultures the message should certainly not come from a high-level manager. When analyzing resistance like this in large change processes, you often come to the conclusion that people tend to resist the way in which the change is sold to them rather than the (logic of the) change itself.

Lewin's force-field analysis model (Lewin 1951) is useful when trying to understand that there are several forces in an organization that support change, as well as several forces within the organization that resist change (Figure 10.1). The job of the change manager is to increase the forces that aid change, while simultaneously reducing the forces that oppose change. That sounds easy.

You would expect that, by default, the restraining forces in some cultures would be bigger. For example, cultures with high scores on uncertainty avoidance would tend to be conservative and maintain the status quo, as exchanging this for an unexpected situation would increase uncertainty. People prefer stability in their lives and careers, and they prefer to be able to predict and control their environment. On the other hand, cultures with low scores on uncertainty avoidance see uncertainty as normal: the future can bring about change and uncertainty, but we will deal with that when it comes.

There is an increasing base of research that gives evidence of the opposite. For example, Schneider and De Meyer (1991) have postulated that in high-uncertainty-avoidance cultures, managers are likely to engage in proactive behavior, as this helps them control and adapt to their future environment. The same is suggested by Geletkanycz (1997), who argues

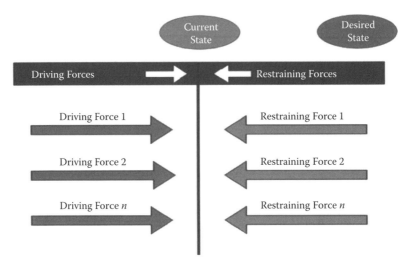

FIGURE 10.1
Force-field analysis, displaying the forces that are driving and restraining the desired change.

TIP 84: APPLY THE FORCE-FIELD THEORY

For any change you are driving in your direct work environment—or even for any change you are driving in your personal life—draw up a list of the forces that aid or resist the change. Take a piece of paper and just do it. Ask yourself which of these forces are significant and which are of minor importance. Which of the resisting forces exerts most influence on your chance of success? What do you need to contribute in order to change this force into a supporting force? Which supporting forces are the strongest, and how can you gain more benefit from these forces in order to realize the required change? Now ask one or two other people who are involved in the change to help you complete your force-field analysis, and discuss the above questions with them as well. What is your final conclusion on how you spend your time as an agent of change: What should you do more, and what should you do less?

that managers in high-UAI cultures look actively for ways to deal with dynamic environments, rather than focus their efforts on opposing the dynamics of change. Adapting to the changing environment is then a way to reduce the feeling of uncertainty, and to avoid losing control.

Risk aversion is also to be expected in established, high-power-distance cultures such as the Chinese. The combination of high power distance, collectivism, and a certain degree of uncertainty avoidance in China results in managers who maintain the status quo (and their privileges in this) (Fang and Hall 2003). The dominant American literature on change predicts the opposite: that change is stimulated by the combination of individualism, low power distance, and low uncertainty avoidance (Sun 2000). For this reason, managers of state-owned, large enterprises in China are allegedly not open to change, but rather oppose it. The combination of collectivism and high power distance makes the established management in large Chinese firms reactive: they tend to respond to orders from their superiors rather than proactively changing the company to deal with rapid environmental change.

In all cases of resistance, the interpersonal communication toolbox mentioned in Chapters 1 and 2 will help you deal with resistance in a constructive way:

- Apply more of the you- and we-dimensions when confronted with resistance. Ask questions in order to understand the opposition and connect to them, rather than rebuff them by stating that their resistance is not justified. It is. Now understand why this is, connect with them, and help them deal with it.
- Framing and reframing. Get into meta-position, and from this position ask yourself: What is going on here between them and me? Then change the frame of reference: In which other way can we look at this change, and does that shine a more positive light on the way change is perceived?
- The four levels of communication. Do not introduce more content and explain over and over again that the resistance is not justified. Again, it is! Switch to process and propose alternative ways to discuss this change with your team.
- The common reality. Get back to the facts and the things that both you and they can clearly observe. Now examine—in conjunction with your team—how you can interpret those data, and which conclusions you can draw from that. The best manager of change is the

manager who is able to make his team propose the changes that he wants to realize. Help them in deciding that this is the best way forward.

Finally, resistance is often more difficult to counter when driving multisite change processes (multiple locations where different national and company cultures dominate). Here the following practical guidelines have proven to be very helpful to me:

- Remember that, in multisite change processes, your aim is to make all the different sites and people collaborate in unison on the same objective, contributing through their own unique way of working. With this mindset, you can regard yourself as an orchestrator of change: your main challenge is to get everyone to work in unison to realize the end goal. What is required for this? This mindset helps to avoid the trap of losing the big picture: it is so easy to focus on one change required at one particular site, rather than focus your attention on the big picture.
- Build a community that collectively works on the change. Communicate to all sites involved (not only the most important sites) and keep everybody continuously updated on the status of the change and the actions that are taken (concrete actions are what people at lower levels in the organization can easily relate to). Invite people to collaborate, and look constantly for dialogue through multiple media (email updates, status reports, success stories, public announcements, Q&A sessions, lunch with a selected group of people involved in the change, etc.): make the change live!
- Identify the main barriers to change per site. It is key to realize that the total change effort, to be successful, requires that all sites buy into it and change the way they work. Overlooking a major obstacle in one of the sites can ruin the entire effort. From American headquarters it is easy to decide that there will be rewards to all who support the change and that, in your yearly performance evaluation, you will rate people on their attitude and behavior in relation to the proposed changes. But if you forget that changes in performance management processes require formal approval from workers' unions in France, and that German labor councils will need to be involved from the early stages, will need to give their advice and approve the changes, the change will not be adopted in France or Germany. Identify the

barriers to change per site, and involve the sites early on in order to start addressing these barriers.

- Work intensely and correctly with local leaders, local managers, and influential local people. Engage them in the change efforts you are driving. You are relying on their help to be successful, and if you do not have the local leaders behind your plans (especially in high-PDI local cultures), the change will not take off.

REFERENCES

Beer, M., and Nohria, N. (2000). *Breaking the Code of Change*. Boston: Harvard Business School Press, May–June 2000, 133–141.

Bridges, W., and Bridges, S. (2009). *Managing Transitions, Making the Most of Change*. Philadelphia: Da Capo Lifelong Books.

Fang, Y., and Hall, C. (2003). Chinese Managers and Motivation for Change: The Challenges and a Framework. Presented at Proceedings of the 15th Annual Conference of the Association for Chinese Economics Studies Australia (ACESA). Online source: http://mams.rmit.edu.au/yynfpoqj2vtk.pdf

Geletkanycz, M.A. (1997). The Salience of "Culture's Consequences": The Effects of Cultural Values on Top Executive Commitment to the Status Quo. *Strategic Management Journal*, 18(8), 615–34.

Hiatt, J.M. (2006). *ADKAR: A Model for Change in Business, Government and Our Community*. Loveland, CO: Prosci Learning Center.

Kotter, J.P. (1996). *Leading Change*. Boston: Harvard Business School Press.

Kübler-Ross, E. (1969). *On Death and Dying*. New York: Routledge.

Lawrence, P.R., and Ronken, H.O. (1952). *Administering Changes: A Case Study of Human Relations in a Factory*. Division of Research, Harvard Business School.

Lewin, K. (1947). Frontiers of Group Dynamics: Concept, Method and Reality in Social Science, Social Equilibria, and Social Change. *Human Relations*, 1(1), 5–41.

Lewin K. (1951). *Field Theory in Social Science*. New York: Harper and Row.

Schneider, S., and De Meyer, A. (1991). Interpreting and Responding to Strategic Issues: The Impact of National Culture. *Strategic Management Journal*, 12(4), 307–20.

Sun, J. (2000). Organization Development and Change in Chinese State-Owned Enterprises: A Human Resource Perspective. *Leadership and Organization Development Journal*, 21(8), 379–89.

Trompenaars, F., and Hampden-Turner, C. (1997). *Riding the Waves of Culture. Understanding Cultural Diversity in Business*. London: Nicolas Brealey.

Trompenaars, F., and Woolliams, P. (2003). A New Framework for Managing Change across Cultures. *Journal of Change Management*, 3(4), 361–75.

11

Managing Negotiations

This is a classic negotiation technique. It's a gentle, soft indication of your disapproval and a great way to keep negotiating. Count to 10. By then, the other person usually will start talking and may very well make a higher offer.

—**Bill Coleman**[*]

On an annual basis, we were negotiating the prices of a full package of products with a major client in the electronics industry. They had scheduled a two-day meeting to come to agreement on the pricing and conditions for the coming year. We knew their negotiators quite well (we thought) and we knew their tactics: they enjoyed using all the tricks of the negotiation trade to gain maximum benefit—and they were usually very successful with their approach. Unfortunately this would happen again this year.

Instead of waiting passively for their tactics to unfold, we decided to take the lead and steer the negotiations toward the result we aimed for: a maximum overall price reduction of 5%. Instead of having long discussions about individual products and prices, we decided to lay our cards on the table. Two weeks before the negotiations, we sent an article to the client, which underpinned our case: it stated that prices in our industry were hardly coming down anymore, and that prices were incidentally increasing. This tactic is called managing expectations: we adjusted the expectations of the other party (at least that is what we thought we did) by citing an independent source claiming that price reductions would not be possible. We also told them that we preferred to discuss an overall percentage for the entire package rather than individual prices: this would save time and result in a much more straightforward process. They accepted our proposal. This meant we

---

[*] www.quotehd.com

would not discuss individual products this year, and would efficiently agree to a total price reduction of a few percent. We thought.

The negotiations started and both parties made their opening statements: we proposed unchanged pricing for next year while they insisted on an overall reduction of 10%. After a day of negotiating we agreed late in the evening on a price reduction of 3.8% for the whole package: although a bit more than what we had realized with other clients, we were happy with this result. We were satisfied that we had reached agreement within a day, and we had ended up with an overall result far below the 5% we ultimately would have agreed to. Our tactics had worked. We thought.

The customer indicated that they wanted to discuss a few minor things the next day and some delivery conditions, etc. Although we had hoped this would no longer be necessary now that we had reached agreement, we were not worried: the deal had already been made to the contentment of both parties. We thought.

When the customer entered the next day, we started to feel uncomfortable. Instead of two guys and a few papers, they arrived with six purchasing people, all armed with thick files with our company name on it. They asked us whether we would always stick to firm agreements that had been made in the past. Of course we said we would. Later we realized this was our main mistake. They brought up every individual product they had bought from us and confronted us with pricing projections that some of our colleagues had anticipated for this particular product in previous years. Price erosions of 8–12% had been communicated for some of these products. Our internal processes at that time were not such that pricing agreements with customers were centrally stored and administered, and pricing agreements were made by a large variety of commercial people all over Europe.

Although we protested that we had reached agreement yesterday on the pricing of the entire package, the customer held us to our promise that we would always honor firm agreements made in the past. When all discussions were finished and we looked back on a long day, it was clear the customer had employed very smart tactics again. By agreeing on an overall 3.8% first and then reneging on previous agreements, they had now realized an overall reduction of 7.7%. The painful mistake we made had cost us more than $1 million and had surpassed by far the 5% mandate we had received from our management for this negotiation.

What went wrong? Our mistake was the result of painfully bad preparation: we did not know the individual pricing agreements our colleagues had made in the past, and had hardly studied the history of our company with this client. Moreover, we had also made a few—perhaps reckless—assumptions with our strategy of one total price for the whole package: these assumptions turned out to be wrong. For example, we had assumed that it was also in the interest of our customer to come to one overall price for the entire package. However, the biggest problem was that we were negotiating with a win-lose mindset. We were prepared to outsmart the other side of the table with our tactics. Over the years, a pattern of win-lose negotiations had been established with this client, and our assumption was that we had to win the negotiations by using tactics that were smarter than our opponent's. Alas, the client proved to be smarter again: this mistake had just cost us about $1 million.

11.1 TWO TYPES OF NEGOTIATIONS

Negotiation is about conflicting interests between two or more parties for which a solution acceptable to both parties has to be found. These negotiations can be about anything where two parties have different interests: the price of a new bicycle, delivery of a few tons of steel to a construction company, or solving border conflicts between two countries. Also, temporarily making available a few of your engineers for a different business unit within your company is done through negotiation: there are conflicting interests everywhere, and the toughest negotiations are often internal. A lot of the commercial negotiation approaches, strategies, and tactics apply to internal negotiation with stakeholders as well. More details about this are presented in Section 11.9.

To determine the best negotiation strategy you need to understand the aims of both parties: What are they after and when will they be satisfied with the result?

We distinguish between two kinds of negotiations: distributive and integrative negotiations. These have already been introduced in Chapter 4. In this chapter we discuss these two extremes in more detail, and give guidance to the cultural aspects of using both forms of negotiation.

11.1.1 Distributive Negotiations

The characteristic feature of distributive negotiations (also referred to as positional bargaining (Fisher and Ury 1999)) is that a fixed amount of

Distributive Negotiation

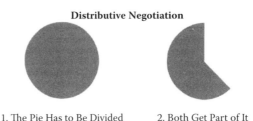

1. The Pie Has to Be Divided   2. Both Get Part of It

FIGURE 11.1
Schematic illustration of distributive negotiations.

goods or services is to be divided between two parties (Figure 11.1). This can be the price of an individual product, such as a secondhand car that you want to get rid of, for example. In this kind of situation, the seller looks for the highest possible price, while the buyer has an interest in a price that is as low as possible. These two are related and in direct competition: profit for one is loss for the other.

Both buyer and seller are likely to know the boundary they do not want to cross in order to reach agreement. The seller has a minimum price he wants to get for the car (directed by his management), and the buyer does not want to spend more than a certain maximum (directed by his partner). Between these extremes is an area of possible agreement (see Figure 11.2).

It is important to get to know the limit of the other party in order to be able to determine your maximum gain, and to determine your strategy. You will have to do much research in advance: you need to know the market conditions, and prepare arguments that will support your price points. During the negotiation you will need to test your assumptions: "I hear from a lot of car sellers that the market for gasoline cars is limited

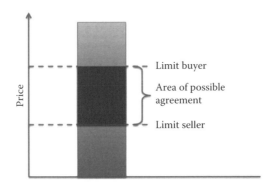

FIGURE 11.2
The area of possible agreement in distributive negotiation between buyer and seller.

and that not many are sold these days: Is that your experience as well?" And you will need to ask a lot of questions about the limits the other person has in mind. The challenge in distributive negotiation is to influence the limit of the other party. You could leave an advertisement on the table of a similar car, where you subtly underlined the low price. Or you can display your knowledge about all the hidden imperfections of this type of car. Also, mentioning your brother who coincidentally has a high position at the national car dealer control body can help. Your aim is to adjust the expectation of the other party, and the chance of successfully doing so is highest in the early phases of negotiating. Obviously the experienced car dealer is doing the same thing to get to know your limit: "Just looking for something new, or did the previous car break down?"

Characteristic of distributive bargaining is the fact that both parties realize there are limited means and that you will need to fight to get your share of the pie. The atmosphere in purely distributive negotiation is generally one of distrust and inflexibility. As profits for the other party equal your losses, you will be careful and you will not trust the other party too easily. The fear of dealing with a very smart seller who knows all the tricks of the trade will paralyze some people. They may unconsciously choose for the strategy of avoidance or of accommodation (see Figure 4.1).

Some cultures will avoid distributive bargaining more than others. In cultures where the relationship between the two parties is of the utmost importance (collective, long-term-oriented cultures), the parties will want to avoid adopting confrontational positions. They feel uncomfortable breaking the harmony of a personal relationship based on trust, and will seek mutual satisfaction with regard to the outcome rather than personal gain (think of cultures in Latin America or in Southeast Asia). The presence of an interpersonal relationship in these countries underlines the fact that you have to find a mutually acceptable outcome, so the parties will not tend to use purely distributive tactics. Very masculine, collectivistic countries can form the exception: although the relationship is important, the masculine characteristic is to compete and win. This drive can be so strong that playing tough in order to get the best possible deal for yourself is well-accepted behavior: showing you are prepared to fight proves that you are very serious about reaching agreement. This holds for countries such as Russia, for example.

On the other hand, haggling is commonplace in many collectivistic cultures: giving and taking and long deliberation often confirm the relationship of mutual interdependence. The distributive tactics that are

TIP 85: WHAT WOULD I DO IF I WERE THEM?

In any negotiation or conflict, force yourself to think first from the position of the other party. Ask yourself: "What would I do if I were in his position?" Place yourself entirely in the shoes of the other person and temporarily park your own interests. If you were him, what would you do to get maximum benefit for yourself? Which weakness do you see in your own proposition? How would you take advantage of that? Always force yourself to think from the perspective of the other person first, before trying to get your own needs satisfied.

frequently used in other countries are not accepted in this setting. Once the other party discovers your tactics and notices that you are only going for personal gain, the relationship can be harmed forever.

Communication in distributive bargaining takes place mainly at the level of content (see Figure 2.1). When the level of communication switches to interaction or climate/feeling this will usually be smart tactics rather than a real intent to strengthen the quality of communications and the relationship of trust.

Being aware of the position of the other party often leads to new possibilities, to give the negotiation an integrative character, for example, and to find common ground from which both can benefit. Think from the position of the other person and enter a new pattern where mutual gains can be much bigger: integrative negotiations. Before we introduce these, we should clarify the difference between positions and interests.

11.1.2 Positions vs. Interests

In negotiation it is important to focus on mutual interests, not on individual positions. The case presented at the start of Chapter 1 provided a good illustration of this principle.

Interests are the things that are of real value to you at the end of the day: gained market share, higher profit margins, or increased customer satisfaction. Positions are the things you demand so that your interests are realized: these are defined in a much narrower form, and are never the things you are really after. Positions are temporary; interests are lasting. In the example at the start of Chapter 1 it was in the interest of both parties to realize a long-term business relationship where the partners would bring a continuous stream of innovative products to the market, hereby increasing their individual market shares at the expense of other competitors. The positions both parties took in realizing this were embodied in the price of products for next year, which was determined in such a way that their individual businesses would be able to grow with profit. However, there are many alternative ways to realize the common goal: a shared roadmap of product innovations for the next two years, for example.

At all times, a negotiator should stay focused on his interests and the interests of the other party, and not be distracted by long debates about positions. Sticking to your position leads to a war in which both parties forget why they are at war, which is a pity, as nobody is satisfied when his positions are met but his interests ignored. The battle has been won, the war lost. A discussion about interests creates connection: in the discussion, the goals of both parties are openly argued and energy is focused on constructing an outcome that helps both. This is what integrative negotiation is about: unifying interests. This could involve actions such as jointly excluding a competitor from the market by joining forces and using each other's distribution channels. The long-term interest cannot be discussed in harmony when there are loud discussions going on about positions.

TIP 86: UNDERSTAND INTERESTS

Each time you hear people taking firm positions about things (usually starting with "I want …" or "We should …" or "It is important that …") teach yourself to try to understand their real interests first. Before you have understood their real interest, do not spend energy on arguing or attacking other people's positions. When it is not possible to know their real interest, there are three things you can do:

- Ask: Directly ask the other party what he is really after and why. After each answer, ask "Why?" again until you understand his real interest.
- Assume: Assume the most likely interest of the other party and then start testing your assumption by asking questions.
- Build scenarios: List a few of the other party's possible interests and test which of the positions he has assumed matches these interests. In the course of the negotiation, some scenarios will prove unlikely, and hopefully only one will remain.

11.1.3 Integrative Negotiations

In integrative negotiations (also called principled negotiation (Fisher and Ury 1999)), the challenge is not to maximize, but to integrate different interests (Figure 11.3). These negotiations often are referred to as win-win negotiations and are characterized by mutual effort to maximize the gains for both. For example, the supplier of office materials and the large retailer can engage in endless negotiations about the pricing of individual articles for next year, but they can also put their efforts into setting up a new online distribution channel that leads to more revenues for both.

A nice analogy is the one with a pie that needs to be divided by two parties: you can engage in distributive negotiations and try to grab as much of the pie as you can (at the expense of the other party). You can also approach this integratively and first try to maximize the total pie before you start dividing it. Working on a solution that benefits both parties is often referred to as soft by negotiators in large international firms. This is nonsense. Integrative negotiation has nothing to do with soft; rather, it contributes—in a much more effective way—to the hard business targets of revenue growth and maximization of profits.

Negotiations in real life are hardly ever purely distributive in their nature. See the earlier example of negotiating over a new car. Although this negotiation looks like a pure win-lose (it is all about price), this is not necessarily the case. In many cases, the garage is open to discussing a fixed-price maintenance contract for the next few years, a set of winter tires is quickly sold, and the assessment that a satisfied customer will also return in three years for a new car is relevant. There is integrative potential here. Unfortunately, the pattern is that experience has often taught negotiators to think in terms of win-lose. I have to admit my mindset was often win-lose during large negotiations, while this should not have been

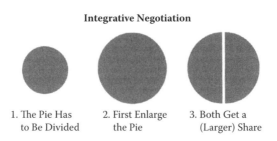

Integrative Negotiation

1. The Pie Has to Be Divided   2. First Enlarge the Pie   3. Both Get a (Larger) Share

FIGURE 11.3
Schematic illustration of integrative negotiations.

the case. Breaking the pattern of distributive thinking by programming yourself to think win-win is the main challenge to every successful international negotiator.

Integrative negotiations are characterized by mutual trust, creativity, openness, and focus on the relationship. Only when these conditions are met can both parties work effectively on a solution that truly benefits both. In integrative solutions, the three dimensions of communication (introduced in Section 1.2) are used differently from the way they are used in distributive negotiations. Although the I-dimension is still activated to argue, to request, and to promise, it is balanced by frequent use of the you- and we-dimensions: the negotiator is truly interested in learning about the interests of the other party and wishes to do so on the basis of strong interpersonal trust and respect.

It is inevitable that any integrative negotiation will also display some distributive characteristics: after the pie has been enlarged and maximized, it will still have to be divided. So even for the negotiator who is constantly very much focused on creating win-win solutions, learning and practicing the techniques of distributive negotiation are still useful activities.

A focus on creating integrative potential (win-win) fits collectivistic, long-term-oriented cultures that are not too masculine. Collectivistic cultures think in terms of the interest of the whole group. Long-term orientation helps to prioritize, step-by-step, long-term benefit above short-term gains. And cultures that are too masculine tend to think in terms of competition and winning, which does not help the integrative, win-win mindset. And although we would generalize far too much if we said that low-IND, low-MAS, and high-LTO countries are in the best position to negotiate win-win, it is my experience that Asian cultures that fit these criteria (such as Thailand, Vietnam, Singapore) think much more in terms of win-win than negotiators from the United States, Australia, and the UK, for example, do.

11.1.4 When to Use Which Style?

Negotiators all have personal preferences on which they first rely. Guided by the personality characteristics that we introduced in Chapter 4, they will have a preference for building up relationships or for closing a deal. In individualistic cultures, this personal preference will be more obvious: I often do not need much more than a first handshake and the exchange of a few pleasantries in order to assess the preferred style I am dealing

TIP 87: YOUR PREFERENCE

Decide for yourself which negotiation style best fits your personality: Are you naturally looking for true win-win, or are you more competitive by nature and do you strive to meet your individual targets first? In negotiations or in conflict situations in the office, your challenge is to make sure it is not your personal preference that drives the choice of your negotiation strategy, but the requirements of the situation. Decide for every situation whether a win-lose or a win-win approach is most appropriate.

with. Verbally everybody will talk win-win, but nonverbal language (body language, tone of voice) often tells you immediately which style of negotiator you have encountered. In collectivistic cultures, individual preferences fade into the background, but the trained eye (ear) is able to quickly pick up the signals that tell whether the group on the other side of the table is negotiating win-win or win-lose.

It depends on the kind of negotiation whether or not it is wise to choose an integrative position from the outset. This depends to a large extent on the intentions that you think drive the other party (see Section 11.1.2). A win-win mindset generally helps you to step into the shoes of the other person and avoid focusing on only one variable (such as price). Only when

TIP 88: INTEGRATIVE POTENTIAL

In disagreements or situations with different interests, our primary response is usually to fight for what we need. Before you start to fight, learn to identify at least three options for mutual gain and benefit. Allow yourself to enter the discussion only when you have done this short exercise and you have three win-win options in mind. Even if you later decide not to use any of the three options (although I don't think you would if you have done this exercise seriously!), you have made a major investment into your personal development. Any leader needs the ability to think in terms of win-win in difficult situations: making this part of your natural response to disagreement and conflict is an important investment in your own leadership potential.

the situation is really win-lose, and your objective is to win whatever it takes, should you avoid losing time speaking integrative language. Spend time thinking about how your company will benefit in the long run from winning the negotiations. And maybe then you will realize that there is more than price alone.

11.2 PREPARATIONS

Thorough preparation gives you an immediate advantage in any negotiation for the simple reason that the other party may not have prepared properly. This statement is not meant to be provocative or cynical, but rather reflects the reality of international business. Here, deadlines and milestones alternate at a very high frequency, and marketing managers, purchasing managers, and salespeople work day and night to follow up on actions in every part of the world: calls in the middle of the night, team meetings during the day, and paperwork and preparations in between. A constant stream of urgent and important actions siphon off your energy from solid preparations of an upcoming negotiation.

Many international negotiations are only prepared when—after a long and tiring flight—you meet your colleagues in the bar of the hotel upon arrival. These kinds of meetings often have the character of a quick exchange of information, while the real strategy, team roles, and opening positions are not discussed. Everybody feels it is already too late to make thorough preparations. The same is the case with internal negotiations with other departments or divisions: in the turbulence of daily work you often walk into meetings unprepared, relying on your knowledge and experience to improvise on the spot.

The choice is as simple as it is confronting. Ask yourself which of two options has the most benefit to your company in the long run: extinguishing fires or preparing negotiations. Answer the question honestly and act accordingly. Good chance you will decide to break the pattern of extinguishing fires.

It is important to be absolutely clear in your preparation about what you want to achieve: a solid strategy is the main outcome of a good preparation phase (Cox 2012). This strategy includes your overall goal and plan, a detailed planning schedule for the opening of the negotiations, and the first offers and concessions. If you only have a vague notion of what you

TIP 89: BLOCK PREPARATION TIME

Plan the preparation of the negotiation as rigidly in your agenda as the negotiation itself. Block the time for preparation, and do not compromise when other actions come up. As a guideline, any complex negotiation needs at least half a day of your individual preparation time, and at least half a day with the entire team: this excludes the time for information gathering, up-front communication with the other party, etc. Consider going off-site with your team for your preparations, in order to concentrate on work without interruption.

want to achieve, you will achieve a similar outcome: a vague agreement, and quite likely far from the best outcome you could have achieved.

Good preparation of negotiations leads to increased self-confidence. And the other party will detect from your nonverbals that you are self-confident (defined as having inner peace of mind and full trust in yourself and your team). This is about inner trust: knowing that you have done everything possible during your preparations to be a full and professional communication partner for the other party. Teams negotiating large international contracts often hire a consultant to help them in the preparation phase of the negotiation. This is a good idea, as this person is often able to identify integrative potential in the negotiation, and contributes his experience with similar negotiations. This person can help the team define a strategy, define team roles and responsibilities, and define the first moves that will need to be made once the negotiation has started.

11.2.1 Interactions before the Start of the Negotiation

Most negotiations have already started before you realize it. Even before the first appointment is noted in the agendas, the parties have influenced one another's positions. Expectations are influenced and ambitions tempered in an early stage. A simple question can be asked even in a first phone call with the other party: "Give me a rough indication of your pricing for next year. Of course I won't take this as an official number, but I need to know roughly what to expect." The number you then give in good faith will be the first reference point in the negotiation, and it is unlikely you will still be able to achieve a better price. When you refer to your first indication being "off the record," the other party will tell you that your number has already been used for budget estimations and that senior management approved the financials of this business case yesterday. The first call up front was an integral part of the negotiation.

A well-known tactic that parties often apply before they meet is that of the "reluctant seller" (Karrass 1996). When a potentially new client indicates he wants to buy from you, you answer him that this probably is not the right moment as you have a lot of requests from the market lately, that you are running short on stocks, and that you will be happy to inform him at a later stage when you are able to take on new clients. Before you hang up the phone the buyer has adjusted his expectations and is prepared to do an opening bid that is more interesting to you. When people are confronted with the reluctant seller they are usually prepared to give up a large share of their negotiation space, simply because they want to stay engaged and not miss a good deal with you.

Never underestimate the influence that prenegotiation interactions can have on the final outcome. We refer to the example at the start of this chapter: our indication that we wanted to negotiate a price reduction for the total package rather than for individual products set the tone and determined the final outcome of the meeting (although not in our favor). Parties usually reveal their negotiation strategy in these first contacts.

The preparation phase also is the phase in which you need to decide whom to bring to the negotiations.

11.2.2 Who Should Participate?

Assembling a negotiation team is an important factor influencing the final result of your negotiation. The negotiation team should be selected carefully, especially when the team needs to operate in an international context. It is beyond the scope of this book to go into full detail of how to assemble (international) teams and how to prepare these teams for their task. We limit ourselves here to the most important, practical roles that need to be represented in the negotiation team (Table 11.1).

Obviously each of these different roles can be performed by one or a few people on the team. You will need to assign multiple roles to one person when you work with a smaller negotiation team. The size of the team you assemble depends greatly on factors such as the industry you are in, the number of people you expect on the other side of the table, and the extent of the mandate you have. Sometimes it is enough to have a team of only two people. But even when only two people are active, you should still

TABLE 11.1

The Different Roles and Functions within a (International) Negotiation Team

Role	Responsibility
Team leader	Responsibility for the end result and leading the negotiation team.
Representative	External representative of the team: this person is often the spokesperson to the outside world. This role often is combined with the role of the team leader.
Process owner	Looks at the negotiation process (level 2 in Figure 2.1): timekeeper and the person proposing and facilitating procedural interventions.
Bookkeeper	Keeps track of the overall results so far (spreadsheet with all agreements, concessions, and results): based on his administration, the final contract is easily formulated.
Data owner	Assembles all relevant information (intelligence on the other party, market data, competitor data), keeps track of it, and makes sure the relevant people on the team are updated on the same information.
Mirror	Has a good feel for human behavior and interaction and is able to give direct feedback to all members of the team: acts as a mirror and source of reflection for the team.
Specialist	Has specific expertise and experience relevant to the team and uses this during the negotiation.
Creative person	Has content knowledge and uses this to think about smart ways to structure concessions and proposals: breaks patterns.
Relation builder	Analyzes the other party, understands roles and responsibilities within the other team, and establishes good relations with individual team members of the other party.

discuss the above roles together and decide who will primarily take which role.

After the team has been assembled, all roles should be discussed and divided. An important point is to discuss the role of the specialists who will join the team: these are usually people who are not used to operating in commercial roles and who focus on the content in every statement or question. As a negotiation team you will need to be clear about the role of these specialists: Can they ventilate their opinion at any given time? Do they represent the team externally? Are they only giving advice within the team? It is these people who—with the best intentions of the world—can put your interests and positions openly on the table as they value an open discussion. They find it hard to accept that some information ought to be withheld from the other party and not openly discussed.

Other factors can also play a role in deciding how to assemble the negotiation team. Especially when many members in the team have never previously worked together, it is good to perform an analysis of personal preferences according to the personality aspects mentioned in Chapter 4. It is certainly advisable to have a mix of task-oriented and relationship-oriented people, as well as a mix of people with a preference for and experience with integrative and distributive negotiation styles. Another criterion should be whether or not the negotiators themselves are responsible for implementing the negotiation agreements: this can be disadvantageous to smooth and timely implementation when the result needs to be transferred to another team later.

In intercultural negotiations, it could be wise to include somebody on your team who understands the different aspects of culture and who has much experience of cooperating and negotiating in an intercultural context. The role of the specialist in Table 11.1 could be the one of intercultural specialist. When negotiating with parties that come from a country with a completely different cultural profile than your own, it is particularly valuable to have a person who knows the customs of that country (a native speaker) on your team. If it is difficult to include an outsider in your team during the negotiation, you should at least have the person work with your team during the preparations and eventually in the breaks during the real negotiation. But even including an outsider in your team often works well, provided you explain to the other party why the person is there. I worked with a Korean intercultural specialist on some complex deals with major Korean customers, and although an outsider who was

**TIP 90: TEAM ROLES INSTEAD
OF PERSONAL PREFERENCES**

When assembling a team—whether it is for a small project or for a large negotiation—focus on the team roles that the team will need, rather than rely on your own preferences for some people. Of course you have your preferences, but choosing team members on the basis of this criterion only will form homogeneous teams that miss the creativity and problem-solving competences that diverse teams can offer. You should decide on the team roles and then look for the right people, not the other way around. Ensure a good mix of task- vs. relationship-oriented people, for specialists and generalists, for introverts and extroverts, etc. Once all team roles have been assigned, ensure that you spend time with each member of the team to clarify your expectations of his or her role.

initially regarded with suspicion, he was eventually very much respected by the Korean team (and by us) for the bridges he could build between the two parties.

One aspect of culture that requires attention is the power distance profile of the team you are negotiating with. In countries with a high power distance (see Section 6.2) you should first ensure that decisions can be made, before even worrying about strategy, tactics, and other aspects of the negotiation. Understanding the mandates of the other team is of primary importance. In Saudi Arabia, for example, you should expect the final decision maker not to join the negotiations at all. If you don't know this and try to obtain concessions from the other party, you will become frustrated. Regardless of what you do, you will not get any guarantees before the other party has had the opportunity to align internally and propose your solution to the final decision maker. When the decision power is high in the organization (as it is in most countries of the world) you should make clear agreements about the availability of the decision maker, and look for clarity about the mandate his negotiation team has. You should expect that, in many high-PDI countries, even the smallest details will need to be agreed on with senior management, and this takes time.

Obviously not every negotiation team you deal with will talk openly about its internal decision-making structure. You should then rely on your own assessment of the power structure on the other side of the table. And this requires serious observation of the nonverbals, listening very carefully, and interpreting what you see. You will need to know who is the eldest person in the tribe in Eastern Africa in order to understand whom you will need to speak to, just as much as you will need to understand the internal organization structure and responsibilities when dealing with a major Japanese client. This is different in countries with low power distance: although there will obviously be internal hierarchy relevant to making major decisions, you can expect that the team you are negotiating with will have a clear mandate, and that they will have short lines to the final decision makers when needed. In these countries, the members of negotiation teams are selected for their competences, experience, and specialisms, and much less for their status and rank in the internal hierarchy.

In addition to power distance you will need to know whether your negotiation partner originates from a high-context or low-context culture (see Sections 6.3 and 6.7). When you yourself come from a low-context culture (very direct and open communication) you should have people on your team who understand high-context communication: they have the experience to translate what is said into what is meant. To many Western cultures, interpreting the meaning from the context of the spoken word is very difficult, while the right interpretation is of crucial importance for the success of your negotiations. The statement "Reaching a conclusion will be difficult today" can mean just that (low context: it will not be easy), or it can mean "We will not reach a conclusion as our senior manager has blocked a deal for now: our mandate has changed."

If teams from high-context cultures are not satisfied with the process, or if they encounter major hurdles in the negotiation, they may not be able to inform you frankly of this: it would mean losing face or showing internal weakness. At a moment like this they will say, "Maybe this specific product is so complicated that we need to analyze this later in more detail." This can mean: "We cannot or do not want to discuss this right now." Your reaction of "This product is not complicated at all: let me explain again" will not help the negotiation process.

In dealing with individualistic cultures in particular, you should agree on the various roles in your team. In these cultures, people are used to speaking up about what they personally think is relevant at that point in time, regardless of whether they represent the team opinion or not. You should make clear agreements about moments when people are allowed to speak up individually and about the kind of situations in which the group should be consulted first. Make clear agreements about the roles that people take on. In collectivistic cultures, people are more careful with this aspect of the negotiation, as they have a natural focus on harmony in the group and understanding the group dynamics.

Other cultural aspects obviously also play a role in assembling the team. People from uncertainty-avoidant countries, for example, will want much clarity about roles and responsibilities. People in these cultures also take the preparation of the negotiations more seriously: they have the mindset that the more you plan up front, the more ambiguity and uncertainty you avoid in a later stage of the process. You can expect people from Austria, Germany, Japan, and Belgium to be much more precise on preparation, planning, and assigning roles than people from China, India, and the UK.

11.2.3 Information Gathering

When two parties negotiate about common interests, they ideally have equal information. They work toward the best possible solution for both parties, based on the common information they have. But this is theory. In real life, there always will be information asymmetry: one party has more information or more valuable information than the other. This information can be used in different ways. The information is used primarily to underpin offers and concessions, or make them fit the interests of the other party. But information asymmetry can also be used to gain emotional advantage. The party with the most information (whether the information is right or not, and whether it is accepted by both parties or not) has more power and gains psychological advantage by using the information tactically in the negotiation (see Section 11.7 on power balance).

A big part of the information asymmetry can be cleared by the Internet: a lot of general information about companies and markets is publicly available once you spend enough time looking for and finding it. And although these public sources give you a lot of information about a country (demographic information, economic indicators, government processes, and organization charts), it will be more difficult to find information about a specific region or subregion and virtually impossible to find all you need to know about your business partner in Congo, Mali, or Burkina Faso. You will need to find your own information sources that are willing to tell all about the power distribution within a certain region, province, company, or tribe. But the time you invest in information gathering will pay off—functionally inasmuch as this information gives you more understanding, and emotionally as it is much more fun to understand why the world around you works the way it does (Table 11.2).

Information gathering is an important step in the preparation of any negotiation, regardless of culture. It is to be expected, however, that cultures with a high uncertainty avoidance score (high UAI) will take the preparations much more seriously than cultures with a low UAI. Having the right information and being well prepared is a means to

TIP 91: DELEGATE INFORMATION GATHERING

Do not assemble all required information yourself, but assign somebody from your team to help you gather the majority of information. With this, your role changes from assembling all information to analyzing the information, interpreting, and drawing conclusions, and this is exactly what you will need to do during the negotiation. Prepare yourself for your main role: analyze all information and steer the next steps on the basis of your conclusions.

TABLE 11.2

Overview of the Information Teams Should Assemble and Interpret before Negotiating with Another International Team

Preparation	Description
Market information	Relevant information about developments in the market, trends, market shares, and prices.
Competitor information	Relevant information about the positions your most important competitors take in the market and specifically about the party you are negotiating with. In technical companies, people should realize that this is not only about product or application information; prices, market shares, financial indicators, and quality data are also very relevant when deciding on your strategy and assessing the potential for win-win.
Shopping list	A list of all your wishes, everything that you would like to achieve best case in your negotiation.
List of concessions	An overview of all concessions that you are prepared to make when needed, including priorities and consequences of your concessions. For every concession you do make, ask the other party to give you one item from your shopping list.
Assumptions	An overview of all assumptions (about content, decision makers, market information, tactics of the other party) you made while preparing. Have your bookkeeper (see Table 11.1) keep the list and keep it updated. Test your assumptions continuously.
Interests and position of the other party	Usually you are not informed about what the other party exactly wants to achieve in the negotiation. Nevertheless, a brainstorm session within your own team about the interests of the other party can provide much new insight. Why does the other party want to negotiate and cooperate with you?
Decision makers	Who are the people on the other team who make the decisions? Are these people physically present in the negotiation or not? What does the so-called decision-making unit (DMU) look like?
Cultural aspects	Analyze the cultures you expect on the other side of the table. Discuss the (potential) consequences of the different Hofstede dimensions (see Chapter 6). Analyze your own cultural competences and discuss the potential consequences of a lack of some of these with your team. Find people who have had specific experiences in the culture you are dealing with.
Experiences	Inventory the earlier experiences your company has had when negotiating with this party. Find out who in your company or network may have this experience. Which style are they likely to use? What are their favorite tactics? Which cultural patterns (also company culture) should you be aware of?
BATNA (best alternative to a negotiated agreement)	When the negotiations break down and you cannot reach agreement, what is the best alternative for you? Knowing this strengthens your negotiation position and makes you less tempted to accept a less favorable alternative.

Source: This list is partially based on an overview in the book Hazeldine, *Bare Knuckle Negotiating: Knockout Negotiation Tactics They Won't Teach You at Business School*, Great Yarmouth, UK: Lean Marketing Press, 2006.

reduce uncertainty. If you yourself come from a culture with relatively low or average UAI (Western Europe, United States), it is important to realize that there is a good chance the other party will be much better prepared than you are, and for this reason, they may already have an advantage.

It is also to be expected that in collectivistic cultures, the information that has been assembled will be shared with the rest of the team. In such cultures, it is customary to think in terms of benefits to the group, and any important piece of information that is relevant to the negotiation will be immediately shared within the group. This is different in individualistic cultures, where the assumption knowledge is power has firmly taken root. In these cultures, there is less information sharing, and people tend to use important pieces of information themselves when this is relevant in the negotiation. People in individualistic cultures are more focused on their own role, and on what they need in order to perform well in that role.

11.3 OPENING

There are still a few details that need to be prepared before negotiations can start, and they should be discussed in the opening phase of the negotiations.

11.3.1 Relationship Building

Western managers (Western Europe, United States) will usually be very much focused on the content of the negotiation: the price reduction they hope to achieve for 1 million liters of liquid gas, the demarcation line between two countries at war, or the delivery conditions for a shipload of cacao from Ecuador. However, we have seen in Chapters 6 and 7 that in many cultures—especially (long-term-oriented) collectivistic cultures—building up a long-term relationship is of primary importance. Of course, every company doing business has a commercial interest. But in countries with a relationship-oriented culture such as Costa Rica, Vietnam, and Pakistan, the negotiation will primarily focus on strengthening the relationship before they are prepared to talk business.

When this is the case, it is not appropriate to bring your lawyers to the first meeting. An eventual contract is not at all relevant in this phase, as the first exchanges between you and the other party will be dominated by building up the relationship rather than discussing business. The goal of the negotiation is above all to establish a mutual relationship of trust and confidence. Likewise, the goal of negotiation can be to fix procedural issues, such as when negotiating the protocol for the visit of a head of state, or on a smaller scale, to fix the terms of payment for a new car. Even negotiating which people should join an upcoming negotiation is procedural: establishing the ground rules for an upcoming negotiation can be a negotiation in itself.

Western cultures (like Western Europe and the United States) find it hard to realize that in some cultures, building a strong interpersonal relationship is the end goal of a negotiation, or is at least a nonnegotiable condition for discussing business at all (think of Japan, but remember that also Italy, Brazil, and many African countries put the personal relationship first). With the Western mindset, you tend to see relationship building as a necessary condition that must be fulfilled quickly so that you can then move on to the next phase: the real negotiation. With this mindset, you tend to engage in a quick exchange about family, children, sports, and holidays. The real challenge to many Western businesspeople is to learn to accept that relationship building is a goal in itself, takes

**TIP 92: BUILD RELATIONSHIPS
BASED ON MUTUAL TRUST**

Intercultural success relies on building solid relationships with people, on a basis of mutual trust. If you are from a Western background yourself, there is a good chance you will underestimate this part of your job. Accept that to be successful in cross-cultural work environments, your main focus should be to establish personal relationships with others: invest in interaction, build trust, accept that this takes time, and resist the temptation to speak about work. Reread the country descriptions in Chapter 7 and realize that in almost every other country you are dealing with, personal relationships are the dominant factor. Then reread Section 9.2 on building trust and familiarize yourself with the different forms of trust that people in different countries use.

time and cannot be rushed. Western businesspeople making commercial deals abroad have to learn to appreciate relationship building as an integral aspect of doing business. They should get into a quiet and relaxed state of mind that tells them "I'd like to get to know this person really well": they should learn to see this as the main focus of their foreign visit to a partner, supplier, or customer.

In fact, any person negotiating with another culture should check beforehand how this culture scores on the dimension of long-term orientation (LTO): this is a good indicator of the time horizon this culture draws out for an important business deal, and hence for the amount of time they spend on building a long-term relationship with you. With high-LTO cultures—such as most Asian and African cultures—you can expect that one meeting will not be enough to reach a deal: it will take many. Spend the first meetings establishing contact, building trust, setting the ground rules, and understanding the mutual interests. Take the time.

11.3.2 Seating Arrangements

An aspect of preparation we easily forget is how to arrange the table and seating for the negotiation. This will not be an issue in many countries. In casual (business) cultures especially, this would not be something you worry about up front, and only when people enter the negotiation room do you start pulling chairs and assigning seats. This is not the case in countries where the business culture is more formal and strict, and where power distance plays a large role. Here, it would be easy to make a major mistake by sitting down yourself before somebody of higher position does so, or by not having enough chairs available, or by choosing random seating rather than carefully organizing who sits where. It is beyond the scope of this book to describe how to do this in each culture. However, some general advice can be given.

Make sure you know the size of the delegation that you are receiving, and arrange a room large enough, with sufficient chairs. Make sure the guests are registered, that they receive directions on how to get to your office (better: pick them up or arrange transport), that they are well received at reception (and do not have to wait), offer them drinks, assign seats, and ensure a pleasant climate in the negotiation room. These are signs of hospitality that will be respected and much welcomed. If your guests are not taken care of, this can easily cause discomfort or, worse, radiate disrespect. Not taking care of these details can be interpreted by the other party as dirty tactics (see Section 11.8).

11.3.3 Making Introductions

Introducing the two negotiation delegations should be taken seriously in more formal cultures (typically high-UAI cultures) and especially in cultures where hierarchy is valued (high power distance). It is in this phase of the negotiation that you can find out a lot about the decision-making unit (DMU) of the other party, by carefully observing how the introductions go, which titles everybody has, and who takes the lead in introducing the team. In more casual business cultures, this is easily forgotten when people hand each other their business cards and sit down. Make sure your eyes and ears are wide open. It is likely that the person introducing the others on his team will be in charge, or at least occupy a higher-level position than the others.

11.3.4 Atmosphere and Climate

Be aware of your nonverbal communication (see Chapter 3), especially in the opening phase. It is here that you need to establish a collaborative atmosphere and express your desire to engage with the other party. Your style of communication—not only the words, but also the "music" and the "dance"—determines the kind of relationship you generate in the meeting. It is your attitude that makes the other party feel trusted or not. When you take a tough, competitive attitude (firm handshake, loud and sharp voice, dominant body position) this can damage the relationship,

---

TIP 93: BE OPEN

In integrative negotiations in particular, you should ensure that you are clear about the composition of your own negotiation team. (Who are part of the team? What are their roles? What mandate do they have?) Communicate this up front to the other party and reconfirm this in the opening phase of the negotiation. Your openness will send a signal of honesty and radiate your integrative intentions: it becomes clear to the other party that you are transparent and that you expect this from them as well.

especially in collectivistic, long-term-oriented cultures that value modesty and harmony. In masculine cultures, a competitive attitude and assertive approach will be valued, while in feminine cultures modesty and a relaxed atmosphere will be more respected.

11.3.5 Surfacing Concerns

Besides clarifying opening positions, it is also important to share the concerns that you have. These can be concerns about the decision-making power of the other party, the presence of the right experts at the table, or whether or not both parties have the relevant information at hand to make decisions. Any concerns—or anything you do not agree with from the start—can best be ventilated at this stage. You will need to do this in a respectful, neutral way and avoid accusing the other party, especially in cultures that are sensitive to the harmony between the parties (collectivistic cultures). Putting your concerns on the table and inviting the other team to do so too will bring you into the position to help each other right from the outset, and again underlines your integrative intentions.

11.3.6 Agenda/Timetable

Making agreements about the negotiation timetable is often tricky, as any reference to timing might be interpreted as tactics (and quite often it is tactics; see Section 11.8). Nevertheless, it is in this phase of the negotiation that you need to clarify how long you expect to negotiate, the flight times, and which transport and logistic details should be organized. Which ground rules will you follow? Which negotiation times will you stick to? Who makes notes? How do you deal with eventual deadlocks? What is the policy on breaks to have discussions with your own team members without the presence of the other party? Are there agreements from the past you need to be aware of? Which topics are nonnegotiable? The list can be much longer, but all these kinds of things can best be clarified in the opening phase to avoid misunderstandings later on.

Now that all preparations have been finished and the opening of the negotiation has gone successfully, it is time to take position.

Sharing Experiences

Gauthier Hanquet, Senior Advisor Middle East and Asia for Borealis,
Abu Dhabi, United Arab Emirates
LinkedIn: http://www.linkedin.com/pub/gauthier-hanquet/2b/879/
48b

Gauthier Hanquet *is senior advisor Middle East and Asia at Borealis,*
providing expertise relating to Borouge (joint venture (JV) between Abu
Dhabi National Oil Company (ADNOC) and Borealis) in the area of
project execution, company governance, and business partnerships.

My first experience in the Arabian Gulf brought me to Yanbu in
Saudi Arabia. I was working for ExxonMobil Chemical at that time
and I was part of the project organization implementing a large investment in a petrochemical site.

As in any large project, it is crucial to understand the work processes and who is involved to achieve a result and to have impact on
the organization. One of the concepts that I struggled to understand
at that time was related to the decision process within the project
organization.

We needed to facilitate construction works in a specific part of the
plant. Obviously a work permit had to be in place with a clearly agreed
on work package that was prepared up front. But after four clarification meetings involving the lead production engineer, the shift leader,

and up to the unit superintendent, new requirements came to the surface every time.

After the fourth meeting, nothing was moving yet: the permit was not signed and the works were still on hold. But I made a discovery! That same week, I saw all three senior operations people together in the small office of another person: a process engineer who was much lower in the hierarchy of the unit operations. I learned he was the guy who was there since day 1, when the plan had been started up in the eighties. His Indian nationality did not make it possible for him to grow in the organization (these things often happen in the Gulf where nationalization programs are heavily under pressure), but he was clearly a crucial player and a point of reference for many people. The senior operations people had difficulties to openly involve the person in our discussions; this would have made them be seen as less knowledgeable and capable, and the loss of face associated with acknowledging this would need to be avoided. On the other hand, it was clear they needed his input in the project.

In the end, we managed to involve the engineer informally at the correct level of discussion, and when he endorsed the preparation packages, everything went seamlessly and we did not face any more delays. The work packages were signed and the project continued smoothly.

Practical advice for the international manager:

- Identify how people are making decisions besides the formal decision process. Even in hierarchical cultures, the "top guy" is not always the real decision maker. On paper, he will be signing off (ultimately), but he will involve and rely on one or more people who are critical to endorse the decision. The identification of these key people may or may not be easy depending on the fact that decision makers may lose reputation (lose face) by relying on them.
- Ensure you understand some of the basic reasons why people have to save face depending on their cultural background. The saving face concept is very complex and can be analyzed from many different perspectives: client/customer perspective, difference in expertise, specific cultural or ethnical divisions like, e.g., caste systems, tribal hierarchy, etc.

- When you reach a breakdown in communication, try to be creative and set the scene differently: Who else is in the background? Can you subdivide the discussion in different groups or at different levels to solve the issues step-by-step?

11.4 POSITIONING

We have made an important distinction between interests and positions in a negotiation. Once you are clear on your interests, you should determine your strategy and tactics. Part of this is to determine your opening position in the negotiation. The opening bid is more than just the first move you make. It really sets the tone for the rest of the negotiation. The way you present your opening position determines the climate in which the rest of the negotiation will be conducted. We go through several important aspects of the opening bid.

11.4.1 Communication Style for the Opening

A successful negotiator knows how to formulate his opening bid in such a way that it highlights the advantages for the other party. He will not say: "Our delivery term is three weeks: we really cannot go any faster, as our distribution centers are not equipped for that." Instead he will say: "We

---

TIP 94: THINK FROM THEIR INTERESTS

A very useful thing to learn in communication in general—and certainly in cross-cultural communication—is to formulate your proposals, questions, and statements in terms of the needs of the other party. Not only should a negotiator learn to formulate his concessions in terms of advantages to the other party, but also a manager of a team should learn to think and speak from the perspective of his employees rather than rely on his own frame of reference. Before making proposals, concessions, statements, or requests, you should step into the shoes of the person to whom you are speaking: think about his interests, his culture, and his personality. Formulate your contribution to the discussion in terms of his frame of reference.

always deliver within four weeks. Guaranteed. Your production line will not experience the risk of discontinuity and you have enough time for solid quality checks. We can give you safety stock to secure your production line 24/7." You will have to place yourself in the shoes of the other person and ask yourself: "How should my offer be formulated in such a way that it ideally meets their needs?" You can only do this when you understand what the other party is really after. Present your options such that what the other party chooses will be something that meets his needs and is exactly what you want to achieve.

Negotiators can learn to observe language patterns of the other person, and use this to their advantage. And smart communication is the key to receiving much useful information from the other party. When your opponent says, "Our delivery time is almost always a minimum of four weeks," you respond automatically by asking, "When is it less?" rather than saying, "Four weeks is unacceptable and this way we cannot do business and…." Learn to link your proposals and questions to what the other party has already said. The consequence is that the other party feels heard: this strengthens the bond (rapport) between the two of you, and he can understand your proposal much better.

Using the literal words of the other person is very powerful: this strengthens the connection between two parties (and is of value not only to negotiation but also to any cross-cultural interaction). So when the other party talks about "I need value for money, and for this reason yak yak yak …," you do not talk next about "added value," "premium," "top-of-the-bill pricing," but you use his words: "Our service has provided value for money to several clients: the value is our guaranteed delivery, the money is on a par with the pricing of all our competitors."

11.4.2 To Open or to Respond?

It is generally believed that the party that does the first bid has an advantage: take the initiative and you grab power. The underlying belief is that everything that happens next will be anchored to the first bid. In addition to this, you have the chance to set the scene, you have enough opportunity to explain your position, and there is a psychological advantage of leading instead of following. On the other hand, there can be an equal advantage in letting the other party make the first bid: you are the first party with the opportunity to reject a proposal and attack (if that is what you want), you gain important information about the position and underlying interests of the other party, and you have the chance to ask lots of questions. This provides you with important information and puts the other party on the defensive (again, if that is what you want). A rule of thumb is to take the initiative yourself when you know the position of the other party reasonably well. If you have little information about them, let them put their cards on the table first. Be sure to discuss with your team in advance whether or not you want to open, and make a process intervention as soon as you have the chance: "May I suggest you share your proposal? Then I will explain our position immediately afterward."

Whether or not you take the initiative depends on the negotiation strategy you decide to use. When you follow an integrative (win-win) strategy, take the lead and do all you can to show the other party that you are sincerely working toward shared success. When convinced that you want to follow a distributive (win-lose) approach, it is wise to have the other party make the opening bid, and have your portfolio of (dirty) tactics (see Section 11.8) ready to respond.

11.4.3 Scale of the Opening Position

Negotiators are often hesitant when it comes to opening negotiations with an extreme position: they are afraid of the response of the other party. They can start laughing about "such a ridiculous position," may refuse to take you seriously, or threaten to end the negotiations on the spot and walk away. Nevertheless, experts agree that even when this happens, you have an advantage: you have cast out an anchor that will be the reference for the rest of the negotiation. The principle he who asks for more, gets more applies, and this principle is independent of culture. When you take the position that prices will need to drop by 25% next year, it becomes hard for your opponent to go for a reduction of only 2%. Many people unconsciously make the assumption that after an opening bid of 25%, you will end up halfway, so around 12–13%. The anchor has been put out.

It is important not to focus entirely on the "right response" to the opening bid of the other party. You will get more credit from making concessions in later phases. So do not respond with an overmodest bid. Buy sufficient room to make concessions in a later stage by doing an extreme opening bid. On top of that, you can sometimes be surprised when an extreme opening position turns out to be not so very extreme after all, and forms a serious starting point for asking a few concessions from your side. Ask for more, because maybe you will get it. However, you will need to prepare your arguments for retreating from your extreme opening position in a later stage, and you should know what you want to ask in return for relinquishing your extreme opening position. If you adjust your opening position without good arguments, you will no longer be taken seriously in the opening phase of any future negotiation.

Especially when dealing with rational cultures that value objective facts (Australia, Germany, Canada, Finland), you will need to have good arguments to adjust your position or to underpin the position you take. Your logical arguments, data, and facts will be appreciated, and can help you get what you want: here, the information gathering you did in the preparation phase is of advantage. In more emotional cultures (Brazil, Greece, Indonesia) subjective feelings usually win from objective logic, and here you can convince the other party by explaining your offer in terms of advantages to the other party and references to the long-term benefits of your proposal.

It also depends on culture whether or not negotiators have difficulty with an extreme opening position: Russians, Koreans, and Saudis do not usually have any problem with this (although they may react very emotionally when confronted with your extreme demands). In these cultures—where competition and winning are important concepts—you have to show that you are a serious negotiator and that you are willing to fight for what you believe in. They appreciate competitiveness and a good debate. Feminine cultures—especially when collectivistic as well—tend to look at this as play: they prefer modesty to argument, and good relationships to competition. They value discussion about positions as a means to explore how mutual concessions can bring the two parties together or—even worse in the view of the masculine cultures—go for a quick compromise.

11.4.4 Response to an Opening Bid

"I offer you a price of $20 for this product." Every experienced negotiator knows that the response should be: "That is really unacceptable to me. Anything above $10 is highly unrealistic in this market. You have to do better than that." Good chance that the other party will respond immediately with a concession. This tactic (called "the Krunch" (Karrass 1996)) is much applied for the simple reason it works so well. Without any debate about content you put the other party in a defensive position and you adjust his expectations: the offer he just made is no longer of any relevance, as he has to do better. You ask for an immediate concession, and many—especially less experienced—negotiators will give it. However, when you have read this book, you will know that this is not yet the moment to do concessions: this is the moment to still explore and learn. "Could you explain what the $10 price is based on?" or "It seems you have a clear view of the bottom price you can accept, which I understand is well above $10. Could you explain more?"

Your team should be prepared to analyze everything the other party brings to the table: what they say contains valuable feedback for you. It can be hard to isolate these signals from "background noise," especially when dealing with an indirect, high-context culture, and that is why somebody in your team should be assigned the single task of observing and interpreting what the other party is doing (the relation builder in Table 11.1). All feedback you receive helps you understand how to adjust your position next time. The key to this is to practice observing and listening rather than speaking (you-dimension in Section 1.4), so that you can interpret signals from the other party correctly and use these to your advantage later on.

In an intercultural setting it is important to realize that low-context cultures will always take your offers literally: they focus on the content and take your offer seriously. What you say and what you intend to say are the same. As low context means you literally say what you mean, the position the other party takes is taken for granted and the receiving party will accept it and start thinking about a response. People from low-context cultures will need to learn that high-context cultures (most—collectivistic—cultures in the world) will continuously wonder about the information hidden in the context of the spoken word. The counter-questions you get from a negotiator from a high-context culture will give you valuable information about the way in which the other party perceives your bid, and the thoughts and worries of your negotiation partner.

Now that preparations have been made and the opening positions have been taken, the real battle can begin.

11.5 EXPLORING

The exploration stage is about testing all possible options in order to arrive at a good agreement that satisfies both parties. The key activities in this phase are asking for concessions and making concessions yourself, which is not possible without valuable information about the interests of the other party. Although a lot of this information has already been gathered in the preparation and opening phases of the negotiation, a good negotiator will also keep his eyes and ears open for valuable intelligence in the exploring phase.

11.5.1 Gathering Information

With the short-term focus on reaching quick agreement, Western managers often forget to spend time on listening and gathering information. However, negotiation simulations (Brett 2007) have demonstrated that the parties that gained the best results for both were mostly the parties that were genuinely interested in gathering information about the other party. They usually had a conscious strategy for gathering, processing, and using valuable information. It is wise to designate somebody in the team to administer all the information gathered on the other party (the data owner in Table 11.1). However, accumulating information is the task of everybody on the team, and a few simple yet powerful techniques can be used to do so.

Asking many questions is the most obvious and powerful method of gathering information. Both open and closed questions can be used to gain the information you need from the other party, and more often than not they will (feel obliged to) provide an answer. A negotiator should not limit himself by convictions such as "I'd better not ask this as then they'd think I don't understand" or "I don't understand completely, but that must be my problem: I'm sure I'm the only one." You are not. The willingness to ignore personal discomfort and ask anything you want to know is an important competence of the intercultural negotiator. To him, it has become an automatism to respond with a question. When the other party states, "We want 1,000," you can counter this with "That's way too much," but more effectively you can counter with "How did you get to 1,000?" In the latter case, you will get much more relevant information, while you implicitly underline your intention to cooperate rather than battle.

The so-called "what if" tactic is also very useful for information gathering. When the discussion is stuck on one item (usually price), the question "What if I were to offer you payment in installments?" can be enough to break the pattern and find common ground again. The question will usually give you a lot of insight into the interests and internal dynamics of the other team. When your opponent is willing to discuss the alternative payment scheme, it becomes evident that price is not a breakpoint but just

TIP 95: PRACTICE WHAT YOU ARE GOING TO SAY

Negotiators with limited experience—although this equally applies to seasoned professionals—benefit from a practice session to learn these communication techniques. This can be a short training course in which a few cases are practiced and where participants help each other in countering arguments and asking questions. When done shortly before the real negotiations take place, participants will benefit from their learnings while at the negotiation table.

one of the variables that needs to be negotiated. Looking for an answer to your question has the important side effect that it forces people to think creatively about their situation and tell you about any problem they have with accepting your "what if": again, you gather relevant information.

You can train yourself to see opportunities for asking questions at everything the other party says. Without making it resemble an interrogation, you can ask questions about every deletion, distortion, or generalization that you notice in the language pattern of the other party. This Neuro-Linguistic Programming (NLP) technique (Bandler and Grinder 1975) is very useful, and has been of huge benefit to me in many situations:

Deletion: You want clarification of everything the other person deleted from his sentence. So the statement "We really need a better price for our products" is immediately countered with (1) Who is "we"? (2) Better than what? (3) Which products?

Distortions: You point out all inconsistent logic or every half-truth. The remark "We cannot agree to your proposal as our procedures do not allow for that" sounds quite reasonable. However, the content of the statement is quite vague (although in high-UAI countries people are used to assigning power to procedures). Your counter-question should be: "So why are procedures so important to you in judging the proposals of suppliers?" Although this sounds like a grammatical power game with the other party, very often it will lead to new information being provided to you. Also, incomplete logic belongs to the category of distortions: "It is better to first agree on price and only later on delivery times." After reading this book you will ask: "Did you ever agree on a delivery time before agreeing on price?

What happened?" Even your counter-question "How do you know this is better?" is simple yet very effective.

Generalizations: Train yourself to hear internal alarm bells in your head at every generalization. "We always work with payment terms of three months" is a generalization. The appropriate next question is: "Always?" and the other party will say, "Yes, most of the time we do." Your next move is clear: "When is this not the case?" Most of the time this linguistic strategy will give you useful information (although this is a generalization in itself). A bit subtler is probably more effective: "Did you ever get into a situation where you had to accept two months? What would we need to do in order to realize that?"

There are many more tactics you can use to get the information you want. When the other party is not readily giving you the information you are looking for, you can formulate your assumptions as facts and see which response you get. When you state, "I understand you work with a cost price of $3.50, and with your target margin of 30%, your minimum selling price should be around $4.55," this will either be received with a nonverbal sign that you are right or be followed by an attack on your statement about the margin ("Our margin on these products is no more than 18%") or an attack on the cost price ("After the last increases in prices of basic materials our cost price increased to $3.80"). Good to know.

TIP 96: DELETIONS, DISTORTIONS, AND GENERALIZATIONS

Teach yourself to notice the above-mentioned three linguistic patterns in your communication with others. Address these and see what it brings you. You will be surprised how quickly you learn this new technique and unconsciously start to notice such patterns in many conversations. Evaluate how much information you gain by applying this technique. A few days of practice is enough to train your brain to spot them. Start with deletions for a day, add distortions the next day, and so on.

11.5.2 Concessions

A concession is an adjustment of your position in such a way that your interests are still served. Concessions are an important aspect of intercultural negotiation, as the willingness to make concessions and the way in which you do this are culturally dependent.

Concessions are usually enforced by logical argument and reasoning: "Market prices in this segment are diminishing by 2.5% a year, as we have just seen. Hence, your position to pursue a price reduction of 3.5% is not realistic. I have to ask you to accept 2.5%." If you wish to persuade the other party through logic, your arguments should be formulated shortly and precisely (see guidelines for the I-dimension; Chapter 1). After presenting your argument, shut up and let the silence do its work. Many people have a tendency to continue talking, and avoid silence by bringing in more explanation, logic, and reasoning. However, your position will benefit from being short and concise—and then enjoy the silence.

When making a concession, you should expect return on investment: you want something in exchange. Just making concessions without demanding something in return is almost never a wise strategy and can, in masculine cultures, even have the opposite effect: you have to fight for a good result, and not doing so reduces your credibility.

Try to make concessions (and your demands for concessions) very concrete: the way in which you present your concessions is generally more important than the content of the concession itself. For this reason, you should practice making concessions and practice demanding concessions with your fellow teammates in advance: in negotiation training, this aspect often does not receive enough attention, although even the most experienced negotiators can genuinely benefit from practice with an actor on effective communication about concessions. Teach yourself to present concessions from the point of view of the other party: think about his interests and positions when making a concession.

A well-known tactic to force concessions is to say something like: "Let's be honest and not spend too much time. Instead of giving and taking the whole day and making a game out of this, let me give you my final offer: I'm willing to accept $4.10. I cannot go any lower, this is the very best I can do." It is up to you to judge whether this is a genuine offer or pure tactics (it is likely to be tactics: if it was his best position he would not openly share it with you). When this tactic is applied convincingly it can immediately force you into a major concession. This is not what you want. So before countering, ask questions such as "What is your best proposal based on?" before stating that your best, final offer depends on many variables that you would like to discuss now.

11.5.2.1 Making Concessions

Take your time when making concessions. Move cautiously and never make concessions too quickly. Avoid concessions in the opening phase of the negotiation: in this phase you exchange information and look for underlying interests. Only in a later stage should you start to move from your initial position. Do not make too many concessions in a short time interval: if you do, you make it clear to the other party that your previous concession was not serious, as you are now already willing to adopt a new position. You reduce your credibility. Make only small moves when doing concessions, and remember that in many cultures trust and the quality of the relationship are more important than the content of your discussion: concessions made too quickly can break the trust, as it is proof that your previous offer was not serious. Always present a small concession as if it is a big step for you!

Small concessions can turn out to be very big. Be careful with what Karrass (1996) calls "funny money." A concession of 0.1% on the purchasing price sounds very small. However, on a total contract of $60 million it still represents the price of a nice sports car. Always translate concessions into real money and see whether it is worth the exchange.

TIP 97: CONDITIONAL CONCESSIONS

Always attach conditions to your concessions: "I could agree to a guarantee period of two years provided I have the guarantee of a minimum order. To secure my risk I would need 200,000 units minimum. If this is OK, two years is fine." When making concessions, you give information about your interests to the other party: if he is well prepared, he will be able to understand your interests by listening to your concessions. Many negotiators use this principle to their advantage and make concessions look smaller or larger than they really are in order to influence and manipulate the perceptions of the other party.

11.5.2.2 Responding to Concessions

Always assume that the concessions offered by the other party have some value for them. So don't say no immediately, even though the concession is far from what you had hoped for. Always express your appreciation for the other person making a concession (he is giving you something of value). However, you should also express that it will not help the parties come closer, unfortunately. Do not reject the offer: you appreciate the move while rejecting the content. Then use the discussion to get back to your interests: "I appreciate the concession, although the gap between our positions has not yet decreased. Let's step back, have a small break, process this into the total result so far [work for your bookkeeper; see Table 11.1], and then move on." This is a procedural reaction that enables you to move on after taking advantage of the concession just made.

Don't say yes to a concession too easily, even when the offer is too good to be true. Never let go of the opportunity to gather information: How did they get to this concession? What does it mean for them? Why is their offer exactly 10% and not 9.8 or 10.2%? Again, switch off your own agenda temporarily and learn more about the position (and interests) of the other party.

Another tactic you can consider when the other party makes a concession is to look really worried and say, "You'll have to do better than that." It is best is to look very disturbed and use a low, disappointed voice (Karrass 1996). When confronted with this response, many people tend to do another concession straightaway, or weaken their statement and mumble something like "… and maybe we can even do a bit more." Although often very effective, I would not recommend this tactic: first of all, you miss an opportunity to react to the content of the proposal of the other party. And by using this tactic, you have proven that you are taking a distributive position and only going for your own benefit. Still, you need to be prepared for any confrontation with this tactic. You could consider the response: "What were you thinking of?" You bounce the initiative back to the other side of the table, and you ask the other person to return to the content of the discussion, rather than lose yourself in tactics.

Finally, a tactic that is often used in countries where haggling is very common: think of bazaars in Turkey, street markets in North Africa, or outlet channels in China. As soon as the other person makes a concession you should ask, "And what else can you offer me?" By asking the other person to think immediately of another concession, you cash in on the previous concession and make that one nonnegotiable. Very transparent, yet very effective.

11.5.2.3 Enforcing Concessions

There are many ways to ask a concession from the other party, varying from a vague hint to a tough demand. We present a few techniques: you will notice that the difference between a genuine request and dirty tactics is tiny. You will have to choose which techniques to use and which ones not to use. The advice is to stay away from these tactics as much as possible when you have a truly integrative win-win negotiation in mind. Cultural aspects also need to be taken into account: collectivism, masculinity, and long-term orientation are dimensions of culture that are directly relevant to deciding whether or not the use of tactics would be wise, and when evaluating the potential consequences of using these tactics.

The easiest tactic to force a concession is the so-called flinch (Karrass 1996). When the other party mentions his price, you react full of disbelief and say: "How much?" See the description of this tactic under Section 11.5.2.2. The party confronted with this tactic will almost always start to rationalize (read: defend) his offer, and it is likely this will be followed by a concession.

When you make a proposal and the other party responds by saying, "No, I cannot accept that," stop yourself from rationalizing and explaining why your proposal was such a good one. You have a perfect opportunity here for forcing a concession by saying, "That's a clear answer. What do you propose as a next step?" or more directly by saying, "I understand you cannot accept this. What can you accept?" Assuming the other party has an interest in closing the negotiations successfully, he will not stick to a blunt refusal but feel that it is now his turn to make a move.

When the other party makes a proposal, you can also shake your head and indicate that you are astonished by his ignorance. Then you say: "You've got to do better than that." After this, remain silent and wait for what comes (Dawson 2001). Somebody who is not aware of this tactic can easily feel compelled to make the next move and "surrender," as he notices he will have to do more to remain a serious partner for you. However, the experienced negotiator will simply ask: "How much better did you have in mind, exactly?" Your turn.

Good negotiators—or people from cultures where negotiating is part of daily life—are very good at continuously asking for concessions. They have no problem operating in the I-dimension (Section 1.3) and ask: "Could you give me …?" or "What if you were to offer me …?" Their natural response after a concession by the other party is to immediately say, "What else did you have in mind?" or "Is there anything else you can give me?" These are all techniques that quickly lead to a new concession in many cases.

Asking for concessions by acting as if you are emotionally affected is a tactic that is not recommended: at the very best it will put you in a better position temporarily, but more often it will lead to a smile, as the other party understands your tactic. Emotions cannot be faked. Unless they are real, you should not try to gain advantage by feigning anger or frustration. It comes across as very unnatural (the words, music, and dance are quite likely incongruent) unless you are a very good actor. This is different for Brazilians or Italians: here, an absence of emotion is something to worry about. In some countries, people are far more emotional (this often comes with high scores on uncertainty avoidance), and when working with these cultures, you should not interpret the expressions of anger or frustration as tactics: they are real.

When it is part of your culture to control emotions and not display these openly (as is the case with the Dutch, Austrians, and Swedish), it is better to rely on your strengths: bring the discussion back to the content by sharp and rational analysis. In this case, your most effective response to emotional outbursts is to say that you recognize the emotion. You should respectfully acknowledge the feelings of the other party, and switch the discussion to another level of communication (see Section 2.3: the four levels of communication). A procedural proposal is likely to be a good response, although mentioning what is going on between the two of you (interaction) or expressing your uncertainty of how to deal with the emotional outburst (feelings/climate) can be very valid as well.

11.5.3 Practical Tips

The lion's share of negotiation consists of gathering information, taking positions, making concessions, and responding to the moves made by the other party. Each of these steps relies on effective communication. In previous chapters, it became clear that culture largely influences the way we communicate (Lawson and Rudd 2007): How directly do we formulate our opinions and proposals? Should we confront our counterparts or maintain harmony? Should we focus on the task or the relationship? My eight rules for effective communication during negotiations are:

1. I-dimension: Speak loudly and clearly about your own interests and positions, in such a way that the other party understands these unambiguously. Do this in an open and honest way: do not play a role. Be constructive and professional in every contribution you make to the negotiation; do not criticize the other party (giving feedback is allowed) and do not attack the other party for the positions they assume. Formulate briefly, clearly, and concisely.

2. You-dimension: Listen actively and attentively to everything the other party says. Be curious about everything that motivates the other party and work from the intention that you want to fully understand them. Ask open questions all the time. Be alert for deletions, distortions, and generalizations used by the other party: clarify these. While listening, temporarily park your own agenda.

3. We-dimension: Invest time in building up a good relation with the other party. This is not a nice-to-have item but an absolute condition for effective cooperation. Building mutual trust takes time: invest this time. This holds for every culture, but you should realize that without this mutual trust, there will never be a long-lasting business relationship in collective, long-term-oriented cultures.

4. Assemble feedback: Continuously assemble information about how the other party receives your proposals and which behaviors from your side are and are not appreciated. When alert and sensitive to this, you can flexibly adjust your approach and establish a better connection with the other party. Do not judge the feedback you receive, but use it to work toward a better (mutual) result. Appoint somebody on your team to observe, gather the feedback, and act as a mirror to make your team function better during the negotiation (see Table 11.1).

5. Neutralize emotions: When the other party increases the pressure by giving emotional responses, do not defend your standpoint. If you detect that you are emotionally affected yourself (or somebody else on your team points this out to you), propose a break: neutralize what the other party is saying by focusing on facts and figures. Take meta-position (see Section 2.2). Reposition attacks as attacks at the content level, and not at the personal level (even when you feel it was personal).

6. Focus on interests: Avoid a continuous battle for position and focus on the interests behind the positions. Positions can be attacked; interests should be respected.

7. Draw a line: When communication is not constructive or when your values and integrity are not respected, seize the power to stop the negotiation temporarily, and take a break. Leaving the negotiation table is allowed—with your head high and with respect for the other party.

8. Avoid misunderstandings: However unclear the communication is, in your opinion (think of the way high-context cultures formulate in an indirect way), do not feel tempted to do the same. Be honest and crystal clear without being blunt. This is always possible, and when done respectfully it will be tolerated (and appreciated) by the other party. Make sure language does not become a barrier: write on a flipchart, project images on a screen, or even sit down next to your opponent to clearly explain your view.

11.6 CLOSING THE NEGOTIATION

The last phase of the negotiation often gets messy: both parties feel that the talks are coming to an end and start to prepare for the rounding off of the negotiation. It is my experience that the biggest concessions are made in this phase of the negotiation. The same holds for the amount of mistakes. People often later regret the "quick and dirty" way they closed the negotiation with substantial concessions, vague final agreements, and no proper administration of what had been achieved.

The closing phase of the negotiation not only deals with closures in the positive sense of the word. A deadlock where both parties seem calcified in their positions or even a deadlock where parties decide to stop the negotiation and walk away is also a way of closing the negotiation.

11.6.1 Deadlock

In every negotiation there are moments when it seems that nothing can be done to move on constructively: an outcome that will satisfy both parties no longer seems realistic given the positions that both parties have adopted, and you find yourself in a deadlock. The most difficult aspect of dealing with deadlock is to assess whether you are really stuck and the process has stagnated, or it is merely a matter of tough tactics. The response in either situation should be different.

When you are relatively certain it is a matter of tactics, you can decide to test the relationship with the other party, and try to verify their commitment to do business with you (in spite of the temporary deadlock you are in). I remember negotiations with a French customer where the leader of our team decided to use this response. The customer had played take it or leave it for the last two hours. Various attempts from our side to get the discussion going again and get back to constructive talks had only resulted in a more rigid approach from their side. We were quite surprised to see our own account manager (the leader of our team) close his laptop, take his bag and coat, and shake hands with the people on the other side of the table. In a very respectful way he indicated to regret this but also confirmed that, indeed, it made no sense to continue: he indicated that he respected their openness and thanked them for their hospitality. Before we had reached the door, the other delegation called us back in and indicated that that was not the intention: they invited us for lunch and proposed to continue after lunch. Their tactics had failed completely because now they had indicated that there was certainly room for further movement from their side. Their position was definitely weaker from that moment onward in the rest of the negotiation.

The deadlock also can be very real and have nothing to do with tactics: in that case we refer back to Chapter 2 for strategies to break through the ineffective pattern within which you are confined. This is done by continuing the negotiation after you have used some smart techniques and a lot of creativity. This can be:

- Discussing the process of the negotiation, the interaction between the delegates, or even the climate and feelings that are playing up. Staying away from the content temporarily and negotiating the negotiation itself can lead to increased mutual understanding and the breakthrough you are looking for (see Section 2.3).
- Changing focus from the big picture to the details or the other way around (framing or reframing; see Section 2.2).
- Creating a common reality and looking for solutions again in this new arena (the ladder of inference; see Section 2.4).
- Changing the composition of the negotiation team. Sometimes this brings a new dynamics and can lead to the different mindset that is required to get out of the deadlock. Be careful with this decision, however: in some cultures where mutual trust is important, changing the negotiation team can be to your disadvantage. The other

party will need to learn to trust the new people and get to know them extensively, and this can be a matter of months if not years.

- Changing the way you discuss the content (instead of negotiating cash or real money, discuss percentage price reductions, etc.).

11.6.2 The Deadline

The closer you get to the end of a negotiation, the more important the factor of time will be. This is especially true for Western negotiators who are in a hurry. But they often deal with cultures where relationship building is known to take lots of time (usually collectivistic, long-term-oriented cultures): here, people take the time that is needed to achieve the end result. In these cultures, people feel less pressured to come to a quick deal: they know that if no result can be achieved today, a result will come next time. The Western world (usually the more individualistic, short-term-oriented cultures) has a different concept of time: time passes by, there is never enough of it, and it should be spent wisely and efficiently. People are focused on an immediate result: they want to reach a deal and end the negotiations before they fly back home.

Pressure of time can be real or it can be used as tactics (Lewicki et al. 2010) to force you into a quick last-minute concession. A car seller can certainly be influenced with the factor of time by doing a last offer for the car on Saturday afternoon, just before the shop is due to close. When the end of the month is also coming close, sellers will certainly be eager to have this sale within their monthly revenue figures, and are therefore keen to make a quick deal.

When the factor of time is consciously used by the other party in the negotiation, you will need to assess whether the time pressure is real or it is just being used as pure tactics. Quite often it is the latter. "I need your confirmation before the weekend, to be able to process the order in time" sounds very reasonable. However, in most countries, nothing will be done with your order over the weekend. Don't be forced into quick concessions when there is no need for this.

The negotiator who does not feel pressure of time has an advantage. Western people do themselves and their company a big favor when they organize their schedules in such a way that they feel no time pressure. I know successful negotiators who always make multiple flight reservations: they inform the other party in the negotiation that they will be flying back the same evening. However, they have reservations for the next day as

TIP 98: RELAX

You achieve better results when you are sharp, but relaxed. Teach yourself—before you step into any important discussion—to step back. Close your eyes in a quiet place (a desk in an open-plan office is not the best place) and think of a moment of great happiness or a setting of extreme beauty. To me, the picture of driving a sledge with huskies through the snowy forests of Finland helps, but find your own! Focus briefly on this moment, take a few deep breaths, and try to place your work task in this setting. Now enter the discussion. For some people it helps to regularly take a deep breath and remind themselves of the sentence "I am in control." If you find that these suggestions sound vague and soft, you are right: they do indeed seem out of place in the head of a business professional. But they are not. I challenge you to try first and then judge.

well. In this way, they do not feel any pressure to meet a tight deadline. This is their way to ensure they will be relaxed and comfortable—the best possible mindset for negotiating a good result.

11.6.3 Closing the Negotiation

In the last phase of the negotiation, many mistakes are made by tired negotiators who want to close the deal before they fly home. Appoint somebody in your negotiation team who is responsible for the procedural side of the negotiations (the process owner; see Table 11.1) and agree with this person that he should keep the team (and yourself) sharp especially in this phase. This person is not actively involved in the giving and taking. However, he is very active in the background, guarding the process and making interventions within your team where needed. The person who can restrict your freedom in this last phase and force you to stay sharp will save you a lot of money and prevent you from making moves that you might regret later.

To close the negotiations and make the final agreements, you need to get back to your original goal in the negotiations: your interests and the interests of the other party. Only when these interests have again become the focal point can you close the negotiation to full mutual satisfaction. Even if you have not reached complete consensus on everything, it is still very valuable to speak again about your mutual interests and to emphasize your good intentions to make this business relationship work. In this stage, you should ensure that you satisfy both the task-focused and relationship-focused people: both need to have the feeling that significant progress has been made. This will ensure that both parties are confident that they will reach complete consensus on all outstanding issues in the next encounter.

In the last phase of the negotiation, the parties usually have a tendency to compromise and quickly find middle ground between the two latest positions they have taken. When a new bicycle is worth $800 to me while the seller sticks to his minimum $1,000, we have a tendency to compromise at $900. We find this fair. But fairness is subjective at the negotiation table. A good salesperson will see your offer to close at $900 as a concession (a temporary position) and not as a closure of the discussions. He will emphasize that $1,000 really is his minimum. By now we are looking at $900 vs. $1,000, and before you know, you now want to offer $950. You can guess what the sales guy will tell you. When making deals in the last phase of the negotiation, you should always make conditional concessions: "I am willing to accept $900 provided that closes our commercial discussion and I can take the bike this afternoon. Can you agree to that?" You will probably not reach immediate agreement, but at least you retain negotiation space by making the deal conditional. Renegotiating the price will mean that the conditions also need to be negotiated again.

Just before the closure of a big and complex negotiation, you should take a time-out and take stock of all agreements you and your team have made so far. Four questions should now be answered:

1. What is the sum result of all concessions until now? Which final concession is possible (or required) to reach conclusion?
2. Did we achieve the goal we had for this negotiation? (Have our interests been met?)
3. Is the other party satisfied with the result, and does it meet his or her interests?
4. Under which conditions do we conclude the deal, and which concrete agreements should we make for the future?

Another way to close is to break up when it is clear you cannot reach a satisfying conclusion. This step requires courage and should never be taken on the basis of emotion. It is important to do this in a courteous and constructive way, respecting the other party and regretting that you could not reach agreement content-wise. Never forget that if the subject of discussion was of interest to both parties, you will likely meet again in the future.

11.6.4 Contract

When all agreements have been made, these need to be administered in such a way that the final document meets the needs of both parties. Bringing your own standard contract will often not be appreciated—certainly not when this is full of legal constructions that are not very meaningful in the cultural context you are dealing with. You should learn in advance about the way people work with contracts, letters of intent, and other legal documents in this country. In the United States, for example, legal experts check that all contracts and all clauses and conditions in the contract are such that all possible risk is minimized. In the Middle East, on the other hand, contracts are short and generally describe agreements rather than specifics. In African countries, people will not ask for a contract: they value looking you deep in the eye and personally commit to a good business exchange with you as a person. You will need to know these customs in other countries and know what is the most useful way to seal your business agreement. Discuss with the other party the sort of agreement you are pursuing: "I know it is not a habit for you to sign a formal contract. I know we trust each other and that our mutual trust is far more important to you. However, to get internal commitment in my company, I will need a written statement from you with a signature. So I propose putting the main agreements we made on paper. Can you help me with that?"

Be prepared for the fact that in many countries, it is quite common to renounce earlier agreements and to reopen contractual discussions before the official end date of the contract (and sometimes before the ink of your signature is dry!). This is very common in some cultures (China) where the contract is seen as valid until the circumstances change (which can be long before the expiry date defined in the contract). When the other party indicates that they want to renegotiate contractual terms and agreements, do not react emotionally but go for a constructive discussion. Explain your own interests and explain also that in your own country, previous agreements are not discussed again. After expressing this, ask them what the issue is for them and whether there is anything you can do to help them. You will need to enter into discussion: do not ignore the request, as this would be very impolite. It can be a very honest call for help to a respected business partner.

11.6.5 Evaluation

We close the negotiation with an evaluation of the negotiation. Similar to the preparation phase, this phase often is skipped because daily pressures again make their presence felt. Nevertheless, this is the phase in which you can learn to negotiate better the next time. Always evaluate with your team, and review the content of your negotiation, the process that was followed, the way the parties interacted, and the climate in which the discussions were held. You learn more from critical evaluation than from any course on negotiation techniques.

The best way of evaluating I have ever witnessed was carried out by a former manager who deployed a very professional but assertive style during negotiation. It visibly frustrated him that he could not reach agreement with the other party. After the negotiations—which failed—he went to the delegation leader of the other party and asked him: "This didn't go very well and I regret I was not able to help you realize your objectives. What should I have done differently to get to an agreement with you?" Then he took the time to really listen to what the person told him and closed with the words "Thank you for sharing this with me. I still have a lot to learn." Three months later he still acquired the business from this customer.

11.7 POWER BALANCE

The division of power between negotiating parties has such a large influence on the final negotiation result that I devote this chapter entirely to power division. In every negotiation, power balance is of relevance: negotiators use the power they have. And often they feel that the other side of the table has more power. When negotiating within the context of one single culture, the power balance is already hard to deal with, but in a cross-cultural context, we know that different cultures deal with power in different ways. Power distance was introduced in Section 6.2 where we defined it in terms of the natural inequality between people and the degree of acceptance of this inequality among those who have less power.

Apart from the hierarchical power distance, there are also other ways in which the power balance is established. In this context, it is important to make a distinction between real power (which you can have because products are wanted but in short supply, because you have a hard deadline to reach a deal, etc.) and perceived power. The latter form of power is particularly tricky: there are no fixed criteria that will tell you how power is distributed, but it is certainly a fact that one person has more power than another.

Putting yourself in a position of low power leads to a continuous feeling of having to defend yourself during negotiations. This will certainly not benefit the outcome of the negotiation. With this, the negotiation becomes distributive: you have already concluded that one will have to lose (which is you)—and hence that the other party will win. In this situation, you have to find a way to change the mindset to integrative and start looking for common interests. Putting yourself in a (perceived) position of too much power leads to arrogance and often to a disturbed relationship. In task-focused cultures, people can accept this to some extent: they find it irritating but do not draw further conclusions. It is the end result that counts. In relation-focused cultures, however, the disturbed power balance can damage the relation and, with that, end the business relationship. Many cultures perceive the Americans as dominant: their behavior is interpreted as if they are sure of having all the power on their side, and certainly in more modest cultures (Asian cultures), this attitude is wrongly perceived. The Japanese often perceive Americans as dominant and even arrogant: in this climate the Japanese cannot build up the relationship that is essential to doing business together later. Americans should be aware

TIP 99: POWER DIFFERENCE: ARE YOU CONVINCED?

Explore the cases where you perceive a difference in power with the person with whom you are interacting. Complicated relationships with coworkers, managers, and partners are especially suitable for this. Now find out what exactly causes this perception. Which convictions stimulate you to perceive a difference in power? Which experiences with this person underlie this perception? Which attitudes and behaviors make you feel as if you are in an inferior position? Which attitudes or convictions about this person could help you to change the power balance?

of this, and they would often be wise to adjust (even if only temporarily), rather than stick to their comfort zones.

There are other forms of power that play a role in negotiations:

- Power of the market. When supplies are lower than market demand—when there is a shortage of raw materials or submanufacturers, for example—power can be derived from the market. Prices can be increased in times of scarcity.
- Power of a third party. Some cultures can give power to astronomers or to the position of the stars before they make an important decision. Others prefer to give power to a financial advisor or lawyer. An interpreter or intermediate party can also have power in a negotiation, certainly when he has an interest in the outcome.
- Power of the location. The power balance can shift, dependent on the location that is chosen for the negotiation. Whether you negotiate in the comfortable executive suite at the headquarters of a big multinational or in the hot odorous canteen of a manufacturing site will certainly influence the expectations that the visiting party will have of the negotiation. Bringing a customer into your factory and showing him around before the negotiations start can be a powerful tactic to shift attention from price to other factors, such as production quality, logistics, or service agreements. In this way too, you acquire power from the location of negotiation.
- Power of a person. This is the most common form of power display, in which power is given to a real, live person or to a nonexistent "vague body." You will have to find out who holds the power and on which basis, and you will need to decide whether this is real or merely tactics. By referring to an external party when making the final decision in a negotiation, you can request a very good offer from the other party without having to confront him yourself. The right response in situations like this is to continue to gather information: "Who in the executive management team should I call to explain our position?" or "When is your highest management able to make a final decision?"

Cultures with low power distance have difficulty with public displays of power. When this is done on purpose for tactical reasons they are not impressed. In these cultures, people see hierarchy in companies as purely functional (you have to divide the roles and responsibilities; otherwise, it becomes a mess) and temporary (the person who is the boss today can be asked to leave tomorrow). People from these cultures need to realize that in the majority of countries in the world, hierarchy is taken very seriously, and that power and status are of much greater importance than they are in their home country.

In negotiations, the misunderstandings between cultures with different power distance can be considerable. For example, when one party states that they have limited mandate for the negotiations and that today they will not be able to conclude as the manager who will be making the final decision is not at the meeting, how do you respond? People from a low-PDI culture will tend to respond with "Get him in" or "When you can't decide, we are wasting our time here. Let's stop this." The reference to external power is easily labeled as unfair and tactics, and the interpretation is that the other party is employing tactics by using an external decision maker. However, the same situation will be perceived by a high-PDI culture in a totally different way. They are likely to understand the problem of the other party and will see what they can do to help. They could do this by offering to get one of their senior executives to contact the missing decision maker. Or they could do this by together proceeding with the negotiations, and working out a joint proposal to be sent to the missing manager to decide. Or they could sympathize with the other party and propose coming back next week to proceed with the negotiation. They will understand the relevance of involving the decision maker in the proper way: the reference to external power is often entirely legitimate.

There is obviously an expansive gray area between natural use of power and tactical use of power. When I make a concession in a negotiation and the other party responds with "This sounds reasonable to us, but my boss will never agree, I believe," I find myself in a dilemma. Is this a legitimate response of a person telling me that he is happy with my proposal, but that he thinks his manager is looking for something else? Is he afraid that he will fail to get formal approval from his manager later, and is he therefore indirectly asking for my help now? Or is this pure tactics of a win-lose negotiator who just received my concession, accepts it, and immediately asks for more? Somebody from an Arab country or China will completely understand the response to my concession and accept that a higher official will need to approve it. Somebody from the Netherlands, Israel, or Denmark, however, will perceive this as dirty tactics: he will not trust the remark and probably blame the other party for not having a proper mandate. Confronted with this response to a concession, the right way to proceed is to ask open questions about the way decisions are made by the other team: "In my culture it is not common to involve high-level management in these kinds of decisions: they delegated the responsibility to decide to us. I also know this works differently in your setting. Could you explain when your boss is ready to decide, and can you help me understand what information he needs from us?"

11.8 TACTICS

Tactics are the activities that translate your negotiation strategy into concrete actions and real results during negotiations. This is the area where inexperienced negotiators learn that content, reasoning, and logic alone are not enough to make the other party change its position and make concessions. Tactics can be much more than logic, and some of these tactics are discussed here. With each of the tactics, you should ask yourself whether you find its use appropriate or not. The answers of people in different countries will be different, and that is why we now spend an entire section on this topic. The aim is not to give a complete overview of all the possible tactics and moves you can make, but to discuss a few and deliberate on the appropriateness of these in various cultures.

One can argue that these tactics should not be used in integrative negotiation (win-win), as the aim of most of these tactics is to outsmart the other party and gain personal advantage. When you go for true win-win—most books would argue—you don't need these kinds of tactics. This view holds until you put the books away and take your place at a real negotiation table. In everyday life, the fight for individual gain is on and all soft talk about win-win is very far away. Parties try to meet their own needs by driving a hard bargain. People are set up against each other, the details of deals are changed before they get hidden in a contract of 68 pages, and people use all kinds of tricks to get their own needs met. However much you strive for win-win (and I will always encourage you to do so), you will need tactics to get a good result, and you will need to recognize and effectively deal with the tactics used by the other party. Whether or not you use these tactics depends on the value of your relationship with the other party. And when you conclude that you do not want to use dirty tactics to reach your goal, this is fine. But then it is even more advisable to work your way carefully through this chapter.

The other party may smell blood when they sense that your focus lies on agreeable outcomes, and they may not hesitate to use some tactics to their own advantage. Be prepared!

11.8.1 Take It or Leave It

This tactic is very efficient: it saves a lot of time. You explain you are not interested in spending the whole day negotiating, and you tell the other party you will just give them your best offer straightaway. But of course, this really is the best you can do. "Take it or leave it." The goal is to make the other party believe they have no choice and that they should choose between two bad things: accept this offer or have the negotiations fail and leave with empty hands. This tactic fails more often than it succeeds: every manager knows that there are always more options than taking and leaving. What about negotiating? Also, no true negotiator gives his best offer right at the beginning. The party using this tactic knows very well that they have more to offer than this so-called best offer; otherwise, they would not even bother to meet. An effective tactic to counter this is to use the fake misunderstanding: you pretend you misunderstood the offer and instead ask conditional questions. So the declaration "I cannot go lower than $20, that's my final offer—take it or leave it" should be answered with the question "What if we agree to $18 and I commit to buying at least 10,000 units?" Apart from the content, the reaction will teach you a lot about the position of the other party: there are more options on the table now. If they were really serious about their take-it-or-leave-it announcement, they would immediately reject this proposal and stop the discussion: there is nothing more to discuss. However, it is much more likely that they will start asking questions.

11.8.2 Give Me a Realistic Price

Some tactics can easily convince you to make a bigger concession than you were planning to make, because the other party wants a realistic price. However, realistic prices do not exist. The price is simply a sum the other person is willing or unwilling to pay. Whether a price is fair, decent, realistic, or good is very subjective, and it is up to the two of you to decide on the realistic price. Price is subjective, and the price you discuss in a negotiation is often a position, not a real interest (see Section 11.1.2). Behind every price there is a real interest: market share, profit margin, or simply the satisfaction somebody gets from reaching agreement about a deal (that is also an interest that drives people). So always try to steer the discussion about price toward one about real interests: when focusing on this, there are many more ways to help each other than with price alone.

11.8.3 The Bogey

A tactic that is used a lot is called the bogey: "I find it a good proposal and would love to agree, but my budget is only $200,000. How can we solve this?" The one using this technique is quite often successful: he involves the other party in solving his own problem (which is that he failed internally to negotiate enough budget from his superiors). Instead of negotiating together, you ask the other person for help in considering this common problem that you have, but you also simultaneously lay down your fixed budget of $200,000 as a boundary condition. Another reason why this tactic works so well is that the power lies with a nonpresent third party: "An external power has decided on a fixed budget of $200,000; we obviously cannot change that here." When the tactic is presented in a pleasant and honest way, many negotiators will understand it and tend to accept: we all work on a daily basis with budgets and obviously understand these kinds of problems. The reality is that a budget is just a number agreed between two people—and hence negotiable.

11.8.4 The Best Offer Wins

In Asia especially, customers sometimes summon three suppliers at the same time, put them in different rooms not too far from each other, and set them up against each other: "Your competitor just made a really good offer." Or you just invite all three, allow them to meet each other "accidentally" in the corridor, and tell them you will make your decision at the end of the day. The best offer wins. For the buyer this is a good way to learn a lot about the products they want to buy and about the different competitors bidding for their business. "We have an offer of $68,000. If you cannot go under that, we're done." This is a very difficult tactic for the seller, who has to estimate whether or not this offer has indeed been made, and how far he wants to go to get the business. The emotional and economical pressure that is put on the seller is high, and helps the buyer get the best possible deal. The tactic can be used in any culture, but some knowledge of cultures can help you determine the probability that you will indeed lose the business if you do not lower your price. A Japanese company will ultimately opt for the most reliable partner in the long run. Price is important of course, but it is certainly not the only factor to be taken into account. Trust is important for building up a relation with a Japanese customer: so it is advisable to ask how you can help him make the best decision. Then help him. There is a good chance you can help your business partner with knowledge, experience, and information, and you will thus build up a better position than the party with the lowest price.

This works the same with European clients, but here you need to keep in mind that if price were indeed the only variable, they would have had you send a quote by means of an email with your best price. They did not. Use the moment that you are face-to-face to ask lots of questions, build up the relationship, and openly admit how hard it is for you to compete against a party you do not know: "To be able to judge their service level, I would need to know things like how they handle the defect products that they regularly need to take back. I want to be able to compare their method to ours." Take a positive position, but do not hesitate to openly admit the difficulty you have with the tactic. The best response in my experience is to give the seller a difficult dilemma as well: "I perfectly understand you want the best price. To me, a long-lasting business relationship with a client like you is of paramount importance. I would like to discuss the total package of delivery conditions and quality guarantees, and the price as well of course. But I will fully understand if you decide to go only for the lowest price." Good chance the other party will indicate a willingness to discuss other options as well. And as soon as they do, you have found out that their lowest price tactic is just that: tactics.

11.8.5 Change the Procedure

In Section 2.3 we discussed the fact that a nonproductive conversation can often be brought back on track with a procedural intervention. Changes in procedure can be good tactics also in negotiations. A procedural intervention can consist of, for example, a switch to details at the moment the discussion is about general conditions and the big picture. The other way around works just as well: when you get stuck in the details, you can propose taking a look at the big picture: "Let's approach this holistically." For a person with a preference for detail and concrete information (see Section 4.3.4.1) this is a very difficult proposal. Hence good tactics.

However, changing procedure can also have a much more positive and constructive effect. Low-context cultures with a monochronic time orientation (see Section 6.7) have a preference for discussing issues one-by-one; they first close the discussion on one item entirely before moving to the next issue. The disadvantage of this approach is that major, difficult issues are parked until the last moment, and once you get there it is hard to reach agreement. In a culture like this, you can help by proposing that you first put all the issues on the table, and take a look at the big picture. This is an uncommon intervention, but one that helps unearth the integrative potential that can be found in any negotiation.

11.8.6 Use Time to Your Advantage

Asking the other party for the time of their return travel is a very successful tactic against people from short-term-oriented cultures such as those in the United States or Western Europe. People from these cultures like to reach an agreement and fly back home directly. When the other party knows this deadline, it can ask for big concessions just before their counterparts have to rush to the airport. It is important to realize that in most other cultures, people have more time and patience than you do. Do not get rushed.

Another way to use time to your advantage is to make the other party travel far to the site of negotiation. An eight-hour negotiation session once started directly after my intercontinental flight into Korea, a train trip of four hours that brought us to Gumi in the south, and a subsequent car ride of one hour. You are far from fit when you arrive, and this works to your disadvantage. The other party can consciously decide to take advantage. Not nice of them, but very effective. Be prepared and travel a day earlier: this will cost you much less than one too-quick concession.

11.8.7 How to Deal with Dirty Tactics

The use of so-called dirty tactics (things you say or do to get the other party to meet your needs, whatever it takes) always aims to adjust the power balance to the advantage of the party using the tactic. Our natural response is to fight back. The pattern of repeatedly trying to shift the balance to your own advantage should be broken. We discuss only a few responses here, all based on the same approach: indicate that you have fully understood the tactic and return to a constructive and professional level of negotiation. When the pattern of continuously adjusting the power balance is not interrupted in good time, this leads to an endless game of both parties employing a win-lose approach. The moment will come—sooner or later—when one of the parties will withdraw from the negotiations. Especially collectivistic cultures focused on long-term relationships will have little patience with these tactics.

One approach often used is to directly counter unreasonable tactics with unreasonable tactics. This way, you show you have understood the tactics and also that you are not afraid to go for maximum profit as well. This restores the power balance and indicates to the other party that they have to take you more seriously. This is a must especially in masculine cultures: not countering the tactics in the same tough way would be perceived as a sign of weakness, and brings you into a less favorable position.

Negotiators often have to counter a personal attack that comes with lots of emotions and accusations. The other party hopes to weaken your power and strengthen his own position in this way. My experience is that—even in cultures where expressing emotions is commonplace—you do well by expressing your surprise of the use of this tactic. When the other party accuses you in an emotional tone of voice, articulating statements like "You think you can smartly use the hierarchy to get what you want and now you have ruined the credibility of our team and …," you should not go for the predictable answer: "No that's not the case, I just…." Do not defend. Instead, choose a vulnerable position: "I'm sorry to hear that this is how you have perceived my offer. What did I do that gives you this perception?" You seem to put yourself temporarily in a weaker position, but you repel the attack in an effective manner. Stay calm and ask questions: do not defend yourself.

You can do the same thing in short breaks rather than in the big meeting. In the break, put your pride aside, assume a vulnerable position, and explain that this is not your intention: "What did I do that created this perception? I'm upset, as this is not what I want. My apologies. What do you need from me to move on now?" is an example of such a response. This often leads to an improvement in the relationship between the two parties, and it halts the accusations that aim to disturb the power balance. Your calm and professional response will generate a lot of respect in many cultures.

Countering dirty tactics can be very effectively done by just expressing openly what is going on. In many companies—where the quality of

cooperation and interpersonal relations is not openly spoken about—
this is a disruption of a pattern in itself. "What you are doing now is
clearly the take-it-or-leave-it approach. I'm familiar with that. I think
there's more advantage to be gained for both of us than just me sur-
rendering on price. I suggest a 10-minute break before we take time to
go through our common interests in this negotiation again." You have
demonstrated that you understand the tactics and you now propose professionally and constructively to get back to your shared interests. In the
break, if you walk up to the head of the other delegation, shake his hand,
and express your appreciation for the cooperation, the power balance
will be more than restored and the other party likely will refrain from
using these tactics again.

11.8.8 Cultural Considerations When Using Tactics to Your Advantage

Of the different dimensions of culture described in Chapter 6, a few
are relevant for the choice whether or not to use dirty tactics in the
negotiations.

11.8.8.1 Power Distance

As we argued before, using people who are higher up in the hierarchy to
achieve your goals is not a matter of tactics but common practice in many
cultures. In these cultures, the use of power that is based on someone's
position is not tactics but normal business practice. In a high-power-distance environment, you can use the hierarchy to achieve your goals, even
when this feels unnatural to you. Ask superiors directly for their support
or agreement: their involvement in the negotiation will likely have more
effect than your efforts, and you should not hesitate to use the higher levels
in the organization to get what you need. Nobody will be offended. This is
different in countries with small power distance: here people will not easily resort to tactics that involve the use of positional power—they do not
feel at ease with this course of action. Be careful yourself when interacting
with low-power-distance cultures: involving superiors here will often be
interpreted as direct escalation and will sometimes be seen as an offense.
"We should be able to solve this together" is the dominant mindset here.
Only use the higher levels in the organization when there is no alternative,
and then explain to your counterparts why you are involving a superior:

"Without his agreement now we cannot move on: our mandate is limited."
When people from low-power-distance countries see why you are involving the higher levels (a functional reason) they will accept it, but when
they interpret your move as tactics it will likely have the opposite effect:
resistance and distrust.

11.8.8.2 Group Orientation

Direct confrontation should be avoided in collectivistic cultures. These
cultures often use indirect communication that preserves harmony.
Direct confrontation (which low-context cultures usually value as honest
and to the point) does not fit this picture. The tougher tactics usually come
with aggressiveness, direct confrontation, and potential loss of face on the
other side of the table. Group-oriented cultures will avoid this: they value
negotiating in harmony. In the meantime, they will spend their energy
evaluating whether or not they have found a long-term, reliable business
partner in you. When you decide to use tactics to get what you want in
these cultures, always make sure you have thought about the possible
adverse effect this could have on the relationship. When interacting with
individualistic cultures, you have to be less sensitive about this: they are
generally used to direct communication and can handle open opposition
and disagreement. They will not interpret this as a threat to harmony but
much more as a sign of openness and honesty, and your very direct communication might even be appreciated.

11.8.8.3 Masculinity

In masculine cultures, assertiveness and competition are the norm: here
it is OK to use tactics to get the best possible deal for yourself. It is even
expected that you use proper tactics. This does not mean that masculine
cultures always go for win-lose: it means that—in their efforts to come to
a good mutually acceptable result—they will fight hard to protect their
interests and get their share. In the same way, they expect you to be proactive and assertive in going for what you need. My experience is that masculine cultures will be more prepared to use tactics in everyday life, and
that people from feminine cultures will tend to perceive these tactics as
dirty tricks. You walk a thin line when using tactics in masculine cultures:
although they expect you to fight for your interests, a damaged personal

relationship will be very difficult to restore. Russia is a good example here: tough negotiators are appreciated, but not at the cost of the interpersonal respect that the Russians value even more.

11.8.8.4 Long-Term Orientation

Countries with long-term orientation will be much less willing to use the short-term tactics we have described in this chapter (although there are exceptions!). They evaluate your potential relationship in the long run and will quickly conclude that dirty tactics will not help them achieve their targets.

In Western cultures, people are often tempted to associate the approach of long-term-oriented cultures with tactics, whereas it is nothing more than a fully legitimate way of working in their culture. When I closed the negotiations with a Chinese partner several years ago, to the full satisfaction of both parties, they returned a month later and said that now they needed more price reduction as their market had changed. I was angry and upset: we had signed a deal for a year! It was not proper to come back after the contract had been signed and have our highest bosses talk about a new price agreement. Later I learned to understand and appreciate the actions of our Chinese partners. In a business relationship where you trust and respect each other and where you have cooperation for the long term, you are expected to help each other in difficult times. They "helped" us previously by accepting our prices for the coming year, but now they returned with a counterrequest to help them in the difficult circumstances in which they now found themselves. Their request was a fully legitimate one to a partner they had come to trust. Competition had unexpectedly increased in Southeastern China, as new rivals entered the market: the products the rivals were offering on the local market had been produced under lower-quality standards, and consequently formed a threat to our partner's market position. Their appeal for help was clear: help us in this difficult battle and then we will both get better in the long run and dominate this Chinese market. This obviously does not mean you should immediately give price reductions as soon as your partner asks for it, but you will need to enter the discussions with a constructive attitude to show what the long-term partnership means to you. And you should attempt to help.

Sharing Experiences

Danny Wilms Floet, Technical Manager at Teijin Aramid Asia, China
LinkedIn: cn.linkedin.com/pub/danny-wilms-floet/0/965/6b9

Danny Wilms Floet *is technical manager in Shanghai for Teijin Aramid, a Dutch producer of the high-performance fiber Twaron and part of the Japanese Teijin group. In his current role, he has been setting up a customer support laboratory for the company's markets in APAC and works closely together with Chinese as well as Japanese colleagues on a daily basis. Before that, Danny was based in the Netherlands for the same company and gained international experience as a sales and technical manager for Europe, the Middle East, India, and South Africa and, prior to that, as an innovation manager. Before he joined Teijin in 2002, he worked as a sales engineer for Melles Griot, an American producer of high-end optics and lasers. Danny studied applied physics in Groningen and got his PhD in the same field from the Delft University of Technology. Part of his PhD research was performed at the Jet Propulsion Laboratory in Pasadena, California. His first international experience dates from 1983 when he moved with his parents to Grasse, France, and experienced the high-PDI index of the French in various confrontations with his teachers at school.*

Looking back, I had no idea what to expect when asked to set up a customer support laboratory in China. And neither did the company. They had a sales office in Shanghai, led by a driven and entrepreneurial

Dutch commercial manager with substantial China experience. That was about it.

The facility itself had to be set up practically from scratch. Part of the infrastructure still had to be implemented, equipment from suppliers all over the world had to be purchased, and staff had to be hired and trained.

A remarkable learning experience during the construction phase of the facility was the relation with the building contractor. He and his team worked very hard, but unfortunately, the esthetics of the work did not always get the highest priority: utility tubes placed slightly misaligned, sealings not neatly done, and cheap-looking materials used in an otherwise brand new, shiny lab. Every time when I made a comment that it was not good enough because things did not look nice, the reaction from the contractor would be: "Why? It's working fine. What's the problem?" Over and over, I had to explain that it was an open innovation lab that would be visited frequently by customers, and as such the lab was a business card for our company. For him (and his coworkers) this was hard to understand. They simply didn't see why I was so much bothered with what in their eyes were irrelevant details. The point was not that they were not willing to see it. They simply didn't. In their eyes, functionality counts, not the looks.

Nevertheless, the authority of my position ensured that my critical comments were followed up, although often several iterations were needed to reach the desired result. Of course, I was the customer and he was the supplier. But there were many instances where he could have drawn the line and could have said, "Whether you accept it or not, this is it." I learned that the best way was to stay on top of the process and communicate in an early stage when I saw something was not developing according to my expectations. Getting angry was an ineffective emotion. Humor often would do the job, as long as it was clear that no concessions were made with respect to the end result. And I always was generous with compliments when the job was completed satisfactorily. It was impressive to see how he and his team dealt with the combination of the time pressure and my quality expectations. No single deadline was missed, and the lab looked great.

Some time after the successful opening of the facility, I was talking about the process to the Chinese manager of the lab and mentioned to her that most likely the contractor was completely fed up with all my comments regarding small and irrelevant details. The reaction was rather surprising. The contractor had actually told her that he learned a lot from me, and had started to appreciate "Danny's standard," as he referred to it. Without me actually realizing it, a deep mutual respect for each other had developed.

Today, the contractor is still visiting our lab regularly with potential new customers to demonstrate the capabilities of his team. He enthusiastically points out how nice everything looks, and that all had been delivered right on time. The lab had also become his own business card.

Practical tips:

- Do not criticize another person when he behaves differently than you expected. Rather, accept the person simply sees the world in a different way than you do. Learn to see the world as he does, and build bridges between the two worlds.
- When things do not go according to expectations, address this early. Communication is key. Use humor, give compliments for what is going well, and build up personal trust this way. Both parties will benefit from this.
- Don't worry too much about how others will perceive you in the process of reaching your goals. You may be completely wrong. As much as you may learn from the other, they may learn from you. Bridging cultural gaps is a bidirectional responsibility. Don't be afraid to be your "cultural self."

11.9 NEGOTIATING WITH INTERNAL STAKEHOLDERS

One particular type of negotiation is worth discussing separately: the interaction and negotiation with internal stakeholders. Managers will constantly need to influence and negotiate within their own company in order to get support for the projects and activities for which they are responsible. And while you would expect—certainly in comparison to external negotiations—the internal negotiations to be integrative, reality is often far from that. Within an organization—when budgets need to be fixed or resources need to be allocated—the most constructive managers can change into the most creative sandbaggers or the toughest opponents of your plans. Many of the (dirty) tactics discussed in Section 11.8 are applied to secure people's own interests, with two main differences compared to external negotiations. First of all, there is an escalation path to the highest management where shared interests will often converge again. In addition, the internal pressure to come to an integrative solution is often greater. Whereas an external negotiation can be terminated when interests cannot be unified to mutual satisfaction, an internal negotiation will need to be decided on, as internal commitment to your projects and activities is necessary to move on.

Just as is the case for external negotiations, internal interactions also need to be carefully planned and prepared. Stakeholders—the important people or groups that have an interest in the organization—should be accurately identified, as a manager cannot afford to miss important stakeholders if he wishes to win the support he needs for his projects. There are several methods to identify stakeholders and—once identified—decide where you should focus your energy. We zoom in on two powerful tools to map the relevant internal stakeholders.

1. Decide which categories of stakeholders are present in your organization. This can be done by identifying stakeholders in terms of the power they have in the organization, and their interest in seeing your particular project succeed (Mendelow 2001).

   Based on this, you can set a strategy for dealing with the stakeholders. Of the very influential stakeholders, you should concentrate on the really interested ones: they have the concern and the power to support you in meeting your goals. The less interested ones, although a very influential group, will simply need to be kept satisfied. They

---

TIP 100: QUALITY OR QUANTITY?

Stakeholder management is often interpreted as "I need to get as many people as possible to support my plans." Although the quantity of supporters is a relevant parameter, quality is much more important. Rather than starting to talk about your project to anybody in your direct circle of influence, step back and identify the few people who are most critical to the success of your project. This generally includes people that you do not know so well, or people that you do not think of immediately when deliberating about supporters of your work.

should not be actively involved, but you should avoid their power being used against you, now or in the future.

Either the less powerful stakeholders will need to be kept informed (as long as they have an interest in the outcome of your project) or you will need to monitor them on a continuous basis to see if their power or influence is perhaps increasing.

2. Once you have identified the most important stakeholders, you will need to decide whether they are in agreement with your proposals or not and the extent to which you can trust them (Block 1987). This is shown in Figure 11.4.

This is a way to scan the political environment in which you operate, as you want to know who are your adversaries and who are your allies. Those you can trust bring the least worry: here, your main challenge is to actively work and spend time with them (they agree). You should convince your opponents of the benefits of the project to the company in such a way that they become allies (or remain opponents, but at least you can trust them, and therefore make agreements with them on how you handle your differences of opinion). The situation is trickier with those you cannot trust for whatever reason: your main challenge with these people is to establish a relationship of trust before you start your efforts to make them agree with your plans. Somebody who seems to be in agreement but who is not reliable can turn into your worst internal enemy, so your key priority is to build trust (see Section 9.2 on this topic).

Identifying your most important stakeholders and defining how to deal with them is a key activity for (project) managers, especially when they work in an intercultural context. In cultures with high uncertainty avoidance, managing your stakeholders is a way to reduce uncertainty in projects and, for this reason, is generally taken very seriously.

But other cultural factors are also relevant in identifying the right stakeholders and working with them:

Power distance: In cultures with a high power distance (high PDI), the managers above you will be important stakeholders in terms of Mendelow's grid (Figure 11.4) as they have power. Your task is to keep them satisfied or actively involve them and treat them as key players. Especially when you yourself come from a low-PDI culture, this can be a challenge: accepting someone's power when this is

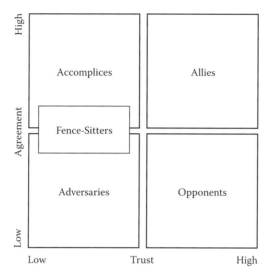

FIGURE 11.4
This stakeholder map categorizes stakeholders according to criteria of trust and agreement. (From Block, *The Empowered Manager: Positive Political Skills at Work*, San Francisco: John Wiley & Sons, 1987. With permission.)

purely based on status and background is not very common in your culture. The limited attention that low-PDI managers tend to give to key stakeholders higher up in the organization can often work against them, as their power and support are definitely needed to get things done. The managers are not used to delivering the respectful communication that is expected by higher-level people from high-PDI cultures, and can easily make mistakes by openly disagreeing with their superiors.

This problem is less relevant for managers who come from a high-PDI culture: they are programmed to think continuously about people with more status and power, and how to get their agreement for their plans.

Individualism/collectivism: In collectivistic cultures, relationships prevail over tasks, and managers from collectivistic cultures will be accustomed to focus on the interpersonal aspects of the interaction with their stakeholders rather than focus on the content alone. In the same way, this is what the stakeholders in these cultures expect: they primarily expect a good relationship with the project manager before being informed of the content of the project. Accordingly, you should not only focus on the departments and other organizational entities whose support you need, but also carefully select the most influential stakeholders and establish personal relationships with them.

On the other hand, in individualistic cultures the task prevails over personal relationships: here the people are separated from the tasks. Your stakeholders will expect to be informed about the content of the project, the current status, and the concrete help you expect from them. Establishing a personal relationship—although appreciated—will not necessarily help the support for your project.

With regard to the above statements, one warning is appropriate: corporate culture and personal preferences may very well override (national) cultural bias, and you certainly cannot predict—based on national culture alone—what stakeholders may expect from you while they are involved in the project. Some degree of relationship building and establishing trust will always be required, even when this is only to get to know what the individual stakeholders expect from you.

We finally zoom in on what stakeholders from different cultures will expect from you in the interaction between the two of you:

11.9.1 Power Distance

High-PDI culture: A stakeholder with more status and a higher position in the hierarchy will expect you to report to him and to take instructions from him in the management of your project. He will most likely not appreciate to hear from you in a very direct way what you expect of him. This means that the help and actions you need from the stakeholder will have to be the result of indirect influence: recruit the help of another person who has a status similar to that of your stakeholder, or adjust your approach and take a respectful and less direct way of communicating your expectations.

Low-PDI culture: Here the stakeholder will be less occupied with status differences and the hierarchical positions of the two of you: he will be more concerned with his role as a stakeholder (which can obviously still be a result of his functional place in the hierarchy within the company). He will expect to receive updates on the project, just as he expects to hear from you about what he can do to support the project. Your interaction with the stakeholder will tend to be on a more equal basis: you both have a purely functional reason why you are interacting. Mutual expectations can be openly discussed and argued about.

11.9.2 Individualism/Collectivism

High-IND culture: Stakeholders in individualistic cultures will expect to be consulted and involved on an individual basis. They are likely to operate with their personal targets in mind rather than as a representative of a certain department or function. The stakeholder will not be loyal and supportive of your project by definition: he will continuously make his own judgments and draw his own conclusions regarding whether to support you or not.

Low-IND culture: In collectivistic cultures, it may be harder to get personal support from a stakeholder, as this person has many interests to take into account (such as the interests of the other groups to which he belongs, like teams, departments, or business units, or the entire company interests). Decision making takes time in collectivistic cultures, and this manager is likely to need time to balance the goals and objectives of your project with the interests of his other activities. Once this step has been taken and you have his support, you can expect this stakeholder to be very loyal and actively support you in your needs. Be understanding about the time it takes, and openly ask this stakeholder about the help he may need from you to convince others in his in-groups that your project is important. Invest in the relationship with this stakeholder. Allow it time before you expect it to start paying off. In addition, it is important to communicate carefully and not too directly in any interaction with stakeholders from collectivistic cultures: high-context communication is likely to prevail in this culture.

11.9.3 Masculinity

High-MAS culture: A stakeholder from a masculine culture can be expected to challenge you when you report on the status of your project. Make sure to be well prepared and be ready to debate with this stakeholder, both at the detail level and on the overall project status. This stakeholder sees it as his role to be very critical and put you to the test. This effect will be stronger when he is also from a high-PDI culture where he will also use his authority to put pressure on you. Adjust to his culture and expect to have to fight to get what you want: he will appreciate that.

Low-MAS culture: In more feminine cultures, the stakeholder can be expected to have more eye for relationships; he may also challenge you on the content, but he will not make it a personal matter. Project managers from a masculine culture dealing with this feminine stakeholder will need to "put up their friendly face" and spend more energy on the question as to what he and the stakeholder should jointly do to support this project.

11.9.4 Uncertainty Avoidance

High-UAI culture: The uncertainty-avoidant stakeholder will expect you, in your reports, to demonstrate that you are very well aware of all the details of your project, and that you are presenting solid plans and thorough risk analyses with a great deal of accuracy. He will take his role as a stakeholder very seriously, as he himself has a role in reducing uncertainty regarding the success of your project. When you yourself come from a low-UAI context, you may have difficulty living up to the detailed expectations of this stakeholder and you may find that he is micromanaging your project. However, this is not really the case. Be understanding of his attention to detail and his focus on procedures, and work with him to clarify all the questions he has about your project. You will also learn from these questions, as you will quite likely have overlooked some of the details he considers important.

Low-UAI culture: This stakeholder expects less detail and most likely expects you to focus on the big picture rather than on the content and details. Do not provide this stakeholder with more detail than he can handle. His support does not depend on the amount of content information you provide him with: it depends on the overall impression he has of your project. Focus more on the big picture and provide more casual, informal updates about the project rather than formal reports and structured meetings.

In the above-sketched situation, the warning about cultural bias and generalization should obviously be repeated: personal preferences and company culture can completely override the behavior you expect from this stakeholder on the basis of his culture of origin.

Now that all stakeholders are in agreement with your project and their support is guaranteed, there is no longer anything impeding your success as an international manager. Good luck with your fascinating cross-cultural activities: always value the strength that diversity brings to a business!

REFERENCES

Bandler, R., and Grinder, J. (1975). *The Structure of Magic: A Book about Language and Therapy*. Palo Alto, CA: Science and Behavior Books.

Block, P. (1987). *The Empowered Manager: Positive Political Skills at Work*. San Francisco: John Wiley & Sons.

Brett, J.M. (2007). *Negotiating Globally: How to Negotiate Deals, Resolve Disputes, and Make Decisions across Cultural Boundaries*. San Francisco: Jossey-Bass.

Cox, G. (2012). Negotiations: How to Achieve Win-Win Outcomes. In *Financial Times Essential Guides*. Harlow, UK: Pearson.

Dawson, R. (2001). *Secrets of Power Negotiating: Inside Secrets from a Master Negotiator*. Franklin Lakes, NJ: Career Press.

Fisher, R., and Ury, W. (1999). *Getting to Yes, Negotiating an Agreement without Giving In*. London: Random House Business Books.

Hazeldine, S. (2006). *Bare Knuckle Negotiating: Knockout Negotiation Tactics They Won't Teach You at Business School*. Lean Marketing Press.

Karrass, C.L. (1996). *In Business as in Life, You Don't Get What You Deserve, You Get What You Negotiate*. Beverly Hills, CA: Stanford Press.

Lawson, D.R., and Rudd, J.E. (2007). *Communicating in Global Business Negotiations: A Geocentric Approach*. Thousand Oaks, CA: Sage Publications.

Lewicki, R.J., Barry, B., and Saunders, D.M. (2010). *Negotiation*. New York: McGraw Hill.

Mendelow, A. (2001). Stakeholder Mapping. Presented at Proceedings of the 2nd International Conference on Information Systems, Cambridge, MA, 407–417.

Appendix: Country Cultures Classified

This appendix contains classifications of all cultures of which Hofstede determined the scores on each of the five dimensions of culture. The relative country scores are taken from Hofstede's *Cultures and Organizations* (Hofstede et al. 2010) and cover five categories: low, moderate-low, neutral, moderate-high, and high. Keep in mind that the Hofstede scores are already relative. The exact position of a country in these tables does not mean a lot. However, the overall differences between the various categories are relevant. Use this appendix as a quick reference guide when reading the other chapters of this book.

TABLE A.1

The Power Distance Index of the Countries for Which Hofstede Determined the Scores

Low	Moderate-Low	Neutral	Moderate-High	High
Austria	United States	Canada (Quebec)	France	China
Denmark	Canada (Tot)	Italy	Portugal	Russia
Israel	United Kingdom	Spain	Switzerland (Fr)	India
New Zealand	Germany	Malta	Belgium	Malaysia
	Netherlands	Japan	Hong Kong	Philippines
	Switzerland (Ge)	Taiwan	Singapore	Bangladesh
	Ireland	South Korea	Thailand	Indonesia
	Sweden	Argentina	Vietnam	Mexico
	Norway	Jamaica	Brazil	Venezuela
	Finland	Trinidad	Chile	Suriname
	Luxembourg	Lithuania	Peru	Guatemala
	Costa Rica	Latvia	El Salvador	Panama
	Estonia	Hungary	Colombia	Ecuador
	Australia	Czech Republic	Uruguay	Serbia
		Greece	Bulgaria	Slovenia
		Iran	Slovenia	Romania
		Pakistan	Croatia	Arab Countries
		South Africa	Turkey	West African Countries
			Poland	
			East African Countries	
			Morocco	

TABLE A.2

The Individualism Ranking of the Countries for Which Hofstede Determined the Scores

Low	Moderate-Low	Neutral	Moderate-High	High
China	Portugal	Spain	Canada (Quebec)	United States
South Korea	Hong Kong	Malta	France	Canada (Tot)
Taiwan	Russia	Austria	Germany	United Kingdom
Singapore	Malaysia	Luxembourg	Finland	Italy
Thailand	Philippines	Japan	Switzerland	Belgium (NI)
Vietnam	Chile	India	Norway	Netherlands
Indonesia	Brazil	Argentina	Denmark	Hungary
Bangladesh	Mexico	Suriname	Ireland	Australia
Peru	Uruguay	Czech	Sweden	NewZealand
Venezuela	Jamaica	Estonia	Belgium (Fr)	
Guatemala	Romania	Lithuania	Latvia	
El Salvador	Croatia	Slovakia	South Africa	
Costa Rica	Turkey	Poland		
Ecuador	Greece	Israel		
Trinidad	Serbia	Iran		
Panama	Slovenia	Morocco		
Colombia	Bulgaria			
Pakistan	East African Countries			
West African Countries	Arab Countries			

TABLE A.3

The Masculinity Ranking of the Countries for Which Hofstede Determined the Scores

Low	Moderate-Low	Neutral	Moderate-High	High
Sweden	Portugal	Canada	United States	Italy
Norway	Finland	Spain	Germany	Switzerland (Ge)
Netherlands	South Korea	Malta	United Kingdom	Austria
Denmark	Russia	France	Ireland	Japan
Costa Rica	Thailand	Switzerland	Belgium (Fr)	Venezuela
Latvia	Vietnam	Belgium (Nl)	China	Slovakia
Slovenia	Chile	Luxembourg	Philippines	Hungary
Lithuania	Guatemala	Hong Kong	Mexico	
	Suriname	Taiwan	Ecuador	
	Uruguay	Singapore	Colombia	
	El Salvador	Malaysia	Jamaica	
	Estonia	Indonesia	Poland	
	Bulgaria	India	Australia	
	Croatia	Bangladesh	South Africa	
		Brazil		
		Argentina		
		Peru		
		Panama		
		Trinidad		
		Romania		
		Serbia		
		Greece		
		Czech		
		Turkey		
		Israel		
		Pakistan		
		Arab Countries		
		Iran		
		New Zealand		
		Morocco		
		East African Countries		
		West African Countries		

TABLE A.4

The Uncertainty Avoidance Index of the Countries for Which Hofstede Determined the Scores

Low	Moderate-Low	Neutral	Moderate-High	High
Denmark	China	United States	Germany	France
Singapore	Hong Kong	Canada	Italy	Belgium
Jamaica	India	Norway	Luxembourg	Spain
	Malaysia	Finland	Switzerland (Fr)	Malta
	Vietnam	Switzerland (Ge)	Austria	Portugal
	United Kingdom	Netherlands	Taiwan	Japan
	Ireland	Philippines	Thailand	South Korea
	Sweden	Indonesia	Brazil	Russia
		Bangladesh	Ecuador	Argentina
		Trinidad	Venezuela	Mexico
		Slovakia	Colombia	Costa Rica
		Estonia	Latvia	Chile
		Iran	Czech	Panama
		Australia	Croatia	Peru
		New Zealand	Lithuania	Suriname
		South Africa	Morocco	El Salvador
		East African Countries	Arab Countries	Uruguay
		West African Countries	Pakistan	Guatemala
				Hungary
				Bulgaria
				Turkey
				Slovenia
				Romania
				Serbia
				Poland
				Greece
				Israel

TABLE A.5

The Long-Term Orientation Ranking for the Countries for Which Hofstede Determined the Scores

Low	Moderate-Low	Neutral	Moderate-High	High
Argentina	United States	United Kingdom	France	Belgium
Colombia	Canada	Spain	Italy	Germany
Venezuela	Denmark	Malta	Netherlands	China
El Salvador	Norway	Sweden	Luxembourg	Japan
Iran	Finland	Austria	Switzerland	Taiwan
Morocco	Ireland	India	Hong Kong	South Korea
Nigeria	Portugal	Bangladesh	Singapore	Russia
Ghana	Thailand	Vietnam	Indonesia	Ukraine
Zimbabwe	Philippines	Malaysia	Latvia	Belarus
	Mexico	Brazil	Bulgaria	Estonia
	Peru	Romania	Czech	Lithuania
	Uruguay	Serbia	Slovakia	
	Chile	Croatia		
	Poland	Hungary		
	Israel	Greece		
	Saudi Arabia	Turkey		
	Australia	Slovenia		
	New Zealand	Pakistan		
	South Africa			

Source: These data are taken from the World Value Survey (WVS). See Section 6.6 for more details.

REFERENCE

Hofstede, G., Hofstede G.J., and Minkov, M. (2010). *Cultures and Organizations. Software of the mind. International cooperation and its importance for survival.* New York: McGraw-Hill.

Index

About the Author

Frank Garten is an independent business consultant, specializing in cross-cultural communication and cooperation. He advises and helps companies improve their cooperation with people from other cultures, and gives workshops, lectures, and training courses (both open and in-company) on this topic. Before publishing this book, Frank published the Dutch book *Werken met Andere Culturen* (Working with Other Cultures), and he frequently publishes blogs and articles on intercultural cooperation.

Frank is based in the Netherlands, but facilitates personal development programs across the world in the areas of leadership development, communication, influencing, conflict management, and negotiation.

Frank acquired his practical experience largely from a career with Philips Electronics (Philips Semiconductors, which later became NXP). There he fulfilled roles in engineering, commercial and technical marketing, program management, and general management, heading a 68-million euro division with 15 direct reports. Prior to working as an independent consultant, Frank made a conscious choice to switch to human resources management, where he focused on the design of talent programs as well as on implementing a learning curriculum for all employees.

With a PhD in physics and chemistry, Frank's career has followed an extraordinary path with many switches: Frank calls himself a specialized generalist.

Frank lives with his (French) wife and two children in Utrecht, the Netherlands, and enjoys wine tasting, saxophone playing, traveling (especially Asia), and reading.

To exchange thoughts on cross-cultural cooperation in your company, please contact:

Frank Garten BV
The Netherlands
info@frankgarten.com

Frank frequently posts blogs on his website www.frankgarten.com, presenting new insights on cross-cultural communication and cooperation. Events, open training courses, and articles can also be found here.